The Woman in Question

OCTOBER Books
Joan Copjec, Rosalind Krauss, and Annette Michelson, editors

Broodthaers, edited by Benjamin H. D. Buchloh

AIDS: Cultural Analysis/Cultural Activism, edited by Douglas Crimp

Aberrations, by Jurgis Baltrušaitis

Against Architecture: The Writings of Georges Bataille, by Denis Hollier

The Woman in Question: m/f, edited by Parveen Adams and Elizabeth Cowie

Painting as Model, by Yve-Alain Bois

The Destruction of Tilted Arc: *Documents,* edited by Clara Weyergraf-Serra and Martha Buskirk

Techniques of the Observer: On Vision and Modernity in the Nineteenth Century, by Jonathan Crary

The Woman in Question

m/f

edited by PARVEEN ADAMS and ELIZABETH COWIE

An OCTOBER *Book*

The MIT Press
Cambridge, Massachusetts

This book was set in Garamond by DEKR Corporation and printed and bound in the United States of America.

Inquiries about back issues of the journal *m/f* may be addressed to: *m/f*, 24 Ellerdale Road, London NW3 6BB, England.

Library of Congress Cataloging-in-Publication Data

The Woman in question : M/f / edited by Parveen Adams and Elizabeth
  Cowie.
    p.   cm.
  "An October book."
  ISBN 0-262-01116-6
  1. Feminism. 2. Feminist criticism. 3. Women and socialism.
  4. M/f. I. Adams, Parveen. II. Cowie, Elizabeth.
  HQ1154.W83   1990
  305.42—dc20   90-6076
                                                      CIP

Contents

Acknowledgments

First we would like to thank the women who worked with us on *m/f*'s editorial group: Rosalind Coward, who made it possible to plan and publish the journal in 1978; and Beverley Brown, who joined us later that year and made an invaluable contribution to shaping and sustaining the journal over the next seven years.

We would like to acknowledge the support we drew from our advisory group between the years 1982 and 1986: Diana Adlam, Maud Ellmann, Mary Kelly, Chantal Mouffe, Constance Penley, Nancy Wood. We thank them for their help and advice.

We offer thanks to those close to us personally: Parveen Adams to Mark Cousins for all the forms of his allegiance, especially his wit and criticism; Elizabeth Cowie to Anne Cottringer, Celia Cowie, Nancy Wood, and Glenn Bowman for their help, support, and encouragement

We thank many other people for their moral and material support of *m/f*: those who made the first issue of *m/f* possible through their donations; our subscribers, both personal and institutional; the purchasers of single copies; our contributors and translators; those who have helped at conferences, workshops and with sticking down envelopes; our printers, Billing and Sons of London and Worcester. To Norma Kitson and Red Lion Setters, our typesetters from the beginning, we have always felt a deep gratitude. We owe many thanks to Ben Brewster for his help and for the translations, which he was always ready and willing to do for us.

Joan Copjec and Ernesto Laclau encouraged us to pose some questions again and so made *The Woman in Question* possible. We thank them both; and very special thanks to Joan for looking after this book.

We are grateful to the holders of copyright to the French texts for permission to print translations: Michèle Montrelay, "Recherches sur la fémininité," *L'Ombre et le Nom*, Editions de Minuit, 1977; Moustafa Safouan, "L'Oedipe est-il universel?" *Etudes sur L'Oedipe*, Editions du Seuil, 1974; Moustafa Safouan, "Les hommes et les femmes," 1983; Catherine Millot, "Le surmoi féminin," *Ornicar?* no. 29, 1984.

Introductions

CHANTAL MOUFFE

When the first issue of *m/f* appeared in 1978, the relation between Marxism and feminism was very much at the center of the debate among feminists who, unlike those of the radical-feminist tendency, wanted to conceive their struggle as part of the socialist project. A socialist-feminist current was being organized, distinct from both the class reductionism of orthodox Marxism and the sex reductionism of the radical feminists. Many socialist feminists viewed women's oppression as a consequence of their position with respect to two structures of domination, the economic class structure of capitalism and the sexual hierarchy of patriarchy with its male dominance over women. Many attempts were made to articulate a theory of "capitalist patriarchy" that would account for the necessary link between capitalism and women's subordination. Such a theory alone, it was said, would provide the basis on which the political unity between feminist and socialist struggles could be grounded. While situating itself within the socialist feminist current, *m/f* argued forcefully against those views. It took the view that not only was a theory of that kind impossible but also that it was irrelevant for politics. The articulation between feminism and socialism had to be the result of specific alliances, not the necessary effect of a common cause. It was misleading to search for a principle of unity; unity could only come about through the *construction* of common interests and goals. There was no need to prove that the subordination of women was caused by capitalism in order to justify such an alliance.

Several contributions to *m/f* pointed out that all the different versions of the theory of capitalist patriarchy presupposed a unitary phenomenon of "women's oppression," which was considered to be the effect of a cause that had to be explained by a theory. These versions implied both the existence of a pre-given unitary subject "woman" already available to be oppressed through various mechanisms, and a unity of subjects, "women." *m/f* opposed this essentialism. One of its main tenets was that there was no pre-given unity of women to which would correspond a simple notion of women's oppression. Instead, *m/f* argued that "legal, medical, political discourses each construct different definitions of women rather than being the expression or representation of pre-given objects, women and men. This means that there can be no 'feminine discourse' representing or reflecting a pre-given object, woman" (editorial no. 2). *m/f*'s objective as a feminist journal was to study the construction of the category women within the specific practices that produce sexual difference in many different ways and to scrutinize the way women's subordination was produced in diverse practices, discourses, and institutions. This required analyses of the production of sexual difference in all social practices where the distinction between masculine and feminine existed as a pertinent one, including economic, cultural, political, and legal practices as well as in the family and the specific domain of sexuality. This was quite an original position.

Another important departure from current political thinking was the deployment of a multiplicity of theoretical frameworks to address the diversity of discourses where sexual difference was produced. So while *m/f* recognized the crucial importance of psychoanalysis, it did not use it as the master theory that was to provide the key to women's oppression. Freud and Lacan were central, but so were Foucault and Hindess and Hirst's post-Althusserian critique of Marxism. *m/f* also published several translations of a variety of French writers and established a lively and productive dialogue with different varieties of post-structuralist thought in France. It made a general theory of women's oppression a thing of the past.

A decade later, the panorama has changed but the crucial issues posed by *m/f* are still as relevant as before, and the publication of this volume is extremely timely. "Capitalist patriarchy" has now lost its appeal and the crudest forms of reductionism are rather marginal, but the struggle against essentialism is far from having been won. Essentialism takes more sophisticated forms today, but it remains the backbone of feminist discourses. The great attraction of the work of Nancy Chodorow and Carol Gilligan among North American feminists, for example, indicates the permanence of a problematic that postulates that women *as* women have a specific "gender identity" or share a common model of moral development; this is the attraction of essentialism. Among feminist political theorists the popularity of the view that opposes a feminine "ethics of care" to the male individualist "ethics of justice" as well as the call from Carol Pateman for a "sexually differentiated" conception of citizenship that recognizes the specificity of women *as* women, not to speak of the various forms of "maternal thinking," testify to the resilience of that essentialist and unitary view of the "feminine" that was *m/f*'s target ten years ago.

For the increasing number of feminists who are aware of the aporias and the political limitations of the essentialist approach and who advocate the development of a "postmodern feminism," *m/f* will provide an alternative framework whose fruitfulness for feminist theory and politics has not been equaled. Indeed, if there is one thing that unites the feminists of the different currents of thought that are now referred to as "postmodernity," it is their common challenge to essentialism, which is precisely the central theme of the otherwise diverse interventions made in the journal during its nine years of existence.

Rereading those articles today I am struck by their utter relevance to our current debates. I will give three examples. First, the disputed question of equality versus difference. *m/f* posed the question of sexual difference in relation to feminist objectives and argued that in some cases equality required the disappearance of sexual difference as a pertinent distinction, while in others it required the recognition of the distinction masculine/feminine. It would be beneficial to take up and explore this in a more detailed way.

Second, the feminist critique of liberal individualism could distinguish itself more clearly from the communitarian one by using the critique of the unitary subject as it is worked out in *m/f* in relation to many issues of political theory relevant to feminism.

My third example touches closely on my own work. Despite the misgivings I have always had about a too one-sided emphasis on the dispersion of subject positions in *m/f*, its lack of recognition of the hegemonic forms of the articulation of these positions, the journal has been for me a constant source of inspiration. I touch here on the point at which, in my view, *m/f* has opened up an immense field of action for feminist politics. It has done this by denying the existence of a feminine essence and hence of a pre-given sexual division and by focusing on the organization of sexual differences in social relations. The multiple strategy avowed by *m/f* as the only one adequate to deal with the complexity and variety of the forms of construction of women's subordination both at the theoretical and the political level strikes a chord with the current attempts to articulate a radical democratic project that recognizes the multiplicity of forms of subordination linked to class and race as well as gender without deriving them from a single cause.

m/f's undoubted contribution to feminism and to democratic politics is not yet at an end. This book will be the opportunity for a new generation of readers to take up the theoretical and political direction that *m/f* staked out.

CONSTANCE PENLEY

m/f may have gone missing, but the ideas and debates that drove the journal are far from lost. The journal's project was founded on the belief that the stakes of feminist and socialist theory and practice could best be gauged, in the 1970s, through a fiercely focused examination of key terms such as subjectivity, sexual difference, identification, and desire. Within this belief, *m/f* for nine years scrutinized the language of feminism and socialism, including some of the prize slogans of the '60s and '70s—such as "every woman's right to choose" and "the personal is political"—with the aim of showing how discourse shapes action and response, makes certain strategies possible while limiting others.

To *m/f*'s critics, however, one term crucial to the debate—the female subject—was typically slighted in the zeal of the journal's investigation of essentialist ideas. It is indeed true that *m/f* eschewed any founding subjectivity for feminism as a movement—be it "Woman," or perhaps even more radically, "women." But this was because its project was precisely to study all claims for a feminine or feminist subjectivity, a project of "deconstruction" in the broadest sense of the term that frequently had to meet accusations of theoreticism, indifference to political urgencies, or worse. Compounding it all, of course, was *m/f*'s adoption of psychoanalysis (historically anathematized by many feminists), with its particular account of subjectivity, as its chief analytical approach. *m/f* chose, however, not to go on the defensive about its allegiance to psychoanalysis, but instead proceeded forcefully to extend and rework psychoanalytic ideas for feminist theory.

What has been the fate of the kinds of ideas generated within *m/f*? It is heartening to see how they have proliferated. In pointing to some of the latest work on the debate around essentialism that has followed in the wake of *m/f*, I do not mean to suggest that *m/f* was the only source of all the newer work on questions of identity, subjectivity, and sexual difference. Rather, *m/f* served as an *example* (it was even *exemplary*) in the way it presented the most condensed and focused critique of the terms of the debate during a particularly crucial period in the development of feminist theory, from about the mid-1970s to the mid-1980s. Some of the strongest work that appeared later included arguments ranging from Joan Scott's avowal of the usefulness of the nonessentialist term "gender" to feminist historical studies, Denise Riley's claim that the category "women" is as constructed as the more metaphysical category "woman," Donna Haraway's polemical call for a new hybrid and nonorganic "cyborg feminist" identity, Diana Fuss's demonstration of the way in which essentialist ideas inform all constructionist arguments and vice versa, and Paul Smith's attempt to formulate for feminism a nonessential notion of "agency."[1]

Looking back, one of the main strengths of *m/f* as a feminist project was the way it kept psychoanalysis at the forefront of feminist theory. To argue for the usefulness of psychoanalytic ideas to feminist theory was an often difficult and unwelcome task. But it was a necessary one, and the enormity of the loss of *m/f* as a kind of theoretical beacon can be seen quite clearly in the face of the recently renewed will to purge feminism of psychoanalysis (or at least of certain less desirable parts of it). Frequently this takes the form of a call to substitute "gender" for "sexual difference" as an analytical category for feminist theory—thus displacing the role of the unconscious in the formation of subjectivity and sexuality—or to substitute a theory of a *socially* divided and contradictory subject for one that is psychically split. Gender is seen as a more capacious and less loaded term than sexual difference, particularly insofar as gender is seen as a way of "referring to the exclusively social origins of the subjective identities of men and women . . . [and] emphasiz[ing] an entire system of relationships that may include sex, but is not directly determined by sex or directly determining of sexuality."[2] The call is fueled by the presumption that theories of sexual difference, indebted as they are to Freudian and Lacanian psychoanalysis, are no longer adequate (if, for these writers, they ever were) to the needs of contemporary feminist theorizing, especially when that theorizing is extended to include the categories of class, race, ethnicity. While few feminist theorists would want to reject psychology altogether, the search is on to find a theoretical account of the construction of the female psyche that would be more readily "articulable" than psychoanalytic theory with social and historical accounts of women's position within class, race, and so on. Almost automatically, with scarcely a look backward, feminists are turning to those psychoanalytic theories which, because they are already sociologized, appear to allow an easier link with the other categories, presumed to be entirely social. The work of Nancy Chodorow and Carol Gilligan, for example, is quite frequently cited in the effort to find psychoanalytic theories that fit with a more apparently pluralistic account of modern femininity. While Chodorow and Gilligan do not offer pluralistic accounts of female subjectivity, their sociologizing of the psyche puts the mechanisms of the unconscious acquisition of sexual identity on the same level as supposedly more social forms of acquiring identity (the effects of class, race, etc.). A similar impulse shapes Teresa de Lauretis's call for a theory of the "multiple" subject rather than the split subject of psychoanalysis, which thus reconceives sexual difference as only one strand among many in a pluralistic array of (purely social) differences.[3]

Whether it is intended or not, what gets lost here are certain emphases that feminists drawing on psychoanalysis have considered crucial to the theorizing of subjectivity, feminine or otherwise, that is, the insistence on the role of the unconscious in the assumption of sexual identity, and the instability of that identity, imposed as it is on a subject that is fundamentally bisexual. Psychoanalysis gives us not only the most complex account of sexuality and subjectivity that we have, it also suggests how that imposed sexuality and subjectivity is *resisted* by the subject. This is not to say that a positive or immediate politics can be constructed on the resistant tendencies of the unconscious (an unconscious that is in no way radical, and is even quite conservative), but that many lessons can be learned here about both the need to have a fixed sexual identity and the ways that identity is never in fact fixed. While it is indeed important to extend feminist theorizing to take account of class, race, ethnicity, and sexual orientation (itself a crucial counter to essentialist thinking of another kind), it does not have to be done at the price of a theoretical leveling in the name of pluralism. Not all differences are the same; not all (if any) can be accounted for purely sociologically.

New developments in feminist cultural studies make it particularly important to keep the psychoanalytic account of subjectivity in mind. To take one instance, the last few years have seen a marked increase in feminist interest in popular culture. Rather than theorizing about "subject positions" or "textual operations," or even "the subject in the text," feminist critics of popular culture are now asking fans, readers, and viewers how they *use* popular culture, what they *do* with it in relation to other daily life activities. In the rare instances when these theorists invoke psychoanalysis (in the anxiety that the statements of users of popular culture may consist of more than their face value), it is usually more sociologized versions of it that are called up. Thus consumers of popular culture are seen to be using it to work through, in a very immediate way, the problems of everyday domestic life (for example, soap opera viewing as a living out of revenge fantasies against the constrictions of women's lives under patriarchy),[4] or they are seen to rely on popular culture to gain moments of controlled pre-Oedipal regression (for example, female romance reading as escape into a space of nurturance socially denied women in their role as caretakers).[5] Seldom in this new feminist work on popular culture do we see an account of the vast range and complexity of fantasies, desires, and identifications suggested by psychoanalysis, an account that could help to describe both the unconscious construction of subjectivity as well as crucial mechanisms for resisting subject positions imposed from the outside. It is undeniable that introducing psychoanalysis into the study of popular culture and its uses can make for a messy and even contradictory account of subjectivity and subject positioning, because psychoanalysis does not patly categorize subjectivity as "progressive" or "reactionary," for example, (a kind of categorization that Meaghan Morris has decried as the "banality of cultural studies"),[6] but focuses instead on the subject's complex and intricate negotiation of psychical and cultural forces.

Through the sharpness of its critique of essentialism and its commitment to the importance of psychoanalysis for feminist theory, *m/f* offers a retort to the continued urging, both within feminism and outside it, that feminism must "take the risk of essentialism" or that it must "reject psychoanalysis." In contrast, *m/f* put forward the demand that we take the risk of psychoanalysis. It took that risk and showed, again in an exemplary way, what a modern feminist rethinking of psychoanalysis could offer feminism.

Notes

1.   Joan Scott, "Gender: A Useful Category of Historical Analysis," *The American Historical Review,* vol. 91, no. 5 (December 1986), p. 1056; Denise Riley *"Am I That Name?": Feminism and the Category of "Women" in History,* University of Minnesota Press, 1988; Donna Haraway "A Manifesto for Cyborgs: Science, Technology, and Socialist Feminism in the 1980s," *Socialist Review,* no. 80 (March–April 1989); Diana Fuss, *Essentially Speaking,* Routledge, 1989; Paul Smith, *Discerning the Subject,* University of Minnesota Press, 1988.
2.   Scott, p. 1056.
3.   Teresa de Lauretis, *Technologies of Gender,* Indiana University Press, 1987.
4.   See, for example, Tania Modleski, *Loving with a Vengeance: Mass-Produced Fantasies for Women,* Methuen, 1984.
5.   Janice Radway, *Reading the Romance: Women, Patriarchy, and Popular Literature,* University of North Carolina Press, 1984.
6.   Meaghan Morris "Banality in Cultural Studies," *Discourse,* vol. 10, no. 2 (Spring–Summer 1988), pp. 3–29.

m/f, or Not Reconciled

JOAN COPJEC

Before the sublime *ekphrasis* always fails, but—if we are to believe the literature—it fails more miserably in the mouths of women than men. The accidental
tourist who accompanies Coleridge on one of those many Romantic expeditions in
search of the sublime displays, it seems, not an accidental inability, but a typically
female one, when she stumbles in her description of the awesome waterfall that confronts her and her companion. To Coleridge's precise observation that it is a sublime
object, "in the strictest sense of the word," which they now behold, this lady traveler
assents, while trying to better the description: "Yes! and it is not only sublime, but
beautiful and absolutely pretty."[1] The words in quotation stand pathetically, not daz-
zlingly alone (negative *ekphrasis*?) as the narration pulls away from them; Coleridge
cringes.

"The logic of soup, with dumplings for arguments,"[2] Freud will say many years
later, as if in reaction to the lady traveler's ill-conceived remark; and he, too, will
cringe. According to Freud, the familiar homeliness of feminine logic is a sign of the
woman's structural difficulty in giving up the Oedipal bond with the father. Because
the father cannot threaten her with the loss of what she knows she does not have,
he remains the object of her love. She continues to demand his love in return (this
is a simple, household account) and to believe that some other person—her father
or a substitute—can give her what she too concretely wants. As she presses her mun-
dane demands, the truly sublime demands of the superego go unheard by her. For
she does not—or does not easily—develop a superego, having already located the
source of significant power outside herself. The feminine woman, then, experiences
neither the morbid pain of ethical accusation, nor the joy of ethical exaltation. The
sublime field of the ethical is, in general, closed to her. By this account it would
appear that feminism is foredoomed to fail as an ethical project.

It is, perhaps, the clear and sustained refusal of this prognosis that most defines the work of the British feminist journal, *m/f*. In ten issues published over nine years (1978–1986), *m/f* carefully articulated a position that can accurately be called an ethical feminism. This is not to say that the journal ignored the quotidien concerns of women, the malpractices that shape our everyday lives. Analyses of specific practices—legal, political, representational, educational—in their specific historical and geographical times and places are a central part of *m/f*'s investigation, the putting into practice of its belief that the concrete forms of the limiting and denial of women's accession to social entitlement are essential targets for critique. To insist that feminism must be an ethics is not to propose that the middle regions of basic social existence be forsaken in favor of a contemplation of Mont Blanc; rather, it is to say something specific about the way social existence is to be thought. It is to say first of all that intersubjective relations do not structure social practices but that social practices, instead, decide the structure of intersubjective relations. This being so, the temptations of moralism—the temptations to make one's own or the affections of other people the object of one's political analysis—need to be scrupulously avoided. Moralism is a kind of moraine upon which analysis can only run aground.

Nor is the appeal to ethics meant to invoke some ideal form of reason that escapes its own embeddedness in the contingencies of social existence. That there is no universal reason that can be ubiquitously deployed, that reason itself has a history—this is one of the guiding principles of *m/f*'s analyses. The principle is now often associated with the work of Foucault, but it was first articulated by others and is, of course, held by a whole tradition of theorists. In "Canguilhem, philosopher of error," for example, Foucault himself sketches the outlines of this tradition. The introduction, around 1930, of Husserl's work into France sparked a research— mainly among historians of science, such as Canguilhem, Cavailles, Bachelard—that would produce powerful arguments against the logicism that then prevailed and would inspire work in fields as diverse as psychoanalysis (Lacan), Marxism (Althusser), history (Foucault), sociology (Bourdieu, Castel). This work, which Foucault describes as a "philosophy of *savoir*, rationality, and the concept," was radically distinct from that of a simultaneous tradition—developed by philosophers such as Sartre and Merleau-Ponty—described as "a philosophy of experience, meaning, and the subject."[3]

It was by isolating the *concepts* of science (rather than a science's description of the world) as the focus of their research that the historians of science were able to demonstrate the existence of radical discontinuities within the history of any science and among the various sciences themselves. It was argued that each science constructed its own objects of study as well as the procedures for operating on these objects and for ratifying the truth of their findings. In other words, it was argued that there was no general epistemological method, no general practice of observation, no monolithic category of the real upon which all sciences operated. The differences between looking through a telescope, looking through a microscope, and looking through the viewfinder of a camera cannot, in effect, be charted on a continuum of vision.

One will find this "mode of work," this location of discontinuities, in operation throughout the pages of *m/f*. The specificity of individual discourses is always respected, the norms of one never imposed on the study of another. In terms of its feminist project, this means that *m/f* never assumes a general category of woman. Rather, it attempts to determine, through analysis, the specific concept of woman that each discourse constructs and the specific actions it directs toward her. The oppressive notion of "woman's oppression" thus vanishes and is replaced by detailed descriptions of the practices that bring a particular category of woman into being, exclude her, make her visible, invisible, valuable, redundant, dangerous, etc. Vanished, too, is the dream of a total revolution that would deliver woman's freedom. Dreaming is replaced by intervening—one by one—in practices that can only limit power, never totally deny it.

This labor alone—this "Foucauldian" labor we might call it, subscribing to popular perception—undertaken by *m/f* in its analysis of a *range* of practices (legal, cinematic, educational, etc.) has made considerable contributions to feminism. But surely one of the most representative claims of the journal is that this labor is not enough. The analysis of the inscription of the woman in different social practices must be supplemented by a psychoanalysis of the construction of the female subject. Not only a claim, a description of its own theoretical practice, for *m/f* positions itself—extraordinarily—at the join between social practices and psychoanalytic processes. It is the critical relation between the psychic and the social that is the ultimate concern of this feminist project. By doubling its investigation in this way, *m/f* effectively argues that the subject position inscribed by a discourse is *not* the same as the position of the subject who is engaged by that discourse, no more than the "I" of the statement is the same as the "I" who speaks it. It is in light of a widening trend in contemporary feminism that this argument continues to be extraordinary. For it has once again begun to seem to some feminists that psychoanalysis is dispensable, that an analysis of the multiple, often contradictory, positions inscribed by institutional practices can substitute for a psychoanalysis of the woman's relations in the social.

It is often urged, in short, that the subject must be conceived as "multiple, *rather than divided*."[4] Since only psychoanalysis has ever proposed a divided subject, it is clear that this coded exhortation is intended as a challenge to psychoanalysis. What is implied by the proposed substitution is that a social theory such as the one formulated by Foucault (along with the adjustments necessitated by his androcentricism) offers an adequate theory of the construction of the subject. It does not. The problem with believing that it does, of believing that the subject can be conceived *as* all of those multiple, often conflicting, positions that social practices construct, is that the ex-centric, or equivocal, relation of the subject to these discourses is never made visible and the nature of her conflict in the social is seriously misconceived.

In order to grasp the *difference* between the Foucauldian and the psychoanalytic assertion that the subject is always a construction of discourse, it will be useful to return to the introduction to Canguilhem's work to which we referred earlier. As his title indicates, Foucault pinpoints the source of Canguilhem's contribution in the privileged attention that the historian of science gives to the operation of error. Canguilhem treats error not as an accident of life but as its necessary and positive condition, not as an eradicable foible but as "the permanent chance around which coils the history of life and of men" and women.[5] Life *is* that which errs.

Foucault makes the advocacy of this concept of error the distinguishing feature of the tradition of theorists to which he belongs. And, in fact, we do recognize the traces of this advocacy in a mode of "poststructuralist" argument, whereby one term—commonly considered to be the negation or privation of another—comes to be seen as its positive condition. Thus: Derrida will argue that absence is the condition of presence; Althusser will argue that misrecognition provides rather than hides one's relation to the social; Lacan will demonstrate that the failure to remember a dream produces rather than erases the material to be analyzed and that Freud's theory of the death drive—death is the goal of life—is a basic fact of psychoanalysis; Foucault will teach us that transgression is the very implantation of the law.

Given the fact, then, that Foucault sees this activation of negation as crucial to the kind of work in which he is involved, his well-known rejection of the "repression hypothesis," the denial of the negative force of the law, which is his most ringing refusal of psychoanalysis, would almost (except for the prominence it has in his work) seem anomalous. For when Foucault argues that the law does not operate negatively by forbidding, censoring, or neglecting to acknowledge the subject, its actions and desires, but positively by furnishing the conditions of their possibility, he is not turning a negative into a positive force in the way that Canguilhem recommended; that is, Foucault is not analyzing the positive operation of negation, he is instead *elim-*

inating negation and replacing it with the purely positive force of "construction." Negation is here extracted from the process that installs the subject in the social. At this point Foucault jettisons one of his own basic principles and commits himself to the conception of construction as a process that has no internal constraints and that must then always result in its own realization, in the production of determinate properties and positions.

Only an external force can oppose such a process. This external force seems to be what many who rely exclusively on Foucauldian theory for political analysis count on. It is the discrepancy between different subject positions or between woman as representation and woman as historical being that holds out for them the promise of our being able eventually to discard ideological misrepresentation. The notion that we can cast aside our subject positions, that the terms of a contradiction can work to expose each other or the fraudulence of ideology, depends on our seeing these various positions as external to each other.

Ironically, Foucault sees things quite otherwise. For according to him, it is the very instability of the system, the discrepancies and anomalies in which it inconsistently consists, that ensures the success of the system's functioning. Here Foucault is "Canguilhemian" again; here he makes negation productive, productive precisely of the internal normativity of the social. The process of normalization—of disciplinary power—is only initiated by the abnormal, by deviations from the norm. The process is caused by failure. Thus, the multiple and contradictory subject positions that women assume do not hold out the hope of our escape from relations of power, they merely cause us to believe there is an outside. It is precisely this belief that catches us up in the normative mechanisms of power.

It would be unjust, however, to accuse those who celebrate the "multiple (rather than divided) subject" as a liberating notion of basing their position on a misreading of Foucault. In a sense they have read him very well, perceiving in what he tries to say what, in fact, he says. For having cleansed the law of its power of negation, he has himself turned negation, contradiction, error into terms external to the law. It is at least partially because Foucault is thus at odds with himself that his critics are so at odds with each other: some seeing resistance as a possibility he uniquely opens up, others seeing it as a possibility he ultimately denies. Either, as we have observed, the original abolition of negation forces us to read negation as external, or it forces us to read every negation as simply the affirmation of what it would deny, every disavowal as at heart a straightforward avowal. In this latter case negation is taken neither as external nor as internal, but as fundamentally impossible. Every resistance to the law another occasion of its instantiation.

Psychoanalysis provides a different scenario. It does not deliver the doomful pronouncement that there is no negation that is not an affirmation, but rather the more complex statement that there is no affirmation without a negation internal to it. This difference can be clarified by returning once again to Foucault's dismissal of the repression hypothesis. The law works, Foucault argues, not by forbidding a desire that already exists—an incestuous desire, let us say—but rather by inciting us to speak about incest and thus constructing a desire that had no prior existence. In one respect, psychoanalysis's claim is similar to this, for it also contends that desire is a product of the law. In another respect, psychoanalysis's claim is profoundly different; it states that the subject produced by the law is not one who simply has a desire—who desires incest, say—but one who *rejects* this desire, who desires not to desire it. Psychoanalysis, in other words, includes in the process of construction the negation Foucault leaves out, and this negation shows in the resulting discordance between the subject and its desire. Though it is, in the psychoanalytic sense, an *effect* of the law, *desire is not a realization of the law*. It is by maintaining this crucial distinction between effect and realization that psychoanalysis distances itself from all other theories of the social construction of the subject.

It is important to see that this distinction is strictly dependent on the concept of repression—not the one Foucault polemically misrepresents, but the one psychoanalysis formulated in light of the philosophical precision of Freud's teacher, Franz Brentano. As is fairly well known, Brentano was one of the founders of the theory of intentionality, or, as we might now say, of the theory of the relation of the subject to the signifier and to the real. The argument that most profoundly influenced psychoanalysis was that in which Brentano insisted that "presentation" and "judgment" had to be seen as separate instances. In presentation, he argued, something (which linguistic science has since taught us to call a signifier) is simply made present or manifest to consciousness. Presentation, or the mere appearance of the signifier, contains in itself neither truth nor error; it is only through judgment that truth or falseness is attributed to presentations. Yet, if the first judgment were conceived as mere affirmation, then judgment would collapse back into presentation, the distinction between them could not be marked and could not practically be upheld. The first judgment, therefore, had to be conceived as negative, i.e., there had to be an original negation for judgment to be able to exist at all.

This originary negation is then reconceived by Freud as repression—the repression that founds and simultaneously splits the subject. What repression, or negation, denies is the *reality* of the signifier. This denial establishes the order of the signifier as radically distinct from that of the real. The real is thus "expelled" (as

Freud says in his essay on "Negation") from the symbolic order, yet it is this very expulsion that enables the signifier to function as a signifier, to come to designate (rather than be) the real for the subject, or (as Freud says, again in "Negation") this expulsion enables thinking, in general, to begin.

Two points must now be made with reference to this definition of negation: 1) It is clear that the negative and affirmative judgments that thought may render are of a different, secondary order from the "negative judgment" that precedes and, indeed, is the condition of their possibility. When Foucault rejects that definition of the law that sees it as a negation, his target is negation in its secondary sense: that which is opposed to affirmation. He thus neglects consideration of the originary negation that precedes this symbolic opposition, and his rejection thus misses its psychoanalytic mark. 2) When psychoanalysis says that repression splits the subject, it should now be evident that this split occurs between the symbolic thinking, or consciousness, that signifiers make possible and the real that they expel. To say that the subject is the effect of historical discourses is to say that it is the effect not only of what these discourses make possible, but also of the real that they make impossible through expulsion. In other words, that which a discourse disallows does not merely define the exterior limits of the subject, that which the subject is not, but rather what the subject is: the subject *is*, in part, the positivization, the interiorization, of that which is impossible for it. The subject includes its own desire, the impossibility or unrealizability of its goals.

There are some who would argue that psychoanalysis surrenders itself to ahistoricism by centering its analysis on the essential nature of the signifier. But psychoanalysis argues that the signifier is the very source, or material cause, of human history. It is only in the symbolic order that human history is composed. It is its very commitment to the historical determinations of the subject that leads psychoanalysis to consider the signifier and the split subject that is one of its most problematic effects—problematic mainly for those histories that have erected themselves on the elimination of the contradictions this subject implies. The consequences—for history, for political theory, for feminism—of the introduction of the divided subject into history are only now, and only slowly, being articulated.

Something can be briefly said, however, about the general significance of the split subject for an *ethical* project. One of the problems of historicizing the question of ethics is that one often ends up endorsing some version of a "naturalistic" or relativist theory: a statement about what is right or just is often seen to be merely an empirical generalization about what people at various moments, in various places, of different sexes were interested in, what it was they valued. To conceive the field of ethics in this way, however, is to picture it as little more than a kind of "used clothing store, where the diverse verdicts that have dominated the aspirations of men are displayed."[6] As everyone knows, such a position seldom yields the tolerance it is supposed to foster. "Just as well another as this," leads too easily to its contrary: "Just as well this as another"—and why not?

Once one conceives the subject as cut off from its desire, desire becomes detached from value. What one desires is no longer simply what society currently deems most valuable, some good we would like to have, but rather something society has caused us to lose. Now, an ethics based on this *impossible* good—lost, irretrievably lost, because it is only *as* lost, as gone, that it is good, *as* rejected that it is desired—will be radically different from an ethics based on a good that defines an ideal future. Unlike the latter this other ethics does not crusade for the cause of harmony; it stakes itself neither on the hope that there will be a time when values will be universal, nor on the pluralist conviction that the space that contains contradictory values is itself neutral, devoid of conflict. In brief, this other ethics is not founded on the belief that an ultimate resolution of conflict is possible, but rather on the insistence that the subject's essential conflict with itself cannot be reduced by any social arrangement. Further, that the attempts at such a reduction are the source of some of the worst ethical misconduct. It is, for example, in the attempts to structure the relations between men and women as a resolution of conflict, as a cure for it, that we will find the motivation for the greatest injustices against women. It has always been in the name of harmony (of insuring against woman's being wolf to man) that woman has been conceived as the complement of man, that which completes, fulfills, and heals him. The conception of the sexual relation between men and woman in these terms—man desiring woman and woman supplying with her being the means of his fulfillment—erases the question of *her* desire and deprives her of the powers and privileges that always, morganatically, revert back to him.

m/f has never tried to reconcile the split that divides the subject and makes harmony impossible. On the contrary, the journal has successfully made visible to us both the fact of this division and the many unhappy consequences—for women—of the various attempts to ignore it. Placing the desire of the subject—the female subject, particularly—in the forefront of its investigations, *m/f* has produced some of the most rigorous and powerful work feminism has to offer.

Notes

1.   Samuel Taylor Coleridge, *Biographia Literaria;* quoted by Frances Ferguson in "The Sublime of Edmund Burke, or the Bathos of Experience," *Glyph* 8 (1981).

2.   Sigmund Freud, "Observations on Transference Love," in *The Standard Edition of the Complete Psychological Works of Sigmund Freud,* vol. III, p. 167; see also Catherine Millot, "The Feminine Superego," this volume.

3.   Michel Foucault, "Georges Canguilhem: philosopher of error," *Ideology & Consciousness,* vol. 7 (1980), p. 52.

4.   This phrase (emphasis mine) is taken from Teresa de Lauretis, *Technologies of Gender,* Indiana University Press, 1987, p. x. The phrase has often been quoted in support of a new social *rather than* psychoanalytic position that seems to be gaining wider acceptance in the United States.

5.   Foucault, p. 61.

6.   Jacques Lacan, *L'Ethique de la psychoanalyse,* Seuil, 1986, p. 24.

m/f sees its work as a contribution to the development of political and theo-retical debate within what is loosely called the Women's Movement. Any political and theoretical argument that places itself within the Women's Movement commits itself to a concern with what is specific to women. But some theoretical formulations of women as a specific social group entail positions with which we must disagree. One such formulation is in terms of essential femininity. This can take two forms; either the idea of transhistorical oppression of women at all times, or the idea of an "orig-inal" femininity that is repressed or suppressed. Another approach is to assume that women are a social group, but one whose history has been suppressed. The rein-statement of this history is then assumed to be a sufficient political practice.

In other words the concern with what is specific to women both provides moments of political unity and at the same time operates to obscure very real polit-ical issues. The unity of the Women's Movement lies in the belief that the sexual divi-sion of labor between men and women, as it is constituted at present, has profound and adverse effects on the social position of women. But attempts to consider sexual division from within existing political and theoretical frameworks cannot provide the analysis that is needed.

The "Marxist-Feminist" position constitutes a recognition of this inadequacy. Traditionally, in this country, Marxist politics have stressed not only the organization of capitalist society in terms of class division, but also the primacy of the class division as the determinant of political action. It has also been argued that the transformation of this division will necessarily bring about significant changes for women. But the problem of women cuts across class division. Given this traditional definition of soci-ety in terms of class and politics, the problem of women is always secondary to the problem of the class organization of society. This placing of a politics of women has left some of us in difficult political straits, since we have no desire to dissociate ourselves from a politics that aims to erase the class basis of society. But neither can we accept the empty promise that the transition to socialism will in itself bring about a change in the relations between the sexes.

Within Marxist-Feminism there are three distinct tendencies that emerge directly from the theoretical and political priority given to the concept of class. There are problems, however, with the direct importation of Marxist terms into feminist analyses.

First, there is the attempt to argue that women as a consistently deprived social group constitute an economic class. And because of a certain position within Marxism that asserts that transformations will be effected when a class becomes conscious of itself as a class (a class for itself), this position assumes that political changes in the position of women will be effected when women become conscious of themselves as a class. The consciousness of belonging to an oppressed class is seen to be the basis for political action. Against this argument it can be simply stated that class divisions cut across "women as a social group."

A second tendency in the application of classical Marxist ideas of class to women can be seen in any political project that claims that it is working-class women alone who will form the vanguard of any feminist politics. Doubly exploited, at work and at home, it is these women who will become conscious of their exploitation and form the vanguard of a transition to socialism. While no one would want to dispute the double pressure on working-class women, it cannot be said either that they are necessarily politically progressive or that they are the only women who are exploited. The operations of the law, education, and employment discriminate against women of all classes. To ignore these areas is to miscalculate the current situation.

The third tendency within Marxist-Feminism is the one that is dominant at the moment. The oppression of women—across all classes and through many different social practices—is seen as having one common function. That function is the maintenance of capitalism. The arguments put forward in support of this view concern the economy and the family. At times the family is seen to perform a direct economic function. It "services" the workforce, a service that the capitalist state would have to pay for otherwise. At other times the family is seen primarily in terms of its role in socialization. The definitions given within the family make women amenable to manipulation by the capitalist state, by which the employment of women can be used to deflate incomes and produce a reserve army of labor.

These arguments may seem attractive, but they are subject to the objections against any functionalist argument that necessarily implies an "intention" of the social structure to reproduce itself. Within the functionalist argument the family is instrumental in the maintenance of capitalism. But the collapse of the nuclear family by no means entails the collapse of capitalism. The Swedish example points to the possibility of a capitalist social democracy in which the traditional family might have no place. The "liberation" of women from the family need not in any way commit them to a socialist politics and to the overthrow of the existing society. In the functionalist argument the organization of sexuality within the family is also seen as a function of capitalism. But the organization of sexuality for reproductive ends is by no means exclusive to capitalism. It also exists in primitive societies and in socialist countries.

An examination of these tendencies within Marxist-Feminism thus produces the necessity to challenge and develop existing theories within Marxism. It also indicates the need for new work that can adequately theorize the production of women's subordinate position in the social formation in relation to and within a theory of class.

It is in the area of this work that *m/f* has placed itself. We are interested in how women are produced as a category; it is *this* that determines the subordinate position of women. Some feminists have taken up psychoanalysis as providing an account of the process of the construction of the sexed subject in society. This is seen as important because it is with the construction of sexual difference and its inscription in the social that feminism is concerned. But psychoanalysis has had little to say on the relationship of this construction to particular historical moments, or the effect that considering the historical moment might have on psychoanalytic theory itself. Thus psychoanalysis is not a sufficient theory for understanding the construction of women as a category.

The particular historical moment, the institutions and practices within which and through which the category of woman is produced, must be addressed. This is not a problem of origins but of the continual production of the sexual division within those institutions and practices.

The problem of the production of sexual division has been addressed in this issue in a number of ways: through an examination of how psychoanalysis constructs the category of woman, how Marxism conceptualizes the sexual division of labor, and how discursive practices such as film produce the category of women.

We hope that *m/f* will be open to questions that will advance theoretical and political considerations of women today. *m/f* places itself as a predominantly theoretical journal, and we believe that at this moment this work is of major importance for feminism. But we also believe that a politics cannot be "read off" from theory and that theory can never be a substitute for politics. One of our foremost aims therefore will be the development of a theoretical debate on women's politics; a debate that must take place in relation to existing socialist and feminist politics.

Parveen Adams, Rosalind Coward, Elizabeth Cowie

The practice of the Women's Movement depends on a notion of "the feminine" whether in feminist therapy, feminist politics, or even in the production of a feminist journal. It is the specificity of these practices, and the concept of the "feminine" within them that must be addressed. In the first issue of *m/f* we argued that the category of woman is not a pre-given unity. To the extent that feminist theory continues to rely on such a notion, there are problems for feminist politics concerning the formulation of pertinent political demands.

When feminists explain the present position of women in terms of a point of origin of sexual difference, they deny specific practices and politics any effectivity since these are thereby expressions of a fixed and unchanging essence. Sexual difference is then not instituted within specific practices but functions outside it.

A feminist history that positivizes the position of women merely expresses this point of origin in a celebratory fashion. What is important, rather, is to consider how specific practices have produced sexual difference, in a multiplicity of ways.

More recently, feminists have sought to theorize an alternative place from which to "speak." Feminist therapy, for instance, argues the primacy of a feminine experience. It assumes that what is repressed is alternative to and outside the given order and therefore subversive—but the terms of its "otherness" are, precisely, formulated within that order. Consequently, the assertion of an alternative closes off questions about the nature and constitution of such alternative femininity.

If the particular site of experience is located in the body, it then takes on the function of an origin. It becomes the source of a true speech, a "woman's discourse." But psychoanalysis has shown that the body has no language of its own, though the body can "enter the conversation." Psychoanalysis accounts for that possibility through the theory of the unconscious and its relation to discourse. It is concerned with the production of the feminine (and the masculine) through the discourse of the unconscious.

However, such a production is not itself determining across other discourses. Legal, medical, political discourses each construct different definitions of women rather than being the expression or representation of pre-given objects, women and men. This means that there can be no "feminine discourse" representing or reflecting a pre-given object, woman.

The Women's Movement is by definition about sexual difference and, in particular, the category of women. But the relation between women and sexual difference is always a *constructed* one, and it is therefore not inconsistent to conceive of a strategic homogeneity of women *and* to insist that women are constructed in a variety of practices. It is the shifting ground between the construction of the category woman that we have at present and that category that feminists struggle to construct that gives rise to the temptation to fall back on the notion of a pre-given unity of women and a simple notion of women's oppression. The unity of women's oppression results directly from that unity of women, women seen as the entity that the state, patriarchy, or capitalism oppresses. The questioning of such unities at a theoretical level is relevant to feminist politics, though theory cannot dictate that politics.

This is of immediate concern to *m/f* as a journal within the Women's Movement and addressed to it. A central tenet of the politics of the Women's Movement has been autonomy, from the established male-dominated left (or any other) political groupings, and autonomy as a women-only movement. Nevertheless there are notable exceptions where feminists have worked together with men and with specific left groupings—the National Abortion Campaign, or the Working Women's Charter Campaign. The problems this has thrown up, on precisely feminist grounds, have been discussed extensively in the Women's Movement. The necessity for collaboration and its difficulties remain crucial issues. Thus autonomy, while at times constructed in terms of a sex war, as a response to "essential antagonisms" between men and women, is also more pragmatically a recognition of the effects of sexual difference as sexual *division*.

This is especially relevant to *m/f*'s project as a theoretical journal inasmuch as theory has been the traditional preserve of men, with rare incursions by women. Our political response to these problems has been to work as a women-only group with a commitment to encouraging and developing work by women. Yet we are also publishing work by men. That is, within *m/f* we are drawing on and developing theoretical work by men as well as by women. Theory is not sexually differentiated, is not male or female. But we wish to emphasize the importance of the appropriation and production of theory by women for women. Hence the basis on which men contribute to *m/f* raises a number of difficulties both for the editorial group and for the journal's relation to the Women's Movement. It raises the question of in what way men can, and should, contribute to the elaboration of the strategies and objectives of the Women's Movement. What would it mean to confine any contribution by men to the area of theory, the area of their traditional dominance? Or, on the other hand, to publish direct interventions by men in feminist politics? The balance being held within *m/f* is, we hope, one between autonomy as isolation and a collaboration that subsumes and submerges the specific problems of women.

Parveen Adams, Beverley Brown, Elizabeth Cowie

If feminist analysis is to concern itself with women as a category, as opposed to a sum of individuals comprising a group by virtue of their common features, then it is necessary to consider women in terms of the organization of social relations. This is not to say that women are always and everywhere produced in the same way since the field of social relations does not have a necessary topography. As a category woman does not consist of a fixed content but of a multiplicity and diversity of forms in which "woman" is constructed.

This can be considered in relation to one way in which reproduction is set up as a problem of sexual *division*—in terms of a disputed control and possession of a feminine body, a politics of opposition/antagonism. Struggle in this area is defined in terms of women gaining back from men control over the reproductive capacity originally invested in the feminine body. What is implied is an absolute possession of the body by individuals and rights and responsibilities conferred by nature. We also see rights and responsibilities as conferred but through particular social practices in which possession is always constrained. "Individuals" are therefore the site of different rights and responsibilities that are concomitant with different forms of possession. It becomes impossible to speak of *a* body because it is not the same body that is constructed in different practices. Therefore there cannot be a feminine body whose control would secure a liberation of women.

If possession is usually thought of as the more or less absolute control of a unitary thing by a unified subject, then we are challenging all three of these elements. The subject of possession is not a naturally occurring masculine or feminine individual or sum of individuals but an agent defined relative to particular practices; the relation of possession is never absolute, but it is always a specific form of control relative to governing protocols; the object of control is fragmented, that is, defined as accessible only in certain specified terms. Agents of possession may *not* be summed and mapped back onto a recognizable and coherent entity. In seeking to return their bodies to women's control feminists are therefore in search of a position of subject that does not exist.

If there is no one subject position there can be no *sexual division* between feminine subjects and masculine subjects, for sexual division always requires full subjects already sexually differentiated, that is, organized into two unitary groups. It can never function as an explanation of anything because it always returns to its starting point. The problem then is not that of a feminine body and not that of a feminine subject. What is at stake is the organization of *sexual differences* in social relations. The law, medicine, social policy, policy-making agencies, etc., do not operate on a pre-given, coherent entity woman; however, the organization of these practices does involve forms of possession and control that are intricated in a series of sexual differences.

If we accept this, the feminist demand for individual choice must be rethought, insofar as this involves three interconnected elements. First of all, the demand assumes the possibility of a totally unconditional choice; second, this means that the choice is outside social structures, is a purely personal choice; finally, it is assumed that the power of such a choice would enable a true expression of femininity. But if we consider the notion of motherhood, for example, analyses are made in terms of individual women as mothers; hence rights and responsibilities in terms of abortion, access to family benefits, and custody of children are demanded that actually reinforce the notion of motherhood as devolving upon individual women alone. At the same time, it is demanded that the burden of childcare should not fall on maternal shoulders alone, that is, the necessity for a redistribution of certain responsibilities is recognized. However *all* rights, even those claimed by individual women as mothers, are not ours through our individual nature, but are already part of our construction as social agents—which involves the recognition of the effectivity of social definitions and social practices that have produced the category of motherhood. Calling for a redefinition of motherhood might well involve depriving mothers as individuals of a wide range of choices that they presently enjoy (in the name of collective decision-making, for example). The exact nature of the redefinition is, of course, a political question for feminism to decide on.

It may be thought that a level of social determination is introduced through considering woman's place in the family rather than as an isolated individual, and it is in this context that Engels's treatment of the family has been valued for its materialism. But in Engels this materialism is specified in terms of an economy derived from the successive divisions of Man's species-being, and the family is seen as the economy in miniature—and so the family is effectively asocial. For this is to ignore the possibility that the family may be seen as the contingent effect of the intersection of social practices, which produce different "families." The specificity of woman's place in these different families could never be recognized in the former analysis.

The distinctions we have been trying to make are relevant to feminism's *evaluation* of its gains and losses, in which the pessimism of "recuperation" always threatens. For an absolute right is evoked that contradicts the construction of rights within social relations. Such a nostalgia produces an evaluation of failure—we can never achieve a right so incontestably ours—and anything less is always seen as in "their" interests. When it is images that are seen as recuperated, the structure of the argument is comparable. A fixed content available to possession is assumed—either we possess it, and therefore it is progressive, or "they" possess it, it is taken back, divested of any progressive meaning or implication and thus recuperated. But images do not exist in isolation, their meaning given once and for all; they are constituted within a system of representation that itself is a social practice.

Parveen Adams, Beverley Brown, Elizabeth Cowie

This issue of *m/f* carries work on political objectives, forces of struggle, and sites of intervention and what it means to pose definite problems about them. We would like to take up what is at stake in this designation of "definite problems" through engaging with some of the appraisals of *m/f* and its project in comments, letters, and reviews (*Marxism Today,* December 1974, *Camera Obscura,* no. 3/4, etc.). Our position has consistently been that there is and can be no *general* grounding of feminism, no essential femininity, no eternal forms of oppression and patriarchy—which has led to accusations that we have thereby removed the basis for feminism. We would like to look at this problem.

Our arguments against such groundings of feminism have insisted on the multiplicity of ways in which the category of woman is constructed in social relations. This means that there are no *a priori* reasons for regarding all constructions as innately oppressive, and this has two consequences. First, it is necessary to demonstrate in any particular case the means by which an oppression is constructed through different social practices. Second, it rules out any "different but equal" formulation precisely by refusing to make a judgment in advance. Otherwise the dilemma would be: either *all* constructions, inasmuch as they produce differences, are automatically instances of oppression, discrimination, etc., or *no* construction is, and we have mere descriptions of differences with no reason for taking these as anything but "equal."

A feminist position that grounds its arguments in a general notion of oppression and, for this, introduces a terminology of "differences" and "inequalities," sees a demand for the production of similarities, equalities, as progressive. We will argue that the objectives of feminism cannot be seen in terms of equalization. (Although the Equal Pay Act could be better, there is no Equal Pay Act that could resolve the problem of women's low pay. Equality can only be constituted through the terms of an existing framework. Given the problems for women of "part-time" work and "over-time" earnings, it is that framework that has to be evaluated and restructured.)

It is our rejection of oppression as a universal ground that has been criticized as leaving feminists stranded. The question is whether we can ground our political objectives in a notion of oppression or whether we have to identify what will count for us as oppression—locate sites of intervention and analyze them in order to construct political objectives. Seeing oppression in the evident differences, the inequalities between women and men, leads to a politics of redress. But this is dangerous, for this theorization in terms of equality for women sets up a context where many feminist demands could themselves be criticized for giving rise to other inequalities or discriminations. Thus to argue for financial responsibilities for fathers and *at the same time* to argue for the right to custody of children for mothers might be construed as discrimination against men and hence as a contradiction. But, politically, for feminists, this is not a contradiction as we will show, and we must beware of producing, in the context of equality arguments, ammunition for our opponents. Indeed, we must look ahead to circumvent possible attempts at equalization whose rationale lies not in a feminist discourse but in the discourse of liberalism. An example here is the possibility, in the wake of the Paton case, of a change in the 1967 Abortion Act, which assigns no rights in abortion decisions to the father. The flood of letters in the press that followed the decision contained many that were expressions of a feeling of injustice done to Mr. Paton—given that the conception had been a joint decision, was it not only fair that termination should also be a joint decision? [This is discussed further in "The 'Subject' of Feminism" in this volume.]

If equality arguments are rejected, then there are still alternative means for constructing political objectives, for instance, by construing oppression as consisting simply in the denial of individual women's desires and choices, irrespective of any comparison with male choices. But, if even this possibility is unsatisfactory (as has been argued in "The Feminist Body and Feminist Politics," *m/f,* no. 3), then we are faced directly with the question of what it means to construct political objectives without recourse to general grounds. If we reject this as the reason for the maternal custody objective, then we see that the construction of political objectives is a necessary and complex task (in which theoretical argument has an inextricable part). One reason for right of custody by mothers would be to safeguard the women who by virtue of their sexuality—for example, lesbians—are outside the group of socially acceptable mothers. This is to say that in the present practice of choice between mother and father (and state agencies), certain categories of mothers will not be assigned custody because of the definitions and structures of sexuality in our society.

The custody demand is a demand for legislation, yet it is not sexuality itself that is framed in the law. The question therefore remains of what effects such legislation could have in altering the structures of sexuality. (The emphasis on the area of sexuality in feminist politics will of course have its own determinants. The political objectives of feminism have not always been posed within this domain.)

It is not only sexuality that escapes—something else escapes demands on the law posed in terms of each and every woman. A formal demand for custody would exclude any space for custodial arbitration. But is it clear that there is *no* need for such a space? If there is such a need, what would be required is a way of representing feminist interests within that space. We don't yet know how to do this. We can now see that demands posed as demands for each and every woman are not necessarily informed by an essentialist position. Nonetheless there are problems with such demands.

m/f has not removed the grounds for our struggles by questioning oppression, equality, etc.; we want to point out that such notions did not ever, in the first place, successfully ground the political objectives of feminism. Indeed, to follow through such notions would produce effects that feminists would not want. However, what it means to specify political objectives in other terms remains a highly complicated question.

We have argued that the posing of definite problems for analysis involves a number of considerations, none of which can be said to be exclusively either theoretical or political. It is necessary to consider existing possibilities, to make judgments about priorities, to deal with constraints operating on programs, and to think about the nature of political objectives. This means thinking through strategies that are not merely responses to events but involve calculations about sites and forces of intervention, and we hope that articles in this issue will contribute to this.

A further criticism has been that our analysis produces a political problem of the unity of the Women's Movement. Clearly the Women's Movement is not a coher ent expression of oppressed womanhood or a universal condition, but itself a system of alliances between groupings of interests of mothers, workers, lesbians, battered wives, etc., and this does produce the problem of the basis for these alliances, a problem already recognized within socialist feminism. Once this is recognized, it is surprising that the very possibility of using the term "woman" across a range of constructions is itself raised as an insuperable problem unique to *m/f*.

In relation to this discussion we would like to emphasize that the work of *m/f* is work-in-progress, developing lines of argument in order to specify terms for feminist struggle. Insofar as a coherence has marked our previous issues it is not the closed finality of a fully elaborated position, but may be seen as the result of the rigor with which we have sought to develop each stage of our arguments in relation to specific practices. This work has taken place in "internal" debate, public meetings, and working groups, as well as in detailed discussions with authors about their articles. If the outcome of this process were known in advance, the work *m/f* has demanded would not be necessary.

Parveen Adams, Beverley Brown, Elizabeth Cowie

In this issue of *m/f* the question of sexual politics is addressed both directly, through analyses of rape, pornography, motherhood, and homosexuality, and indirectly by posing the relation between psychical relations and social relations. In order to set out our approach to sexual politics, certain issues must be clarified. *m/f* has been accused of denying the existence of concrete men and women, or worse, of claiming that they are made not of concrete but of words. Of course we have never denied the existence of concrete individuals. What we have done is dispute the usefulness of using the notion of the individual woman or man to analyze the complex relations of sexual differences. What we have questioned in particular is the use and the blind perpetuation of the category of the subject as the site and explanation of those relations.

Our analyses in terms of the production of the categories of masculinity and femininity, whether in psychoanalytic terms or in terms of discursive practices, are not a way of demonstrating the nonexistence or illusoriness of individual women and men. Rather, speaking of categories is a means of stressing that masculinity and femininity have effects even though they have no clear unity of content or reference. For we would insist that although discursive practices clearly have relations with each other, there is no way in which they produce any fixed abode for the feminine and the masculine. Equally, we have argued that psychoanalytic theory does not produce the concepts of femininity and masculinity fitted out with simple contents, and certainly not as ones that can be made consistent with any general idea of domination/subordination. The effect of our argument, then, is hardly to say that individuals do not exist.

But while the "subject" cannot be the site and explanation of social relations, social relations cannot produce effects out of thin air. There must always be some material to work on; it may indeed be other social relations. But in the case of humans it has to be recognized that the social also works on a heterogeneous psychic material. The issue of a sexual politics forces the question of the forms of connection that might exist between psychic relations and social relations.

Some of the articles in this issue directly address this relation between the psychic and the social, opening up the question in a number of different ways. Other articles address particular problems of sexual politics where analyses of specific practices, legal, educational, political, representational, displace the question of the subject.

This issue of *m/f* thus contrasts with and disrupts some of the ways in which psychoanalytic theory has been used for a sexual politics. For in posing the question of the connection between psychic relations and social relations, it gives no priority to psychic relations and does not treat these as the cause of women's subordination. Yet social subordination has indeed been argued to stem from the unconscious read in terms of patriarchal structures—and the unconscious itself has been suggested as object of reform, subject of a socialist future and a feudal past. The psychic has thus been put forward as that which provides a given content, masculinity and femininity, which is tantamount to the social subordination of women. It has also been used to provide structures that ensure willy nilly an asymmetrical production/positioning of sexed subjects. But these asymmetric structures are always finally provided with contents that yield inequality. For what is claimed is a *general* link between subjects and social practices in that asymmetric psychical structures are taken to predetermine the subordination of women. When psychical structures are illegitimately given a content, this robs the social of any effectivity.

But what has been argued in previous issues is that the moment of sexual difference as conceptualized by psychoanalytic theory does not in itself produce fixed sexualities nor a definite and consequent set of social relations. Rather, the moment of sexual difference is about the necessity, in humans, of a psychical domain—of the unconscious and of desire. The inauguration of sexual difference thus makes it possible to *raise*, rather than to close off, the question of the connections between psychic relations and social relations. But these connections will take no general form. The social must necessarily work on psychical material, but it cannot be said to work on a finalized, sexed psychical entity. What we call sexuality—the object of a sexual politics—emerges from the interplay of sexual difference in the psychoanalytic sense and social relations.

We suggest then that the psychical and the social do not meet as fully determinate domains whose relation is then one of causality, overdetermination or parallelism. Thus they cannot substitute for each other and they cannot have any

necessary relation between them that can be stated in advance. To be concerned with
sexual politics must necessitate tracing the *particular* forms of connection between
psychical relations and social relations in specific areas as widely different as consciousness-raising, motherhood, or pornography.

To take consciousness-raising as an example, we would say that its effectiveness depends on the form of organization of the women's group involving a specific
formation of libidinal ties. The psychical and social relations involved in motherhood or pornography would be differently specified.

What will be true for all these, however, will be that social relations and psychical relations, while not the same thing, are nonetheless inseparable. Thus we would
argue that the radically different politics that feminism has claimed *is* radically different precisely in that it will have consequences both at the level of social relations
and also at the level of psychical relations.

Parveen Adams, Beverley Brown, Elizabeth Cowie

This is the last issue of *m/f*. The journal began as an intervention, committed to publishing articles that involved different ways of thinking about feminism. From the beginning we took certain concepts to be a problem and not a solution for feminism and we initiated a certain polemic with what had been understood as the first steps toward feminist theory at the time. As socialist-feminists we were opposed to the much-discussed union of Marxism and feminism; on the other hand, committed as we were to the exploration of psychoanalytic theory, we did not think there could be any simple union of psychoanalysis and feminist theory. Above all, it seemed important to problematize the notion of sexual difference itself, to suggest an analysis that went beyond the obvious division of "men" and "women."

We had hoped to open up possibilities, and now our initiatives have begun to be taken up elsewhere. But if *m/f* has had its successes, these are bound up with certain failures. It can be said that where there was a measure of political agreement our theoretical effect has often been slight, and that where we have been theoretically welcome the political point has not always been sustained.

Though it was not clear at the time, *m/f*'s project had an inbuilt time limit. It was the kind of project that surfaced at a particular time and in a particular theoretical and political space. That space no longer exists in the same form. It was a project organized on the margins, outside any institutional support or constraint. The journal has been self-financing and has never been linked to any academic, publishing, or political group. At a particular time, on the margins—and perhaps this was our strength—*m/f* was able to make its specific contribution.

The moment of *m/f*'s project has now passed. Like all feminists we continue to feel the discontents of women and we continue to feel the need for a feminist discourse that does not lose sight of that discontent. The concerns that cover the area first designated by feminism with the phrase "the personal is political" remain important. Certainly, "the personal" now seems to span a great complex and "the political" seems a much more fragmented field. As feminism articulates itself, the difficulty of its task becomes more apparent. We remain committed to these difficult concerns.

Parveen Adams and Elizabeth Cowie

The Nature of Feminist Argument

The articles in this section are drawn from the first three issues of *m/f*. They are an assault on old ways of thinking, an attempt to clear the ground for feminist thought. The first editorial was a strongly worded argument on the limitations of Marxist-Feminism; it stated that just as there was no reason to rely on Marx for the development of concepts for feminism, so there was little reason to carry the burden of traditional sociological and philosophical concepts. A fresh set of questions had to be asked and many "givens" cast aside in the process; we had no wish to hand down the same old conceptual clothing. Some concepts simply did not seem to fit the problems identified by feminists; concepts are not endlessly elastic. Other concepts that had seemed to be made to measure were also suspect; the very problems themselves stemmed from these ready-made ways of thinking. So a large part of the first few issues was given over to an elaboration and criticism of traditional concepts that seemed to us an obstacle to feminist analysis and argument. These included the concepts of experience, the subject, patriarchy, and its associated theme of origins.

This formed part of *m/f*'s argument against essentialism. Yet, while many endorsed an anti-essentialist position, these particular arguments were not generally given their due. For the question of essentialism provokes a deep ambivalence within feminism. On the one hand, there is an eagerness, especially among socialist feminists, to take a distance from a crude division by sex, an initial sorting from which the rights and wrongs of women would follow. If sex is not determining, then an analysis of the organization of social relations can explain the distribution of rights, powers, etc., and feminism can strive for changes in those relations. Of course, this argument is unexceptional. On the other hand, the trouble is that the analysis almost always fails to be made fully in terms of the social because there is recourse to the pre-given and homogeneous groups of men and women.

It is precisely concepts like experience, the female subject, and patriarchy that were and still remain quite central to feminism, which enable this sorting into two monolithic groups prior to the work of any analysis in terms of social relations. To avoid this, *m/f* accompanied its dismantling of these concepts with the idea of the construction of women. At the time, this move was met with disbelief, hostility, and derision.

Even today a sophisticated essentialism remains the hallmark of much feminist work. *m/f*'s dissent from essentialism of any order left its quite different mark on both our thought and our practice. Our anti-essentialism guided us into decisions that were necessarily independent of those of socialist feminists in the late 1970s. A first decision, as we have already seen, was to question what women are. If categories of women are constructions, then there is no necessary unity of women and no necessary definition of feminist issues. Feminism has to forge a unity for political ends, and this requires a conceptual apparatus to do the job. The point still stands, its force all the more obvious today.

A second decision, concerning the analysis of social relations, was complementary to the first. Social relations are not homogeneous; women are differently constructed through different discursive practices. It is therefore necessary to analyze practices such as law, medicine, social policy, in their own terms. It is not that the law, for example, *does* things to women; rather, it is a question of women as they are *made* by the law. The law works by constructing a reality that cannot be said to pre-exist the law. What is important are the *means* of representation,[1] for they produce their own effects; it is not a matter of representing a pre-existent reality.

A third decision concerned the question of male authorship in *m/f*. We did not doubt that men might produce valuable work toward feminist analysis and we thus accepted their contributions; we include two of our male authors in this section. This decision is consistent with our anti-essentialist position. For it is not a question of a man's thinking or a woman's thinking, but of thinking the category women *otherwise* than both women and men had thought it before.

To take women for granted is to fail to understand the construction of categories of women and to blind ourselves with the obvious. This section is dedicated to seeing beyond the obvious.

Parveen Adams

Note

1.   The work of Paul Hirst and Barry Hindess and their co-authors was an important influence on our thinking at the time of setting up *m/f*. See B. Hindess and P. Hirst, *Mode of Production and Social Formation: An Auto-Critique of Pre-Capitalist Modes of Production,* Macmillan, 1977; A. Cutler, B. Hindess, P. Hirst, and A. Hussain, *Marx's 'Capital' and Capitalism Today,* vols. I and II, Routledge and Kegan Paul, 1977 and 1978. See also Rosalind Coward's review in *m/f,* no. 2, 1978.

Natural and Social Division of Labor: Engels and the Domestic Labor Debate

BEVERLEY BROWN

The Concept of Human Nature

In recent years the notion of humanism has been under attack from various quarters, and in the following article the characteristics of a particular form of humanism, and its embodiment in the concept of natural division of labor, will be considered. There is in fact no coherent doctrine that is humanism, although its marks are easily recognizable in many discourses. For all its possible variants, what is unhesitatingly picked out as humanist are appeals to the dignity and freedom of humanity, hope for the future based on a utopian past, and abstract conceptions of the sanctity of human life. The most general definition that can be given is that humanism begins with some notion of an essence of humankind, its basic nature or innate properties, and proceeds to deduce from this the way things must or will be.

In spite of the lofty aims apparently espoused by humanism, it has been shown that this doctrine invariably functions as a theoretical and political obstacle. The precondition of Marx's *Capital* was the overcoming of a particular form of humanism by which the human essence was identified with reason and freedom, where the essence of the species-being of man was discernable in every human being. It was similarly necessary to eradicate the effects of humanism at the political level, where it obscured the necessity of altering control of the state by appealing instead to the good will of human nature to redistribute its products voluntarily.

In this article another form of humanism is identified and some of its consequences noted, with special regard to certain questions initiated within the women's movement. This is a form of humanism that arises out of attempts to pinpoint the emergence of the specifically human or social out of a posited state of nature. Compared to many simple humanist arguments that *claim* to locate human nature in some set of properties or other, this version is quite complex, for the human is located in opposition to and yet as deriving—"naturally"—from the natural.

One immediate effect of this view in the women's movement is its tendency to construct an essential "Womankind" to correspond to the spurious unity "Mankind" and therefore to repeat many of the previous humanist errors, assuming a monolithic set of questions and hence a unitary set of answers concerning women's issues. History—the history of an oppressed sex, and in particular the moment of emergence of its oppression—while originally providing a corrective to idealist and voluntaristic solutions, comes to function as a universal explanation.

It is, I hope, unnecessary to address the simple form of feminist humanism by which a basic female nature is posited (whether to women's benefit or detriment). Such simplistic conceptions may be taken to be almost universally discredited. In either case the correct procedure must be to analyze specific issues or particular obstacles to this theorization, as in the present article.

It is one of the characteristic things about even the simple form of humanism that it always functions by reference to a posited nonhuman term that is subsequently identified as part of humanity itself. The spate of books in the 1960s on the innate nature of aggression or territoriality (Ardrey's *African Genesis* and *Territorial Imperative,* Lorenz's *On Aggression,* Alex Comfort's *Nature and Human Nature,* etc.), for example, all argued back and forth between human and animal forms of organization, anthropomorphizing animals by equating territory with private property and then reading back the results onto the human species, which is thereby seen as a (reconstructed) animal essence. Ridiculing such comparisons, Engels remarked a century ago, on the question of the innateness of monogamy, that:

> if strict monogamy is to be regarded as the acme of all virtue, then the palm must be given to the tapeworm, which possesses a complete male and female sexual apparatus in every one of its 50 to 200 proglottids or segments of its body, and passes the whole of its life cohabiting with itself in every one of its segments. (Engels, p. 476)

However unacceptable such attempts at defining the human may be they do display this common feature of humanist arguments quite clearly—in practice, a humanist development usually takes as its starting point an *indeterminate* state, neither human nor inhuman but both, and proceeds to show how the essentially human is born out of this. Hence the usefulness of the ape as starting point, for it is neither completely animal nor yet human. The development of adults out of infants is another frequent model for the development of the human race in general or of particular social forms, and this, too, involves the idea of the as yet unfulfilled but already implicit (human) nature that must follow a set pattern of development.

Thus two of the major characteristics of humanism have been outlined—its positing of a human essence and its ambivalent relation to its nonhuman opposite. Since this appeal to essence may be either an appeal to forces of change or a justification of the status quo, the indeterminate half-human state frequently functions as a utopian past or future. The nature of the origin of humanity is taken as the guarantee of the possibility of a certain kind of future.

The two texts considered here represent two ways of dealing with the problematic of the emergence of the social out of the natural. There is a superficial resemblance between them as both present a history of the early stages of humanity, both see the institution of a form of division of labor as the moment of passage. Both are in the end concerned not with the social in general but with civil society (*bürgerliche Gesellschaft*), as the other side of the natural/social couple. The two texts are Rousseau's *Discourse on the Origins of Inequality,* and Engels's *The Origin of the Family, Private Property and the State.*

Apart from questions of detail, the difference between them is the status accorded to the term "nature," which for Rousseau signifies a set of conditions embodied in the state of nature and a constant set of human qualities preserved beyond it. While Engels on the whole avoids according any such absolute status to nature, regarding it rather as a constantly changing set of conditions in perpetual interaction, it will be seen that a residual form of it is nonetheless preserved in his use of the concept of natural division of labor and its supporting concepts.

The Natural and the Social for Rousseau

First, an examination of Rousseau's *Discourse on the Origins of Inequality,* in order to see the way in which the question of origins is classically posed. This text has been said to address "the central problem of anthropology, viz the passage from nature to culture" (Lévi-Strauss, p. 173). This passage is chronicled in the second part of the *Discourse,* where a speculative history is presented as a possible mode of transition. It is not intended as a literal history but as a set of enabling conditions. The end product—civil society with its fully developed system of social inequality—is made possible only "by several prior ideas which only spring up gradually one after another" (Rousseau, p. 212).

The mode of transition is both continuous and discontinuous, beginning with the "natural" man whose capacities for self-preservation and pity (compassion) combined with the freedom to adopt noninstinctive modes of behavior lead through an "insensible" progress to various forms of self-improvement and technological

advance. This tendency for gradually cumulative change by which man's inventive-
ness supplements and consolidates past achievements is augmented by a series of
disruptive events or "revolutions."

The first revolution, which "produced the establishment and distinction of families, and which introduced a species of property," (*ibid.,* p. 216) consisted in the
establishment of dwelling places for extended family units. Whereas before, men
and women, like all animals, had been more or less independent, a sexual division
of labor is instituted by which women stay at home and perform other domestic tasks
while the men take care of subsistence (hunting and gathering); there are corresponding developments of the sentiments and morality. At this point, "each family
became a little society," while the powers of cumulative change coagulate around
this revolution, creating society-by-contiguity at least. This is envisaged as a collection of rustic huts where work is organized non-cooperatively: "as long as they
undertook such works as only a single person could finish, and stuck to such arts as
did not require the joint endeavour of several hands, they lived free" (*ibid.,* p. 220).

The second great revolution was brought about by the introduction of agriculture and metallurgy. The tilling of land "naturally" gives rise to its individual distribution and so private property is born, if not yet legally and universally instituted.
Natural inequalities of strength and advantage are now developed into artificial ones
until, by the process of man's (I use the term "man" advisedly) cumulative nature
taking advantage of chance events, competitiveness, avarice, and desire for power
eventually produce a universal state of war, from which the only recourse is the social
contract and the institution of a juridical society. This is the

> moment when right taking the place of violence, nature became subject
> to law . . . that chain of amazing events in consequence of which the
> strong submitted to serve the weak, the people to purchase imaginary
> ease, at the expense of real happiness. (*ibid.,* p. 176)

It will be asked first of all why this is a *humanist* text. The answer is to be found in
the operation of the terms "nature" and "society" (or "culture"). Nature is identified
as the not-social, while natural man is the not-animal. Although invested with some
instincts, the differentiation from animals exists from the start with the capacity for
compassion and the capacity to adapt and invent (which is all that "natural" liberty
amounts to, for in a state of nature it is otherwise meaningless—cf. Althusser, p. 121).
What is shared with animals is the *state* of nature, that of being "alone, idle and always
surrounded by danger" (*ibid.,* p. 185), while at the same time there is a milieu of
abundance in which every need is satisfied. Thus, while "nature" is a certain set of

conditions shared with animals, as well as the physical and mental results of living under those conditions, natural man is from the start different and human.

This state of nature, by definition the non-social, remains within the social. Coincident with the positing of a far distant original state is its present existence in the human heart, an essence that may still be encountered by stripping away every artificial, social attribute by the process of introspection.

> If I strip this being ... of all the supernatural gifts which he may have received, and of all the artificial faculties which he could not have acquired but by slow degrees; if I consider him, in a word, such as he must have issued from the hands of nature. (Rousseau, p. 179)

Society exists both because of a natural development of human qualities, yet right within it, in the human heart is an original core that may still be discovered.

The history of the development of society consists in the interplay of the development of natural human capacities in response to certain natural events. Even the discovery of iron, for example, is attributed to volcanic eruption (*ibid.*, p. 221). Thus nature signifies both an original condition and set of capacities and also the means to their disruption. Artificiality is merely that which has been produced by the interaction of natural events and natural capacities. The establishment of private property in its first agricultural form is itself described as "natural":

> This origin is so much the more natural, as it is impossible to conceive how property can flow from any other source but work; for what can man add but his labour to things which he has not made, in order to acquire a property in them? (*ibid.*, p. 223)

Yet this same moment is simultaneously the first step on the inevitable road to civil society. "The first man, who, after enclosing a piece of ground, took it into his head to say, *this is mine,* and found people simple enough to believe him, was the real founder of civil society" (*ibid.*, p. 211). No external agency is called upon to establish human society; it is rather drawn out of humanity itself.

This same drama is played out again in terms of the relative development of the intellect or the passions, for Rousseau is at pains to point out how it is the latter, natural, form that has always taken the lead, by providing the motive for innovation and change. Similarly, language develops out of the first cries elicited by a spontaneous recognition that others (first animals, then human beings) are like oneself, and only subsequently does reflection and order produce a fully constituted "logical" language. No *a priori* knowledge need be instituted in advance, merely a certain capacity for adaptation and freedom from the trammels of instinct.

The problem therefore arises of how the terms "nature" and "society" can be set up as an absolute difference, or, if they are, how the transition between them is to be possible. The key to the argument lies in the relation between natural and social inequalities, for it is natural inequalities, which, in combination with the accidents of culture and climate, originally bring about the difference between rich and poor and the resulting "horrible state of war" (*ibid.,* p. 226). The only recourse from these property disputes is the universal institutionalization of that very form of private property that gave rise to them. The social contract is itself simultaneously established by universal consensus *and* is the mechanism by which such consensus is brought into existence.[1]

Finally, natural man is required to be not only an original starting point but present to this day in the human heart, this being the starting point of introspection. Therefore the effect of humanism as manifested in this particular text is the setting up of the two terms "nature" and "society," which are originally posed as opposites but which are also required to be continuous, the artificial deriving from the natural. Therefore the opposite term (society, violence, *écriture*) is implicit from the first and the state of nature can only be posed atemporally. Natural man is both eternally lost and eternally present within.

It is this duality that explains the ambivalences and sequential shifts concerning the point of the break between nature and the social. The emergence of private property, of language, and of the intellect all occur "before" the absolute juridical sanction of the social contract, and yet they gain their significance only retrospectively, in its light. They are ambivalent terms, all equivalent with each other—rudimentary possession/universal private property, *cri passionel*/fully constituted language, natural inequality/social inequality. In a sense, there is never a time that was not social and natural as well.

This is reflected in Rousseau's plans for resurrecting the state of nature, for it is not the absolute, utopian, and innocent form that is his prescribed reform, but a very specific vision of the period of independent, self-sufficient households.

Rousseau invokes as a practical solution to his problem (how to suppress the existence of social classes) an *economic regression* towards one of the phenomena of the dissolution of the feudal mode of production: the independent petty producer, the urban or rural artisanate, what the *Discourse on Inequality* describes in the concept of "independent commerce" (a universal economic dependence, permitting a "free" commerce, i.e., free relations between individuals). (Althusser, p. 159)

Engels and the Natural Division of Labor

The Origin of the Family is a text much respected for its theoretical formulations and ideological consequences. Making use of a classification of precapitalist societies formulated by Morgan as a set of "ethical periods," Engels demonstrated the intimate connections between the social organization of those periods and the organization of production. While some of the concepts, group marriage, for instance, are no longer accepted by anthropology, "the necessity of the gentile form of social organization in the more advanced variant of primitive communism" has been argued for as recently as 1975 (cf. Hindess and Hirst, *Precapitalist Modes of Production,* ch. 1).[2] Equally, Engels's arguments that monogamy is natural neither to the animal world nor to the early forms of social organization have been important in combating the view that women are naturally inferior, or that society can be inaugurated only on condition of the subjugation of women.

In spite of its honorable history, this text itself makes use of a concept of natural division of labor in such a way as to inscribe property relations within the very heart of supposedly primitive communist societies. It is thus no surprise that Marx and Engels find in the family the nucleus of class society, for the family is portrayed by them—not just from the institution of the monogamous family—as the primary site of the natural division of labor. If, as I shall show, this division of labor in at least some of its appearances in *The Origin of the Family* entails exclusive possession of certain of the means of production, then, despite the overall position of the text, "nature" is already invested with class forms.

That this is not the general position of *The Origin of the Family* can be clearly seen from the way in which "nature" does not signify for Marx and Engels a given and eternal set of human or material properties to stand over against the social. Nature functions rather as the continuing but continuously altering set of material conditions. The entire polemical argument explaining the *origins* of the family, private property, and the state would be vitiated by any overt argument that nature already contained property relations. Indeed the primary effect of the text, when we turn our attention away from the set of confusions contained in the natural division of labor, is to show that precapitalist forms of organization involve neither exchange nor exploitation, nor the production of a regular surplus that could make these possible. Thus the treatment of the natural division of labor must be regarded as an anomaly, but one that must be examined and accounted for.

Its anomalous character does not prevent the concept of natural division of labor from having serious consequences for the theory of gentile organization, of which it is originally an incidental feature. For if the terms in which the natural division of labor is theorized requires the existence of exclusive possession of at least some of the means of production on the part of men and women, then the whole conception of primitive communism as a form of collective ownership is put at risk. How can the gentile form of ownership be said to be collective with respect to the tribe in general but divisive between individual men and women?

The existence of this contradiction is disguised by Engels's shifting descriptions of the form of domestic organization of precapitalist households, so that sometimes they are left unspecified, sometimes described as comprising many families, but, in cases where the division of labor is concerned, invariably defined as consisting of only two main individuals. In these cases the subsistence economy appears as if it were a form of patriarchal autonomous household, supplying all its own wants and engaging in external relations with no one.

Apart from its appearance in *The Origin of the Family,* this notion of the self-sufficient household in which each member contributes equally to a joint labor process should also be familiar from certain romantic conceptions of precapitalist societies, which equally fail to consider the form of reproduction of the social formation as a whole. Instead a contrast is posed: where capitalism dehumanizes, alienates, divides; the precapitalist utopia is complete in itself, as innocent of exchange as of any other form of external social connection. The persistance of such an ideal may be detected in remarks like:

> Firstly, a historical pre-requisite of the capitalist mode of production was that the domestic family economy of workers ceased to be self-sufficient and self-reproducing. (Gardiner, p. 52)

> Practically all the family's needs were supplied by its members. The producer and consumer were virtually identical. The family was the economic unit, and the whole system of production was based upon it. (Tyson, quoted in Braverman, p. 272)

It makes little difference that one author is talking about pre-capitalist society in general, and the other about America in 1810.

The prevalence of such visions of a petit-bourgeois paradise and in particular its appearance in *The Origin of the Family* have inevitably had their effect upon the conceptualization of domestic labor. As with Engels, this conception does more to conceal than reveal, and it will be shown that the terms necessary to analyze domestic labor are somewhat more complex than this.

The Origin of the Family

Engels gives a summary of Morgan's periodization, which is a set of categories identified through human achievements:

> *Savagery*—the period in which the appropriation of natural products, ready for use, predominated; the things produced by man were, in the main, instruments that facilitated this appropriation.
> *Barbarism*—the period in which knowledge of cattle-breeding and land cultivation was acquired, in which methods of increasing the productivity of nature through human activity were learnt.
> *Civilization*—the period in which knowledge of the further working up of natural products, of industry proper and art was acquired. (Engels, pp. 472–473, my italics)

Each of these stages is connected with a form of marriage. There is first of all group marriage, prohibiting intergenerational incest to begin with and subsequently sibling incest as well. These correspond to the stages of middle and upper savagery (see table). Group marriage has the consequence that the paternity of a child is necessarily unknown, and therefore all forms of kinship must be calculated through the relatives of the mother. There is, of course, no private property, so this form of matriarchy is not an inverted precursor of patriarchy, a right of inheritance and succession through the mother. Group marriage is an organized system of access to a fairly large but well-defined number of "wives" and "husbands."

The movement to pairing is one of Engels's weaker arguments. He claims that to the extent that the increasing density of population must have made the traditional sexual relations seem more "degrading and oppressive" to women, "the more fervently they must have longed for the right to chastity, to temporary or permanent marriage with one man only as a deliverance" (Engels, p. 492). The period of matriarchal group marriage is already seen as if it were oppressive, something from which

Savagery/Group Marriage		*Barbarism*/Pair Marriage	

1 Lower
   transition from
   animal;
   articulate
   speech
	probibition on
	intergenerational
	incest
		1 Lower
		   cattle and
		   horticulture
		   slavery;
		   occasional
		   exchange
			transition to
			father-right

2 Middle
   hunting and
   foraging bands
		2 Middle
		   irrigation;
		   first social
		   division of
		   labor (i.e.,
		   pastoral and
		   other tribes);
		   exchange of
		   slaves
			communistic
			household

3 Upper
   bow and arrow;
   settlement;
   fixed wealth:
   tools and house-
   hold goods;
   food procured
   each day
	prohibition on
	sibling incest
	
	communistic
	household
		3 Upper
		   large-scale
		   agriculture;
		   population
		   increase;
		   second great
		   division of
		   labor (i.e.,
		   agriculture and
		   manufacturing)
			monogamy

the woman "purchases her redemption . . . and acquires the right to give herself to one man only" (p. 491). Such an argument makes sense only on the assumption that women are "naturally" monogamous.

While kinship is still traced through the mother (lower stage of barbarism), the seeds are sown for the overthrow of matriarchy with the institution of pairing. With the combination of increased wealth in the male-dominated spheres of production and the knowledge of paternity afforded by pairing marriages (even if only temporary) it is not long before the father "insists" on the right to pass on his newly acquired wealth to his children.

> In the beginning they [the children] inherited from their mother, along with the rest of their mother's blood relatives . . . but they could not inherit from their father, because they did not belong to his gens, and his property had to remain in the latter . . . as wealth increased, it, on the one hand, gave the man a more important status in the family than the woman, and, on the other hand, created a stimulus to utilise this strengthened

> position in order to overthrow the traditional order of inheritance in
> favour of his children. (Engels, pp. 494–5)

The overthrow of mother right and the establishment of inheritance through the
father are the conditions for the eventual institution of monogamy, a life-long bond-
ing in which faithfulness and a condition of semi-slavery are formalized for the wife.

Whereas Morgan had seen the transition from one period to another as "a history of the successive transformations effected by the products of men's mind, of
innovation through the effects of invention" (Hirst, p. 35), Engels transforms it into
a history of the effectivity of the forces and relations of production. Each stage from
lower to middle to upper savagery to lower to middle to upper barbarism is seen in
terms of this interaction. Hence in preclass society, according to Engels, marriage
relations are not simply a reflection of economic conditions but are themselves an
integral part of the organization of the production process, and also the condition
of its reproduction.

Thus in the lower and middle stages of barbarism, matrilineal or patrilineal
kinship structures determine the division of labor in the tasks performed, the coordination required in the performance of those tasks, and the distribution of the product of that labor (cf. Hindess and Hirst, *Pre-capitalist Modes of Production, ch. 1*). As
the gens as a whole is communistic, this access is collective, that is, all ownership is
in the name of the tribe. Ownership can be designated as access to the means of production, and the capacity to set them in motion. This implies not only simple possession but

> the "power to appropriate" the objects on which it acts for uses that are
> given, particularly the "means of production" and the power to dispose
> of the products obtained with the help of those means of production.
> (Bettelheim, p. 69)

The means of production in the case of the tribe would be either moveable property
(tools, cattle, or slaves) or land.

The movement toward private property by which certain agents are excluded
from access to the means and products of production is, as we have seen in connection with the overthrow of matriarchy, connected with the first appearance of private property in herds.

> But to whom did this new wealth belong? Originally, undoubtedly, to the
> gens. But private property in herds must have developed at a very early

stage. . . . One thing, however, is certain, and that is that we must not
regard him [the individual] as a property owner in the modern sense of
the term. (Engels, p. 493)

However, alongside this problematic relationship between collective ownership and
emerging private property, there is another, prior relationship. Not only do cattle
come to belong to the men as opposed to the tribe, they belong to the men as
opposed to the women. In the case of the collective/private property distinction,
there is a genuine question to be settled about what form property takes when it is
in this transitional stage. But the property relation between men and women, such
that women are automatically excluded from the ownership of the cattle, is justified
on the assumption that the division between men's work and women's work is
already a differential access to their respective means of production. Hence even
before the introduction of cattle men and women must have been prescribed limited
forms of ownership, since the automatic male right to the cattle is justified as merely
an *extension* of their previous sphere. It is this assumption that justifies the transition
to father right on the basis of inheritance, since the male wealth suddenly increases
in value with the introduction of cattle and becomes the subject of inheritance.

That the natural division of labor between the sexes is actually seen as a "natural" form of differential access from the start can be seen here: "According to the
division of labor then prevailing in the family, the procuring of food and the instruments necessary thereto, and therefore also the ownership of the latter, fell to the
man; he took them with him in the case of separation just as the woman retained the
household goods" (Engels, p. 494).

While the distribution of the product may be collective, and the distribution of
the means of production may not favor any one individual man or woman over others, in this division between male and female labor there is already presupposed a
form of class society.

The basis of this sexual exclusion from ownership of certain of the means of
production is the "natural" division of labor by which men and women have separate
spheres of activity. It is something that claims to be located in a simple fact of difference, and around which is accumulated a history of customary tasks.

> there develops the division of labour which was originally nothing but
> the division of labour in the sexual act, then that division of labour which
> develops spontaneously or "naturally" by virtue of predisposition (e.g.,
> physical strength), needs, accidents, etc. Division of labour becomes

> truly such from the moment when a division between mental and manual
> labour appears. (Marx and Engels, p. 51)

Here two sorts of difference are established: one through primary sexual differentiation, the other through secondary characteristics conceived as strength/weakness
(childbearing capacity, etc., could be added here).

These differences evolve "spontaneously" or "naturally" into a division of
labor. "The division of labour was a pure and simple outgrowth of nature: it existed
only between the two sexes" (Engels, p. 577).

It should be emphasized that "natural" is not the opposite of "social," for the
same activity may be both natural and social at once.

> The production of life, both of one's own labour and of fresh life in pro-
> creation, now appears as a double relationship: on the one hand as a nat-
> ural, on the other hand as a social relationship. By social we understand
> the co-operation of several individuals, no matter under what conditions,
> in what manner and to what end. (Marx and Engels, p. 50)

When Engels uses the terms "natural family," "natural economy," this does not imply
that they are pre-social, for each of these employs forms of cooperation through
social relationship. It merely implies pre-class and, by implication, pre-private property. Similarly with group marriage, pairing, and monogamy. None of these is a first
social event. Therefore, when Engels uses the term "natural division of labor" it does
not imply that it is independent of social forms, for it represents one of the first
modes of cooperation.

Nonetheless, the arguments that purport to establish the existence of a natural
division of labor elide many separate considerations. We may, without raising the
question of differential access to the means of production, consider first of all a
purely technical division of labor, that is, simply the division between different tasks
or functions in a labor process. Where Marx speaks in *Capital* of the division of labor
in a workshop, considering merely the way in which production is subdivided into
different tasks, this is essentially technical. Although this division itself may be
thought to be determined by the relations and forces of production, this does not
prevent it from being considered in isolation.

To speak of a natural division of labor, refers, in a minimal sense, to the distribution of previously divided functions over the sexes. It is natural only insofar as
the mode of distinguishing between the sexes is natural, and does not necessarily
imply any essential reason why specific tasks should be assigned to specific sexes.

It is possible to construct an instance of such a nonprejudicial form of natural division of labor by reference to the case of the hunting and foraging collective of middle savagery (Hindess and Hirst, *Precapitalist Modes of Production,* ch. 1). If the population is so unstable and diverse that the only guaranteed differentiated members are men and women, then one would have a genuine case of a division of labor on a sexual/technical basis, with no reference to the secondary sexual characteristics of men and women.

There are certain problems with this conception, however, which arise partly from the transference of a concept of technical division of labor first formulated in terms of a capitalist workshop onto a subsistence economy. A workshop, like any form of capitalist enterprise, has a definite product, and therefore the division of functions is always subordinate to the constraints governing the production of that particular product at any one time. While there may be several possible ways of dividing the work, these will be within certain definite limits. In a subsistence economy, however, it is not clear what is to count as the whole labor process to be divided, as there is no "natural" designation of what constitutes the end product. Thus it is not clear whether the prepared food—the combined result of both male and female activity—is the entire end product, or whether the growing or catching of the food is one thing and its preparation another. Therefore, it might even be suggested that the division of labor in a subsistence economy ought really to be compared to the division of social labor, a division between different branches of production.

More important, however, is the fact that while any technical division of labor is determined by production relations, this does not mean that it is the only possible division of the same labor process. This leads to the idea that secondary sexual characteristics might themselves have some effect on the technical division of labor, affecting the way tasks are divided up in the first place. This is more akin to Engels's arguments, for it is clear that the "minimal" technical/sexual division of labor based on difference alone would not serve Engels's purpose, as it cannot tie men and women permanently to their division of tasks. Once hunting and foraging is superseded, another set of reasons have to be found for assigning an analogous set of relations to households in permanent settlement, and this is why Engels (like most defenders of the natural division of labor) attaches the technical division of labor to secondary sexual characteristics.

In terms of the relationship between the technical and natural division of labor, therefore, it can be said that the technical division of labor between the sexes should be seen as bearing as much relation to biological sex differences as kinship structures do to biological parenthood. Sexual difference in this sense has effects on both the forces and relations of production and may be comparable to any other such "natural" force. Variations in strength, child-bearing period, etc., are merely factors to be taken into account in considering the totality of determinants in the organization of production at any one time.

Marx and Engels make the transition to class society through the concept of the social division of labor, which is "the division of economic positions between classes of agents coincident on the distribution of the means of production" (Hindess and Hirst, *Mode of Production and Social Formation,* p. 77).

"Social" in *this* sense refers not to the simple coordination required even by a technical division of labor, but to the differential access to the means of production by different classes of economic agents, that is, different forms of ownership by different classes.

> The various stages of development in the division of labour are just so
> many forms of ownership ie the existing stage in the division of labour
> determines the relation of individuals to one another with reference to
> the material, implement, and product of labour. (Engels, p. 43)

Thus it is only with such a social division of labor that one can legitimately speak of class or private property.

We have already noted, however, that this seems to apply equally to the natural division of labor in the family. What *prevents* one from saying that the natural division of labor is also a social division, since it assigns certain means of production to certain classes of agents (men collectively and women collectively), is the condition implicit in the social division of labor that exchange take place between the two sets of agents and that production be at least in part for exchange.

Engels identifies the first great social division of labor with exclusive pastoralism, which allows both the substitution of new means of subsistence for the old ones and surplus for exchange (primarily for slaves). The products of women's work are never surplus and never exchanged.[3]

The following anomalous set of propositions therefore arises from this analysis of *The Origin of the Family:* 1. sexual division of labor is not social because it does not entail exchange or the production of a surplus; 2. the sexual division of labor may therefore be conceived as a division of subsistence labor centered around an (as yet unspecified) household; 3. the division of labor is defined in terms of exclusive possession of certain of the means of production (a possession so exclusive that women are automatically witheld from a share in the crucial surplus-producing cattle): "Hence he owned the cattle, and the commodities and slaves obtained in exchange for them; the women shared in consuming it but she had no share in owning it" (Engels, p. 579).

Thus domestic labor is conceived both as one part of the total production process and as an exclusive sphere of activity with its own means of production. The sphere of male labor outside the household is both natural (i.e., pre-class) and social (i.e., involves exclusive possession and therefore private property). Thus there is a problem not only for the opposition domestic/outside labor, but also for the relation between collective/exclusive ownership. In other words, the natural division of labor itself appears to harbor the private property supposedly exclusive to the social division.

The Household Economy

These contradictions are able to coexist in the same text through their cohabitation of the scene of subsistence production, the communistic household, which subsumes and disguises their opposing tendencies. Insofar as it is communistic, there must be no exclusive possession since all ownership is mediated through the kinship structure and hence the tribe as a whole. Yet in the very passages that assert this communality, the exclusive possession characteristic of the natural division of labor is simultaneously asserted:

> The men went to war, hunted, fished, provided the raw material for food and the tools necessary for these pursuits. The women cared for the house and prepared food and clothing; they cooked, weaved and sewed. Each was master in his or her own field of activity; the men in the forest, the women in the house. Each owned the tools he or she made or used; the men the weapons and the hunting and fishing tackle, the women the household goods and utensils. The household was communistic, comprising several and often many families. Whatever was produced and used in common was common property: the house, the garden, the longboat. (Engels, p. 577)

Communality is therefore established only *between families,* totally ignoring the fact that domestic as well as outside work is undertaken collectively. In spite of the fact that the women's work is collectively organized through technical division (of household functions), the natural division of labor is usually presented as between "the man" and "the woman," with private access to the tools he or she has produced. The "natural" division of labor therefore does not even recognize the presocial matriarchal communal household as a form of division between women's work and men's work in general, but posits instead a division between two primary *individuals.*

Similarly the collectivity of the social formation as a whole is dissolved into a simple domestic model of production:

> At bottom, every household contains an entire economy, forming as it does an independent centre of production (manufacture merely the domestic subsidiary labour of the women etc). (Marx, *Formen,* p. 79)

Just as the term "communistic household" is used indifferently throughout *The Origin of the Family* to characterize all forms of premonogamous household, so women's work exists as an unlocated—hence timeless and "natural"—set of activities.

The only form of household that appears to unite collective and individual labor as an explicit form bears certain similarities to the Asiatic, Slavonic, and German transitional forms of social organization. The household organization is described as follows:

> It embraces several generations . . . who all live together in one household, till their fields in common, feed and clothe themselves from the common store and communally own all surplus products . . . the master of the house (*domàcin*), who represents it in external affairs may dispose of smaller objects and manages the finances, being responsible for the latter as well as the regular conduct of business. He is elected and does not by any means need to be the eldest. The women and their works are under the direction of the mistress of the house (*domàcica*), who is usually the *domàcin*'s wife. In the choice of husbands for the girls she generally has an important, often the decisive, voice. Supreme power, however is vested in the Family Council. (Engels, p. 497)

The antagonism between collective labors and individual possession is settled by establishing a supreme authority in the respective realms of master and mistress who presumably organize the collective labor of the male and female members of the different generations.

The suppressed phrases in the above quotation are: "the descendants of one father and their wives" and "The community is under the supreme management of (the master of the house)." In other words, the household community that fits the requirements of the natural division of labor is the *patriarchal* household community, which Engels sees as the transitional form between mother right and institutionalized monogamy. What was supposed, if not as an original state of nature, at least as a material given with a limited history connected with prepatriarchal forms, arises only with the emergence of a primitive form of property and surplus and, most significantly, with the institution of patriarchy.

The family is well described as the nucleus of class society, for its conceptualization derives from that society and is subsequently read back onto its preclass forms:

> With the division of labour, in which all these contradictions are implicit, and which in turn is based on a natural division of labour in the family and the separation of society into individual societies opposed to one another, is given simultaneously the *distribution,* and indeed, the *unequal* distribution, quantitative and qualitative, of labour and its products, hence property: the nucleus, the first form of which lies in the family where the wife and children are slaves of the husband. (Marx and Engels, p. 52)

The characteristic of this transitional form is the breakdown, on the one hand, of the primitive means of reproduction through a complex kinship structure, and its anticipation of a not-yet-developed state. In the case of the Asiatic mode of production, this is manifested as a state whose existence is purely formal, its forms of exploitation being covered by the social organization itself. With this communistic household, unconnected by either marriage or exchange with any other household, and in fact used to characterize all precapitalist social structures, there is more than just a failure to consider the question of its reproduction, for it is used to disguise the non-naturalness of the natural division of labor. The unspecified character of the household merely confirms the indeterminacy of this concept of the division of labor.

In fact the concept of the patriarchal household owes less to a schema of transitional forms in early society than it does to the influential concept of the patriarchal household in seventeenth-century political philosophy. The authority that the head of the household exercises over wife, children, and servants is taken as the type of authority the monarch exercises over his domain (cf. Tribe, ch. 3). The version of this offered by *The Origin of the Family* is an economic one, positing a master and mistress in charge of their respective domains, with the mistress, however, subordinate to her husband, who is concerned with the overall management of the household. "Just before" the birth of class society ("just before" the birth of political economy) there is posited a unit of the economy that can function as pattern for the whole. It is Engels's equivalent of the way isolated economic man is posited by political economy and it is subject to the same strictures. Just as Marx railed against classical political economy for positing as "primordial condition" the very thing whose historical conditions needed to be explained—isolated economic agents—so Engels can be criticized for positing a primordial isolated family. The precapitalist family does not correspond to this model, nor can any economy be constructed as a series of totally self-sufficient household production units.

It must be asked therefore why this myth exists, in other words, why the contradictions in the conception of domestic labor exist? They reveal a failure to take into account the relation, or rather, the changing relation, between production and reproduction, subsistence and surplus. This is manifest in the way a division of labor originally seen as an equal participation by *groups* of men and *groups* of women in production for subsistence can come to be described retrospectively in the following terms:

> *Gaining a livelihood* had always been the business of the man, he produced and earned the means therefore. The herds were a new means of gaining a livelihood and their original domestication and subsequent tending was his own work. (Engels, p. 579, my italics)

Showing the way in which domestic/outside labor has been "naturalized" into production for consumption/"gaining a livelihood" does not mean giving up the sexual division of labor as a concept but necessitates a reexamination of precapitalist forms of subsistence production, taking into account the collective organization of domestic work and the role of women in nondomestic work. This will also affect the conceptualization of male work; it is illegitimate simply to redescribe it as "gaining a livelihood."

Integrating Precapitalist Formations

In those texts in which Marx and Engels consider these precapitalist forms, the coexistence of such contradictions is found to be facilitated by certain features of the organization of the texts themselves.

The exegesis of *The Origin of the Family* and *The German Ideology* is organized around a series of social divisions of labor. In *The Origin of the Family,* these are, first between pastoral and prepastoral tribes, and second between manufacture/handicrafts and agriculture. In the *German Ideology,* mental and manual labor is the overall form of division, shown first as the division between town and country, then town against town, the separation of production and commerce, and so on. Given the form of development of the "narrative," it is inevitably the progressive one of the pair that is analyzed and that is the subject of the succeeding division of labor. Apart from the division between labor and capital, no coherent account is given of what happens to the superseded member of the pair, thereby neglecting the transformations that necessarily appear in all spheres with each successive division of labor; it also ignores the traditional forms of combination of "backward" spheres—domestic work and handicrafts, for example. Thus, if we start from an original division of labor *within* the family, and then proceed to a subsequent division of the outside labor performed by males into pastoral and prepastoral forms of labor and so on, there is no account given of the way in which this affects the division of labor *still* obtaining in the family.

One should employ the same principle Marx employs of the institution of generalized commodity exchange:

> The process of distribution which turns a mass of individuals into a nation, etc., into potential free wage-labourers . . . does *not* presuppose the *disappearance* of the previous sources of income. . . . On the contrary, it assumes that *only* their use has been altered, that their mode of existence has been transformed. (Marx, *Formen,* p. 105)

In the transformations of domestic labor the same set of historic activities is performed perennially and yet their *use* is altered.

> This division of labour (in the family) remained unchanged, and yet it now puts the former domestic relationship topsy-turvy because the division of labour outside the family had changed. The very cause that formerly made the woman supreme in the house, namely her being confined to domestic work, now assured supremacy in the house for the man: the woman's housework lost its significance compared with the man's work in obtaining a living. (Engels, p. 579)

Just as the pastoralist, the hand-weaver, the petty commodity producer, does not function under capitalist social relations as an isolated and anachronistic survival, neither does the domestic worker. Their "original" relations to the means of production will of necessity be altered, and differences of scale will also have occurred. The selling of petty commodities, for example, could not fail to be affected by capitalist market relations.

It is, of course, possible to reduce to capitalist relations even directly incompatible ones. The self-sufficient peasant for example, is, for the purposes of calculation, "cut up into two persons":

> As owner of the means of production he is capitalist, as labourer he is his own wage-labourer. As capitalist he therefore pays himself his wages and draws profit on his capital; that is to say, he exploits himself as wage-labourer, and pays himself, in the surplus-value, the tribute that labour owes to capital. (Marx, *Theories of Surplus Value*, p. 408)

This, however, is not to deny the existence of the peasant, nor the specificity of his noncapitalist relations, and indeed, these are essential to the reduction itself.

In the case of domestic labor the problem of theorizing the effects of successive divisions of labor is compounded in a number of respects, not least by the lack of an adequate account of precapitalist domestic labor. Such an account is necessary in order to establish the specificity of the domestic/subsistence form. An account of precapitalist domestic labor is a prerequisite for the conceptualization of its relation to subsequent forms including capitalist production relations.

One difficulty in conceptualizing domestic labor is that of dealing with the transformed status of "preserved" economies. This sphere of activity is no longer one element in a subsistence economy but is now subordinated to the demands of production for surplus. A second difficulty relates to the fact that subsistence production was organized around the kinship structure that determined the reproduction of the entire social structure, but now domestic labor and kinship relations relate only to the reproduction of individual wage workers. Reproduction of the workforce as a whole is thus no longer the function of an all-embracing lineage system, but is atomized like the individual workers themselves. Previously there was no separation between the conditions of reproduction of the social organization as a whole and the reproduction of the individual worker; under capitalism these have become separated.

The Domestic Labor Debate

All these considerations have had their effects on the domestic labor debate. Attempts have been made to assimilate domestic labor to wage labor, petty commodity production, and unproductive labor, but none of these solutions escapes the fact that something that is paid no wage, has no specific marketable product (use-value) as its end, and has no formal relation to the production process or the labor market cannot be slotted into one of these preexisting categories. While the historic set of activities that makes up domestic labor *could* be socialized, this does not sanction an analysis of them as if they were so at present. A service industry is an enterprise employing wage-laborers and producing a profit. Domestic labor is a set of services and consumer activities performed in the house and local community. The domestic labor debate (which is usually couched in terms of the labor theory of value) may be reduced to a conundrum, if that is not too impertinent a term.

According to the labor theory of value, the profit that accrues to the capitalist in production derives from the difference between the amount of labor performed by the laborer and, ultimately, the amount of labor necessary to reproduce the laborer—the cost of the provision of food, shelter, and emotional necessities as well as the provision of new laborers when the old ones wear out—the cost of labor power in other words. The wage paid covers only the cost of reproduction of labor power, whereas the labor performed (which is what the wage is supposed to remunerate) is worth more than this. Both labor and labor power may therefore be considered in terms of commodities, the commodities necessary for reproduction and the commodity, labor, for it is only as a commodity that labor may be sold by a wage-laborer.

Under capitalist relations of production the only way in which labor may be so regarded as a commodity is if it is sold directly to the capitalist enterprise, for only then is the unequal exchange effected from which profit derives. (The labor that goes into the production of use values in petty commodity production is not sold as such—only the resulting commodity.) While the actual commodities necessary for the reproduction of the wage-laborer have themselves been previously produced in a different branch of production, and are therefore calculable at a specific cost, the domestic labor of preparing these commodities has never been sold directly to any capitalist and is therefore never productive labor. (Even though the same tasks, if separated and organized into different service industries, would arguably be part of the production process in Department II, it is not the content of the work but its social organization that counts.)

Therefore while one can in principle reduce the reproduction of labor entirely to the cost of consumption commodities (taking service industries as one of these), the privatized form of domestic labor itself cannot be included in this schema because the only way in which it could possibly be a commodity would be if it were sold on the labor market, which it evidently is not.

For the same reason—the nonsocial organization of domestic labor—it cannot be calculated as *either* labor *or* as an element in the reproduction of labor power because both require a direct relation to the means of production. One can neither demand wages for the unpaid labor of housework nor claim that payment is already implicit in the laborer's wage.

The origin of the problem lies in the conceptualization of the transition from production for subsistence to production for surplus. What is ignored is a "double separation": for not only is the domestic laborer separated from the means of production (even her own, for the tools of domestic labor are no longer produced by the laborer but acquired by exchange of the male surplus), but the reproduction of the individual laborer is separated from the reproduction of the conditions of production as a whole. This corresponds to the separation of enterprises under capitalism.

The domestic laborer is no longer working in a sphere of parallel subsistence production and no longer connected through kinship with the generalized form of reproduction. This is the true site of the overthrow of matriarchy, and the final separation obscured by the "naturalizing" influence of the patriarchal/communistic household.

Conclusion

In the discussion of *The Origin of the Family,* two particular mechanisms that operate as obstacles to analysis have been isolated. First, although the natural division of labor, may be given what we have called a "minimal," inoffensive reading, Engels's use of it serves to cover the distinction between a technical division of labor, organized around a subsistence economy, and what is effectively a social division of labor organized around the production of a surplus. By labeling the sexual division of labor "natural" it is possible for him to pass from an economy in which no member can be said to have exclusive access to the means of production, to one in which men and women have a differential access, based upon their respective spheres of operation. By retrospectively labeling male work, even in the collective subsistence economy, as "gaining a livelihood," the question of whether women, their production partners, might equally accede to ownership of the herds, is already a closed issue. Joint production for subsistence has been redefined as if it entailed a distinction between production and reproduction from the start.

The use of the autonomous household obscures these distinctions in a second way, since it enables Engels to pass from the collective household consisting of several families to the autonomous unit dominated by "the man" and "the woman." Once again the technique used is the retrospective definition as if this division between individuals had always been the case in the communistic household. What are lost are the crucial work relationships holding between men and women collectively, between men and men collectively, and between women and women collectively. Instead it appears that society has always been organized in autonomous household production units with no external relationships.

As a result of this it can be seen that the present state of domestic labor is different in at least two respects from its starting point in primitive communism, firstly in that female labor in a subsistence economy could not be labeled "reproductive," since the term "productive" can only have a distinct meaning when we begin to speak of the production of a surplus; secondly in that it could not be considered as privatized since domestic production is, for the most part, organized collectively.

I should here like to point out a number of consequences of the position taken in this paper. In the work on Engels a number of different issues were raised. While the presence of such a concept as the natural division of labor, which implies an independence from social forms, in such a classic text may be worth remarking in itself, it serves to draw attention to the fact that feminist issues are not a separate domain and that the failure to conceptualize them adequately leads to problems in the text as a whole. In this case, failure to work out the implications of the terms in which the natural division of labor within the family was defined led to problems in locating the emergence of private property from the collective ownership of the tribe.

Conversely, it must also be recognized that feminist issues have in themselves no necessary unity and should therefore be related to parallel problems in other theoretical areas. The myth of the self-sufficient household, already noted for its political significance in Rousseau, represents a common focus in questions concerned with the existence of a peasant economy, the concept of the Asiatic mode of production and other transitional forms, and romantic conceptions of precapitalist forms in general.

This questioning of unities should be extended to the separation of some of the commonly associated concepts of the domestic labor debate itself, for example, the complex: domestic labor/women/privatization. These do not necessarily and absolutely belong together and the historical reasons explaining their conjuncture must be established apart from any *a priori* assumptions of unity. It should be noted that the privatized nature of domestic labor or rather, of the reproduction of the labor force, would remain an issue even if it were performed equally by men and women and even if an equal number of men and women were engaged in wage-relations. Analysis of privatization, on the other hand, might more profitably be linked with other forms of privatized labor, notably out-work (so-called cottage industry), which are not necessarily performed by women and are not necessarily in the sphere of reproduction.

Finally, a word on "patriarchy." As has been indicated, this concept cannot be used to denote any form of precapitalist society. In particular, we must be warned against the notion that society may be seen as consisting of a series of isolated households or, conversely, that any household may be seen as the microcosm of society as a whole. Social and economic relations always extend beyond any particular family unit, which therefore cannot be conceived as autonomous. Avoiding any suggestion that the term may denote an economic system, "patriarchy" may be preserved only as a reminder that there is still room for some form of *extra-economic* explanation of that which precapitalist and capitalist social formations have in common— the residual connection of women with certain specific forms of labor.

I would like to acknowledge a debt to Judith Ennew, whose comments on this article and discussions concerning this theoretical area in general have been invaluable.

Notes

1. This and related arguments are set out in *Politics and History,* part 2, ch. "Rousseau."
2. The analysis of primitive communism provided here is the basis of my interpretation of Engels's gentile organization.
3. The definition of surplus would also depend on the definition of the production/subsistence unit, and here I have taken the family. However, Coulson, Magas, and Wainwright, taking the woman herself as the unit whose subsistence is to be the measure of surplus, claim: "Women produced a surplus, i.e., goods over and above what was necessary for their maintenance, and the exchange between their labour and the labours of other members of the family was on the basis of marital or filial relations, dominated by father or husband."

References

L. Althusser, *Politics and History,* New Left Books, London, 1972.

C. Bettelheim, *Economic Calculation and Forms of Property,* trans. J. Taylor, Routledge and Kegan Paul (1970), 1976.

M. Coulson, B. Magas, and H. Wainwright, "The Housewife and her Labour under Capitalism—a Critique," *New Left Review,* no. 89 (Jan./Feb. 1975).

J. Derrida, "Nature, Culture, Ecriture: la Violence de la Lettre de Lévi-Strauss à Rousseau" in "Lévi-Strauss dans le 18e siecle" (part 1), *Cahiers pour l'analyse,* no. 4, Sept./Oct. 1966.

F. Engels, *The Origin of the Family, Private Property and the State* in *Marx-Engels Selected Works,* Lawrence and Wishart, 1968.

J. Gardiner, "Women's Domestic Labour," *New Left Review,* no. 89 (Jan./Feb. 1975).

B. Hindess and P. Q. Hirst, *Pre-Capitalist Modes of Production,* Routledge and Kegan Paul, 1975.

B. Hindess and P. Q. Hirst, *Mode of Production and Social Formation: An Auto-Critique of Pre-Capitalist Modes of Production,* Macmillan, 1977.

P. Q. Hirst, *Social Evolution and Sociological Categories,* Allen and Unwin, 1976.

C. Lévi-Strauss, *Totemism,* trans. R. Needham, Pelican, 1969.

K. Marx, *Pre-Capitalist Economic Formations,* ed. E. Hobsbawm, Lawrence and Wishart, 1964.

K. Marx, *Theories of Surplus Value,* part 1, Lawrence and Wishart/Progress, 1969.

K. Marx and F. Engels, *The German Ideology,* part 1, ed. J. C. Arthur, Lawrence and Wishart, 1974.

J. Rousseau, *The Social Contract* and *The Discourse on the Origins and Foundation of the Inequality among Mankind,* ed. and intro. by L. G. Crocker, Washington Square Press, 1967.

K. Tribe, *Land, Labour and Economic Discourse,* Routledge and Kegan Paul, 1978.

P. M. Tyson, *Household Manufacture in the United States: 1640–1860,* Chicago University Press, 1971 (cited it H. Braverman's *Labour and Monopoly Capital,* Monthly Review Press, 1974).

from *m/f* 1, 1978

Material Arguments and Feminism

MARK COUSINS

Two questions are frequently posed: what is the material basis of women's oppression and what is the materialist explanation of women's oppression. In this way two themes are linked in feminist analyses: that women's oppression shall be considered as the effect of a cause, or base, which can be identified and that the theoretical means of analysis shall be according to a doctrine of materialism. The doctrine is taken to be historical materialism even if a historical materialism in need of some repair. This paper questions the way in which these problems are constructed and questions the form of argumentation that is deployed in their service. If the problem of women's oppression is posed as being a unitary field of effects of a unitary cause, and if in addition it is proposed that this can be specified by historical materialism, then the problem is incapable of solution.

This assumes that what is conventionally invoked by the term "materialist explanation" is in fact historical materialism. But what frequently appears is an appeal to a materialism in general, partly because it is averred that Marxism has "neglected" the problem of the organization of sexual difference. So a banner of general materialism is raised to advance where Marxism has failed. But this is purely gestural. In respect to the analysis of social relations there is no clear and singular form of materialism as a doctrine, still less as a methodology with which analysis can proceed. This is not to deny that materialisms have registered successes, but it is to deny that there is any unequivocal materialism awaiting use. In its absence, it is the materialism of historical materialism that seems to be invoked, though with a certain equivocation.

Indeed, Marxism has specified a system of social and economic relations and their necessary effects as the "material base." It is this that distinguishes it from other "materialisms," which provide other bases such as "biological need" or "technique" as the ultimate level of determination. Marxism has involved a theory of causality or determination and the specification of objects that appear in it, together with the theoretical means whereby the "real" can be appropriated in knowledge. To support such a claim the Introduction to the *Critique of Political Economy* of 1857 has frequently been held up as an exemplar, as the epistemological ground of a theory of modes of production.

But such a definition of materialism renders the quest for a Marxist theory of women's oppression paradoxical. For the basic elements of a theory of modes of production do not require any specific form of sexual divisions or of the sexual division of labor. The concept of mode of production requires, in noncommunist modes, a class division and a social division of labor. But there is no requirement that it shall be realized by any definite sexual division or indeed any other division as a necessary effect of that primary division. To attempt to refute this by evidencing instances of such sexual divisions in concrete analysis is to miss the point. At this level of generality and abstraction of the concept mode of production, sexual divisions are not pertinent. Of course, if the concept of mode of production is itself displaced, then the question could be opened up. If the question of the possession of and separation from the means of production as constitutive of classes as both economic agents and political forces is dropped, then it would be open to investigate how the organization of sexual difference is implicated in the formation of agents and their position in respect to the means of production. Yet even here it could not be assumed that the concept of sexual division, that is, a division between males and females, was coextensive with the organization of sexual difference. While the question is that of components of the concept mode of production and a simple concept of sexual division, there is no way in which the latter can be written into the former with any theoretical necessity or coherence.

This difficulty takes on an acute character in feminist analyses that have, obviously, insisted upon the problem of the relations of sexual difference. To the extent that this question does not appear in classical Marxism at the level of its leading categories, it is declared to problematize Marxism itself. Two solutions are frequently posed to overcome this: both may be seen to involve further and insoluble difficulties. First, it is held that Marxism has merely "forgotten" sexual division, and that its analysis can proceed with traditional categories after being "reminded" of sexual division. This is to demand that Marxism deal with a problem through concepts whose objects do not involve that problem. "Woman" cannot be added into the pages of *Capital* as the postscript that will then afford a solution. This is simply because "men" are not in these pages either. The capitalist and the laborer are personifications. Marx may be accused of adopting contemporary literary usage in designating such personifications "he," but he cannot be accused of omitting women. Those personifications of capitalist relations, the capitalist and the laborer, are abstract to and indifferent to the problem of sexual difference. Attempts to simply force the concepts to respect that problem merely result in the distortion of the concept. Again, it may be necessary to displace the concepts themselves, but they cannot both be maintained and compelled to work in a different way.

The second solution has been to argue that indeed Marxist concepts of the mode of production do not provide an explanation of the relations of sexual difference and that concepts have to be provided that are adequate to the task. The term patriarchy has been widely accepted in this context. It is granted that Marxist concepts do not locate forms of sexual division as necessary effects of modes of production, and the term patriarchy stands for those necessary effects within and across different modes of production. Patriarchy is thus the "material basis" of women's oppression. The first consequence of this is that the question of women's oppression is deployed as a historical problem. But constructing a concept that refers "across" modes of production while not being one of its elements reveals that what is at stake is the continuity of the effects of patriarchy in time. Not only does this reduce the problem of modes of production to one of the sequence of time. More importantly, it means that the problem of the relations of sexual difference is captured by the terms of continuity and history. Patriarchy is the great chain of women's oppression.

The construction of such terms for the problem has notorious consequences. Patriarchy must be considered as the effect of a cause, and the cause functions as an origin. It does not matter for the structure of effects what content is given to the origin, whether violence, property relations, or the incest taboo. The origin always functions as a cause by the retrospective ascription of phenomena to this cause-as-origin. The cause is then ever present in its effects this side of its overthrow. The origin thus establishes a realm in which its singular effect is registered, is represented. The realm is then time, the duration of its epoch, and social relations, the medium of its effects. History and social relations are thus a homogeneous substance in which the effects can be deciphered. The form of causality and the form of the social that are necessitated as theoretical supports bear a clear similarity to concepts of human nature that operate overtly and covertly in the social sciences. An entity is proposed as a cause or controlling instance and it is then declared that everything is its effects, by which procedure the truth of the entity is passed off as being adequately secured. The vacuous circularity of this is clear.

In fact, in this position there are no separate classes of cause and effect. The effects are part of the cause. That they are held to be separated by time is not a real distinction, for historical time is merely functioning to display the cause as its effect. Since historical time is considered to be a homogeneous entity, chronological distance cannot be made to provide a separate realm of effects, only one in which the origin repeats itself. Time itself is reduced to being the elongation of the identity of the origin. Attempts to circumvent this necessity, by developing concepts of variants of patriarchy according to different modes of production so that the effects of patriarchy are divided into periods, fail precisely because they are merely variants, variants of an identity that is given in its origin. Historical differences are sublated by the controlling identity. The time of patriarchy is repetition.

A further consequence of the concept relates to the medium within which the effects of patriarchy are to be represented, social relations. This can only be assured in a stable fashion on condition that social relations, all social relations, are themselves a product of patriarchy. Since few have attempted to argue that patriarchy was the origin of society, most have settled for having its origins in society. The problem then arises that since social relations are not themselves products of patriarchy, they must still be constrained to function as the means of representing the effects of patriarchy. And furthermore, if the action of the means of representation can affect the representation, how can any definite means be proposed for reading the representations as effects of that which is represented, patriarchy? Clearly, this point is hardly restricted to the concept of patriarchy; it concerns any position that posits a realm in which effects are realized or represented.

Lastly, another difficulty with the concept of patriarchy compounds this. In order to function as a cause, the concept has to assume the very thing it is supposed to demonstrate. Since the moment of the installation of patriarchy initiates an epoch and its realm of necessary effects, the "moment" cannot be considered as an accident, but rather must be the realization of an immanence already given in the relations of sexual difference. The concept of patriarchy purports to explain the relations of sexual difference, but has to assume that they always already exist in a form in which patriarchy can be installed. Ironically, it thus assumes a primary and originary form of sexual difference prior to its differentiation. This is not to question sexual difference in a conventional sense, but to question the discursive necessity whereby it is conceived as necessarily already existing in a form capable of being subjected to the "moment" of patriarchy in a unitary and exhaustive fashion.

In general, patriarchy is advanced as the "material basis" of women's oppression, taking as its referent the "universality" of that oppression. But because of the inescapable circularity of the concept, it stands as little more than an assertion of that universality. Given the basis which it locates and the causality that it adopts, it cannot escape tautology. Patriarchy is a system of effects of a cause in which all the effects can be read off from the cause, and the cause is constructed by reading off its effects. That its all-pervasive character is something less than an advantage is tacitly accepted in many analyses where it is considered as standing in need of a supplementary theory of women's oppression that is related to definite modes of production as conceptualized in Marxism. As a consequence of this, it is frequently the case that there is an impossible recourse to two "materialisms": on the one hand, the concept of patriarchy with its corresponding causality of cause as origin, and on the other hand, a Marxist concept of social totality with its corresponding causality of determination in the last instance by the economic. In so far as they locate a different "material basis" and do so through a different concept of determination, they cannot be coherently sustained as being complementary. Modes of production cannot realize things other than themselves; they cannot be subordinated to the general function of realizing patriarchal relations unless, of course, the whole concept of modes of production is reduced to a mere set of variant mechanisms for the realization of patriarchal relations. But in this case, the whole concept of determination in the last instance by the economic would have been transformed by a determination in the last instance by the superior instance of patriarchy. If complete indeterminacy is to be avoided, one must be structured by the other in a hierarchy of determination. This is not to privilege the concept of mode of production but simply to register that while it is maintained it cannot be logically articulated to a general theory of patriarchy.

The attempts to articulate the two can be illustrated by reference to capitalism. Often, either a general concept of reproduction is invoked or it is declared in reference to production, that the very concept of capitalist economy already requires for itself a definite distribution of tasks and labors such that a certain sexual division is inscribed in it. Both such positions are taken to be Marxist and both are held to confirm the determination of patriarchy. The concept of patriarchy and a Marxist concept of the necessary conditions and effects of capitalist economy are held to arrive at an identical conclusion, if by different means. This convenient correspondence can frequently be read in discussions of family forms. On the one hand, the family form of capitalist social formations is analyzed as an effect of patriarchy, that is, an effect of an originary cause. On the other hand, it is analyzed as being the cause of women's oppression, a social form necessitated in and by capitalist economy, which has as its effect the oppression of women. The problem of the two forms of "material base" and two forms of causality can be registered in the incoherence. The fact of the very convenience of this intersection, that it permits a wide agreement that the family is a *locus classicus* of women's oppression, is itself an obstacle. The contradiction would have to be registered and displaced if the "family" is not to be treated in an essentialist and sociologistic fashion.

Nor does that very appeal to the concept of reproduction or to the concept of necessary effects of capitalist economy upon the organization of relations of sexual difference escape its own difficulties in respect to Marxism. To take Marxism as a general theory of production and its conditions leads to disastrous theoretical consequences when the conditions are simply expanded by fiat to encompass sexual difference. The argument that a theory of reproduction must include childbirth is based simply upon a pun. It is one thing to list what every child knows is necessary for the continuation of an economy: it is quite another to give any one of them a discursive priority in relation to the problem of reproduction. The availability of oxygen and, within present practices, the continuation of sexual intercourse, could both be counted as conditions. Childbirth does not have any pretheoretical priority over them. Nor can the problem be circumvented by calling upon the "reproduction of labor-power." As a Marxist concept it refers only to a definite and limited number of objects. That the owner of labor-power is mortal and that its labor-power must be replaced by that of owners who are ex-children is bracketed off as a given by Marx. The problem of mortality is not treated as a theoretical problem in *Capital*. Old labor-powers do not die, they are withdrawn from the market. Fresh labor-powers are not born, they appear in the market as substitutes. The reproduction of labor power is conceptualized as a cost, not as a problem. If the social organization of childbirth and childrearing is forcibly intercalated into the concept, the concept ceases to be the thing to which an appeal is made. Ironically, it is only by reversing the terms of the feminist argument on reproduction that the problem of human reproduction could be made determining in the problem of the conditions of production. That would be if it were claimed that the fact of childbirth imposed an ineluctable and necessary social form upon the organization of production and its conditions—the very position feminists have so roundly attacked.

Furthermore, when the problem of reproduction is posed in a general way, it threatens Marxism with the functionalism and teleology of much sociology. Reproduction is there its general problem to the extent that it poses social order over time as central. This results in the assignation of functions to agencies that then realize them (or fail to realize them) in an ordered equilibrium. Such a problem simply does not arise in Marxism, though it does in much Marxisant sociology. In Marx, capitalism reproduces itself. Certainly, precapitalist relations of production require the intervention of noneconomic forces, according to Marx, but this is not equivalent to any problem of reproduction. There is not a limitless class of objects that can be specified as the conditions of reproduction of a mode of production, for in Marx, those conditions are secured as an effect of the mode. The relations of sexual difference cannot be tacked on either as conditions or as effects unless it can be demonstrated that a necessary form of their organization is inscribed in the relations of production. And it is the very concept of relations of production that has been indifferent to sexual division. The logic of this is clear: it is not a question of "excluding" the relations of sexual difference, it is rather that if they are to be treated in respect to the relations of production, then there is a further reason for displacing the concept of mode of production. But those relations of sexual difference cannot be saved for the concept of mode of production either by "adding" them in or by the detour of reproduction.

The other means whereby the economy, in this case the capitalist economy, is currently compelled to require a certain organization of the relations of sexual difference is by reference to the organization of the division of labor. This concern revolves around the question of domestic work and the position of women in employment. Attempts have been made to conceptualize the former problem around the question of the production of surplus value and its conditions, and the latter around the problems of the value of women's labor-power together with the concept of the reserve army of labor. What is promised is a political economy of women derived from Marxist categories that will deliver an analysis of the basis of women's subordination within the economy and hence in general. As a corollary of this, it is frequently argued that "ideological" phenomena, popular representations of women, forms of training and evaluating women, that is, the apparatuses of "sexism," find their material bases in women's position in the economy. Hence these phenomena are treated not simply as forms of oppression themselves but also as signs of oppression, the representations of an oppression that originates from elsewhere.

Each of these propositions involves a series of difficulties. First, in regard to Marxist categories there is frequently recourse to a reductionist functionalism. Certain characteristics of, for example, the majority of family units are abstracted and hypostasized as functional requirements of the capitalist economy in general. Whatever is, is made into a structural requirement. Thus attempts to demonstrate that capitalism cannot "socialize" domestic work often rest on the fact that it is not "socialized" and that therefore its nonsocialized character must be in the "interests" of capital. Leaving aside the quirk of a capitalism serving its "interests" by not capitalizing something, the reasoning imposes a tautology. Second, in those discussions that center upon the relation of domestic work to the constitution of surplus value— though it is largely agreed that domestic work cannot both be regarded as outside the realm of the law of value and at the same time constitutive of surplus value—the discussion proceeds as if there is no problem of the category of domestic work itself. It is assumed there is a homogeneous domain of work even outside that of socially necessary labor. But while Marxism involves a concept of labor it is not a doctrine of work. It does not provide any criterion of demarcation of what shall be treated as work and what shall not in regard to domestic work. It can hardly be desired that the principle of purpose shall be used to justify a realm of such labor, the means whereby the worst housewife shall be distinguished from the best bee. But in the absence of a criterion it is by no means clear what should count as domestic work and what should not. Neither a principle of the expenditure of energy, the dictates of common sense, and still less the sociological categories of work and leisure could provide an answer. The answer is given in the original feminist assertion of the problem as a political problem, and its treatment is not advanced by hegemonizing it by the categories of labor and value.

Many such arguments have been developed to provide a specifically Marxist explanation for the organization of sexual difference, under the title of a political economy of women. Their theoretical promise was to specify the forms of social organization and divisions of labor as they affected women, as the necessary effects and conditions of capitalist economy. Divided though they may be in their conclusions, they appear united in one assumption. There is an assumed correspondence between certain social forms and positions and their occupation by women. To question this is not merely to point to the existence of female capitalists or male performance of domestic work. It is to question that a social form can be mapped onto a sexual division in a straightforward way. To be able to do that would mean that the organization of sexual difference is at the level of the economy, for example, always able to be conceptualized in terms of individuals of a particular gender. This is the necessary condition of a political economy of women: that women are an entity whose components are individual females. The entity has the consistency of being female, and a finity by differing from men. The consequence is that however unintentionally, the category of the individual returns to a discursive privilege. It may now be a gendered individual, but it is an individual nonetheless, for only individuals may people a gender. This then excludes the possibility of conceiving of the economy as involving a set of relations between agents which are in principle nonreducible to human beings, individual men and women.

The contradictions produced by treating the economy as divisible into ultimate entities of male and female individuals can be demonstrated in certain discussions of women and the "value" of their labor-power. It is sometimes held that this is lower than men's and that this evidences the fact that women are distributed through the economy in a way that reveals their subordination. An equation is made whose terms are women, subordination, and economy as material base. Arising from, or at least corresponding to that material base is supposedly an ideological instance, of "sexism," of representations of subordination. But again such a form of reasoning imposes circularity. Why should the value of women's labour-power be lower? If the answer given is that it is so for customary reasons then this would reverse the whole terms whereby the "ideological" was a realm of representations of an oppression inaugurated at the level of the economy. This circle cannot be broken until the economy is no longer conceived as relations between men and women, and until the representations of sexual difference are no longer treated as expressions of a relation of subordination/superordination that is located elsewhere. This entails that the organization of sexual difference cannot be simply placed over the grid of men/women.

In fact, this difficulty appears in most analyses. It is usually taken as unproblematic what the referent of men and women is. It is the sum total of dead and living male and female subjects. The terms male and female, the organization of sexual difference, even the categories masculine and feminine, are usually tied to a referent in the last instance, the referent of concrete women and men. By this relay of reference most Marxist and sociological work requires that the final object of analysis is persons, women and men. Thus discourses and practices are conceived as ultimately the way in which persons and things have effects upon other persons, where things appear as the frozen residue of the past actions of persons. The objects of inquiry are then humanity and its divisions, that is, groups of persons, what they do, and what happens to them. Classes, women, youth, judges, are all the possible objects of inquiry by virtue of a double criterion. They are human subjects and they share the characteristic that defines the group.

This permits the repetition of all the well-worn sociological themes, the story of things that happen to people. As long as "woman" appears not as a category but as a simple referent, the structure of those themes is bound to recur. It has been by the use of that assumption that the arguments criticized above have been able to be deployed. It is by the use of that assumption that women's oppression is able to be conceptualized as a unitary field of necessary effects. For any such concept requires as its theoretical support and as its ultimate referent an unproblematic totality of women as concrete individuals. "Woman" is treated thus not as a category that might be conceptualized according to the discourse in which it appears, but always already exists as a singular plural, of the many who compose it and of the one fact by which it is composed. Such a unity can only be achieved within the confines of an anthropology of women's oppression, the unity of female pre-given subjects within the field of a subject population.

It is the undisclosed power of that assumption that makes possible the employment of sociological categories, especially of power and oppression. Oppression is conceived in one of two ways. Where men and women are staged as equally vivid referents, the oppression is set up in terms of the oppression of women by men. When it is objected that this reduces a social oppression to one of intersubjective relations, then systematic social relations are invoked as the author and mechanism of oppression. But this second form does not escape the problem, for the concept of oppression still involves the concept of persons as its referent. This entails that standard notion of power, as an entity which can be possessed and is exercised over persons who are the locus of its effects.

Power in the social sciences draws upon a legalistic treatment of power as being a set of capacities that lie with certain subjects and that can be exercised over other subjects. It is essentially a distribution of effective rights. It results in the positing of power as a quantity that exists in a form that may be owned or controlled. It thereby excludes the possibility of treating powers as relational, as sets of relations that implicate humans as their supports, but not as classes of possessors or the dispossessed, in respect to some desirable quantum.

Yet it is the traditional concepts of power and oppression that are used. The concept of the oppression of women often results in an algebra where one man's power is another woman's oppression. To challenge this is to challenge both the treatment of the category "women" as having a simple referent and to challenge that power can be conceived in this way. None of this is to dispute the political problems that are at stake but rather to deny that those problems can be dealt with by the maintenance of these concepts. It is no derogation of the Chinese political slogan "Women hold up half the sky" to note that if it were used as a theoretical protocol it would merely demonstrate that there was nothing new under the sun. But once the organization of sexual difference is no longer tied to the pre-given anchor of women and men, it is possible to deal with that organization in a way that respects the dispersed and heterogeneous places in which it occurs.

from *m/f* 2, 1978

The "Subject" of Feminism

PARVEEN ADAMS AND JEFF MINSON

The demarcation of a definite area and means of feminist politics has been both a necessity and a problem. The necessity refers to the need to argue a specificity to feminism that will resist its absorption by other politics. The problem refers to the fact that the area it designates cannot be theoretically specified in terms of the oppression of a pre-given category women and hence simply and obviously a struggle for women by women alone. Both the necessity and the problem create difficulties for socialist feminists. This problem is investigated in this article, which seeks to displace conventional categories whereby the specificity of feminism is articulated.

For while that specificity is widely recognized and respected, it must be noted that the theoretical means that are currently employed are often widely discrepant. It must be recognized that the theoretical differences within which feminism is constructed create difficulties for any effective evaluation of its practice. Indeed, there is a powerful tendency in the women's movement to evaluate its own past and present practices in a mode of celebration. While this is not true of all such evaluations, the article seeks to demonstrate the dangers of that position in which humanist theories of the subject, together with essentialist concepts of "interests" are reproduced within feminism and which have effects on the formulation and evaluation of feminist struggles. To précis this as a form of celebration is not to imply that anyone thinks that feminist politics are perfect. Rather, it is to make a point about the way in which both progress and failure are interpreted. Once the entities of "women" and "men" are introduced, together with their "interests," and once these categories are taken as given and self-explanatory, the form of evaluation that is adopted frequently falls into a form of measurement of the realization or nonrealization of the capacities and desires of women, in short, their "interests." The obstacle to this is then "men" and their "interests." It is easy to see how this obstacle appears ever-present and thus how the effects of feminist struggles appear to be ever endangered and undermined. Thus the registration of failure itself provides the occasion for celebration since it testifies to the subversive integrity of the movement's goals and the timeless justice of its cause. This form of evaluation is hardly restricted to the women's movement and can be seen at work in many left-wing organizations. It is organized by essentialism and moralism.

The essentialism is revealed in treating the category women as unproblematic in feminist analyses. It is merely a variant of the tradition in which humanity is composed of "subjects" as individuals, and upon which society acts. It thus necessitates a concept of a human essence that exists independently of and prior to the category of the social. The category of women is simply an addition to this. "Women" marks the always already given gender in the category of humanity, a gender to which essential attributes are ascribed. The most extreme form in which this is expressed in feminist writings is to be found in those assertions of female attributes, communality, tenderness, care, etc., to which are counterposed male attributes of violence and competitiveness. As a correlative political position, a feminist separatism is invoked whereby female nature is installed as a norm, as the essence-as-standard, which then functions as the regulation of the conduct of subjects and as the principle by which social practices are judged. It is clear here how essentialism and moralism are entwined.

Although such a position is rejected by socialist feminists, their own positions frequently have implicit recourse to the categories of women and subject, together with the concept of interest in ways that continue to constitute an obstacle. For woman cannot be taken as a transparent name for an eternal object. It will be argued that as a category, it is organized according to the laws of the discourses in which it appears. Thus women cannot be taken as an unproblematic collection of subjects, once the concept of subject is challenged. Nor can the concept of "interest" be sustained once essentialism is challenged. This article concerns itself with the problems of the concept of the subject and with the consequences of rejecting those positions. The immediate consequence is that the category of a unitary moral domain suggested by moral philosophy or a realm of values posed by much sociological theory is dissolved. What has been conceived as the sphere of the moral or of values cannot be sustained in a unitary fashion without positing an essential subject. Whether the subject is conceived as author or effect of the realm matters little is this context; the structure of the topology remains the same.

It follows that analyses cannot proceed from the presupposition of male "values," "power," and "interests." For this presupposition merely takes social forms as the theater in which already known effects are played out. The bulk of the feminist sociological industry has concentrated on "sexism" as an evil value that can be analyzed in terms of an invariant "experience effect." Social life is in this case the place where values are realized; the realization happens in the experience of subjects. "Sexism" as a category of feminist discourse is thus taken as a given and is read off from a society that is conceptualized according to traditional canons of sociology and moral philosophy. There are two problems here; first, that in order for "sexism" to operate in the way that is assumed it is necessary to pose a definite realm of values; second, it is evaluated according to a category of feminist discourse that is already set up in terms of values itself, the values of the realization of the interests of women. There is a certain complicity between the sociological conception and the categories of feminist discourse: the object of analysis is a value, the means of analyzing it is a value. Yet it is precisely the concept of values that is problematic. Both the techniques of moralism and the concept of a moral domain impede political calculation and the analyses of what has been characterized as the realm of values.

This has effects on feminism because accepting as a given that domain of social relations traditionally characterized as morality means that its analyses bear the trace of moral philosophy and its sociological offspring. To displace this and to argue that it has political implications is not to argue that theory can legislate a politics. Nor is it to say that feminism can be reduced to a moralism. It is to say that while analyses and feminist forms of political evaluation refer to "values" in the sense used above, there are definite limitations on those analyses and modes of evaluation.

The complicity between the two can be illustrated with the example of the concept of "socialization," a sociologism widely accepted by feminism in the analysis of gender difference. The concept borrows the traditional tropes of moral and political philosophy. The individual and the social are set up as separate entities and the process of socialization is the problem of how the "values" and "norms" of the social are ingested by the individual. It does not particularly matter what process is described, whether the individual is an active partner or a passive victim of the process. It does not particularly matter whether the individual prior to its socialization is conceived to be egotistic or altruistic, satanic or angelic. It does not particularly matter whether the values of the social alienate or fulfill the individual. What does matter is that the entities are separate. For all such arguments require a common topology: the subject, a realm of values, and a mode of inculcation.

The subject is thus ascribed unconditional attributes: will and a capacity for self-reflection and experience. The first of these makes the human subject an essentially purposive creature. The second makes it an origin and source of knowledge. Much social theory is directed to reconciling this position with the problem of how social order is possible, that is, to providing a mechanism by which the privilege accorded to the subject does not result in an asocial collection of individual wills and consciousnesses. The indispensibility of the concept of common values follows from this, the realm of values society will have to impose to produce order. Socialization is the mechanism required by that theoretical position that starts from the original separation of the social from the individual.

It follows that socialization is common to all possible human societies. Thus the comparatively recent development of the *concept* of socialization in particular childrearing practices, and of particular discourses on the family, is misrecognized as being the discovery of an eternal phenomenon. The difficulty of this position should be clear: if socialization is taken to be a fact, then there is no way of dealing with those discourses on socialization and their effects save by the teleologism and moralism of judging the effects as a "good" or "bad" socialization. There is no social-ization—the "child" as a subject of normal or abnormal development is constructed in the legal, medical, and other discourses of the eighteenth century. The article will illustrate the point through the work of Jacques Donzelot in *La Police des Familles.* As a preliminary to this it is proposed to discuss problems in the concept of the sub-ject and Michel Foucault's concept of the subject of a statement, which affords a means of displacing the traditional problems of the subject and of values of moral philosophy and much sociological theory. This article will end with a brief consid-eration of the influence of certain assumptions of subjectivity on feminism.[1]

A Difficult Subject

From Nietzsche and Marx onward there are a number of theoretical writings in which the notion of "subject" is questioned in ways that represent a departure from its treatment in traditional philosophical writings. The most frequent objection to the concept is to its constitutive role in a variety of accounts of social relations, accounts in which the responsibility for social relations lies with human subjects and where the social is the medium or instrument of human self-realization. But although "subjects" are conceived as part of social relations, no explanation is pro-vided to account for the existence of the subjects themselves or of the faculties whose exercise is alleged to give rise to the phenomena of social life. In other words, the human subject is accorded an unconditional status in these accounts.[2]

It is insufficient to restrict one's interrogation of this category to the denial of unconditional constitutivity. Attempts that confine themselves in this way remain questionable in at least two ways. Firstly, the classical subject of humanist philosophical reasoning is retained along with its unconditional attributes—barring those that confer constitutive power on it in respect to social relations. The only difference is that the subject is given no constitutive work to do; it is restricted to a passive, determined position. The difficulty with this position is that, for all its appeal to a determination by the social, the subject is not a whit less necessary, indeed unconditionally necessary, to the existence of these social relations. Others have pointed this out in relation to Marx's theory of fetishism (Brewster 1976, Hirst 1976). There, the *content* of the will and consciousness of the capitalist is determined by his or her position in the structure of capitalist relations, but the capitalist's *having* a will and his or her possession of the register of experience are unconditional and pre-given in Marx's theory. Furthermore, this relationally determined will-to-profit and "knowledge" of the conditions of capitalist calculation are unconditionally necessary to the "motion" of the capitalist mode of production. A further difficulty is that the work of constitutivity previously accorded to the subject is ascribed to something else, "the social system," "relations of production," "the social organism," or in the case of Foucault's recent work, a global "strategic" but nonsubjective ensemble of "power-relations" where a concept of totality and a unitary meaning are incorporated through a mechanism of the age.[3] The problem of constitutivity is thus still retained.

If the subject/structure opposition is retained, it is necessary to go on to question the imperviousness of the subject to structural complexity. The theoretical recommendation that follows is to construe the subject as a composite ensemble, as an effect, the components of which are related in some definite fashion. But is this move in its turn sufficient? To consider the subject as effect only delays the problem of constitutivity. For the subject to take on a necessary and unitary form, even as effect, requires that it always in the last resort already possesses the means to become a subject. The problem is merely postponed, not solved (Hirst 1976) and cannot be while the concept of subject is retained, even in this reduced form of the unitary locus of effects. This does indeed occur in Nietzsche, as it does in the work whose theoretical armature owes much to him, that is, in Foucault's *Histoire de la Sexualité* (1976) and *Discipline and Punish* (1975, 1978). Since these books are likely to have considerable influence, we should also be aware of their limitations. The most relevant of these is the retention of the concept of the human subject, albeit as an object of historical investigation. Foucault and Nietzsche both "decenter" the subject but it remains a totality and hence exposed to the problems that arise for any theory in which such global concepts figure. What is at stake here is the possibility of a genealogy of the emergence of the human subject that does not assume an unconditional subject in the course of that account.

Since Foucault's recent work bears a relation to texts of Nietzsche, it is necessary to demonstrate that Nietzsche does not escape the problem of the subject despite his hostility to philosophy and its effects. In *Beyond Good and Evil* (1886, 1973), Nietzsche conceives the subject as a multiplicity of powers and perspectives, "a complex of ruler and ruled." The ruling component, consciousness, does not act as a principle of unity by virtue of its possession of the power to subjugate other components. Rather, its power depends on the powers of subordinate components and even on certain incapacities on its part, its relative ignorance of many of the activities of the "ruled." Crucial to the multiple "perspectivity" of subjectivity is the body, which has its reasons. These may be inferred from activity that is inexplicable in terms of consciousness. By this means Nietzsche decenters the subject: "the sphere of a subject constantly growing, the center of the system constantly shifting" (*The Will to Power,* 1968, p. 270). But it is also clear that to decenter the subject is not to detotalize it. If the subject is merely decentered, it is necessary to set up some other principle of unity.

In Nietzsche and Foucault the body provides that principle of unity. In *The Will to Power* Nietzsche wants to accord only "a methodological priority" (p. 357–358) to the body. The problem is that the body's reasons are, so to say, all of a piece. That is, all the forces (powers and perspectives) at work in the body have a functionally determined integral relationship to the body/subject of which they are part. That relationship, the configuration of forces, is precisely the will to power of a particular body. Neither consciousness nor any other faculty may wield the power in this complex of power relations. But maintaining the composite nature of subjectivity is to no avail if *the frame of the body* to which Nietzsche appeals, as if to an immediately given "tangible" datum, is invoked to perform the essentialist task of unification previously performed by the ego. "The body" is not a brute reality but is always conceptually differentiated. The body can only remain a principle of unity in a definite discourse despite Nietzsche's wish to "ground" it, opposing it to spiritual entities such as "the soul-superstition." What differentiates bodies in this schema is the *will to power* of which thoughts, motives, etc., are mere signs that have to be decoded. But then the unifying truths concerning the spiritual aspects of human beings cannot be referred, as Nietzsche tries to do, to the *reality* of the body. Furthermore, while Nietzsche questions the unconditional sovereignty philosophy assigns to consciousness, reason, etc., he maintains that they constitute a limit: "to relinquish these assumptions means no longer to be able to think." Nietzsche's *Genealogy of Morals* (1887, 1969) substitutes for the illusions of philosophical anthropology an antimoralistic philosophical anthropology, since the object of the investigation remains the human subject in its totality. Since this totality is assumed *a priori,* there cannot be a theoretical specification of a set of social determinants for such a totality, for the "subject" must necessarily transcend any particular social relations or determinate combinations of relations.

In Foucault's genealogies the particular mode of action of power on the body is similarly taken to constitute the key to any form of power. He is thus able to challenge conceptions of power and politics such as Marxism on the grounds that they purport to account for forms of domination without reference to the formation of the agents "subjected" to it. Foucault's maxim, in contrast, is, no form of domination/subjection without a determinate form of subjectification (*assujetissement*). Both the forces that exercise power and those contending for it occupy positions defined by "power relations." In this relational conception, points of resistance to prevailing powers are not constituted independently of power relations but "invested" and even demarcated by them. The "strategic," calculated character of these relations makes of them a nonsubjective variant of Nietzsche's will to power. In addition, it implies the immanence of forms of discourse to those power relations. Ensembles of power relations, polymorphous in form yet united according to a global strategy, constitute forms of subjectivity in and through the discursive forms that are immanent to them. In the case of the modern subject at least, subjectivity (consciousness and/or unconsciousness) is taken to be both the effect of these relations and the instrument of the subjection of the body. True to form, the body is implicitly accorded a variety of unconditional and hence ahistorical attributes and capacities. In *Discipline and Punish* (1975, 1978) it is assumed to have an inherently subversive character. In Foucault's text, the body functions as a font of political force. In *Histoire de la Sexualité,* Foucault conceives of the body as a seat of prediscursive pleasures. The "real though incorporeal element" of subjectivity is brought into existence precisely in order to control this force by techniques of normalization, a normalization that operates *through* this subjective medium. Thus both body and soul (prison of the body) have to be presupposed for the account to work.

A further problem with the human subject concerns the concept of origins in humanist theoretical discourse (though the problem is not confined to these discourses). If origins are accorded a constitutive status, it implies that the origin of something contains the key to its nature and composition. Frequently the terms foundation and base work in the same way. The problem with the theoretical employment of such metaphors is raised in connection with the human subject in order to further substantiate the claim that this category is retained by theoretical discourses that posit the subject as *effect*.

The general point may be stated in terms of *conditions* (as did Kant in the section of *The Critique of Pure Reason* entitled "The Antinomies of Pure Reason"—significantly in arguing against the idea of God as First Cause of the Universe. Significantly, because the human subject partakes of the creativity traditionally assigned to God). A totality of conditions cannot itself be conceptualized as one condition among others. By the same token, the origins of a totality of conditions cannot be conceptualized as a part of that totality as, say, its First Cause, the first term in a causal series. Both a totality of conditions and its origins lie outside the realm of conditions—in which case any theory of *social* conditions that requires an explanation for a totality of conditions must *either* designate the totality as a socially unconditioned entity *or* make its existence depend on something else that is socially unconditioned, beyond any explanation in social terms. This socially unconditioned foundation of the social order may itself be a completely separate domain of investigation, for example, the "life sciences." Nonetheless, such a biological domain retains its privileged position vis-à-vis the social domain. This precludes the possibility that the social effects of a biological fact, for example, that only women bear children, may be *variable*. It is contradictory to speak of variable social effects of a biological condition such as this *and* to found women's position on such a condition.

To criticize the metaphor of foundation in this way is to question the privilege attached to what comes first in respect of what comes later. The point to note about this "first" is that it is only apparently a part of the totality that "follows" from it. As soon as the question of the genesis of the subject is raised, what is initially presented as an *ensemble of effects* is resolved into a unity and presupposed in its own explanation. This can be shown by making two points. First, to assert that the unity of the subject is an ensemble, the structured product of many determinations, is an empty gesture when what is to be explained is a totality, the subject. *A priori,* the subject, *qua* totality, cuts across the multiplicity of social relations that may be delineated in or for theoretical investigation and in which human beings are involved in the capacity of agents. Second, it is only on condition that origins are unconditioned that the conditions for the emergence of social forms, for example, a form of family organization, could determine the *modus operandi* and the limits of what may be done with it. The collapse of the composite, subject-as-effect into a constitutive original subject follows from the combination of these two separate points.

Positions for Agents

An alternative mode of analysis can also be found in the work of Foucault, one that is not vulnerable to the problem of the subject as constitutive or totalizing category. It involves a concept of positions for agents in a way that is nonreducible to that of human subjects. Its theoretical treatment can be found in the concept of "enunciative modalities" in the *Archaeology of Knowledge,* and a rigorous demonstration can be found in the *Birth of the Clinic.* It will be convenient to treat that text as an example, though it is a specific example—that of the formation of the objects of medical discourse and of clinical practice at the end of the eighteenth century and the beginning of the nineteenth century.

Although Foucault writes that "a history of the referent is no doubt possible," he is interested in "objects that emerge only in discourse." The distinction, to take psychopathology as an example, is between an analysis that is concerned with *what* the categories of psychopathology bring to attention (or misrecognize) and one in which psychopathology is taken as a form of discourse that in the nineteenth and twentieth centuries *incorporates* its diagnostic categories *into* its human subjects. In this mode of analysis, psychopathological discourse is seen to treat people as so many instances of its categories, thereby *creating* "the homosexual," for example, as a personality type.

Foucault's position is illustrated in the case of what he calls the "grid of differentiation" peculiar to modern medicine, namely, the patient's body. This may sound like a pleonasm. What else could medical knowledge be "about?" Yet Foucault in *The Birth of the Clinic* demonstrates that the "spatialisation of disease" is a variable matter. The modern superimposition of the space of configuration of diseases and the space of localization of diseases in the body of the sick woman or man loses its obviousness if one brackets off our modern knowledges concerning, for example, pathogenic organisms. The idea of opening up human bodies, whether dead or alive, to "see" what is the matter with them, presupposes particular discursive conditions that simply did not prevail in the eighteenth century. *The Birth of the Clinic* discusses an eighteenth-century form of medical practice in which the patient's body patently does not define the space of origin, distribution, and "articulation" of diseases. That the body is the object of nineteenth-century medical discourse is in no way reducible to Nietzsche's selection of the body as the focus of genealogical inquiry and as an unconditionally accessible datum. It is, precisely, the site of a particular discourse.

Nor is the "subject" who subjects the body to the clinical gaze reducible to a human subject. It is the subject of a medical statement, the enunciative modality proper to definite medical discourses. Foucault writes that "the subject of the statement should not be regarded as identical with the author of the formulation—either in substance or in function. . . . It is a particular, vacant place that may in fact be filled by different individuals. . . . If . . . a group of signs can be called a 'statement' . . . it is because the position of the subject can be assigned" (*Archaeology of Knowledge*, 1972, p 95). Determining what position can and must be occupied by an individual if it is to be the subject of a statement consists in posing questions concerning the *sites, statuses,* and *positions* of discursive agents with respect to objects.

Status is closely connected with statement: "Medical statements cannot come from anybody; their value, efficacy, even their therapeutic powers . . . cannot be dissociated from the statutorily defined person who has the right to make them" (*ibid.,* p. 51). The institutional siting of medical discourse underwent a profound transformation in the nineteenth century and the hospital, "a place of constant, coded, systematic observation, run by a differentiated and hierarchised medical staff . . . constituting a quantifiable field of frequencies" (*ibid.,* p. 51), cannot be conceived as a kind of external context to anatomo-clinical medical practice, any more than the status of the doctor is external to the existence of the statements made. The third type of enunciative modality is that of positions with respect to objects. Take, for instance, the perceptual situations it is both possible and necessary for the subjects of statements of medical discourse to occupy: "according to a certain grid of . . . interrogations, he is the questioning subject and, according to a certain programme of information, he is the listening subject" (*ibid.,* p. 52). Analogously, positions for a seeing subject can be defined. Medical instruments, far from being mere instruments of aided human perception, are "instrumental" in situating the subject "at an optimal perceptual distance whose boundaries delimit the wheat of relevant information . . . shift the subject in relation to the average or immediate perceptual level" (*ibid.*).

Subjects of statements also occupy a set of positions in information networks—theoretical teaching, hospital training, systems of oral communication and documentation. In this systematic network of relations and in its articulations with those pertaining to sites and statuses, there is no place for an essential medical human subject to synthesize the total perceptual manifold. This position is thus sharply opposed to the view that puts the human subject at the origin of meaning, value, etc. Medical statements produce a set of positions that can be filled by agents satisfying certain conditions. Obviously, being human is neither sufficient nor defining of the practice. The subjects of medical statements are then dispersed among the various statuses, sites, and positions prerequisite to the articulation of particular medical statements.

To conceive of subjects of statements is not to conceive of subjects in the traditional sense. It is to displace the subject from its position as origin, a source of language, expressivity and will, and in so doing to dismantle the unity of the subject. Neither language nor social relations are means of expression, and the concept of social agent, as opposed to the inevitably totalizing concept of the subject, is introduced here to register our own primary theoretical concern with the construction of positions for agents, agents and positions always being defined with respect to specific social relations or combinations thereof. Agents in this sense are not incapable of "independent" action. But such capacities as are presupposed in so acting cannot be referred to the spontaneity of human free will, but are subject to definite conditions of existence, conditions of endowment of agents, and conditions of exercise.

In this perspective there is no place for a "total" subject that transcends or else is subject to different forms of social relations. On the contrary, in *positioning* agents, in defining a social agent always with respect to one or more specific social relations, we precisely abstract from *other* capacities and relations associated with that agent. For example, the analysis of the doctor-patient relationship would abstract from other social relations in which doctors and patients are involved (financial, domestic, sexual, etc.) up to and until such time as particular nonmedical conditions become pertinent. At this point, it should be an open question how these conditions of the nonmedical components of the doctor-patient relationship should be specified.

That is to say, at no point in the analysis is it necessary to assign a theoretical priority to entities such as "people," "human relations," and so on; they have no explanatory function. Nor is it necessary to refer to a realm of values or to unconditional "moral" attributes such as moral responsibility or free will. Thus the theoretical promise of Foucault's work in the domain of what might otherwise be called the ethical consists in its opening up the possibility of accounting for the existence and functions of rules, principles, and codes in social relations without relying on the assumption of a moral domain, as opposed to other domains of social life to which it is connected. The text opens up the possibility of specifying the "moral" component of social relations in such a way as to undermine its privileged or separate relation to other social relations in the order of social analysis without positing an indeterminate interactionsim or reducing this component to an effect of something other than itself. The latter procedure, common in certain Marxist positions, only confirms the "moral" domain as a definite entity, while at the same time according it a most implausible lack of effectivity.

The implication of Foucault's position is that the domain of morality, the realm of values, is dissolved. This is not to explain it by reference to something else, but to break the conceptual couple subject/values in order that it can be opened up to analysis. Consequently, there is no general problem of responsibility, the self-presence of the subject to its actions. The problem of responsibility is dispersed into the particular sites, positions, statuses, and agents of definite practices. Professional responsibilities, family responsibilities, legal responsibilities, etc., should be considered as specific *conferred statuses,* their ascription by other agents depending on the fulfillment of determinate conditions. To be held responsible, in this view, is no more or less than to be recognized as such in one or more definite discourses. Nor do the agents of recognition or the agents recognized have to be human beings. The problem of recognition and its component of responsibility cannot be unified within a general philosophical/moral concept. Certain responsibilities are thus the components of definite statuses.[4]

Two qualifications must be made to the above formulations. The first is that there are certain forms of "all-purpose" responsibility that cover a multitude of social relations—that persons are held "responsible" in general, in a multiplicity of evaluations (being held "irresponsible" is the negative pole). But however diffuse this all-purpose responsibility appears to be, it is nonetheless still subject to the satisfaction of definite social conditions and "all-purpose" responsibility must be construed as a heterogeneous bundle of statuses. The second qualification is that dissolving the moral domain as an object of analysis is still to leave unspecified the question of the components of moral discourses, their relations and effects.

The Institution of Domestic Responsibilities

Much current feminist and sociological writing on the family conceives it as an intersection between two processes, the needs of capitalism and the effects of patriarchy. The "nuclear family," the object of its attention, is conceived as that intersection, the economic and social form that "serves" capitalism and at the same time enslaves women as housewives and locks them in the privacy of the family. Donzelot's *La Police des familles,* while dealing with many of the problems addressed in such analyses, does so in a way that changes the terms of such a debate.[5] His account of the transformations of familial and surrounding social forms in France from the mid-eighteenth century to the present does so without recourse to essentialist conceptions of the family and to subjectivist conceptions of the positions occupied within them. For his analysis proceeds with reference to agents that take up determinate positions in a range of relations and the positions of agents involve definite attributes as a function of definite relations. Agents are conceived as having responsibilities and capacities that comprise the possibility of their fulfillment of definite actions, though it does not assume that fulfillment. This form of analysis, which eschews both a reduction to the simple entities of women and men and avoids any problem of necessity, renders any conception of analyzing the "family" in terms of the domination of husbands/men and the subordination of wives/women impossible. The oppressive aspects of women's position within the family does not preclude, but on the contrary, involves a set of competences and responsibilities that provide the conditions for action. These cannot be termed "powers" if that implies an automatic capacity to realize particular ends. But *no* social agent has this capacity.

In its account of the transformation of familial relations of the ancien régime, Donzelot locates the supervised liberty of the modern family as the product of a variety of strategies whose objective is the reformation of family life and a formulation for it of criteria for the welfare of children. Crucial in this was the construction of the agency of *housewife* and *mother*, an agency accorded responsibilities and capacities. This involves, not a stripping away of rights and responsibilities, common to accounts of the sociological version of the transition from the extended family to the nuclear family, but on the contrary, a definite displacement of absolute paternal rights and the construction of legal and "moral" attributes of the mother and wife. Those "moral" attributes involve the creation of an agent, the housewife, whose responsibilities are created by the valorization of tasks in respect to a domain of the domestic. This involves a responsibility for the healthy development of the child and for its discipline. It also involves, not simply the provision of domestic comfort for the husband, but responsibilities to maintain him within domestic "virtue." The whole process involved a definite legal, administrative, pedagogical, and political shift *away* from certain paternal powers and a certain provision of maternal powers. Such sets of relations cannot be captured by conceiving the housewife as a term of exclusion from a "man's world," nor as a term simply of exclusion from certain social and economic activities. Both these involve a collapse into that separation of women from social relations whereby social relations are conceived merely as "oppressing" them. Rather than contrast women's positions in these relations to those of the "extended" family and declare that there is a reduction in the presence of women to certain responsibilities and work tasks, it is important to consider how forms of agency are constructed.

Women taken as a pre-given entity are conceived as members of a family, itself taken as an essential form and the result is the current and standard thesis of "privatization" in which the private is contrasted with the public (i.e., social).[6] But this distinction cannot be maintained as a "real" one; it is a conventional distinction. The "privacy" of the marital bed is no less social than the "public" nature of a political meeting. But the "privatization" thesis does suggest that the space of the family is quarantined from some public domain. The nuclear family is treated as a given that is teleologically projected back into the time of traditional "extended" family life. Privatization then follows by numerical subtraction, either as an effect of external or internal pressures.

Insofar as Donzelot maps out transformations within familial relations as transformations of the relations of social agents, the public/private distinction is displaced. The "nuclear family" is not some preeminent reality but rather a locus in a network of relations. What is at stake then, is not so much the transmutation of the form of the family from the ancien régime, but rather the construction of the modern "family" in a series of relations and discourses.

Thus it is in specific interventions of policy, both governmental and nongovernmental, the practices of philanthropic societies, the politics of residential architecture, the conditions of mortgages and insurances, the counsels of hygiene manuals, that this family is constructed. To be able to specify this is to break from the teleology of accounts given in conventional histories of the family. For their discursive materials are frequently taken as referring to "real" objects outside discourse, which are subject to the gloss of contemporary prejudice. Discourses on masturbation, poverty, pastimes, etc., are treated as descriptions of ever-present objects, the objects themselves being a continuous sediment of history. This obscures the construction of entities, their determinants and their relation to other objects. Donzelot does not take the family as a given but considers it as a locus of interventions in which the discourses of the social sciences and of previous "moral" science are invested as the "knowledges" of the family.

Such an approach displaces any idea of "social change" or society influencing the family, as if the family and its members were the eternal cast of a passive drama. The concept of privatization cannot grasp the production of the supervised liberty of the family, which provides for a specific logic of internal and external agents of supervision. The mother/housewife and her appearance as an agent to whom non-familial institutions accord definite responsibilities and capacities is a crucial condition of the existence of an "autonomous" family. For example, responsibilities may be relayed through definite forms of scientific and popular medical discourses. Crucial to the eighteenth- and nineteenth-century campaigns for the reform of family life, particularly where the welfare and development of children were concerned, was the privileged relation to be established between the mother and the medical order. And the "sites" and "statuses" through which medical practice operates now institute the *family* doctor and the doctor's new privileged, "on-the-spot" auxiliary, the mother, who is either deemed to naturally possess special competences or is expected to acquire them. That general strategy of family reform in which the mother/housewife appears, is in full accord with the "private" character of the modern family, for example, its apoliticism, overinvestment in children, and intense emotional struggles.

Such an analysis makes it impossible to have simple recourse to any general view of the subordination of wives to husbands, still less as its being a defining character of the modern family. The legal rights of the father in respect to his children, for example, are cut back after the ancien régime and an "equalization" of rights is effected between father and mother. It is this very change that makes possible controversy between husband and wife in respect to control of children.

The construction of responsibilities and capacities of the housewife and mother permits her, in part, to be the agent of the "civilization" of the worker and the point of the introduction of hygienic and disciplinary forms into a population without the direct intervention of "public" administration. This does not mean that the organization of domestic life is closed away from public scrutiny, but that its "privacy" is the particular term of descriptions of its organization, of the supervised liberty of the family. The whole geography of public/private distinctions does not refer to any essential fact but is a discursive distinction of particular bodies of knowledge. A parallel example can be seen in the distribution of entities of economic sciences into public and private realms. Thus the housewife is not in purdah but is a social agent in the full glare of those discourses on the domestic unit.

The problem with Donzelot's account is that while it effectively displaces conventional categories of subordination within the family, the problem seems to reemerge in relation to the state, which appears to stand in *patriarchate* relation to all other agents, directly intervening in cases of the breakdown of domestic supervision in problem families, in order to guarantee a social stability. This threatens to return to a functionalist account of the state, one which is increased by his tendency to flatten all discourses on the family of the last two hundred years from psycho-

analysis to taxation policy into a strategy for the production of the modern super-
visory family. Since, on his view, familial mechanisms never entirely achieve the
reformer's delirium of stability and since, in point of fact, those "failures" are a continual and necessary condition for the advance of the progress of supervision, it is
difficult to see how the state could ever lose. Success is success and failure is the
grounds for the extension of powers. There is clearly a problem here of unifying and
hypostatizing the state as the personification of a strategy. Once such a unity is
denied, once governmental, administrative, and legal practices are conceived as
being able to move in "contradictory" directions, such a position is untenable. This
denial would not only permit further analysis, but also enable both realistic and
effective political calculation to be made; while Donzelot's account would suggest
that any strategy could be drawn back into the ruse of the state. Having advanced the
problem of the relation of the family to the state, it is then required to advance the
problem of the state in relation to the family.

The Subject of Feminism

The problem of the connection between feminism and the pervasive hold of
certain assumptions concerning subjectivity can be demonstrated by reference to the
feminist slogan "the personal is political." It implies that matters of "experience"
should be treated in a global and undifferentiated fashion. The slogan has two
aspects. Firstly, that "experience" of social relations that can be treated as pertinent
for political struggle should not be restricted. In particular, it should not be restricted
to a category of phenomena that is bracketed off as "political"—experience of trade
union activities, the struggles of or within political organizations, etc. Essentially the
slogan was a protest against an economism and traditionalism that limited the inven-
tory of what was relevant to the struggles for democratic and socialist transformation.
It insisted upon the importance of problems that did not fall within that conventional
syllabus of political struggle. But secondly, it insisted that the form of analyzing and
criticizing social phenomena should be based on "experience," frequently designated "personal experience." Personal experience is thus elevated and privileged as
the origin of knowledge of oppression and also as the source of the will to its transformation. Thus in the slogan "the personal is political," the personal functions in
two ways: as a realm of previously discarded social objects that are now being
inserted as objects for political struggle, and at the same time as the locus of their
recognition and the form of their treatment.

This double character leads to a paradoxical conclusion. While it is able to provide a certain criticism of economism, it does so in a conventional form. While it adds a realm of objects, the organization of the family, sexuality, etc., it does so in a fashion that can actually buttress the conventional distinctions of personal/public or private/social. The concept of "personal," then, can become synonymous with the banal sociological category of "everyday life." While a realm of objects has been asserted as "also" political, it is tacitly accepted that they are "personal." The slogan is thus ambiguous, especially in regard to analyses such as Donzelot's that effectively displace the distinction of personal/public as pre-given. The slogan can also lead to that intense subjectivist exclusion of given political organizations and struggles by restricting politics to only that which is "personal."

Furthermore, the slogan assists in maintaining the category of personal *experience* and privileging it in the hierarchy of arguments that are thought to be acceptable. To contest this is not to privilege something else against experience; it is not to insist that there are guaranteed treasures of knowledge elsewhere, nor to say that experience only ever captures phenomenal forms and thus misrecognizes the real. In sum, it is *not* to make an epistemological critique of empiricism and its limitations. It is rather, that once the concept of the subject is displaced, there is strictly speaking no such thing as pure experience. For the concept of experience is linked to the concept of the subject. This can be illustrated by pointing to the heterogeneity of things that are commonly held to fall within the category of experience, not only matters of perception but a battery of "knowledges" and "judgments." It makes no sense to attempt to restrict the analysis of those "knowledges" to the category of experience. The concept itself needs to be displaced.

If this theoretical point is to have any relevance to a discussion of political questions and their analysis, two general points must be borne in mind. The first is that it is not being suggested that political discourse can be installed and governed by theoretical evaluation, merely that theoretical evaluation will be one component. Second, that theoretical evaluation is *not* functioning as an epistemological court that delivers judgments of truth. That this is not the case can be illustrated by the above example. The slogan of "the personal is political" is not being subjected to an epistemological critique, but rather the reverse. A theoretical argument is made against the incursion of an epistemological category in a political slogan, that is, the personal as source of knowledge. Such an argument cannot claim to be definitive, but it can claim attention, especially in the task of the endless reformulating of a politics, of feminist objectives and strategies.

Given that certain slogans and "demands" are maintained, it is important to recognize that they are never unequivocal. "Women's liberation" could only be specified as a definite state of affairs with necessary effects within the fantasy of utopianism. More relevantly, even apparently concrete demands remain necessarily equivocal. Consider the NAC slogan, "A Woman's Right to Choose." Despite its simplicity and its undoubted capacity to mobilize support, it remains (necessarily) an open question what the best form of meeting the demand would be. There is, in fact, no "true" meeting of the demand. It depends on the way each element of the slogan is interpreted and what weight is accorded to each. At a recent National Abortion Campaign conference differing arguments were made.[7] One argument was for an interpretation of the slogan whereby the pregnant woman should be given full control of the decision on the question of termination and its method at no matter how late a point in the pregnancy. (The question of method is important here because after a certain stage of pregnancy the question of technique will determine the chances of survival of a viable fetus.) Thus the rights of the pregnant woman are considered as unconditional, not subject to limitation until their mutation into the rights of a mother and the rights of a child. The importance of the question of the viability of a fetus is denied on two grounds. Firstly, it is conceived as a ploy of anti-abortionists in the sense that if the viability of the fetus is conceived as an origin of rights, then the march of medical technique will make abortion increasingly difficult by rolling back the point of abortion. Second, the more important, the possibility of a viable fetus having rights is denied. Fetuses are declared to have potential rights, which finally exist at birth and not before. Consequently, the form of legislation envisaged not only removes any constraint on the provision of abortion but insists that abortion at any moment in the pregnancy should be made a statutory right, enforceable against any resistance, such as the lack of facilities, unwillingness of doctors, etc. The contrary argument was that women's rights to abortion should be subject to a limitation, the limitation being that the viable fetus should be recognized as having rights. It was denied that medical technique could, in the near future, push back the point of viability, merely that it could increase the chances of *survival* of a viable fetus. The argument that such a fetus has "rights" rested upon its capacity to survive independently of the mother, and this was elaborated by indicating that such a fetus is already recognized in law, has some form of legal personality by virtue of the necessity to provide death certificates for it after twenty-eight weeks.

Both these arguments are directed towards the formulation of a bill that can be sponsored within Parliament. Both purport to be arguments to support legislation in support of the provision of abortion on demand (subject to qualification in the second case). The first represents itself as a specifically feminist proposal and as such hostile to the second. The strange thing is that both of them, and indeed the anti-abortionists, pose the whole problem in terms of rights. These are essentially moral rights in search of legal recognition. Thus the anti-abortionist position is characterized by ascribing rights to the fetus from the moment of conception. The second argument outlined above ascribes rights to the fetus from the moment of viability, while the first ascribes rights to the child only after birth, before which the rights exist only in a potential state.

The contrariness of the positions is reduced by the unitary way in which they all operate within the space of rights, the distribution of rights, and the relation of rights to the law. All conceive of the law as that agency which both recognizes and makes effective rights that preexist the law's form of recognition. This results in an absurd misrecognition of law in the second argument: the right of the viable fetus "must" exist because the law recognizes some form of personality of that fetus. But law doesn't recognize personality in this way; it creates it. Legal recognition is a real and circular process. It recognizes the things that correspond to the definitions it constructs.

A similar confusion is introduced in the first argument. A law is demanded that "recognizes" and makes effective women's unrestricted rights over their bodies. It is argued that only such a law will remove "state" control over sexuality and fertility, and return it to women. There are two paradoxes here: the first is that the state must intervene to abolish "state" control (the legislation, it should be remembered, is not simply a decriminalization of abortion but legislation for its provision as a statutory right). The second paradox is that the collectivity of women is being defined in essence as a population of individuals, subjects of right, in this case subjects of property rights in the classic sense.

The problems of a unitary realm of morals that would include that of natural rights and that of the concept of the subject have been outlined above. They obviously do not have any direct or necessary implications for such a debate. But nor is it clear they have none. Within contemporary political discourse it is probably impossible to escape the effects of problems being constructed at least partially in terms of rights. But the dangers are apparent. Arguments concerning rights are intrinsically insoluble and have a tendency to narrow the range of questions at stake: the rights of the unborn fetus and the rights of the pregnant woman can be played out in a dogmatic repetition. The further danger is that once the question of rights is allowed to rule all discussions, there is always the threat of the sudden entry upon the scene of a new subject in pursuit of rights. The recent Paton case demonstrates that despite the clear and complete lack of legal rights in relation to abortion, a father was able to claim them with a good deal of public support.[8] It also invites the medical profession to chip in to claim their share of rights. It is not unreasonable to suggest that to permit the question of rights to dominate the discussion restricts the issues that feminism should raise. But at the same time, the problem runs deeper than a possible political miscalculation. For it has to be admitted that many analyses and positions are themselves constructed upon the assertion of rights, rights that are denied, rights that are not recognized, rights that are not respected, rights that are constantly wronged. They return to the account of the rights and wrongs of women, a moralism analyzing morality in the name of an always present unity of womankind. The paradox is that such a unity is necessarily the unity of subjects, of individuals. There is a price to pay for returning to such traditional and conventional ground.

This paper has attempted to trace a circle in which much work is currently caught: the circle of the categories of the subject, experience, and the domain of morality. It has suggested that their displacement permits new forms of analysis of the construction of sexual difference. Once it is recognized that sexual difference is constructed in a variety of practices, it becomes necessary to determine which differences and which practices are oppressive. This is part of the task of setting up objectives for feminism, a task that the analysis of the slogan "A Woman's Right to Choose" has shown to be far from obvious.

We wish to acknowledge Mark Cousins's considerable help in the preparation of this article.

Notes

1.   We are grateful to Denise Riley for comments on an early draft of this section and to Colin Gordon for drawing our attention to Donzelot's *La Police des familles*.

2.   Philosophical tradition does not *invariably* take this notion for granted. David Hume, for example, collapsed subjectivity into a bundle of sense impressions and questioned the sovereignty of reasons. However, this did not prevent him from attributing to the subjective essence of man, the unconditional power to constitute social relations: "our passions are the only cause of our labours."

3.   For this and for an elaboration of some of the following ideas on subjectivity and on the "moral" aspects of social conditions in particular, see Minson 1980.

4.   For the concept of agent see Cutler et al., *Marx's 'Capital' and Capitalism Today*, vol. I, part III, ch. 11.

5.   We refer only to certain aspects of Donzelot's work and in particular those relating to the status of women. The polemical target of *La Police des familles* is psychoanalysis and its supposed connection and commitment to "familialism." For Donzelot, the discourse and practice of psychoanalysis is simply a further step in that production of the modern family begun more than two hundred years ago.

6.   For popular and influential expositions of this thesis, see Oakley, and Zaretsky.

7.   See Butler et al. and Bury and Fairlamb.
8.   Paton v. Trustees of BPAS; Paton came before the High Court at Liverpool on May 24, 1978.
See transcript.

References

B. Brewster, "Fetishism in *Capital* and *Reading Capital,*" *Economy and Society,* 1976, vol. 5, no. 3.

J. Bury and A. Fairlamb, "Why we have Doubts about a Bill without a Time Limit," papers from the NAC Planning Conference held at Sheffield, April 1978.

G. Butler, R. Knight, and B. Beaumont, "NAC stands for a 'Woman's Right to Choose.' What do we Mean by This? And How do we Achieve it in Practice?" paper from the NAC Planning Conference held at Sheffield, April 1978.

A. Cutler, B. Hindess, P. Hirst, and A. Hussain, *Marx's 'Capital' and Capitalism Today,* Routledge and Kegan Paul, 1977.

J. Donzelot, *La Police des familles,* Editions de Minuit, 1977. *The Policing of Families,* trans. R. Hurley, Hutchinson, 1980.

M. Foucault, *Archeology and Knowledge,* trans. A. M. Sheridan Smith, Tavistock, 1972.

M. Foucault, *The Birth of the Clinic,* trans. A. M. Sheridan Smith, Tavistock, 1973.

M. Foucault, *Discipline and Punish,* trans. Alan Sheridan, Allen Lane, 1978.

M. Foucault, *The History of Sexuality, vol. I: An Introduction,* Allen Lane, 1979.

P. Q. Hirst, "Althusser and the Theory of Ideology," *Economy and Society,* 1976, vol. 5, no. 4.

I. Kant, *The Critique of Pure Reason* [1787], 2nd ed. trans. N. Kemp Smith, Macmillan, 1964.

J. Minson, "Strategies for Socialists?—Foucault's Concept of Power," *Economy and Society,* 1980, vol. 9.

J. Minson, *Genealogies of Morals,* Macmillan, 1985.

F. Nietzsche, "*Will to Power* Selections," in *Notebooks 1883–1888,* trans. and ed W. Kaufmann, Vintage Books, 1968.

F. Nietzsche, *Beyond Good and Evil,* trans. R. J. Hollingdale, Penguin, 1973.

A. Oakley, *Housewife,* Allen Lane, 1974.

Paton v. Trustees of BPAS and Paton transcripts of legal argument and decision available from Lee and Nightingale, Liverpool.

E. Zaretsky, *The Family and Personal Life,* Pluto, 1976.

from *m/f* 2, 1978

A Note on the Distinction between Sexual Division and Sexual Differences

PARVEEN ADAMS

Many feminist theories assume that the problem to be addressed is obviously one of sexual division. This obviousness contains many difficulties. For if sexual division is assumed, then a category, that of sexual division, is being imported into the analysis that will govern and limit the form of questions that may be asked. To question that category of sexual division is not, of course, to object to it in a conventional sense, but to object to it when, as a concept, it is promoted to a privileged position, a privilege that is assumed but not demonstrated. Sexual division in this privileged sense refers to the setting up of two mutually exclusive and jointly exhaustive categories that are held to refer to two mutually exhaustive groups, concrete men and women. There are, of course, vastly different and opposed forms of *explaining* sexual division, and it must be recognized that the essentialism that derives division from an anatomical distinction has been challenged by theories that emphasize the space of representation and systems of representation. But it will be argued here that the essentialism that is being attacked in this challenge often returns even if in a more sophisticated form.

This will be exemplified in this note by considering the ways in which feminist work on ideology retains the problems of sexual division. Marxist theories of ideology, of course, emphasize the space of representation, for Marxism itself alludes to a system of representations by which individuals are positioned as social subjects. Feminists have used psychoanalytic theory to outline a theory with the positioning of *sexed* subjects as its central concern and some have gone on to utilize it for a theory of ideology. Both the feminist theory of ideology based on psychoanalytic theory and the Marxist theory of ideology accord to the question of representations—and the mechanism whereby those representations are effective in the construction of the subject—a centrality by virtue of which it was possible for many people to consider a synthesis of Marxism and psychoanalysis possible. For through their joint attention to the category of the subject it was held possible to produce a theory of the relation between psychical and social reality. This possibility can be questioned on the grounds that while Marxism and psychoanalysis deal with systems of representation of reality, the conception of reality is fundamentally different in each of these two theories. What will be questioned here, however, is an assumption common to the way in which the two theories are utilized—that what is represented is reality, that is, a prior and given state of social being.

My argument is that as long as feminist theories of ideology work with a theory of representation within which representation is always a representation of reality, however attenuated a relation that may be, the analysis of sexual difference cannot be advanced because reality is always already apparently structured by sexual division, by an already antagonistic relation between two social groups. And thus the complicated and contradictory ways in which sexual difference is generated in various discursive and social practices is always reduced to an effect of that always existent sexual division. In terms of sexual division, what has to be explained is how reality functions to effect the continuation of *its* already given divisions. (The different ways in which sexual differences are produced is actually denied as a political fact in this position.) In terms of sexual *differences,* on the other hand, what has to be grasped is, precisely, the *production* of differences through systems of representation; the work of representation produces differences that cannot be known in advance. Some further points on the distinction between sexual division and sexual difference will be made later.

To start with the problem of sexual division. It is clear that in radical feminist analyses, which are in terms of the domination of women by men, this relation has always been ultimately determined by a biological distinction. This is made totally explicit in the recent revolutionary feminist literature where the fact of women's reproductive capacity is taken to be determining. What is set up is an antagonism between the sexes, grounded in a biological reality that is taken to preexist and to determine social relations.

The realm of sexual antagonism is also referred to as the realm of patriarchy, and many who are not radical feminists and who would reject an explanation in biological terms nonetheless retain the notion of patriarchy as a general problem to be addressed. This is to say, the conception of the domination of women by men is retained as the problem by many feminists. On the other hand, many feminists would invoke the concept of patriarchy as a set of systematic social relations, as the origin and mechanism of women's oppression. Now while this latter position would appear to offer a means of *not* reducing social relations to intersubjective relations, my point will be that in the end it does not solve this problem. As Mark Cousins has pointed out in "Material Arguments and Feminism" (*m/f*, no. 2), since the field of effects of those social relations is the already constituted group of women and group of men, the social division that was to be explained has already been assumed as part of the explanation.

This can be illustrated with reference to Juliet Mitchell's work, and we find in *Psychoanalysis and Feminism* (1974) an explicit disavowel of the problem of male domination, which as it were, exists from the cradle. What she is challenging is that anatomically differentiated babies are always already men and women. She is also challenging what appears to be a completely opposite view that babies are empty vessels into which are poured the social roles of male and female. Because ironically, these two apparently opposed views which could be respectively called biologistic and sociologistic are in fact two sides of the same coin. The biologistic view assumes already constituted capacities, and while the sociologistic view assumes a *tabula rasa,* it also always has to rely on already constituted capacities of experience, cognition, and purposeful action. Juliet Mitchell puts forward the challenge by taking up the psychoanalytic insistence on a realm of *psychical* reality, a category which disrupts the mechanisms of both the realization of a biological essence and the implacable march of socialization.

The position that Juliet Mitchell espouses displaces the constitutive subject of the biologistic and sociologistic views and, using psychoanalytic arguments, she tries to show that men and women are no longer to be thought of as pre-given, but as the effect of something else. While this is a big step forward, it must be noted that we are back with the problem of masculine domination and feminine oppression. For if the construction of men and women on the level of psychical reality is put to use to analyze feminine subordination, then the construction *is* women's oppression. That is to say, that the theory of ideology Juliet Mitchell sets up itself demands an explanation of the opposition men and women, and psychoanalysis is employed to reproduce precisely these divisions.

It is necessary here to briefly refer to some specific aspects of Juliet Mitchell's argument and to elaborate the problem of representation and its consequences for feminist analyses. To begin with a question: how does the problem of sexual division come to dominate that work of Freud's that started with such a momentous questioning? Freud, of course, problematized the concept of sexuality by postulating an infantile sexuality, which necessarily undermined the standard definition of sexuality understood as an instinct which manifested itself at puberty and had a definite object (of the opposite sex). For Freud sexuality is not an instinct, a hereditarily given pattern of behavior, but a drive. And in the *Three Essays on Sexuality* (1905) he develops the theory of "propping" (so named by Laplanche and elaborated by him as the propping of the drive on the instinct) by drawing a distinction between the reduction of need that is characteristic of instincts and the satisfaction sought for at the level of the sexual drive. Here Freud is concerned with the construction of sexuality itself. While there are problems with this account, what is clear is that Freud demonstrates that the differentiated sexuality of the standard view is the effect of a long history of the drive and its vicissitudes.

Now this is important. For the standard view of sexuality had assumed the distinction between masculinity and femininity whereas Freud saw this as something that had to be explained. There is no masculinity and femininity in infantile sexuality. The necessity for this distinction is an effect of the necessity of the Oedipus complex in psychoanalytic theory. That complex is the internalization of the incest taboo, the incest taboo being the founding moment of society, and in fact, of patriarchal society. The resolution of the Oedipus complex demands that a choice be made between masculinity and femininity, and it is only then that the child takes up its place in human culture. Masculinity and femininity are the psychical reality of the human order. Within psychoanalytic theory this order is patriarchal, the father has the law.

The foregoing is not an account of the mechanisms through which femininity is produced—it is rather an indication of how the idea of construction is present in psychoanalytic theory. And when Juliet Mitchell talks about the construction of men and women she means the psychical construction of masculinity and femininity. Masculinity and femininity have, then, to be always already available for the individual to take up the position. The taking up of masculine and feminine positions is a consequence of a system of representation (known through psychoanalysis), which is the representation of a patriarchal order. What we have then is the construction of the sexual identity of male and female individuals by means of a system of psychical representation through which they are distributed to masculine and feminine positions. The theory of ideology presents masculinity and femininity as representations of a real order, that of patriarchal society. The psychical level of construction is determined by reality. The problem then would be the real distinction between men and women. The categories that have to be accounted for are, in fact, already assumed in reality. This is very clear in the following passage from Mitchell: "The social reality that he [Freud] is concerned with elucidating is the mental representation of the reality of society" (p. 406). In the reality of society, women circulate; in the symbolic order the phallus circulates. (This interpretation of Mitchell is consistent with her claim that the conditions of change lie in reality. She sees the possibility of an alteration in patriarchal ideology under the conditions of capitalism where, according to her, the mass of women are not circulated.)

It must be emphasized that there is a certain use of terms in Mitchell's book that could mislead. Her use of "social reality" and "the construction of men and women" are in the context of emphasizing the importance of *psychical* reality where this is the outcome of the organization of men and women in the "reality of society," an organization around the incest taboo. The mental representation of the reality of society always has the same represented, which is that reality. (This is a problem inherent in the tension within psychoanalytic theory, between an endless productivity of the signifying chain—in Freud, the productivity of the dreamwork; and the return to the phallus as that which orders language—in Freud, the dream can be traced back to the first representatives of the sexual drive.)

What is at stake here is the classical theory of representation within which the represented is always prior to the representation that is its mark. Paul Hirst, in his critique of Althusser (*Problems and Advances in the Theory of Ideology,* 1976), has argued an alternative position where what is represented must be considered to be an effect of the action of the means of representation. Thus representation cannot be subordinated to the position where it is a reflection or distortion of what is represented. For, if ideology is thought of in the classical sense of representation (i.e., the primacy of what is represented), the question arises, where does the form of the representation come from? Two alternatives can be considered: that it comes from the subject or that it comes from reality. If they are not to stem from the constitutive subject, and Mitchell certainly recognizes the importance of the psychoanalytic challenge to such a subject, are they then to be attributed to reality? To attribute the forms of representation to reality leads to a reflection theory of ideology (which can take very sophisticated forms)—but what is lost here is the autonomy of ideology that Mitchell wants to maintain. The autonomy of ideology is not guaranteed by insisting on an autonomy in relation to the economic instance if this latter is merely replaced by the patriarchal instance. The structure of Marxist theories of ideology together with all its problems is here simply transferred to the patriarchal domain.

A second problem with a patriarchal theory of ideology structured along Marxist lines is its retention of the ideological as a homogeneous, unified instance. Femininity is the psychical representation of the reality of society for women and of women's oppression. The taking up of the feminine position reproduces oppression. Femininity as mental representation depends on the ever-present patriarchal order of reality. Nothing else can then affect the ideological positioning of women. There is a priority given to ideology as psychical instance. Women are unified through this psychical instance, unified in their femininity and in their oppression. The patriarchal organization of reality produces a psychical substrate, woman, who can take her woman's place in reality. The unity of the ideological, woman as a unity and a unity of women, are produced simultaneously.

This has important consequences for feminist analyses. First, woman is set up as an entity on which society operates. Men do this or that to women, the law discriminates against women, etc. Second, women are the sum of these entities and what society does to women constitutes their oppression. We can say that this oppression is taken to be homogeneous insofar as it is the oppression of *women.* The theoretical attempt was to ensure the presence and availability of women for oppression. The ideological was substituted for the biological to secure, nonetheless, the unity of women. In other words, for all its sophistication, the end-product is still the same—for the effect of the biological *and* ideological positions is to pick out and and focus on sexual division.

A note of caution is necessary in regard to what is being claimed. The retention of an analysis in terms of sexual division has been shown to be an effect of Juliet Mitchell's *use* of psychoanalytic theory. The theory itself, it is arguable, considerably problematizes sexual division, though it does so in a number of problematic ways. While it can be said that sexuality is unified and organized around the phallus, it must also be noted that the sexual distinction masculine/feminine cannot be directly mapped on to male and female organisms. And while the choice is masculinity or femininity, Freud recognized that "pure masculinity and femininity remain theoretical constructs of uncertain content," that human individuals combine in themselves both masculine and feminine characteristics. Does this not challenge that unity of the feminine that is required to make of the feminine the substrate of subordination?

What has been argued is that the construction of femininity is theorized in such a way as to produce a coherent, unified entity, the feminine subject, albeit that it is explained as an effect. To explain the structure of the unified feminine subject is taken to be tantamount to exposing the mechanisms of patriarchal ideology. It is suggested here that such an analysis makes impossible the consideration of the effectivity of a variety of systems of representation. Now in the present case it is the psychoanalytic notion of patriarchy that is used, and it might be argued that this is why the effects of specific discursive practices can have no place—psychoanalysis being concerned with an unchanging structure of discourse. That is to say, that the effectivity, conscious or unconscious, of a variety of systems of representation cannot be addressed within that particular framework.

This difficulty, however, is not a function of psychoanalytic theory, but rather, it is a function of the centrality of the subject in theories of ideology. How then does this concept obstruct the consideration of the effects of a variety of systems of representation? In feminist analyses, the concept of subject obstructs because it relies on a homogeneous oppression of women in a state, reality, given prior to representational practices. To take account of the different forms of the construction of sexual difference would necessitate abandoning that position. Thus there is a difference between analyses that explain the persistence of representations in terms of a general structure of the subject and its conditions and analyses that emphasize the importance of definite practices and their conditions. Is it not the case that in operating with unified entities we are kept busy explaining unities while the effects of practices of representation are *not*, in fact, unified? To say this is to suggest that a series of sexual differences is constructed through practices of representation and in such a way that sexual distinctions set up under different discursive conditions may vary, overlap, be contradictory, etc.

It is only by examining the workings of particular practices that it can be shown that the concept of subject is inadequate to them. The brief example from legal practice that follows supports the questioning of the concept of a legal subject in general. In the recent case in which Mr. Paton sought an injunction in the Liverpool High Court to prevent his wife from having a legal abortion, it is clear that an individual may be assigned legal statuses that do not add up to the category of the subject. Without a detailed discussion here, it can merely be briefly and baldly stated that the legal argument makes clear that Mr. Paton cannot claim any rights as Mr. Paton *per se*. He cannot be represented as himself and have rights stemming from himself. What his own lawyer is led to demonstrate is that as a member of the public, as a father, as a husband, and as a possible representative of the fetus, he has no rights either. So Mr. Paton has a number of legal statuses but the legal rights that attach to these give him no right to an injunction. And Mr. Paton cannot claim derivative rights through the fetus because though *it* has various legal statuses, the relevant legal rights are not attached to those statuses and the fetus can no more be represented *qua* fetus than Mr. Paton can put himself forward as Mr. Paton.

With reference to this case it is not possible to talk of a legal subject in general and its rights and if this is so it is not possible to talk of a feminine subject as such, in law. The argument of the court was not concerned with men and women *as such*. It is not that the law operates on two groups, men and women, given in reality. This is not to prejudge the relevance of the case to feminist struggle. It is rather to put forward the problem of the *categories* men and women in relation to the law. Categories are not fixed though they may appear to be so at any one time and a category has no necessary unity—in relation to the category woman, for example, it is indeed possible for a concrete individual to be judged a woman for some social purposes and not others.

It could be said that one of the paradoxical effects of feminism as a political force has been to force the recognition of the diverse and unexpected character of the organization of sexual differences. It has proved a difficult and contentious problem as to how to analyze the effects of anything from social policy to artistic practices in respect to the organization of sexual differences. But to reduce these problems to the simplicities of an always already antagonistic relation between two social groups who are frozen into a mutually exclusive and jointly exhaustive division is an obstacle both to feminist analysis and political practice.

from *m/f* 3, 1979

Representations

The issue of representation has been fundamental for the modern feminist movement. Challenging existing definitions of women, feminists confronted the problem of how to define positive or correct images as opposed to negative or oppressive images of women. Feminists were thus forced to examine the construction of images as such and the way meaning is constituted through representation to produce a definition of women. But at the same time as feminists were challenging particular images of women, new theoretical work emerged that undermined the very notion of representation on which much of the feminist critique had been based. This new work demonstrated that there is no "gold standard" for the sign, no guarantee of its truth or reality by virtue of the referent that lies behind the represented. Representation is not a system of signs referring to reality and there can therefore be no recourse to an original essence against which the achievement or shortcomings of images produced by cinema, television, literature, etc., can be measured. As the articles reprinted here indicate, this work was central to *m/f*; it required us to abandon attempts to define the correct way to represent the truth about women, men, or whatever in favor of an emphasis on the *production* of meaning and truth. This raised different questions about feminist strategies with respect to representation.

If images themselves are not transparent, do not reflect a reality prior to and other than them, it is not that they are simply dissembling, but that they are not simply and already meaningful. It is not a question of merely unmasking the constructedness of representations, for this still implies a possible pure form of representation in which meaning exists unmediated by any such construction. It is rather a question of accepting the fact that meaning only arises in the very construction of the representation. For example, if the question is asked: "what does this image of a woman's vagina mean?" and the answer given is "pornography," we would clearly understand this answer, even though it is equally clear that pornography is not signified within the image as such. "Pornography" is a meaning constructed through discourses of representation. It is a reading of the image that places it in a recognizable genre of images—of the pornographic rather than the medical, for example. Some feminists have objected to *any* representation of naked women as exploitative, and the debate that resulted from this claim has been of considerable importance to feminist artists and filmmakers. Yet what is not often acknowledged is that such evaluations and critiques are themselves discursive determinants of the meaning of the image as pornography: for the consumer, the meaning is constituted by the possible pleasure the image can provide and for feminists the meaning ("exploitation") is constituted by the fact that this pleasure is presumed as male. These are not "added onto" the image; the image cannot stand apart from its moment or context of reading as if in a moment of a pure "before" (contrary to Barthes's early claims, there is no moment of pure denotation for the image.) Understanding the arguments and terms by which such meanings come to be constituted is, as Beverley Brown shows, central to work on representation.

But such definitions and meanings are not simply external and objective, available to rational reform. For we ourselves are constituted in the very process by which these meanings are formed. Whether these are images of motherhood or of pornography, we cannot simply accept or reject them through acts of conscious will. It is this which the simple demand for censorship always fails to address.

The issue of representation thus clearly involves another aspect, one that is equally the concern of the articles in this section: namely, a certain power of the image, which exceeds its function as the mere construction of a definition. For, while we are constituted by these images and representations, they themselves are taken merely to stand for, stand in for, something else, an elsewhere, that can only really be known to us through these images. Here is the central paradox or contradiction of representation: by its presentation in this image, we are assured of a real referent absent, elsewhere, but affirmed by its representation here. This is the function—and pleasure—of realist representation. It purports to show reality, whereas in fact it simply organizes images—arranging them according to a point of view that endows them with recognizable meaning—in a way that claims a real referent. By means of realist conventions, the reader or spectator places and deciphers the images and sequences and so arrives at the consciousness of her or his own identity, namely as the point at which the representation makes sense. Here, then, is the lure of realist representation; it is this securing of the reader or spectator's identity as the point of knowledge of the text. This lure is not eschewed by the attempts of critics to "unmask" representation, for such attempts betray the continuing desire for an unmediated and hence uncontaminated representation by which one might "know oneself." Such a representation is, of course, an impossibility. The point, then, is not to condemn realism as a system of deception, but to recognize its role in the construction of identity as unified and to see our relation to realism as one of desire.

It is in this nexus that psychoanalysis has been central for discussions of representation in *m/f*. For, it is psychoanalysis that theorizes the subject as the one who knows very well that the image is only an image, but who all the same takes it for real. This is the subject who misrecognizes in Lacan's mirror phase as well as the subject who disavows. Representation is central to the psychoanalytic theory of identity as formed through a series of identifications: in the mirror phase, it is involved in the subject's identification with itself as an image. Furthermore, it is through psychoanalysis that we can begin to understand the pleasure of the image, and our desire for the image, in a way which is not first and foremost organized in terms of the "meaning" purported to be presented in the image. In cinema, it is the way in which we are captured by the world portrayed on the screen, the way in which we are taken up and into that world which may not only, if at all, seem better than our everyday reality, but which is also and most importantly larger-than-life, other-worldly, even if and at the same time we require it to be realistic. The pleasure of images is not just what they say to us as signification in the traditional, realist, sense, but also what they constitute for us as imagings. In other words, the pleasure of images, in part at least, is the pleasure not of what I come to know—signification—but of what I come to desire, that is, the scenario of desire that I come to participate in as I watch a film, view an image, or read a text. This is a desire not for some thing, but for desire itself. What is signified is thus the position of desire for the spectator. This is the pleasure of images as fantasy. It is this area of work that the discussion in "Fantasia" begins to open up in relation to cinema.

Addressing film as a fantasy structure, that is, as a *mise-en-scène* of desire in which the subject of the fantasy—and the viewing subject through identification—may take up any of a number of positions, introduces the issue of feminine as well as masculine fantasy and desire into discussions of representation. However, a politics of sexual difference might seem to have disappeared, since the significant differences are now between the various positions, masculine or feminine, active or passive, mother, father, daughter, son, successively taken up by the spectator regardless of his or her biological sex. But these positions are not simple alternatives or open choices; they are effects of the film text's narration and function to determine places of desire and positions of identification that are interdependent. A binary structuring of sexual difference is indeed produced for the film and for the spectator. But this production of differences is not equivalent to a division into men and women, for it may involve a phallic/nonphallic distinction between members of the same sex, for example mother and daughter. Fantasy therefore fails to produce the fixed and polarized positions of men and women required for a feminist politics basing itself on a theory of patriarchy.

In any case, whether in the cinema or in everyday life, it is not sexual difference as such that must be challenged—if this is understood as the different relations to lack and to the phallus taken up by men and women[1]—for this does not secure the identity men/masculine and women/feminine. Instead it is the *fantasies* (of women as well as men) that arise as a result of the difficulties of assuming a sexually differentiated position that must be addressed. And it is the way these fantasies translate the problem of the psychical and social organization of difference into a solution of subordination that must be challenged.

The difficulty entailed by sexual difference is not simply a matter of the Oedipus complex and the lack in the mother, the woman. It is also a matter of the lack in the subject and her or his acknowledgment of the lack in the Other. In other words, it becomes necessary to recognize that no one, neither man nor woman, has the phallus. But it would seem that this recognition is never fully achieved by the subject (to the extent that it is, however, the process is described by Lacan as "going-through the fantasy,"[2]), but continues to jostle with disavowal. Fantasy is the means by which, Freud says, the subject "attempts to replace a disagreeable reality by one which is more in keeping with the subject's wishes."[3] Parental fantasies, family structures, and social relations determine the context for this negotiation of differences and the production of all those fantasies that are part of this negotiation.[4] It is the determinations—both social and psychical—of this construction that need to be addressed. The complex function of fantasy requires an equally complex political response.

Elizabeth Cowie

Notes

1.   Moustafa Safouan discusses the issue of lack and castration in his article, "Is the Oedipus Complex Universal?" in this volume.
2.   This is discussed by Slavoj Žižek in the chapter "Identity, Identification and its Beyond" in his *The Sublime Object of Ideology,* Verso, 1989.
3.   Sigmund Freud, "Reality in Neurosis and Perversion," *The Standard Edition of the Complete Psychological Works of Sigmund Freud,* Hogarth Press, vol. XIX, p. 187.
4.   This is discussed further in Elizabeth Cowie, *The Representation of Sexual Difference in the Cinema,* Macmillan (forthcoming).

Woman as Sign

ELIZABETH COWIE

Most work on film by feminists has been in terms of the kinds of images of women represented in films: the stereotypes presented of women, the types of parts women play and the kinds of stories told about women in films. "Women, as a fully human form, have almost completely been left out of film . . . That is, from its very beginning they were present but not in characterizations any self-respecting person could identify with" (Sharon Smith, p. 13). Yet what must be grasped in addressing "women and film" is the double problem of the production of woman as a category and a film as a signifying system. Feminist analysis of film assumes "woman" as an unproblematic category constituted through the definitions already produced in society—as mother, housewife, worker, sexual partner and reflected in film. Women are taken as inscribed in a particular position as women, which then determines all representations of women. Film as a practice is posited as secondary to other practices within society. Social definitions of women's roles are seen as the "lived relations" of women whereas film is taken to be merely a "representation," powerful as ideology yet without the material effectivity of, for instance, employment structures that produce a definition of women as second-class workers suited by virtue of this definition to certain types of work and thereby requiring a lower reward for that work than men.

Woman as a category, as the effect of definitions produced by political and economic practices, is posited as prior to filmic practices, and as then simply reproduced, reflected, or distorted by film. Film itself is asserted as an ideological practice and therefore is assumed to have ideological effects, in particular on the definitions of women in society, the images of women, masking or reinforcing those definitions. It is these effects that feminists have usually addressed. However these are then seen as part of a problem of ideology, which is defined and theorized outside of the specificity of film.

On the other hand there has been a development within the theory of cinema that argues that film is not simply a reflection of other practices. Instead it defines film as a system that produces meaning through the articulation of signifying elements. That is, the work of film is the definition of meaning produced in the combination of elements within that specific film. The *film* produces the definitions of its elements by which they have meaning and are understood (see especially *Screen* special issue, vol. 14, no. 1/2). But when the political project of feminism—to question the representation of women as against men—is brought to bear on film, the object, woman, is assumed already to have a definition, to have meaning, which is produced outside of the system of representation of the film. Thus the same problem emerges: the category "woman" is not seen as produced within the film but drawn from a general placing of women outside the film, in society. Films are criticized for not showing "women as women," or "as fully human." It is criticized as inadequate, as partial and one-sided in relation to a possible definition of women elsewhere, or else it is seen as a negation of that definition. Film is therefore precisely denied as a process of production when it comes to definitions of women, of woman as signifier and signified in the system of the film.

Hence the struggle for definitions of women is placed elsewhere, and film becomes simply the site of the struggle of the *representations* of those definitions, to be replaced or subverted by other, progressive representations. I want to argue, however, that film as a system of representation is a point of production of definitions. But it is neither unique and independent of, nor simply reducible to, other practices defining the position of women in society.

What is at issue is whether it is possible or useful to presuppose a generalized notion woman, whose consistent degradation across all practices justifies the assertion that there is a consistent category woman produced by film. Lévi-Strauss's ideas are particularly relevant in this context. This is because he has put forward ideas that engage both with the question of the position of women in general and also with the question of the production of women as a category within a particular signifying system, in his case, kinship. Feminists have recognized his importance but have often fallen into the traps that are implicit in Lévi-Strauss's own work.

It is from this position that I want to look at the notion of "woman as sign"— a sign communicated by men. This concept originates from the work of Lévi-Strauss on forms of kinship, as a result of which he argues that the exchange of women is the constant term in all kinship structures. Lévi-Strauss is important to consider here because he offers not simply a description of kinship structures but also a theory: that kinship structures are a system of exchange—the exchange of women—which is a system of communication.

> These results [in the understanding of kinship structures] can be achieved only by treating marriage regulations and kinship systems as a kind of language, a set of processes permitting the establishment, between individuals and groups, of a certain type of communication. That the mediating factor, in this case, should be the *women of the group,* who are circulated between clans, lineages, or families, in place of the *words of the group,* which are circulated between individuals, does not at all change the fact that the essential aspect of the phenomenon is identical in both cases. (Lévi-Strauss, *Structural Anthropology,* p. 61)

Kinship is a structure through which men and women are put into place, through the complex rules of familial affiliation and the implications of these for a group in terms of duties and rituals to be performed by each sex as a result of that placing— as father, son, husband, and brother/uncle, and as mother, daughter, wife, sister/aunt. Kinship is also a system of communication, the production of meaning between members of the system, a signifying system, in which women are produced as a sign, which is circulated in an identical way to words.

I want to examine Lévi Strauss' notion of kinship, in terms of his theory of communication and in terms of his presentation of women as the term of exchange and some of its implications. I want to argue that though these two theses are linked within Lévi-Strauss's argument, it is important to disengage them in order to open up questions about women's subordinate position on the one hand, and the representation of women in signifying systems on the other. This is precisely made possible by Lévi-Strauss's work, although he himself closes off such questions. Further I want to look at the way this work has been taken up by feminists, in particular by Juliet Mitchell in her book *Psychoanalysis and Feminism,* which remains one of the most important contributions to feminist theory; and by Pam Cook and Claire Johnston in their article, "The Place of Women in the Cinema of Raoul Walsh," which is one of the first attempts to theorize women in the cinema. Nevertheless in both texts similar problems emerge in relation to their use of Lévi-Strauss: first, the uncritical acceptance of Lévi-Strauss's elaboration of woman as sign; and second, the too literal use of the concept of woman as sign.

For Lévi-Strauss exogamy is fundamental to social life; in discussing structures of reciprocity he states:

> The law of exogamy, by contrast, is omnipresent, acting permanently and continually; moreover, it applies to valuables—viz., women—valuables *par excellence* from both the biological and social points of view, without which life is impossible, or, at best, is reduced to the worst forms of abjection. It is no exaggeration, then, to say that exogamy is the archetype of all other manifestations based upon reciprocity, and that it provides the fundamental and immutable rule ensuring the existence of the group as a group. (*Elementary Structures of Kinship*, p. 481)

Exogamy is the foremost mode of exchange, and for Lévi-Strauss exchange is the giving and receiving of equivalent but different items. It creates "social bonds" that are reflected, for instance, in feasts, where food is distributed on the basis of marriage relationships. For Lévi-Strauss, then, exchange is a principle of culture, and hence exogamy, together with its corollary, the incest taboo, insofar as it is the rule ensuring the exchange of women through marriage outside the group, is the preeminent mode or structure ensuring social life—the rules of kinship *are* the society.

In the kinship structures that Lévi-Strauss has analyzed it is women, and only women, who are exchanged under the rules of exogamy. Lévi-Strauss states that there is no theoretical reason why women should not exchange men, but that empirically this has never taken place in any human society. Yet in establishing his thesis of exogamy as the consequence of the rule of reciprocity the implications of Lévi-Strauss's argument are very different, that is, he asserts that women have a fundamental *value* for the community: "women are held by the group to be values of the most essential kind" (*ibid.,* p. 61). In his discussion of the universe of rules and the system of exchange in primitive groups, Lévi-Strauss places women with food as the most valuable commodities to the community: under the "system of the scarce product," "The group controls the distribution not only of women, but of a whole collection of valuables," and "The methods for distributing meat in this part of the world [by the Eskimo hunters of Hudson bay] are no less ingenious than for the distribution of women." Later, as an example of the "value" of women, he quotes the Pygmies as saying "the more women available, the more food" because of the importance of their role as gatherers of fruit, etc., to the diet of the group. He cites as well a Brazilian village where he saw ". . . in the corner of a hut, dismal, ill-cared for, fearfully thin . . . in complete state of dejection" a young man whose problem, or sin, turned out to be that "he is a bachelor." In other words, it is crucial for a man to have a wife. Nowhere does Lévi-Strauss argue why women are constituted as valuable to the group in this way, nor why women are valuable to women—the group may find women "essential values" but how far does the group here indicate its male members? (Quotations are from *Elementary Structures of Kinship,* Chapter IV, "The Universe of Rules.")

Theoretically it is not required that women rather than men be exchanged, but as Lévi-Strauss himself shows, it is constituted through the principle of reciprocity whose condition of existence is a hierarchy of "valuables," of exchangeable items (a value defined by the group, a value that is not necessarily a function of the "usefulness" of the object to the group but is a socially constituted value), different but equivalent, of which women are the "valuables *par excellence.*" What is important here is that exchange is not itself constitutive of the subordination of women; women are not subordinate because of the fact of exchange but because of the modes of exchange instituted. In arguing the "neutrality" of exchange as a concept, Lévi-Strauss overlooks the fact that while in his theory the principle of exchange itself does not define or "value" the items of exchange, which must always be equivalents although different, the terms of items of exchange must *already be* constituted, in a hierarchy of value, in order to be available to a system of exchange. Yet once constituted as terms in exchange, they are then defined by the mode of the structure of exchange.

Lévi-Strauss posits that women become a "symbol or sign" within exogamy, a sign that is exchanged. There seem to be two aspects to this: first, in relation to prohibitions generally, that the incest taboo, which is the corollary of exogamy, is comparable to other prohibitions:

> For several very primitive peoples in the Malay Archipelago the supreme sin, unleashing storm and tempest, comprises a series of superficially incongruous acts which informants list higgledy-piggledy as follows: marriage with near kin; father and daughter or mother and son sleeping too close to one another; incorrect speech between kin; ill-considered conversation; for children, noisy play, and for adults, demonstrative happiness shown at social reunions; imitating the calls of certain insects or birds; laughing at one's own face in the mirror; and finally, teasing animals and in particular, dressing a monkey as a man, and making fun of him. (*ibid.,* p. 494)

Lévi-Strauss argues that

> all these prohibitions can be reduced to a single common denominator: they all constitute a misuse of language, and on this ground they are grouped together with the incest prohibition, or with acts evocative of

incest. What does this mean, except that women themselves are treated
as signs, which are *misused* when not put to the use reserved to signs,
which is to be communicated? (*ibid.,* p. 495–496)

Thus the incest taboo is assimilated to all other prohibitions as a prohibition on the
misuse of language, a misuse that puts in jeopardy social relations. Hence exchange
is defined as a language in as much as the taboo—incest—which is its corollary, is
defined as a misuse of language, that is, a misuse because there is no exchange. And
this is the second aspect of the concept of woman as sign, that the exchange of
women that is fundamental to all kinship structures is a system of communication:
"In any society, communication operates on three different levels: communication
of women, communication of goods and services, communication of messages"
(*Structural Anthropology,* p. 296). Lévi-Strauss argues that women are signs in as
much as women are "communicated," that is, because they are exchanged in all kinship structures. Primitive groups themselves recognize this by putting the incest
taboo together with other prohibitions that relate, as he says, to a misuse of language.
Incest is the "misuse" of woman as sign since it is not using woman in the way
reserved for signs "which is to be communicated."

Lévi-Strauss obviously doesn't think exogamy is a system of communication of
the same sophistication as language but he strongly associates language and exogamy as two solutions to the same fundamental situation—which could perhaps be
loosely put as the necessity for the resolution of the opposition between the self and
others in order to make possible social intercourse. This leads to the assertion of
universal mental structures, that is:

the exigency of the rule as rule; the notion of reciprocity regarded as the
most immediate form of integrating the opposition between the self and
others; and finally, the synthetic nature of the gift, i.e., that the agreed
transfer of a valuable from one individual to another makes these individuals into partners, and adds a new quality to the valuable transferred.
(*op. cit.,* p. 84)

It is in terms of these structures that Lévi-Strauss sees myths as well as kinship structures as a synthesis of the oppositions involved. Man still dreams of a time when the
law of exchange could be evaded, when one could "gain without losing, enjoy without sharing" and quotes as examples the way the Sumerian and Andaman myths of
future life correspond:

the former placing the end of primitive happiness at a time when the confusion of languages made words into common property, the latter
describing the bliss of the hereafter as a heaven where women will no
longer be exchanged, i.e., removing to an equally unattainable past or
future the joys, eternally denied to social man, of a world in which one
might *keep to oneself.* (*ibid.,* p. 497)

It is in terms of this necessity to resolve oppositions that Lévi-Strauss earlier states
that:

> The emergence of symbolic thought must have required that women,
> like words, should be things that were exchanged. In this new case,
> indeed, this was the only means of overcoming the contradiction by
> which the same woman was seen under two incompatible aspects: on the
> one hand, as the object of personal desire, thus exciting sexual and pro-
> prietorial instincts; and on the other, as the subject of the desire of others,
> and seen as such, ie as the means of binding others through alliance with
> them. (*ibid.,* p. 496)

I have quoted Lévi-Strauss at length because I think that these passages show most
clearly the problems in his argument. By raising a philosophical premise—the
necessity of integrating self and other—language and exogamy are reduced to solutions. The primacy of human essence—here represented in the necessity to integrate
self and others is asserted, from which language and exogamy become consequences. An appeal to humanism is made, so that women can never be simply a sign
since they are persons as well. The human exceeds the sign, which is derivative
of it.

> But woman could not become just a sign and nothing more, since even
> in a man's world she is still a person, and since insofar as she is defined
> as a sign she must be recognised as a generator of signs . . . In contrast
> to words, which have wholly become signs, woman has remained at once
> sign and value. (*ibid.,* p. 496)

Woman as exchange, and hence as sign, is a solution to a contradiction—but the solution is always only partial since Lévi-Strauss poses as part of the same problem of
women as sign the ability of women to be more than a sign, that within marriage and
indeed before it woman is more than a term in a signifying system, exchange,

because of her "talent . . . for taking part in a duet." He qualifies the concept precisely because of that contradiction for which it is a solution. In other words he qualifies the concept of woman as sign because of a humanist notion of woman as already constituted, a position that is also implicit in his notion of the "value" of women. This has important consequences for Lévi-Strauss's use of the concept of sign, a use that is marked by the same ambiguity that is involved in his relationship to the structural approach in anthropology, which he introduced. That is, the dilemma that it is the structures that "produce" man and yet man is still always posited as prior to those structures. Lévi-Strauss refuses the radical implications of his own concepts, which I want to take up here as being of important use to feminists. That is that his theory can be understood as specifying the production of woman within a particular system—exchange—and that this system is a signifying system producing woman as both object of exchange—positioned by the structure as mother, wife, etc.—and as sign within that signifying system.

Lévi-Strauss draws extensively in his work on the theoretical developments of Ferdinand de Saussure and on subsequent structural linguistics; however it is not clear that the sign for Lévi-Strauss is the same as the Saussurean sign. Rather he uses the term interchangeably with "symbol": "as producers of signs, women can never be reduced to the status of symbols or tokens" (*Structural Anthropology,* p. 61). Taken in this sense there is a difference between the signs women produce or speak, that is, linguistic signs, and the sign or symbol woman *is* in the act of exchange within kinship structures. Lévi-Strauss himself is not concerned with this question, but it is clearly important if one wishes to develop his notion of the exchange of women for signifying systems other than that of kinship.

Two questions have to be dealt with, one, whether woman is a *symbol* or a *sign*. Two, whether woman as a sign is a function of a cultural reflection of a natural gender-position of women *or* is specific to the position of women in the particular signifying structure, kinship.

In linguistics the difference between a sign and a symbol is clear; for example, words are signs (which can also be used symbolically) because their relation to the idea or concept is arbitrary and unmotivated. There is no necessary analogy between the word *ox* and the image of an *ox*. In nonlinguistic signifying systems a confusion of the two notions consistently arises. In the symbol the relation of the form of the symbol, the signifier, to the signified, the concept which is communicated by the symbol, is never wholly arbitrary. Thus the scales as the symbol of justice could not be replaced by just any other symbol such as a chariot, since the scales incorporate the notion of balance which is the embodiment of the concept of justice for our social formation.

Within kinship structures of exchange, however, woman must be a *sign,* and not a symbol, inasmuch as "woman" does not represent any notion intrinsic to what is communicated in exchange, that is, to what Lévi-Strauss argues as a "social contract." The term "woman" is part of a semiotic chain of communication with a sender and a receiver and an object of exchange—woman—which is the *sign* produced, signifying the "social contract." In other words, the agreement to give up a present right (to this woman) for a future right (access to all women, or all women in a certain group) and which Lévi-Strauss argues is the fundamental principle of culture, of the possibility of culture as a social structure.

Thus "woman" here is not a sign because of any immanent meaning. Meaning is not some substance contained within the sign "which might be examined independently of the signs in which it is apprehended; it only exists through the relations in which it takes part" (Tzvetan Todorov, pp. 131—138). *Woman* is produced as a sign within exchange systems inasmuch as she is the signifier of a difference in relation to men, that is, women are exchanged rather than men. Saussure emphasises in relation to language that "there are only differences *without positive terms*" (p. 120). Both men and women are positioned in exchange—as husbands or wives, etc., but only women are produced as signs. In other words, that women are exchanged as a sign rather than men does not mean that there is a positive difference that determines this, simply that men are not the term of exchange. The position of women *as sign* in exchange, however, has no relation to *why* women are exchanged. In other words, it has no relation to the "idea" of women in a society—which is what Lévi-Strauss is in fact referring to in his notion of the "value" of women. The sign woman is produced within a specific signifying system—kinship structures—and hence while the form or rather *signifier* of the sign (which in language would be the sounds making up the word) is the actual person, woman, the substance or meaning of the sign, its signified, is *not* the concept woman. One cannot speak of "a" sign—woman—without specifying the system in which it has signification—exchange. Signs are only meaningful within the system of signification in which they are produced, and not as discrete units.

The problem of value is explicit in Lévi-Strauss's use of the concept of sign:

It is generally recognised that words are signs; but poets are practically the only ones who know that words were also once values. As against this, women are held by the social group to be values of the most essential kind, though we have difficulty in understanding how these values become integrated in systems endowed with a significant function. (*Structural Anthropology,* p. 61)

It is the same problem indicated earlier in relation to the question of why it is women who are exchanged. In both cases value is left undefined but Lévi-Strauss signals it as determining in signifying systems.

In associating value in the sign or word with the "cultural" value of women, and posing these as somehow preexisting but then integrated in "systems endowed with a significant function," Lévi-Strauss radically undermines the concept of sign as he uses it. Saussure emphasized that value in the sign is only produced once the sign is truly a sign—arbitrary and unmotivated. Value in the sign is produced *by* the signifying system—language—and is not a determinant of it. "Value" as a notion is unclear in Lévi-Strauss but it seems to be used in the sense of hierarchical values of a society. But then it is a question of certain things being more "valuable" than others, of a cultural hierarchy being formed. In this sense a term or object only has value *to* or *for* someone or some group.

This returns to the question of how women are constituted as "values of the most essential kind," and raises a further question of how the social group is constituted since Lévi-Strauss argues that it is through exogamy that culture, and hence the social group, is possible. Yet exogamy is characterized by the term of exchange involved being uniquely women; women are *already* marked as of value by exchange itself. If, however, women are exchanged in kinship structures because they have value for the group, then the group must have already entered culture to the extent of recognizing women as socially valuable. In ascribing "origins" the trap is set for the inscription of a fundamental sexual difference into the social, even though he appears to be claiming that the mode of inscription is cultural. The exchange of women defines society as human. The act of exogamy transforms "natural" families into a cultural kinship system, thereby ensuring the rights and obligations between groups as kin which incest, that is, sexual relations contained within the biological family unit, can never produce. But sexual division as social must already exist in order for women to be available for men to exchange in an organized way, and for women to be "valued" as an object of exchange. What remains problematic therefore is that the exchange of women, on which culture is based, is itself predicated on a pre-given *sexual division,* which must already be social. The exchange of women is thus presented as the necessity for culture, because man is inherently unsocial, desiring without giving, inherently incestuous and engaged in permanent warfare over "possessions," including women.

Yet it is not the question of origins, of "what came first," which is important here, although this is clearly a problem with Lévi-Strauss's use of the notion of value in his thesis of exchange. Rather, it is a problem of the limits it sets on his notion of exchange as a system of communication, of signification. Once exchange is established in practice and theoretically, as constituted in Lévi-Strauss's work, the questions then raised are ones about the place of women in certain social structures. The question of the *necessity* of the *exchange* of *women* may not be determinant *of* the position of women within exchange. Here what is important is not why but how women are placed in exchange, for which Lévi-Strauss himself gives two answers: as objects and as signs.

Therefore work should be undertaken not simply around the empirical reality of women as exchange objects, that is, placed as wives, mothers and sisters within families, but also in terms of the exchange of women in a signifying system in which woman is produced as a sign. It is here that the notion of value can be taken up again, in the sense Saussure established: "Language is a system of interdependent terms in which the value of each term results solely from the simultaneous presence of the others" (p. 114). The value of words does not lie in their "exchangeability"; in any case words can only be interchanged with each other, and exchanged with a concept or idea:

> Its value is therefore not fixed so long as one simply states that it can be exchanged for a given concept, i.e., that it has this or that signification: one must also compare it with similar values, with other words that stand in opposition to it. Its content is really fixed only by the concurrence of everything that exists outside it. Being part of a system, it is endowed not only with signification but also and especially with a value, and this is something quite different. (p. 115)

Value is the measure of difference; a term has value only relative to other terms in the same system, for instance numbers, where "8" is more than "6," yet the higher value does not indicate that 8 is necessarily preferred to 6, simply that its value in the numerical system is different and higher than that relatively of 6.

The value of a word is produced by the system of language—Saussure gives the example of the word sheep, which he says in French, as *mouton,* has a different value because it serves for two meanings, than in English, which uses two distinct words for those meanings: mutton and sheep. Further, the value of a word is conditional on all other words that surround it, rather than on its signification. For Saussure the value of words is not intrinsic, nor a function of signification, but is a property of the system, thus, "The Community is necessary if values that owe their existence solely to usage and general acceptance are to be set up; by himself the individual is incapable of fixing a single value" (p. 113). Why bother then to suggest that women are signs in exchange systems? What does it add to Lévi-Strauss's argument that women are exchanged and that this is the basis of kinship structures and society? Its importance lies in that exchange is not just an operation—the bodily movement of women from one place to another via a matrimonial ceremony, but a system of communication (Lévi-Strauss), or, more precisely, of signification. I use signification here rather than communication because what is crucial is the notion of a system that posits the sender as well as the receiver of the signified as *part of the system,* rather than as *operators* of the system.

> The fundamental problem with the conception of language as communication is that it tends to obscure the way in which language sets up the positions of "I" and "You" that are necessary for communication to take place at all. Communication involves more than just a message being transmitted from the speaker to the destinee . . . [it] involves not just the transfer of information to another, but the very constitution of the speaking subject in relation to its other. (Coward and Ellis, pp. 79–80)

Thus exchange is not simply the "communication of women," which for Lévi-Strauss is always the act of exchange, of goods, words or women, without attention to the specificity of the system in which this occurs, and hence representing it as neutral or passive vis-à-vis the terms communicated. But rather a putting into place—of culture, and crucially, of sexual relations. Jacques Lacan, writing from within psychoanalysis, has taken this up, relating the exchange of women, as Lévi-Strauss elaborates it, to the Oedipus complex, which together function to institute "subjectivity" in the human animal.

> The primordial law is therefore that which in regulating marriage ties superimposes the kingdom of culture on that of a nature abandoned to the law of mating. The prohibition of incest is merely its subjective pivot . . . This law, then, is revealed clearly enough as identical with an order of language. For without kinship nominations, no power is capable of instituting the order of preferences and taboos that bind and weave the yarn of lineage through succeeding generations. And it is indeed the con-

fusion of generations which, in the Bible, as in all traditional laws, is
accused of being the abomination of the Word (*verbe*) and the desolation
of the sinner. (*Ecrits,* p. 66)

That woman is a sign in exchange and not only an object of exchange has important
consequences. Exchange becomes not just a series of acts but a structure that makes
possible all particular acts of exchange within a group. The structure, its rules, pre-
scribes the kinship relations of a group, producing the positions of men and women
in the group in terms of their marriage relations:

> From a social viewpoint, these terms cannot be regarded as defining iso-
> lated individuals, but relationships between these individuals and every-
> one else. Motherhood is not only a mother's relationship to her children,
> but her relationship to other members of the group, not as a mother, but
> as a sister, wife, cousin or simply a stranger as far as kinship is concerned.
> (Lévi-Strauss, *ibid.,* p. 482)

As a result, "Every family relationship defines a certain group of rights and duties,
while the lack of family relationship does not define anything; it defines enmity"
(p. 482). For primitive groups kinship is *the* structure that defines relationships, produces its members in the position of mother, sister, etc., so that for the Australian
aboriginal group the most important question put to a stranger is "Who is your *maeli*
(father's father)" in order to establish kinship relations; to have no such relations is
to be an enemy, one to whom the group has no obligations. Kinship is thus part of
a system that produces women as object of exchange, which on one side becomes
a sign, of the institution of culture through reciprocity.

> the inviolable debt . . . guarantee that the voyage on which wives and
> goods are embarked will bring back to their point of departure in a
> never-failing cycle other women and other goods, all carrying an iden-
> tical identity. (Lacan, p. 68)

And on the other side exchange becomes the mode by which women are defined,
are placed. Once posited within kinship structures, that is, as a category that is not-
men, women are "produced" as mother, daughter, wife, sister.

A number of complex and different points come together here: that of woman
as sign, through a "negative" difference, as the term of exchange; that of the institution of culture through the establishing of reciprocity—primarily through the
exchange of women; that of the institution of and social/symbolic inscription of dif-

ference through the castration complex. It is exogamy with its corollary, the incest taboo, which enables man to locate himself—and his goods—in relation to others; it produces a *difference* socially secured/secure through the rule of reciprocity. Paternity is therefore a crucial term here. In the realm of the psyche it is the castration complex—the unconscious counterpart of the incest taboo—that establishes difference, sexual and hence also social, in the human animal. It is therefore possible to see "woman" not as a given, biologically or psychologically, but as a category produced in signifying practices—whether through exogamy and kinship structures, or through signification at the level of the unconscious. To talk of "woman as sign" in exchange systems is to no longer talk of woman as the signified, but of a different signified, that of: establishment/reestablishment of kinship structures or culture. The form of the sign—the signifier in linguistic terms—may empirically be woman, but the signified is not "woman."

The question of the nature of the operation of Lévi-Strauss's concept of woman as a sign in exchange systems has thus seemed to me to be of fundamental importance on the one hand for work on the constitution of the place of women within kinship structures, which produces both an inscription of sexual difference within a practice, kinship, and has effects within, for example, economic practices, in terms of the structure of ownership of property within the family and by the family. On the other hand, it has importance in relation to questions of how woman as a sign is produced in other signifying systems.

It is this role of exogamy in establishing sexual difference that Juliet Mitchell draws attention to in her book *Psychoanalysis and Feminism*. In that book she is concerned to show how exogamy corresponds to Freud's theory of the incest taboo and Oedipus complex. She points to the way in which Lévi-Strauss argues that kinship structures are not based on the biological family but on the principle of the reciprocal exchange of women. It is this exchange that organizes difference and thereby inscribes it within men and women.

At the same time Juliet Mitchell seeks to secure her use of Lévi-Strauss from an accusation of sexism by using Lévi-Strauss own defense. Thus she says: "Lévi-Strauss is correct to stress that the given place in a system of communication is no index of inferiority or superiority and that we must not be led astray by the false derogatory connotations of the word 'object'" (p. 372). I have tried to show, however, that this defense—that women are more than objects and signs in exchange because they are also producers of signs, and because of their inherent value over and above their participation in the act of exchange—is highly problematic. Thus Juliet Mitchell

accepts the construction of woman as object of exchange as not itself sexist, while
noting that Lévi-Strauss's repudiation of antifeminism is inadequate although correct
(see here her quote from Lévi-Strauss, p. 371). However the problem is then left as:
"Nevertheless this primary sexual division is an important indicator of difference and
a difference that may well be historically exploited to establish a system of defer-
ence" (p. 372). However, in emphasizing the role of exogamy in establishing difference, kinship is reduced to a more or less fixed structure which has already
produced sexual difference and culture. The implications of the notion that "woman
thus becomes the equivalent of a sign that is being communicated" are not addressed
by her. Rather, kinship is taken as a given structure whose description will expose
the situation of women generally: "What we need is kinship analysis of contemporary capitalist society, for it is within kinship structures that women as women are
situated."

Yet it is not just as structure but also as process that kinship is important. What
Lévi-Strauss's emphasis on kinship as communication has marked, although in an
inadequate way, is that the work of kinship, that is, of exogamy, is a production, of
woman as sign and of men and women "in position" in society. That is, of placing
rather than placed. It is not that women as women are *situated* in the family. But that
it is in the family—as the effect of kinship structures—that women as women are produced, are defined within and by the group. Thus kinship structures should in no
way be seen as neutral or nonsexist, as effectively apolitical; exogamy must instead
be seen as a practice as well as a structure that signifies men and women as mother,
father, wife, and husband, etc.

Juliet Mitchell reproduces problems within Lévi-Strauss's work by failing to
consider the implications of his theory of women as sign. Pam Cook and Claire Johnston use this notion directly in their article, "The Place of Women in the Cinema of
Raoul Walsh" and therefore reinscribe the problems already outlined in relation to
Lévi-Strauss. They seek to translate his concept of women as object of exchange in
kinship structures into a parallel operation in film structures. It assumes that Lévi-
Strauss is adequately talking of a system of signification and that a comparable
exchange of women in another system can be posited that then also produces
women as signs.

They refer in their article specifically to those films produced by the director
Raoul Walsh, but see their argument as applying beyond the Walsh oeuvre inasmuch
as "Woman as signifier of woman under patriarchy is totally absent in most image-
producing systems, but particularly in Hollywood" (pp. 107–9). What is important in
their article is that they take up Lévi-Strauss's point that woman is a sign in exchange

systems, rather than woman simply being the object of exchange. However the structure of exchange is simply seen as taken up by the filmic system: "As an object of exchange between men, a sign oscillating between the images of prostitute and mother-figure, she represents the means by which men express their relationships with each other" (p. 95). Further they continue Lévi-Strauss's confusion about the nature of this sign, hence arguing that woman as sign remains a token of exchange in the patriarchal order of a Walsh film. But in fact in kinship structures the sign is much more than a token of exchange, since its signification *exceeds* simply that of "exchange" or the system of marriage rules, signifying the possibility of culture organized on the basis of kinship structures. The sign "woman" in exogamy is not exchanged but produced in the exchange of actual women. What is raised is indeed the relationship of actual women to the signification constituted within kinship structures, but this cannot be in terms of a "real" signified, woman, in contrast to a distorted or inadequate signified, woman as exchange. As soon as a system of representation is posited—as with film—it is no longer possible to talk, as above, of "woman as signifier of woman" since this poses the system of representation over and against a true signified woman, or, presumably, actual women. What is important is not that film falsely signifies women, or appropriates the signifier (image) woman to another signification, but the particular mode of constituting woman as sign within film. What is of concern is the specific consequences of that mode of constitution both within film and in relationship to other signifying systems and discourses.

In fact this is the implication of their analysis of Walsh's film *The Revolt of Mamie Stover* (1956) where they "attempt to demonstrate that women (e.g., Mamie Stover) in fact function as a signifier in a circuit of exchange where the values exchanged have been fixed by/in a patriarchal culture" (Introduction, p. 94). That the system of the film produces the main protagonist, Mamie Stover, as signifier of lack—castration—around which male desire, and patriarchal law, are organized: "The male protagonist's castration fears, his search for self-knowledge all converge on woman: it is in her that he is finally faced with the recognition of "lack." Woman is therefore the locus of emptiness" (p. 97). However, this does not make "Mamie Stover" an *empty sign* as they claim: "woman is not only a sign in a system of exchange, but an empty sign" (p. 96). The term empty is problematic because it suggests a "fullness" somewhere else. Rather the sign always has signification; on the other hand the signifier is necessarily "empty" inasmuch as it is unmotivated and arbitrary, that is, without an already given meaning. Nevertheless this does not mean that women *are* lack or anything else, but that in a certain signifying system, here in *The Revolt of Mamie*

Stover woman signifies lack in a circulation of desire organized around the male dilemma/fear of castration.

It is precisely this circuit of desire, of signifiers, by which the meaning of the film is organized. However the "values" of the terms in circulation are not simply already fixed "by/in a patriarchal culture" that is outside of the film. The film itself is part of the operation of the "fixing" of the "values." Therefore it is crucial to keep separate the question of the representation of women and woman as a sign, to avoid any simple denunciation of the sign as inadequate representation/signification of the "real" object woman, and rather to take up the implications of certain modes of representations of women for the position of women constructed within society.

References

Rosalind Coward and John Ellis, *Language and Materialism,* Routledge and Kegan Paul, 1977.

Pam Cook and Claire Johnston, "The Place of Women in the Cinema of Raoul Walsh," in *Raoul Walsh,* ed. Phil Hardy, Edinburgh Film Festival, 1974. Reprinted in *Feminism and Film Theory,* ed. Constance Penley, Routledge and BFI, 1988.

Jacques Lacan, "The Function and Field of Speech and Language in Psychoanalysis," *Ecrits,* trans. Alan Sheridan, Tavistock, 1977.

Claude Lévi-Strauss, *The Elementary Structures of Kinship,* Eye and Spottiswoode, London, 1969.

Claude Lévi-Strauss, *Structural Anthropology,* Penguin, London, 1972.

Juliet Mitchell, *Psychoanalysis and Feminism,* Allen Lane, London, 1974.

Ferdinand de Saussure, *Course in General Linguistics,* McGraw-Hill, 1966.

Screen, vol. 14, no. 1/2, published by Society for Education in Film and Television.

Sharon Smith, "The Image of Women in Film: Some Suggestions for Further Research," *Women & Film,* no. 1, 1972.

Tzvetan Todorov, "The Sign," in Oswald Ducrot and Tzvetan Todorov, *Encyclopedic Dictionary of the Sciences of Language,* Johns Hopkins University Press, 1979.

from *m/f* 1, 1978

A Feminist Interest in Pornography: Some Modest Proposals

BEVERLEY BROWN

The object of this essay is to lower the level of analysis of pornographic images. On the general questions of the relation between sexuality and power, sexuality and representation, sexuality and the law, it has little to say. Pornography is after all a definite and limited cultural form with a specific mode of effectivity. If it is to be assessed as a political issue for feminism then there must be some form of distinguishing it and of relating it to possible feminist campaigns. Merely characterizing the pornographic in terms of extremes of explicitness is about as useful and as accurate as characterizing capitalism as extreme misery. In suggesting instead an analysis in terms of pornography's mode of combining the components of genre, sexual fantasy, and cultural objects, I am in a sense no more than restating points that have been made in other forms elsewhere, by "common knowledge," by the recently published *Williams Report on Obscenity,* and by feminism. But this analysis also confronts the terms of liberal political argument to pose the question of formulating the grounds of a feminist policy on pornography.

The "Problem" of Pornography

It would be too formal to say that there is such a thing as an accepted definition of pornography. However, one area of agreement between liberals and antiliberals is that pornography can be characterized in terms of extremes or explicitness, that it is a matter of exposing to view certain acts or anatomies. But it is this common starting point, and the consequences that flow from it, that should be disputed. In producing a "problem" of pornography, already and familiarly demarcated, it preempts a feminist delineation of the problem and its object.

There are two components to this notion of pornography, first that it has a certain content, a range of sexual behaviors along a spectrum differentiated as more or less "extreme"; second, that an exposure of the body is involved, similarly ranged along a continuum in which more or less is shown. Taking the two components together, what is produced is an account of the pornographic as a single and recognizable problem of extremes, something that shows too much and goes too far. It is hardly surprising that, when it comes to a question of adjudication, the decision too is one of "how much," of where to draw the line.

Yet there is clearly a noncorrespondence between degrees of exposure of the body and degrees of "extreme" behavior. Forms of bondage, for example, depend upon the tactical presence, rather than absence, of certain articles of clothing. To pose a challenge to the idea that there is a simple convergent "extreme" is also to challenge the related assumption that objections to pornography will increase along a corresponding scale, as reactions to a content. This is important because it allows us to register the fact that it is often the silly and the sultry—the stock in trade of "soft porn"—that produces the more violent protest from feminism. For the statement "pornography is a part of everyday sexism," it is the everyday that is perhaps more galling than the exotic.

Indeed, even limiting ourselves to one of these supposed continuums it soon comes to seem an implausible characterization. An objection can be made to images of bound and passive women without having to construe the whole range of pornography as incipient sado-masochism. Otherwise sexuality is reduced to a set of acts exemplifying a unified field of the sexual, in which the extreme can be taken as the typical, and the whole domain known by its destination.

Such a notion of a unified field of sexuality motivated along a single line of "need" was popularized in the figure of the "permissive society." Something called "sex" was represented as in the process of emergence, an emergence that could be marked as the increasing visibility of an already-constituted but previously repressed set of behaviors and desires. A variety of phenomena—different forms of sexual conduct, shifts in speech patterns, changes in childrearing practices, the existence of the sexual therapies—were all treated as aspects organically related in a homogeneous field of the sexual in which a logic of derepression urged that the most "outrageous" and resisted be taken as the most truthful and typical. Against this one would wish to protest the distinctness of different forms of sexuality, in relation to which a concept of "extreme" is simply unintelligible, the noncorrespondence between extent of repression and forms of sexuality, and indeed the difference between physical activities, social conducts, and psychic formation.

There are also problems with the idea of a scale of increasingly explicit representation of the body, where representation is thought essentially as a transparent medium giving more or less access to its object. This might seem unexceptionable insofar as we can all recognize pornography "on sight." But let us not mistake recognizability for a simple givenness of content. Recognizability does not depend just upon what and how much is shown—otherwise we would not be able to distinguish between pornographic, artistic, or medical representations of sexual acts and naked bodies (indeed, if it is the extreme that is the test of the pornographic, then medical textbooks or biological cross-sections would be definitive). What makes pornography recognizable are its *non*transparent features, the elements that constitute it as a distinctive representational genre—a certain rhetoric of the body, forms of narration, placing and wording of captions and titles, stylizations and postures, a repertoire of milieux and costume, lighting techniques, etc. Even where the distinctness of the genre is acknowledged—all that the Williams Report glosses as "shallow and trashy"—it is given a secondary status in identifying the pornographic, merely representation's rather nasty shade of coloring or, alternatively, a "knowledge" that something is pornographic. These features are, however, an important element in feminism's objections to pornography.

We have been arguing that it is misleading to begin from an assumption that the pornographic is a literal representation whose content merely happens to exceed certain, disputed, boundaries of acceptability. When such a position is made central, then pornography's distinctive character cannot be recognized and, moreover, feminism's objections to "soft-core" pornography and to the manner as much as the fact that women are therein represented, simply appear as prudishness, as a particularly limited range of acceptability. But if we separate out different forms of objection, then feminism's concern with the more quotidian aspects of the pornographic can be posed as a distinct problem.

And indeed it is not irrelevant to point out that a feminist interest in pornography must be attached to feminist concerns. It is not feminism that has produced pornography as a discrete "social problem," and it is not at all obvious that feminists and their supposed allies would even pick out the same images as objectionable. It may well be that pornography would be addressed only as a small part of campaigns with other, more general objects, which picked up part but not necessarily all of the field of pornographic images. A campaign around representations of women would, one might think, confine itself to representations of women. Another declared interest of feminism, the reform of the personal, might include attention to the pornographic, but once again, this would involve a shift in the domain of comparison and selection and grounds of criticism.

Feminist statements on the subject of pornography often take it to be an exemplary moment of patriarchy. If patriarchy treats women as objects, then pornography does so in a most vivid and incitatory way. If patriarchy consists of an organized system of subordinations, then pornography subordinates women not only to the eye of the camera but to the indignity of a banal range of objectionable fantasies. At this point the language of explicitness offers a temptation to serious parody, a temptation for feminists to claim that indeed "all is revealed" in pornography. But it is not necessary to take up this option and it would be well avoided, for such a generalization of the pornographic would either lose sexuality in a general power relation of subordination or it would eroticize and make fundamental the eroticization of all differentiations of power. Pornography is both more specific and less important than that.

It is not necessary to treat pornography as an essence of patriarchy to grant that it might in some sense typify it. Its exemplary power lies not in its being unitary but in its being discrepant, in holding together distinct ranges of determination. That it holds them together is not nothing: consider, for example, the sorts of connections allowing the play on the word "availability" in the Williams Report, where it designates an availability at the level of commercial transaction, of images in the street, of woman in the image. But recognizing the powers of an accumulation of meanings around pornography does not establish what is specific to pornography. And consequently it is not *as* accumulation that it can be dealt with.

Let us take the statement that "pornography treats women as objects" and examine it in relation to the two features that the Williams Report takes to be essential to pornography, namely that it "has a certain function or intention, to arouse its audience sexually, and also a certain content, explicit representations of sexual material (organs, postures, activity, etc.). A work has to have both this function and this content to be a piece of pornography" (para. 8.2, p. 103). The point about content, taken alone, would amount to an identification in terms of explicitness or extremes, in which it would be impossible to distinguish between pornography and other forms of representation involving nakedness, sexual activity, etc., and impossible to formulate feminism's objection to the *way* in which women are represented.

Considering the question of sexual arousal, an initial sense of the feminist objection to pornography would be to the representation of women as objects of sexual desire. Yet the presence and, more, the promise of an alternative feminist erotica would seem to rule out an objection to women ever being placed in a sexual context. However, there is something more specific about the Williams formulation since it refers to sexual arousal. Even here, made slightly indeterminate by its emphasis on more diffuse and nongenital forms of pleasure, the feminist erotica will once more signal that it cannot be an arousing body of images as such that is objectionable. It is important here not to assume a mapping, at least at the level of practical pleasures, of heterosexuality onto genitality or vice versa. To pose nongenital pleasures is not in itself to oppose heterosexuality or male desire; and to pose homosexuality is not to exclude genital behaviors. This is why countering pornography's construction of women as "objects of male desire" means adjudicating on three separate issues: the possibility of erotic representations in general, the possibility of a form of representation designed to have an effectivity of arousal, the possibility of arousing in a genital (and nongenital) way. It is assumed here that feminists would accept all three of these possibilities in framing an alternative.

In order to capture the precise sense of "pornography treats women as objects," we need to be able to specify not just the coexistence of a content and arousal, as Williams does, but their form of *connection*. The objection surely consists basically in the way in which pornography depends *for* its sexual effectivity on images of the feminine that are constructed as a limited and highly fixed repertoire of postures and props. The connection is thus between sexual fantasy's[1] capacity to hook psychic material onto rigid structures, in this case certain images, and pornography's production of prepackaged erotic visual material, "the way its medium mimics the medium of fantasy" (Wollheim, p. 17). Those aspects of pornography's recognizability so often regretted on aesthetic grounds, far from being gratuitous, are essential to it; it is the way in which the organization and disorganization of bodies operates as a short-cut to desire that constitutes "objectification."

A few caveats need to be entered on the notion of objectification. Initially and tritely, all representation objectifies, all representation fragments. We should also be wary of taking "objectification" to signify an omission, a dehumanization, in which pornography just leaves out or fails to portray other aspects of the feminine or aspects of sexual relations that could be, as it were, simply placed alongside sexuality to give a fuller, more healthy, picture. Given that we accept some possible literature whose interest is sexual arousal, the problem is not that pornography might fail to show women at work—why should it?—or even that it might fail to picture those extrasexual accompaniments to sexuality demanded by "responsible adults." When feminists talk about altering the forms of sexuality, it means changing *sexuality*, not just ameliorating the surroundings. So, curiously, to hold pornography objectiona-

ble in omitting the faces and the feelings is in effect to accept an adequation of pornography to sexuality as such—an equation that pornography does its best to
promote. But if the current sexual regime is said to "objectify" sexuality, then it must
"objectify" feelings as well. In fact, as I shall mention later, it is by no means the case
that pornography can be put forward as "*the* sexual" in contrast to other aspects of
"the personal"; on the contrary. In any case, an alternative literature of arousal would
not at all be committed to representing the whole of life and all aspects of the feminine in order to differ from the pornographic.

Yet it is not even necessary to supplement sexuality with the comforts of
domestic coziness or the ecstasies of religious devotion to dispute pornography's
claims to be the truth of sex. Pornography's relation to sexual relationships is not at
"the level of a photograph." We have already argued in the first section that seeing
pornography in terms of an explicitness of content does not sufficiently distinguish
it from other representations involving bodies or sexuality. But, it might be claimed,
now in virtue of its generic features, that pornography does indeed reveal the truth
of the current regime of sexual relationships and, further, the fact that it "works" is
a tribute to this realism: the objectification of women in the image is the objectification that women experience and men enjoy.

Literalness should be met with literalness, and with qualification. For the first,
it is simply not true that pornography has the status of a "factual" account of what
people are doing at this very moment all over the country. If it were true we would
hear no complaints that women were forced to live up to or out such fantasies. And
in this consists the qualification, for in recognizing that it is at the level of fantasy that
pornography operates, one recognizes that pornography does exist in a certain relation to people's lives. But it would be a literalism of another kind to take fantasy scenarios as blueprints for any existent or future world, to read them as descriptions of
what people would like and endeavor to do and have done to them. There is no point
putting forward a connection between genre and fantasy if fantasy is itself treated as
a content.

If we take "treating women as objects" to refer rather to the intransigence and
fixity with which pornographic fantasy organizes its content, to its repetitive and
fetishistic[2] character, then we return to the question of what specific sense is to be
given to the notion of "object." I would like to suggest that, insofar as it provides an
objection to pornography, the notion of "object" is most appropriately connected
with another aspect of pornography's generic features. This is pornography's capacity and determination to capture and eroticize certain familiar cultural objects. It is
particularly but not exclusively evident in the sort of images in *The Sun* or in "soft-

core" pornography. Indeed it is pornography's construction around those very aspects of life it supposedly omits that is remarkable: elements of personality—the first name, the smile, the biography, and the "interests"—artifacts from the workplace and the home, the realms of hobbies and topical news items (sailing caps in Cowes week, bunting for the New Hampshire primaries), domestic settings ranging from the Gothic castle to the front room.

The trouble is that pornography eroticizes women as well. That is to say it produces them as erotic in precisely the same way it produces objects as erotic. It is as if women *had been* objects on a par with other cultural objects, and had then been subjected to a process of eroticization. This pluperfect formulation is the only one that avoids the hesitation between saying "pornography treats women as objects" and "pornography treats women as sexual objects." If it treats women as objects in the way that porters treat objects as objects, then the claim is merely baffling; if it refers to some process of commoditization, then so does capitalism treat women as objects, just as it treats men as objects. Yet, as we have seen, taking it to refer to being the object of a sexual interest is also not quite right.

To speak of an "eroticization" of women, then, is to say that preexisting cultural elements of the feminine are taken up, subject to certain protocols of definition and emphasis, placed in relation to certain other objects, including men, in a limited syntax of possibilities. The fact that cultural elements, including those elements of the feminine, can and do exist in different forms elsewhere, placed differently, even differently in other erotic situations, does not undermine the specificity of pornography. It is not being claimed that pornography invented sexuality any more than it invented culture.

This new sense of "pornography treats women as objects" thus registers a double objection, both to the initial implicit equation with a thing, impersonal and nonsexual, and to the techniques by which eroticization is produced. It allows us to extend feminism's emphasis on the form of connection between arousal and content by adding the other element it stresses, the "everyday." To repeat this another way: pornography is *a coincidence of sexual fantasy, genre, and culture in an erotic organization of visibility.*[3] The objects that pornography produces as erotic, in a form provocative to fantasy's tendency to accrete and solidify, are familiar objects. Insofar as fantasy does not work without material, there must be *some* object, arbitrary but not random. If that object is already connected with the sexual, so much the better. Pornography essentially provides a stock of visual repertoires constructed out of elements of the everyday, using objects, including elements of the feminine, already placed within definite cultural practices. In re-placing these objects, in making them available or special, as objects around which sexual fantasy can operate without too much wit or effort, pornography simultaneously opens up the possibility of a reversal, of seeing objects return to their cultural niche with a certain afterglow. Since pornography is involved in constructing a form of recognizability or visibility for women within a space of eroticization of everyday objects, it can have effects at the level of ordinary life without having to make a long excursion by way of the "extreme"; a day return will do, and do better.

On this analysis, definite rather than general connections can be made between pornography and other forms of representation, particularly advertising. The reason why advertising images are especially prone to quote from the pornographic genre is that they are by definition in the business of promoting everyday objects, and eroticization offers a means to that promotion. It is not just as commodity that a parallel exists, but as desired commodity.

The Grounds of a Feminist Intervention

The logic of intervention is dominated by the liberal argument that it is only harms that justify intervention, that harms must be demonstrable effects, and that the harm of intervention must always be less than the harm it is to alleviate. The Williams/Wolfenden formula, which itself begins from these premises,[4] is emerging as the current legislative strategy for the management of a range of issues around sexuality. It is thus both useful and pertinent to ask how these principles of argument condition the possibility of a feminist policy on pornography. It is important to emphasize that, although guiding legislative argument, the principles are framed in order to apply as well to extralegal intervention: John Stuart Mill's *On Liberty* speaks equally of the force of moral opinion as a public intervention constraining individual liberty. Thus to prioritize the extralegal as a site of struggle is not in itself to escape the constraints of this form of argument.

Let us try and set out the terms of reference of the debate about pornography as classically conceived. This means locating an effect of pornography, arguing that it is a harm, weighing it against the harmful effects of possible means of action against it. The strongest argument, as conducted by Dr. Court and the Festival of Light, as well as some feminists, is that pornography is a direct cause of undeniable and great harms, namely sexual offences such as rape and sexually inspired murders. The requirement that demonstrable connections be shown urges that pornography have its effects in a very literal way, that certain individuals are inspired to reenact a scene they see in such magazines or that they "mistake" real women for images of women.

Equally the requirement to produce a truly serious harm to justify the harm of intervention pushes the argument toward concentrating on what is seen as the most "extreme" and "explicit" material. Indeed the language of exposure suggests that such "extreme" material is more effective precisely because it is closer to reality; it is a short step from seeing pornography as a reproduction of acts in the image to seeing it as a reproduction of images in the act.

The usual means of intervention being considered is censorship, whether a suppression at the point of production or a restriction on the conditions of availability. While both forms of censorship involve an incursion on the individual's freedoms to indulge "tastes and pursuits," a proven connection between sexual offences and pornography would render availability restrictions merely whimsical. This is why Williams first examines the Court evidence before, finding the connection "not proven," he suggests restrictions on availability.

The harm of censorship by suppression is held to consist in its threat to freedoms of expression and opinion. The danger is not only that a particular object of suppression may have countervailing good properties (even if they refer only to the shortness of life and the limited forms of pleasure it allows) but also censorship's blindness, its incapacity to distinguish between good and bad objects, whether present or future. Clearly the dangers that censorship—of either kind—would pose for feminist images of the body is one reason for wariness. A different but related fear is not of censorship's blindness but its. clearsightedness, that such power, once granted, would fall into the wrong hands—if it is ever in the right ones.

The classic dilemma around pornography is thus a balancing of extreme harms of doubtful direct connection with pornography against the harms censorship offers not only to traditionally conceived freedoms of the individual but now to feminist interests as well. But this anxious irresolution is not the essence of feminism's problems with pornography. It is merely a symptom of the more general lack of fit between feminist politics and liberalism's central terms of reference: individual/society, harms, intervention.

For liberalism, harms attach to the interests of individuals or, less popularly, to society as whole. Yet feminism is concerned with the interests of a constituency of women for whom pornography will have different effects on different individual women. This constituency cannot be simply reduced to a collection of individuals, or made homogeneous with either "reasonable people" or "society." Consequently the level of harm to such an interest is not amenable to liberalism either.

And what is more, liberalism prefers harms to be measurable in something tangible, such as acts against individuals. Yet the harms feminism wishes to mark do not depend for their seriousness on being or resulting directly in acts. The harms indicated by pornography's relation to "a sexist society" are serious in themselves.

The reason why liberalism attaches an importance to the at least notional possibility of measuring harmful effects is that it must weigh them against the harm of intervention. The concept of intervention is posed as absolutely general. It may not be only the state or the law that can act in this way, but it is action of this scale that is premised. Yet feminism has always posed forms of intervention that could be sporadic and local, take the form of campaigns or personal interaction.

In short, liberalism offers neither a means of representing a feminist interest or a harm to that interest, nor a means of reckoning the type of harmful effects feminism seeks to emphasize; nor a way of thinking such a harm in relation to nongeneralized forms of intervention. This is why, in seeking to register its level of interest and complaint, feminism is always placed by liberalism in the position of having to "overstate" its case in order to have a case liberalism can recognize at all. Thus feminism is forced to stake its claim centrally on pornography's power to produce direct harms to individuals in the form of actions. It has to state all its other objections to pornography as if they referred to effects convergent on if not quite expressed in such acts. It has to give its objections to pornography a seriousness of the order of murder or treason in order to weigh in the balance against a possible censorship. And, at the end of it, a prohibition of pornography, even a total policing of the sexist society, would bear very little relation to the sort of changes feminism would wish to see. It is not that feminism is excessive to liberalism, but that liberalism is inappropriate to feminism.

If the emphasis on acts as a direct effect of pornography has been provoked by a form of calculation that finally is irrelevant to feminism, then there is no reason why it should dominate a feminist analysis as such. But shifting attention away from an attempted match between extremes of pornography and extremes of harmful action is by no means to deny that there are individual cases in which pornographic images, like certain religious paintings, may have a particular power to produce deep pathological disturbances,[5] which might take the form of a literal reenactment of images. To count as reenactment there would clearly have to be a high degree of similarity between act and image; indeed it is this literalness that grounds any argument that pornography "puts ideas into people's heads"—otherwise pornography could be held responsible for all sexual activity. But what is being staged in such precise detail is not just a possibly novel arrangement of bodies or acts. It is the scenario *as* scenario, the scene constructed by pornography ritually reconstructed. And to make a specific scenario the object of such theatrical compulsion is to mark a definite order of pathology. The Moors murders, far from functioning as an extreme example of a typical form of effect, are *atypical* because they *are* reenactments. Where pornographic images do have effects in "ordinary" behavior, they will not be of the order of a literal reenactment, but work through a general psychic economy as it orders and disorders conduct.

Reconsidering Effects

Unhooking the possible range of effects of the pornographic from acts of imitation involves rethinking what is meant by an effect. "Acts" are emphasized by liberalism not only because they are an obvious way in which individuals come into contact with and hence may harm other individuals, but because of an assumption that actions are the proper place to look for effects. Yet what makes something an effect is nothing to do with where it happens. It is not *because* something happens in the "real world" that makes it an effect. When we said earlier on that pornographic images could have effects on advertising images, this was not because advertising images were more "real" than pornographic images. Obviously things have to be different from each other before one can affect the other, but being different is not a matter of being more or less real. For that matter pornographic images and advertising images are just as real.

Of course not just anything can count as an effect. In the case of advertising we said that it was possible for pornographic images to be "quoted" because both of them were concerned with the visual promotion of objects. In other words, it was because of pornography's organization of a certain space of visibility that another form also concerned with visibility could borrow from it. And this borrowing is facilitated to the extent that both are concerned with an erotic promotion of cultural objects.

But this means that the effects of pornography could be sought in spaces of "imaging" other than advertisements or, indeed, outside the conventionally limited space of representations altogether. There is no reason why a notion of representation should be tied to the conditions of viewing set up around printed images and darkened auditoriums. We can also consider the viewing of everyday objects, of daydreaming and nightdreaming. To put it crudely, women may be looked at in a certain way—by women as well as by men—and pornographic images may have contributed to that organization of viewing. Thus it is possible to speak of a connection between pornographic images and "everyday sexism" in a way that does not take as its starting point two materially distinct realms, a concrete domain of real acts as against an abstract domain of representations.[6] *Both* these supposed unities can be disrupted. For pornographic images to have effects on the everyday is not more miraculous than their having effects on other forms of representation. And no less specific: for, in saying that pornography can have effects on everyday viewing practices (whether their object is on paper, in the mind, in the street) one is also insisting that it is *just* viewing, precisely the possibility and probability of being looked at in a certain way, that is in question. There may indeed be further effects, as has been mentioned, between modes of viewing and forms of action, but forms of action are not as such the more legitimate space of effects. Forms of viewing are just as real.

A Reform of Visibility?

In thinking about pornography's possible range of effects within "everyday sexism," what has been raised is a much larger issue than pornography as such. In fact, it might be in relation to a possible campaign around the reform of forms of feminine visibility that a feminist policy on pornography could be formulated. It would thus be part of feminism's project of altering (not eradicating) forms of sexuality, in this case as they were implicated in the organization of viewing the everyday. Surely the insistence that the personal is political, that sexuality is not innately private, involves both locating just this sort of "public" configuration and making it an object of "political" reform. And it is pornography's availability at the level of ordinariness that links it to such a campaign.

At this point a certain interest attaches to the Williams Report, which poses the question of pornography in relation to a policing of a "public" space of visibility.[7] Its objection to pornography is that, particularly when displayed in the street, pornographic images expose to view certain private, sexual acts and anatomies, and that this is offensive. Consequently pornography should be returned to the private realm of individual choice by being available only under certain restricted conditions, in bookshops and cinemas with no external displays of material.

Obviously this formulation comes into direct conflict with feminism's refusal to accept that the sexual is innately private. Yet it has not always been easy to formulate what its "publicness" consists in. When we look at the Williams Report it is clear that the sexual is thought primarily in terms of certain acts or parts of the body, and that what is meant by "public" is exposing them to view. Now this is just to apply a notion of public and private to the sort of thinking about pornography we challenged at the start by emphasizing that sexuality was not just a matter of acts and bits of bodies and that representation, or indeed making visible, was not just a matter of what was seen but how that seeing was organized. At least this makes it clear that feminists cannot be thinking in the same way as Williams, since they are not talking about public nudity or sex in the public library.

But the issue is complicated for Williams by an unspoken reliance on certain arguments in the Wolfenden Report. Wolfenden uses the privacy of the sexual to guarantee certain liberties in respect to sexual conduct, specifically homosexuality and prostitution. Yet Wolfenden's formula of "consenting adults in private" tries to do two things at once. It begins from an argument that there are areas in which the law has "no business," so long as no harm is involved, that, with respect to a domain of sexual conduct, it is improper for the law arbitrarily to introduce an enforcement of morals. It then goes on to make a contrast with "public indecency." Yet a "private" space of judgment about sexual conduct is by no means equivalent to or coterminous with an innate privacy of the sexual in a way that can determine its proper and improper venue. Sexual conduct is not just acts, and private domains of judgment are not dwelling places.

Wolfenden functions as the background to the Williams Report. This means that when Williams treats pornography in terms of its making public the private, he has actually confused three different senses of public and private: private in the sense of "not the law's business," private in the sense of "as or in dwelling places," and private in his additional sense, of "not exposed to view."

But Williams uses the principle of privacy of the sexual not only to explain why pornographic images are offensive, especially when publicly displayed, but to insist that there should also be "private" access to pornography in restricted bookshops, etc. The harm of offensiveness is thus not to be outweighed by the harm of a suppressive intervention, and it is with fitting symmetry that private liberties can be matched onto private sexualities. This correspondence itself goes back to another infelicity in Wolfenden, a slide from the general domain of moral matters "outside the law" to the specific domain of sexual conduct. Yet only a very narrow sense of morality would, in allowing that it was not the law's business to enforce morals, assume that only sexual morality was important.

If feminism's challenge to the privacy of sexuality seems at odds with Wolfenden's guarantees of certain freedoms of sexual conduct, then this is because a struggle to define domains of autonomous conduct or "private" judgment has not been rigorously separated from issues around sexuality. And if feminism seems to demand a scrutiny or invasion of these areas, then they must be defended, where defensible, in terms other than unexamined assumptions of some *innate* privacy of the sexual.

The terms of the Williams Report are thus unsatisfactory for any possible feminist campaign around a reform of visibility, and offer no acceptable means of producing a feminist policy on pornography in relation to such a campaign. The most that can be gleaned are certain limited ways of beginning to think about a relation between protocols of everyday conduct and organizations of visibility. As an opening proviso, any notion of a single public/private distinction would have to be jettisoned, particularly when seen as a distinction between acts on the one hand and an exposing to view on the other.

What can be salvaged, with a measure of disrespect to the original, are the following: on the one hand, there is an organization of spaces, civic *and* domestic, not only towns, streets, and country lanes but the internal differentiations of dwelling places. On the other hand, there are domains of "private" judgment whose autonomy rests neither on individuality, or sexuality, but rather the assignment of differential rights and responsibilities, whether by a professional code of conduct or manners for everyday or special occasions.

In both cases, principles of access/exclusion/appropriateness govern conduct, and in both cases conduct includes modes of visibility. In just this sense, then, places and judgments could be the subject or site of reforms of feminine visibility.

Clearly a feminist policy on pornography in relation to such a campaign would involve certain tactical judgments, such as a possible defensive strategy around "appropriateness." But it would also mean developing positions on questions such as whether or not fantasy is "private," what it would mean to talk of a reform of fantasy or a reform of manners, whether action would be considered in relation to pornography as such or in relation to its other levels of effects, whether such intervention might take the form of breaking up its genre elements.

Notes

1.   "Fantasy" is used in this article to refer to certain organizations of psychic material, rather than in the looser sense of wildest, or most secret, wishful ruminations. Nor is fantasy taken to be "unreal" or fiction. Thus I am saying that fantasy involves a general capacity to hook unconscious material onto psychic structures, and that some of those structures take the form of visual scenarios. It is these scenarios, as structures, that I am relating to pornographic images' generic features.

2.   In this article I have avoided any account of the considerable body of work on the relation between representation and sexuality and the structure of the look, for which fetishism is a central moment. Anyone who wishes to pursue a connection between fetishism and the "eroticization" of cultural objects is free to do so, but this is a very different level of analysis. On pornography, see John Ellis's recent article and the reply by Paul Willemen.

3.   Designating pornography as such a combination both makes it specific and identifiable, not simply a manifestation of patriarchy or even everyday sexism, and also allows a maneuvreability for its components. Pornography does not tell us everything there is to know about sexual fantasy, for instance, and there are other organizations of cultural objects, visual and nonvisual, erotic and nonerotic.

4.   For a proper account of the sorts of harms and considerations attaching to them for Mill and Williams, see the extremely elegant essay by Richard Wollheim.

5.   It should be emphasized that pathology as such does not distinguish the normal from the abnormal as a classification of persons. Nonetheless this argument is distinguishing between pathology in a general sense and a particular pathological formation as a contrast between even "deep" disturbance and a fetishizing of the pornographic scenario. Richard Wollheim also raises some questions about pornography and fantasy, attributing to pornography an effectivity over and above a reinforcement and activation of the "volume" of a subject's fantasy; he claims that pornographic images may also independently mold the character of fantasy (p. 17) and regards this as arguably harmful. But this is not an argument of any specific feminist concern.

6.   There is another way in which the normal sense of "effect" has been shifted: on this account the notion of a cause is irrelevant. Instead there is, on the one hand, an availability of a certain effective organization of components and, on the other, sets of conditions under which that availability could be taken up.

7.   For a discussion of the general Williams/Wolfenden strategy and some of its incoherencies, see my article in *Ideology and Consciousness*.

References

B. Brown, "Private Faces in Public Places," *Ideology and Consciousness,* no. 7 (1980).

J. Ellis, "On Pornography," *Screen,* vol. 21, no. 1 (1980).

J. S. Mill, *On Liberty,* Gateway, 1955.

P. Willemen, "Letter to John," *Screen,* vol. 21, no. 2 (1980).

R. Wollheim, "A Charismatic View of Pornography," *London Review of Books,* February 1980.

Williams Report—Report of the Committee on Obscenity and Film Censorship, Her Majesty's Stationary Office, November 1979 and Cmnd 7772.

I would like to thank my friends Parveen Adams, Elizabeth Cowie, and Miranda Feuchtwang for their help with this article.

from *m/f* 5/6, 1981

Fantasia

ELIZABETH COWIE

This article will seek to elaborate some distinctions in relation to the concept of fantasy[1] and to suggest some connections between feminist debates, the field of psychoanalytic theory, and the analysis of films—that is, to bring together fantasy as a political problem, psychoanalysis's specific conceptualization of fantasy, and the film as a particular site of the representation of fantasy. While the problem of fantasy in feminist politics is the starting point, it will not be the focus of this article. Rather, by elaborating its mechanisms and illustrating the functioning of fantasy in film, it is hoped that some of the problems in current feminist argument in this area will be illuminated, and some directions for future work suggested. In particular two points will be argued: one, that the opposition real/not real is wholly inappropriate to a consideration of fantasy, whether it is used to "save" fantasy—because of course one wouldn't want it to *happen*—or is part of a dismissal of fantasy as unimportant because it isn't real. Two, that, while on the one hand fantasy can be characterized as a series of wishes presented through imaginary happenings, on the other hand it is also a structure: fantasy as the *mise-en-scène* of desire, the putting into a scene, a staging, of desire. The emphasis of this article will thus be on fantasy as structure, a structuring of the diverse contents, wishes, scenarios of wishing, and it will draw on psychoanalysis for this description of fantasy. While fantasy has been directly addressed within feminist debates and is a key concept in psychoanalysis, in relation to film the concept has been used either peripherally or pejoratively—pejoratively, in the dismissal of cinema, or at least American cinema, as escapist fantasy; peripherally in that the term is used to describe a genre—the fantasy film—but in which the term simply marks those films that present either the supernatural or an imaginary world unknown to us as yet, for example, science fiction.

Nor is fantasy as such addressed in current studies of film involving psychoanalytic concepts. Rather, in the work of Raymond Bellour, Stephen Heath, or Mary

Ann Doane, for example, the analysis involves uncovering the trajectory of desire constituted by the film text, a trajectory that is shown to position and fix the spectator as subject for its enunciation, an enunciation concerning a masculine Oedipal problem. Fantasy as a concept is then invoked to support analyses that center on the problem of *identity*, of the male subject, whether it is a director like Hitchcock, or a character, neurotic or psychotic.[2] In giving attention to fantasy my discussion will be askance from such studies; the difference opened up will I hope offer another way to considering the fixity, or not, of the sexual positions of cinema-subjects.

Within feminism the discussion of fantasy emerged as a necessity in the context of the demand "the personal is political." However, the issue has never been seen only in terms of male fantasy as a problem for women, for example in relation to pornography, sexism, and the treatment of women as sex objects; it was also addressed from early in the modern Women's Movement as a problem in terms of our own, politically recalcitrant, fantasies—whether as secret pleasures in Mills & Boon style romantic fiction, or in the way one falls asleep with a fantasied scene of romantic encounter or seduction, or the desire when making love for domination or submission. Such "fantasy" was initially seen as the consequence of women's oppression in which we accepted and acted out the distorted fantasies and representations of men. Once a woman was aware of this oppression, for example through consciousness-raising, such reactionary imaginings would be seen as simply that—the trappings of male ideology that we hadn't been strong enough to throw off.

As a result what has emerged in the Women's Movement is broadly two positions: the first, the moralistic, whereby we are exhorted to have strength and break our bonds, etc. This demands that fantasy be seen as simply a question of content that can be changed at will. This has also led to a demand to forsake fantasy, at least any sexual fantasy, altogether. It is condemned as invariably involving using another person as an object, as fragmented and reductive in relation to the full identity of that person. A moral charge is made that sexual fantasy dehumanizes. The second position on the contrary accepts that fantasy is intrinsic to human nature and indeed bound up in some way with sexuality, but argues that its implications remain to be explored.

The first position appears most often represented as an aspiration in relation to which women (and men, for whom the aspiration allows a masochistic breast-beating, which itself often seems part of a satisfying fantasy) bemoan their failure, or appeal for the discovery of a new feminist eroticism and fantasy, for which we are still waiting. And will continue to wait, in as much as such a position misunderstands the mechanisms of fantasy. The partialization of objects in the external world, the external world as a series of objects and parts of objects, is intrinsic to our relation with the external world. Yet it is clearly crucial that we also recognize the unity of objects in the external world, the mother as a whole object, as well as the part object, the (maternal) breast. But our relation to the whole is bound up in certain ways with our relation to the part, as in the example just given. We cannot remove that by fiat. But nor does this psychic structuring have simple or necessary consequences for social relations; and the intervention of moral norms, of social requirements through the agency of censorship by the superego, will be involved in the organization of such cathexes. It is the interplay of this organization across *public* forms of fantasy that I will be concerned to address later in this article in terms of the second position outlined above, of fantasy's intrinsic role in relation to sexuality.

The special issue of *Heresies* (1981) on sexuality presents many of the current and most controversial debates about sexuality, femininity, and feminism. In particular it includes articles on the role of fantasy for women, some of which directly address the "unacceptability" of such fantasies for feminists:

> But what is it that I really like? What is it that I really want, sexually? Why is it that I turn away from him even though I feel pleasure and rising lust? I do know what I imagine when I masturbate. Yet my innermost sexual fantasies, with their emphasis on passivity and total male dominance are frightening, because they are so contradictory to what I, as a feminist, think. (Helle Thorning, "The Mother-Daughter Relationship and Sexual Ambivalence," p. 3)

The fantasied scenarios, with the implied sadism and masochism suggested in this quote, are taken up explicitly by Pat Califia and defended as a valid form of feminist and lesbian sexual activity: "The Women's Movement has become a moralistic force, and it can contribute to the self-loathing and misery experienced by sexual minorities. . . . Like Victorian missionaries in Polynesia they [feminists] insist on interpreting the sexual behavior of other people according to their own value systems." In no way do her criticisms imply a general disaffection with feminism, for she goes on to write, "I think it is imperative that feminists dismantle the institutions that foster the exploitation and abuse of women. The family, conventional sexuality, and gender are at the top of my hit list. These institutions control the emotional, intimate lives of every one of us, and they have done incalculable damage to women." Yet while this argument might lead her to condemn sado-masochism as an oppressive structure, and a given in the dominant patriarchal capitalist society, she in fact argues that S/M relationships are egalitarian.

Some feminists object to the description of S/M as consensual. They believe that our society has conditioned all of us to accept inequities in power and hierarchical relationships. Therefore, that the same system that dressed girls in pink and boys in blue, allows surplus value to accumulate in the coffers of capitalists and gives workers a minimum wage, and sends cops out to keep the disfranchised down.

It is true as I stated before, that society shapes sexuality. We can make any decision about our sexual behaviour we like, but our imagination and ability to carry out those decisions are limited by the surrounding culture. But I do not believe that sado-masochism is the result of institutionalised injustice to a greater extent than heterosexual marriage, lesbian bars, or gay male bath-houses. The system is unjust because it assigns privileges based on race, gender, and social class. During an S/M encounter the participants select a particular role because it best expresses their sexual needs. . . . The most significant reward for being a top or a bottom is sexual pleasure. If you don't like being a top or bottom, you switch your keys. Try doing that with your biological sex or your race or your socio-economic status.

Pat Califia's defense of S/M rests on the sexual pleasure obtained, the fact that it is always very clearly *play* ("Even a minor accident like a rope burn can upset the top enough to mar the scene"), and the interchangeability of the roles—"You can always switch your keys." Choice, consent, and free will to engage in S/M are all emphasized in the article, yet it opens with a powerful confession of the compulsive quality of her fantasies. "Three years ago, I decided to stop ignoring my sexual fantasies. Since the age of two, I had been constructing a private world of dominance, submission, punishment and pain. Abstinence, consciousness-raising, and therapy had not blighted the charm of these frightful reveries" (p. 30).

I do not want to center my discussion of fantasy on sado-masochism as such, although it can be argued that the opposition active/passive is central to fantasy. Rather, I am taking it as exemplary of the problem of fantasy for feminism, a problem brought out in Pat Califia's article precisely because she wishes to argue for feminism *and* S/M practices. As a result, because she is not prepared to make an "anything goes" defense of S/M, she is led to theorize the pleasure in S/M. She challenges the content of fantasy as a simple function of experience, for example in the idea that S/M fantasies are found in those who experienced corporal punishment as children. Pat Califia writes

The key word to understand S/M is *fantasy*. The roles, dialogue, fetish costumes, and sexual activity are part of a drama or ritual. The participants are enhancing their sexual pleasure, not damaging or imprisoning one another. A sado-masochist is well aware that a role adopted during a scene is not appropriate during other interactions and that a fantasy role is not the sum total of her being. . . . The S/M subculture is a theatre in which sexual dramas can be acted out. (p. 31)

Pat Califia comes close to psychoanalysis by implying a splitting of the subject in S/M and in the way she takes up a number of issues in relation to fantasy: the notion of the scene, a theater; a role-playing, that is, interchangeability of roles; the issue of the "unreality" of fantasy as distinct from its "seriousness"; the notion that fantasy involves not an object of desire as in "I want X" but a scenario of activities that depend upon the partner's participation.

Pat Califia is clearly arguing for fantasy in terms of the second position outlined earlier, of fantasy as intrinsic to sexuality. But it is not a simple reinstatement of fantasy. Nor is it a declaration that fantasy is *unreal*, that the nature of our fantasies do not matter because they aren't real and we *know* it. But while Pat Califia recognizes this, her insistence on free will, and on choice—with its consequent problems of knowledge and intention—prevents her from developing its full implications. Nonetheless she has opened up a space and debate which I want to explore more directly through the kind of understanding of fantasy suggested by psychoanalysis.[3]

Fantasy in Psychoanalysis

1. Fantasy is the fundamental object of psychoanalysis, it is the central material for the "talking cure" and for the unconscious: "the psychoanalyst must endeavour in the course of the treatment to unearth the phantasies which lie behind such products of the unconscious as dreams, symptoms, acting out, repetitive behaviour etc" (*Language of Psychoanalysis*, p. 317). Fantasy is an imagined scene in which the subject is a protagonist, and which always represents the fulfilment of a wish albeit that its representation is distorted to a greater or lesser extent by defensive processes. Fantasy has a number of modes: conscious fantasies or daydreams, unconscious fantasies such as those uncovered by analysis as the structures underlying a manifest content, and primal fantasies. These are not mutually exclusive modes; on the contrary, a daydream will at the same time involve an unconscious wish underlying its manifest content and the structure of that unconscious wish will be related to the

primal fantasies. For this reason Freud saw the model of fantasy as being, Laplanche and Pontalis suggest, "the reverie, that form of novelette, both stereotyped and infinitely variable, which the subject composes and relates to himself in a waking state" ("Fantasy and the Origin of Sexuality," p. 13). The difference between these modes does not involve a difference in the objects of fantasy, nor primarily a distinction between conscious or unconscious, but a difference in their relation to repression, and the workings of censorship.

2. The word fantasy is defined in the dictionary (*Chambers Twentieth Century English*) as meaning "an imagined scene," and further listings are "fabulous; fancy [now a separate meaning]; imagination, mental image; love, whim; caprice; fantasia; preoccupation with thoughts associated with unattainable desires." The word derives through Latin from the Greek term meaning to "make visible." However, rather than a notion of revelation, making visible what we would not otherwise be able to see—as with a microscope allowing us to see bacteria, etc., invisible to the "naked" eye—fantasy as a term has come to mean the making visible, present, of what isn't there, of what can never *directly* be seen.

In German "phantasie" is the term used to denote the imagination, but not so much in the sense of the faculty of imaginings as in terms of the imaginary world and its contents, the imaginings of fantasies into which the poet—or the neurotic—so willingly withdraws. As Laplanche and Pontalis note, it is difficult to therefore avoid defining the word in terms of what it is not, the world of reality. The opposition of fantasy and reality however, cannot be reduced to the conventional opposition between the terms "fiction" and "real life." Freud discovered the importance of fantasy, in particular its importance in the neuroses, when he abandoned his theory of sexual seduction by a parent or other adult as a real event, producing a real trauma with all its consequences in adult life. Notorious as this has become for feminists, the importance of Freud's assertion is nevertheless extremely relevant for feminism. For what Freud came to understand, with regard to the fantasy of rape or seduction by the father so common among his women patients, was not that the woman was making something up, pretending, or trying to fake, dupe, us/Freud, but that since the event had not happened, then sexuality in the women could not be thought of as simply the "effect" of outside events, of the seduction or rape, whether pleasurable or traumatic. Rather sexuality was already there, in play. The fantasy and its attendant traumas were not the *result* of a seduction but of the *wish* for a seduction, implying a sexuality already there motivating the wish. Freud is then concerned to elaborate on *how* it is already there. The consequences of this are important: for feminism, it shows again that women's sexuality is not a simple consequence (again, whether traumatic or pleasurable) of male sexuality, of the seduction as a real event. Furthermore the wish is not simply passive—its object is the father. It also implies its inverse, the wish to seduce or rape the father. The father as sexual object is of course the consequence of the Oedipal scenario, and therefore of a wish to seduce/be seduced by the mother. What Freud shows is that it is irrelevant to consider whether the event was fantasied or real, or whether the woman wishes it to be real, for the fantasy refers not to physical reality but to psychical reality. This psychical reality is not simply the internal world, a psychological domain of the mental: Laplanche and Pontalis argue that for Freud fantasy "denotes a nucleus within that domain which is heterogeneous and resistant and which is alone in being truly 'real' as compared with the majority of psychical phenomena" ("Fantasy and the Origin of Sexuality," p. 3) and quote Freud, "If we look at unconscious wishes reduced to their most fundamental and truest shape, we shall have to conclude no doubt that psychical reality is a particular form of existence not to be confused with material reality" ("The Interpretation of Dreams," p. 620).

This psychical reality of which fantasy is the nucleus has an effect on and for the subject just as much as the material, physical world may have. In analyzing fantasy, it is not a criterion that there be any factual basis for the fantasy "in reality" or that there be a wish for it to "really happen," rather the criterion is the level of "reality" the fantasy has for and in the psychical system of the subject. What is refused here, then, is any privileging of material reality as necessarily more important, more serious. A patient in analysis recounts that he is an adopted child and relates fantasies in which, while searching for his true mother, he discovers that she is a society woman turned prostitute. Here is the banal theme of the "family romance," which, of course, might equally well have been composed by a child which had not been adopted.

3. Freud never sought to divide fantasy into conscious and unconscious, for the nature and work of fantasy is always the same. From the work of Laplanche and Pontalis it is possible, however, to see different modes of fantasy, but these different modes do not correspond to the division conscious/unconscious. A different distinction must be made. They argue, following Freud, for a distinction between original fantasies and other, secondary fantasies, whether conscious or unconscious: "the unity of the fantasy as a whole depends however on its mixed nature, in which both the structural, original and the imaginary or secondary are found. From this we can see why Freud always held the model fantasy to be the reverie" (*ibid.*, p. 13). While two modes exist they are generally found in combination in any fantasy, conscious

or unconscious. Fantasy again emphasized as a scene. The importance of this idea cannot be overestimated, for it enables the consideration of film as fantasy in the most fundamental sense of this term in psychoanalysis. The same content, the same activation can be revealed in imaginary formations or daydreams and psychopathological structures as diverse as those described by Freud, such as hysteria, delusional paranoia, etc., and in public forms of fantasy such as film and the novel. This argument is seen of course in Freud's papers such as "Creative Writers and Daydreaming" and "Family Romance." And these forms are not just conscious reworkings, that is, censored representations of unconscious, repressed fantasies. For Freud realized that it is conscious fantasy itself that may be repressed and thus become pathogenic. Freud argues, for example, that fantasy is present at both extremes of the process of dreaming. Laplanche and Pontalis note that fantasy is "On the one hand linked with the ultimate unconscious desire, the 'capitalist' of the dream, and as such it is at the basis of that 'zig-zag' path which is supposed to follow excitation through a succession of psychological systems, leading from the unconscious scenes of fantasies to the preconscious where it collects 'the day's residues'" (p. 12). But fantasy is also present at the other extreme, in the secondary elaboration of the dream, the *a posteriori* reworking of the dream once we are awake, which seeks to place a minimum of order and coherence onto the raw material handed over by the unconscious mechanisms of displacement and condensation. Imposing a scenario, a facade of coherence and continuity—in a word, a narrative—it will thus also draw on those ready-made scenarios, the subject's daydreams. But this reworking is not simply a masking, a mistaken distorting and arbitrary revision, for it will draw on the same impetuses for fantasy as the dreams of sleep. Of course, the same fantasy may not be involved in the initial situation of the dream and in its revision by secondary elaboration, but as Laplanche and Pontalis suggest, the fantasies do seem "if not to link up, at least to communicate from within and, as it were, to be symbolic of each other" (*ibid.*, p. 13).

The distinction, in fact, is not between conscious and unconscious, between the censored and uncensored, but rather between primal or originally unconscious fantasies and secondary fantasies, which may be unconscious or conscious. Primal fantasy does not imply a simple causality, primacy or origin, of *original content*. Rather it is to be understood as originary in the instituting of a structure of fantasy, a scene of fantasied origins—the origin of the child in its parents' lovemaking; the origin of sexual difference, and its corollary castration; in the wish to take the father's place and have the mother, or usurp the mother's place and have the father—thus a parental seduction. The primal fantasies are not so much an inherited prehistory, as a prestructure, which is actualized and transmitted by the parents' fantasies.

> In their content, in their theme [primal scene, castration, seduction . . .] the original fantasies also indicate this postulate of retroactivity: they relate to the origins. Like myths, the claim to provide a representation of, and a solution to, the major enigmas which confront the child. Whatever appears to the subject as something needing an explanation or theory, is dramatised as a moment of emergence, the beginning of a history. . . . There is a convergence of theme, of structure, and no doubt also of function: through the indications furnished by the perceptual field, through the scenarios constructed, the varied quest for origins, we are offered in the field of fantasy, the origin of the subject himself. (*ibid.*, p. 11)

The original fantasy explains the beginnings of the child but thus always preexists the child, for to pose a beginning is also to pose a before the beginning; and there is always an already-there for every child—its parents, grandparents, a history. The original fantasy then as structuring rather than a structure, for it is activated by contingent elements. Laplanche and Pontalis make this clear in their discussion of Freud's first reference to primal fantasies in "A Case of Paranoia Running Counter to the Psychoanalytic Theory of the Disease." In it Freud describes the case of a woman patient who declared that she had been watched and photographed while lying with her lover. She claimed to have heard a "noise," the click of a camera. Behind this delirium Freud saw the primal scene: the sound is the noise of the parents making love, thus awakening the child; it is also the sound the child is afraid of making lest it betray her listening. It is difficult to assess the role of this noise in the fantasy. In one sense, says Freud, it is only a provocation, an accidental cause, whose role is solely to activate "the typical fantasy of overhearing," which is a component of the parental complex, but he then corrects himself by saying "It is doubtful whether we can rightly call the noise 'accidental'. . . . Such fantasies are on the contrary an indispensible part of the fantasy of listening." In fact the sound alleged by the patient was, according to Freud, a projection, the projection of a beat in her clitoris, in the form of a noise. Laplanche and Pontalis suggest, "It reproduces in actuality the indication of the primal scene, the element which is the starting point for all ulterior elaboration of the fantasy. In other words, *the origin of the fantasy is integrated in the very structure of the original fantasy*" (*ibid.*, p. 10). The primal fantasy then as the instituting of this structuring, as a scene in which the child is also present interchangeably with the other participants as onlooker, as one or other parent, or even, as the person who will discover the child looking-on. "The primal scene, this 'foreign' body which is to be internally excluded, is usually brought to the subject, not by the perception of a scene, but by parental desire and its supporting fantasy" (p. 8).

4. What is shown here is the originary structuring of fantasy, but it presupposes a structuring of *wishing* already present in the subject, raising the question of the origin of fantasizing as such. This, Laplanche and Pontalis argue, cannot be isolated from the origin of the drive itself. Reinterpreting Freud's concept of *the experience of satisfaction*, they locate this origin in auto-eroticism, which they define not as a stage of evolution but as the moment of a repeated disjunction of sexual desire and nonsexual functions. That is, "the experience of satisfaction" is separated from the object that satisfies, and the latter is represented as a sign. For the baby, the "breast" becomes the object of desire—as giving the experience of satisfaction—but it is so not as itself but as signifier of the *lost* object, which is the *satisfaction* derived from suckling the breast, but which comes to be desired in *its absence*. This is the emergence of auto-eroticism, for the sexual drive is separated from the nonsexual functions, such as feeding, which are its support and which indicate its aim and object. The feeding still nourishes the child, but the experience of satisfaction in feeding has been split off through the function of representation, and moves into the field of fantasy and by this very fact starts existing as sexuality. It is auto-erotic because the external object has been abandoned, the drive is "objectless" and satisfaction is derived from "organ-pleasure"—the motions of sucking, rather than the instinctual act of sucking and obtaining nourishment.

The importance of relating fantasy to auto-eroticism is to show that desire is not purely an upsurging of the drives but comes to exist as sexual through its articulation in fantasy.

5. As noted earlier, fantasies are wishful; however they are not about a wish to have some determinate object, making it present for the subject. Lacan writes that

> The phantasy is the support of desire, it is not the object that is the support of desire. The subject sustains himself as desiring in relation to an ever-more complex signifying ensemble. This is apparent enough in the form of the scenario it assumes, in which the subject, more or less recognisable, is somewhere, split, divided, generally double, in his relation to the object, which usually does not show its true face either. (*Four Fundamental Concepts*, p. 185)

Similarly, Moustafa Safouan notes "instead of being co-opted to an object, desire is first co-opted to a phantasy" (*m/f*, no. 9, 1984).

Fantasy involves, is characterized by, not the achievement of desired objects, but the arranging of, a setting out of, desire; a veritable *mise-en-scène* of desire. For of course, Lacan says, desire is unsatisfiable, much as Freud commented that there is something in the nature of sexuality that is resistant to satisfaction. The fantasy depends not on particular objects, but on their setting out; and the pleasure of fantasy lies in the setting out, not in the having of the objects. Within the daydream and more especially in fictional stories, the demands of narrative may obscure this, for the typical ending will be a resolution of the problems, the wars, feuds, etc., the achievement of union in marriage by the hero and heroine, etc. Yet inevitably the story will fall prey to diverse diversions, delays, obstacles and other means to postponing the ending. For though we all want the couple to be united, and the obstacles heroically overcome, we don't want the story to end. And marriage is one of the most definitive endings. The pleasure is in how to bring about the consummation, is in the happening and continuing to happen; in how it will come about, and *not* in the moment of *having happened*, when it will fall back into loss, the past. This can extend into producing endings that remain murky, ill-defined, uncertain even. It is thus not modesty that veils the endings of romantic fiction but wise caution. Sternberg's film *Morocco* is perhaps an extreme example in cinema of the refusal to narrate an ending, to consummate the narrative, for it concludes with another repetition of the setting out of a lack to be fulfilled, which has already been played twice over and more, namely, of Dietrich leaving an anguished Adolphe Menjou for an unknowing Gary Cooper. Fantasy as a *mise-en-scène* of desire is more a setting out of lack, of what is absent, than a presentation of a having, a being present. Desire itself coming into existence in the representation of lack, in the production of a fantasy of its becoming present.

It can be seen, then, that fantasy is not the object of desire, but its setting. As a result

> In fantasy the subject does not pursue the object or its sign: he appears caught up himself in the sequence of images. He forms no representation of the desired object, but is himself represented as participating in the scene although, in the earliest forms of fantasy, he cannot be assigned any fixed place in it. . . . As a result, the subject, although always present in the fantasy, may be so in a de-subjectivised form, that is to say, in the very syntax of the sequence in question. (*ibid.*, p. 17)

The subject is present or presented through the very form of organization, composition, of the scene. It is perhaps only the most reworked, conscious daydream that is able to impose the stabilization of the ego, so that the subject's position is clear and invariable as the "I" of the story, which the subject as it were "lives out." Nevertheless it will be argued later with regard to the fiction film that it is not only in these "original" fantasies that this desubjectivization takes place. Both the daydream "thoughtlessly" composed and the more complex fictional narrative join with the "original" fantasies in visualizing the subject in the scene, and in presenting a varying of subject positions so that the subject takes up more than one position and thus is not fixed.

In Freud's analysis of the fantasy in "A Child is Being Beaten: A Contribution to the Study of the Origin of Sexual Perversions" he shows three phases in this fantasy, each involving a different subject-position. In the first phase, the fantasy is "my father is beating a child, whom I hate"; thus, "my father loves me since he is beating the other child" but also "I am making my father beat the other child to show he loves me" in which the subject erases the other, rival child from the father's affections. It is thus egoistic, identifying both father/self-love and father/self as beater of the other child. For this to become transposed into "A child is being beaten" with its third-person syntax, Freud proposed a second phase "I am being beaten by my father"; while the first phase may be remembered through analysis, this second phase is wholly unconscious and can only be inferred from analysis. However, it produces the move from sadism to masochism. (Though the first phase is not yet properly sadistic, or erotic, inasmuch as it is pre-genital.) The implicit incestuous desire of the first phase is subject to repression in the second phase, to produce a reversal: "No, my father does not love me (you), for he is beating me (you)." The beating is not only the punishment for the incestuous wish but is also the "regressive substitute for that relation, and from this latter source it derives the libidinal excitation which is from this time forward attached to it." Guiltiness and punishment are thus attached to the sexual desire; to be punished is to have had the forbidden sexual relation, for why else would you be punished? In the third phase, the consciously remembered fantasy "A child is being beaten," once more appears sadistic

> but it is so only in form; the satisfaction which is derived from it is maso-
> chistic. Its significance lies in the fact that it has taken over the libidinal
> cathexis of the repressed portion and at the same time the sense of guilt
> which is attached to the content of that portion. All the many unspecified

children who are being beaten by the teacher are, after all, nothing more than substitutes for the child itself. (p. 191)

The fantasy escapes repression by a further distortion, the disguise of the third-person syntax. Out there, there are children being beaten (like I should be, for my forbidden wishes). Apparently sadistic, inasmuch as it represses the parenthesis. The stake, the effectiveness, of this third phase of the fantasy is the interchangeability of the subject and the other children being beaten.

Laplanche and Pontalis cite the seduction fantasy as a similar example, which they summarize as "A father seduces a daughter," emphasizing the "peculiar character of the structure, in that it is a scenario with multiple entries, in which nothing shows whether the subject will be immediately located as *daughter*; it can as well be fixed as *father*, or even in the term *seduces*" (p. 14).

6. It is precisely to the extent that desire is articulated in fantasy that the latter is also thereby the locus of defensive operations—it facilitates and can become the site of the most primitive defensive processes, such as turning around upon the subject's own self, reversal into its opposite, projection, and negation. Fantasies provide satisfaction, then, not only by presenting a wish but also by presenting the failure of a wish if the latter has undergone repression. This has been seen in the example of "A child is being beaten." Defenses are inseparably bound up with the work of fantasy, namely, the *mise-en-scène* of desire, a *mise-en-scène* in which what is prohibited is always present in the actual formation of the wish. (Walsh's film *Pursued* can be cited as a filmic example of this.)[4] It is also interesting to consider here Freud's example in his essay on hysterical fantasies (1908); he cites as an involuntary irruption of fantasy, a daydream which was produced by one of his women patients. She recounts that on one occasion she had suddenly found herself in tears in the street and that, rapidly considering what it was she was actually crying about, she had got hold of a fantasy to the following effect: in her imagination she had formed a tender attachment to a pianist who was well known in the town (though she was not personally acquainted with him); she had had a child by him (she was in fact childless); and he had then deserted her and her child and left them in poverty. It was at this point in her "romance," Freud says, that she burst into tears.

Freud does not give any analysis of the fantasy itself, but I would like to suggest that it is an example of a fantasy subject to defensive processes. Consider the moment of the tears; narratively appropriate, tears of self-pity at her imagined loss. But why has she produced a story to make herself cry, and may not the tears be a response not to the pathos of the story but to its satisfactions? The crying thus acting as a defense, brings the fantasy to an end in the same way Freud speaks of waking oneself up from a dream. This becomes even more plausible if the possibility of multiple subject positions in the story is considered. It commences with a pleasant and typical erotic wish in relation to the pianist, together with its happy consummation. But the fruit of the affair, a child, places the fantasy into an Oedipal context, for the child is the one wished for with the father. A forbidden desire has found expression in the fantasy, that it is forbidden is marked by the punishment immediately meted out—not only that the man deserts her and the child, but more importantly they are left in poverty. More importantly, for it marks that it was not enough punishment for the man to desert her, another hardship must be given to her. But even this is not enough, tears intervene to halt the fantasy. This might suggest that the man's desertion is *not* the punishment, but part of the wish, that is, for the eviction of the father, so that the child has the mother to herself, and it is *this* wish that provokes the final censorship of tears. (The outline of the daydream bears an astonishing resemblance to Max Ophuls's *Letter From An Unknown Woman*.) It is in the same essay that Freud presents a series of formulas on the nature of hysterical symptoms, in which he suggests that "Hysterical symptoms are the realisation of an unconscious phantasy which serves the fulfilment of a wish," and: "Hysterical symptoms are the expression on the one hand of a masculine unconscious sexual phantasy, and on the other hand of a feminine one." He restates here the innate bisexual disposition of the human made so visible in the analysis of psychoneurotics. But what is thereby emphasized is that this is not a mixing of the masculine and feminine but the juxtaposition, side by side, of both the feminine and masculine as distinct sexual positions of desire.

Fantasy in the Realm of the Public

Fantasy has, of course, never been simply a private affair. The public circulation of fantasies has many forms, from the publishing of psychoanalytic case studies, to feminist articles such as those in the issue of *Heresies*, or speaking-out in consciousness-raising groups; as well as anthologies such as *My Secret Garden* which, besides their pseudoscientific claims of extending human knowledge, are also offering forms of circulation of fantasy just as much as do the letters in *Forum*, *Men Only*, *Penthouse*, etc. But by far the most common form of public circulation of fantasy is what Freud described as "creative writing" of which film can also claim to be a part. Unlike confessional forms, such as letters, diaries, etc., in the novel or the film the subject of the fantasy and the "author" are differentiated. Fantasy, as a *mise-en-scène* of desire will nevertheless be at work in film, but how, and with what implications? Laplanche and Pontalis have shown how all fantasy involves original fantasies that are limited in thematic, endlessly reworked through the material of the everyday, that-day, experiences:

> The day-dream is a shadow play, utilising its kaleidoscopic material drawn from all quarters of human experience, but also involving the original fantasy, whose *dramatis personae*, the court cards, receive their notation from a family legend which is mutilated, disordered and misunderstood. ("Fantasy and the Origins of Sexuality," p. 13)

And Barthes writes

> If there is no longer a father, why tell stories? Doesn't every narrative lead back to Oedipus? Isn't storytelling always a way of searching for one's origins, speaking one's conflicts with the law, entering into a dialectic of tenderness and hatred. (*Pleasure of the Text*, p. 47)

This appears reductive, for there cannot now be anything more to say of fantasy in general, whether in film or the novel, which is not merely banal. And this is supported by the realization of the enormous repetition of cinema: the same stories replayed before the cameras, always the same but differently, which has been the key to cinema's success as a mass form of entertainment. On the other hand there is the rich diversity of cinema, the world on the big screen, the range of genres, narrative devices, cinematographic techniques.

Between the "limited thematics" of original fantasy and the diverse, often complex webs of modern forms of representation, how to pose the question of fantasy in film? Before considering in detail particular films, I'd like to note certain questions and points, and summarize in relation to these, the important starting point and contribution of Freud's essay "On Creative Writing and Daydreaming."

Freud asks what the role of conscious fantasies, of daydreams is, and argues that they function for adults as play had done in childhood, with all the same seriousness:

> In spite of all the emotion with which he cathects his world of play, the child distinguishes it quite well from reality; and he likes to link his imagined objects and situations to the tangible and visible things of the real world. This linking is all that differentiates the child's "play" from "phantasying." The creative writer does the same as the child at play. He creates a world of phantasy which he takes very seriously—that is, which he

invests with large amounts of emotion—while separating it sharply from reality. (p. 144)

And behind the play, behind fantasy, is a wish: for the child, to be grown-up, which is acted out in scenarios; for the adult, ambitious and erotic wishes are fantasied (in scenarios). These can be infinitely various and varied, shifting with the new impressions received everyday, changing to fit the new situations and contexts to the subject—the kaleidoscopic material Laplanche and Pontalis refer to. The fantasy, Freud suggests, thus hovers between three times: the present provides a context, the material elements of the fantasy; the past provides the wish, deriving from the earliest experiences; the dreamer then imagines a new situation, in the future, which represents a fulfillment of wish. Freud's example is of an orphan boy, going for a job interview, imagining not only obtaining the job but being so successful that he is taken into the employer's family, marries the owner's daughter, and succeeds him in running the business. Ambitious and erotic wishes are both fulfilled. But, whether dreams of sleep or consciousness, censorship and secondary revision are central; in various ways, more or less, the fantasies are tailored to, address "reality" in the sense of Lacan's symbolic, a domain of prohibition, and in the sense of "reality-testing," actualized social relations.[5] Fantasy then as a privileged terrain on which social reality and the unconscious are engaged in a figuring which intertwines them both.

Daydreams, fantasies, are normally very private affairs (which is why their rare forms of public circulation are so fascinating) and a certain amount of "shame" and embarrassment is involved whenever the fantasies are found out, or when we fear being found out in them. A shame not only for being childish (and hence for a denial of reality) as Freud suggests, but also surely because of the cathexis deriving from the archaic, original wishes involved. Despite censoring, the existence of the fantasy as such bears witness to the pressure of a desire itself absent (or rather, which is not represented as such). Yet, as Freud suggests, a publicly sanctioned form of fantasy does exist—creative writing in which all this is in play. In his discussion Freud addresses initially the most despised form of creative writing, popular fiction, where he notes the recurrent feature of an invincible hero "for whom the writer tries by every means to win our sympathies," and that "through the revealing characteristic of invulnerability we can immediately recognise His Majesty the Ego, the hero alike of every daydream and of every story" (p. 150). And the hero always gets the girl, against terrible odds. This remains true even for "serious" literature, where the hero may die nobly on the scaffold, or indeed be no hero at all. Nevertheless the anti-hero too is a centered-ego, the privileged character and the site of a celebration, however negative. Freud similarly suggests that the psychological novel, where there is no centered hero, "owes its special nature to the inclination of the modern writer to split up his ego, by self-observation, into many part-egos, and, in consequence, to personify the conflicting currents of his own mental life in several heroes" (p. 150). Creative writing is thus seen to be the presenting in a public form of the author's own fantasies—and the same time structure as that of the daydream can be seen to operate.

Freud's theses, however, while opening up the study of fantasy in public forms of representation, seem to lead back to the author as origin of the fantasy, and as site for any answer to questions about the organization of fantasy in the text. If fantasies *are* "personal" in this way, how can they work for a general public, for a mass audience? Firstly, fantasy-scenarios involve original wishes that are universal. Secondly, they are contingent, so that just as we draw on events of the day to produce our own, so we can adopt and adapt the ready-made scenarios of fiction, as if their contingent material had been our own. Nevertheless a paradox exists: the disavowal of reality— "I know this isn't real, is only an illusion but. . . ," with an attendant pleasure in the *realism* of the illusionism, to the extent that it is the most typical aesthetic criteria for good film, that is, that it be realistic. Notwithstanding the fact that realism, the realistic, are the effects of, are produced by, filmic and literary conventions,[6] it is still held to be axiomatic by critics and audiences alike that some films are realistic—and good—while others are mere fantasy, and only good because particular qualities redeem them (such as the "fine," i.e., realistic, acting in *Now Voyager*, or the "solidly plausible detail" in *The Reckless Moment*). The vehement demand that we should be able to tell the difference between reality and fantasy even in fiction bears witness perhaps to the fear involved in apprehending the reality of fantasy. But inasmuch as this wish is located in relation to representation it is condemned to a hopeless circularity: reality is realistic in representation insofar as it conforms to the accepted conventions of representing. "Realism" in representation can be seen both as a *defense* against fantasy and as a "hook," involving the spectator in the fantasy structure "unawares," and thus as fore-pleasure. This making real of what isn't real reaches an extraordinary culmination in cinema, the dream factory *par excellence*. For not only does cinema offer the specularization of fantasy, but it offers this as a *real* experience, at the level of auditory and visual perceptions.[7]

The fiction will fail as ready-made fantasy then if it is felt to be too "farfetched"; the criteria for this are not fixed but depend on the conventions of realism, of verisimilitude, pertaining. That is, the norms of motivation for "believable" behavior, the requirements for effects to be shown to have causes, and hence the demand for certain forms of narrative conventions. This of course is slightly different from the demand for realism referred to above, which involves a demand for the representation to have a relation to reality as truth, to actuality, as *distinct* from fantasy. But the difference *is* only slight between the conventions of realism in a Vietnam documentary and in *Apocalypse Now*. Thus it is not the content of the contingent as such which makes it "work" for an audience (thought it may be so for any particular spectator), but the presentation of that material, its form.

Conventions are also the means by which the author reworks his or her fantasy for public consumption. For the author (whether the single author of the literary text, or the collective "authors" of a film) produces a further secondary revision of his or her fantasies that leads us to accept what would otherwise appear as rampant egoism, by altering, softening, and disguising the characters of the fiction. This is carried out by drawing on the conventions of the novelistic.

Thirdly, the main way in which fantasy is reworked in the text is through what Freud describes as the way in which a writer

> bribes us by the purely formal—that is, aesthetic—yield of pleasure which he offers us in the presentation of his fantasies. We give the name of incentive bonus, or a fore-pleasure, to a yield of pleasure such as this, which is offered to us so as to make possible the release of still greater pleasure arising from deeper psychical sources. (p. 153)

Freud discussed this concept most fully in relation to the joke. The simple joke, a pun for example, gives pleasure by the shift of meaning, the substitution implied, which produces a comic effect by juxtaposing an appropriate and an inappropriate meaning (just as cinema audiences unused to subtitles invariably laugh and titter at any misspellings). In the tendentious joke, that is those jokes that have an object, there are additional sources of pleasure through the satisfaction of erotic and/or aggressive feelings, but the means to this additional pleasure is via the simple joke, which opens the way to the substitution of meaning in relation to the object. Freud gives a number of examples, among which are the following:

> Serrenissimus [the name conventionally given to royalty under the German empire] was making a tour through his provinces and noticed a man in the crowd who bore a striking resemblance to his own exalted person. He beckoned him and asked "Was your mother at one time in the service of the Palace?"—"No, Your Highness, but my father was," replied the man. ("Jokes and Their Relation to the Unconscious," p. 68)

The question formally admits the reply, the man naming the correct relative instead of the one wrongly suggested by Serrenissimus, but the substitution of father for mother turns the implicit insult back upon his exalted person, making both a joke against authority and a sexual joke (it also contains some of the elements of the "family romance" scenario in the mutual imputation of bastardy). Anther example Freud gives is the quip "The man has a great future behind him," spoken by Herr N. of a public personage (p. 26), whereby the substitution of one word, behind, for before, presents an amusing "mistake" since futures cannot lie behind us, while also succinctly summing up the man's career, for he once had a great future in store, but no longer has. Another Herr N. joke is a simile that introduces a faulty appeal to (Roman) history: of a man who had been Minister for Agriculture with the sole qualification of having been a farmer and who proved to be the least gifted minister there had ever been. On resigning and returning to farming, it was said that: "Like Cincinnatus, he has gone back to his place before the plough" (p. 27). (In this case *before* substitutes for behind, and thus likens the former minister to an ox!)

Fore-pleasure, then, is that small pleasure of word-play, substitution or whatever in the joke, which enables another, greater pleasure. It lifts inhibitions—aggressive or erotic—which are on the one hand social and on the other hand unconscious. But in the joke and in creative writing, unlike the sexual act which is the original context for Freud's use of the term fore-pleasure, the two pleasures may not be distinguishable as different moments of pleasure. Of the sexual act Freud writes

> This distinction between the one kind of pleasure due to the excitation
> of erotogenic zones and the other kind due to the discharge of the sexual
> substances deserves, I think, to be made more concrete by a different
> nomenclature. The former may be suitably described as "fore-pleasure"
> in contrast to the "end-pleasure" or pleasure of satisfaction derived from
> the sexual act. ("Three Essays on Sexuality," p. 210)

While the two moments come together in the joke, or film, they can nevertheless be distinguished as different elements as the discussion later of *Now Voyager* will seek to show. The audience is opened to the "greater pleasure" of the fantasy by a fore-pleasure produced through the aesthetic or formal presentation rather than by an *a priori* identification with the fantasy as such. The aesthetic is then another level on which conventions of representation are brought to bear, but in this case it does not extend the workings of censorship, but enables it to be *undermined*.

Conventions are thus the means by which the structuring of desire is represented in public forms, inasmuch as, following the arguments of Laplanche and Pontalis earlier, fantasy *is the mise-en-scène* of desire. What is necessary for any public forms of fantasy, for their collective consumption, is not universal objects of desire, but a setting of desiring in which we find our place(s). And these places will devolve, as in the original fantasies, on positions of desire: active or passive, feminine or masculine, mother or son, father or daughter.

The author's unconscious is then only one among several determinants for the fantasy, and the "acceptability" of the fantasy for a mass audience is not dependent on any identification with the author. Two sets of questions arise, however: first, if fantasy is the *mise-en-scène* of desire, whose desire is figured in the film, who is the subject for and of the scenario? No longer just, if ever, the so-called "author." But how does the spectator come into place as desiring subject of the film? Secondly, what is the relation of the contingent, everyday material drawn from real life, that is, from the *social*, to the primal or original fantasies? Is the contingent "dressing" of the fantasy irrelevant? It was argued earlier in this article that fantasy is a unique concept in psychoanalysis in referring to a psychic process that is both conscious and unconscious, and that juxtaposes the social and the psychic processes. Two films will be considered in some detail in order to explore these relationships.

Now Voyager

The "woman's film" melodrama was a staple genre of Hollywood production of the 1930s and 1940s, and *Now Voyager* is an exemplary "quality" production within that genre—even reviewers dismissing the film as escapism admired the acting of Bette Davis, Paul Henreid, and Gladys Cooper. The genre was characterized not only by its centering on women but by the wish-fulfillment scenarios thereby presented, the "worst" examples being described by Molly Haskell as filling "a masturbatory need, it is soft-core emotional porn for the frustrated housewife" (pp. 154, 155). The following discussion, however, will be concerned to explore precisely the workings of such fantasy in *Now Voyager* and *The Reckless Moment*.

Now Voyager,[8] made by Warner Brothers and released in 1943 (shown with an A certificate in Britain), was directed by Irving Rapper from a script by Casey Robinson, based on the novel by Olive Higgins Prouty. The traveler of the title is Charlotte Vale, the not-so-young spinster daughter of a wealthy Boston family. A "late" child whose justification for being born, so her domineering widowed mother says, was to be a comfort to her in her old age. Charlotte's sister-in-law Lisa, worried about her mental health, has brought an eminent psychiatrist, Dr. Jacquith, to see her. Despite her mother's interference and condemnation ("No Vale ever had a nervous breakdown before"), Charlotte agrees to have treatment at his sanitorium. The nature of this is unclear but appears to be therapeutic rather than drug based, centering on building up Charlotte's confidence and sense of identity. Two lines of poetry by Walt Whitman are used to herald her "cure," "Untold want by life and land near granted/ Now Voyager sail thou forth to seek and find." Charlotte's recovery is rewarded by an ocean cruise arranged by her sister-in-law, including all the necessary clothes, lent by the glamorous Renèe Beauchamp. The cruise presents definitively the ugly duckling-become-beautiful princess, the caterpillar-turned-butterfly. Turning the tables on her mother, Charlotte transgresses every prohibition Mrs. Vale had imposed during their previous cruise together—from acting like a common tourist, to consummating a love affair (her mother had ended her earlier romance with a ship's officer, declaring he was not good enough for a Vale to marry). A different impediment now separates Charlotte and Jerry, for he is married. They part at Rio de Janeiro, she to rejoin the cruise, he to his architectural work, after three days together.

On her return to the United States she is met by Lisa and niece June, both of whom can barely conceal their amazement at her transformation. Charlotte is surrounded by male admirers, greeted by friends who insist she stay in touch, praising her as the most popular passenger on the cruise. The niece, having previously taunted her old maid aunt, now gets her comeuppance when she asks Charlotte who her boyfriend is and gets the reply "Which one?" Arriving back home (not without seeing Dr. Jacquith first), Charlotte confronts her mother with her transformation. Meeting with her mother's disapproval, she is about to submit, despite Dr. Jacquith's advice, until she receives a present of a single camellia—a gift from Jerry whose special name for her was Camille. This determines her to remain "true to herself" and she countermands her mother's orders, sends away the drab dress and puts on her own elegant and stylish new gown, for the family dinner. Mrs. Vale demands again that Charlotte return to her role as dutiful daughter; rebuffed the mother leaves but falls on the stairs, twisting her ankle. She is thus made absent from the dinner at which Charlotte is a huge success (taking charge, she lights the fire, until now always left unlit on her mother's instructions because of the smoke); her change is admired by her relatives, and also by another guest, who has recently become a widower, and who asks why they had never met before. Charlotte explains that they had; he stood her up on her graduation day! Charlotte's "rise" is matched by her mother's "decline" into physical illness and invalidism. The widower Elliot Livingstone proposes marriage to Charlotte, a final triumph and delighting her mother since, in thus joining two of Boston's oldest families, Charlotte will finally be doing something her family

The first glimpse of Charlotte is of her feet and legs as she descends the stairs.

Charlotte, the "old maid," as her mother warns her of the "disgrace" her nervous breakdown will bring to the family name.

Charlotte's feet and legs again. The camera pans up to reveal her transformation.

Jerry lights a cigarette and hands it to Charlotte in these three scenes.
The gesture indicates their sexual intimacy.

Through Tina, Charlotte has Jerry. Here she dials his number on behalf of Tina.

Charlotte, the good mother, watches a cured and transformed Tina run down the staircase to her admiring father.

In the final scene, the cigarette Jerry and Charlotte share no longer marks their union, but their agreement to forsake it. "Why ask for the moon when we can have the stars?" asks Charlotte.

(mother) can be proud of. But after accidentally meeting Jerry again, she realizes that Elliot and she could not be happy together. Ending the engagement leads to a final row with her mother, which brings on a heart attack in the latter. Feeling responsible, Charlotte relapses and runs back to the sanitorium, only to find there Jerry's daughter, also a victim of an uncaring mother. Taking up the goal of curing Tina, Charlotte confesses to Dr. Jacquith the reason for her interest. He agrees to her idea of taking Tina home with her only on condition that she forswears any relationship with the father, Jerry. The film's closing scenes are of the Vale house transformed by the happy laughter of a party for Tina, who has blossomed into a delightful and pretty young girl under the care of the lovely and kindly Charlotte. Jerry, visiting for the first time, refuses to let her sacrifice her life—he's ashamed at taking so much from her—but she stops him, saying he will be giving her everything in giving her Tina, that they can be together in the child. "Don't let's ask for the moon when we can have the stars," she says.

It is clear from this summary that a series of wishes, both erotic and ambitious, are presented in the film. First, that of being recognized—as somebody, as worthwhile. This is the role of Dr. Jacquith: admiring her ivory carving, he is a fellow-transgressor of Vale prohibitions on smoking, and he takes her part against her mother, seeing how ill she is and rescuing her. Then, there is the triumph of the cruise, with Charlotte's social and erotic successes, and the subsequent achievement of liberation from her mother, aided not only by Dr. Jacquith's words (Charlotte's voice-over repeats them) but more importantly through the love of a man, signified by the flower he sends. Elliot Livingstone, however, represents a different fantasy, of achieving the love of a man who had previously rejected her, only to be then able to refuse him in turn. Within this there is also the fantasy of remaining true to the "absolute" love, the grand passion which, in being unattainable, is also unsullied by the banality of marriage, housekeeping, and so on. The film ends with an apparently unfulfilled wish, however, for Jerry and Charlotte cannot marry, and their love must remain unacknowledged in the world. The scenario is thus the desire for a secret love, passionate and fulfilling as "reality" can never be, and this *mise-en-scène* is not closed off at the film's end, but remains in place. In contrast marriage with Elliot had been impossible because it could not be passionate, as seen in his response when Charlotte declares that she will want children, or when she asks to go to a bohemian restaurant and he is shocked, being thus confronted by her disorderly desire.

Under the guise of these banal wishes, however, a far more "serious," seemingly "perverse" fantasy arises as the film progresses, though of course all fantasy is perverse in presenting wishes that are prohibited and subject to censorship. (Hollywood melodrama is notable precisely for its ability to thus represent perverse and socially aberrant wishes.) Charlotte not only frees herself from her mother, she also displaces her mother, becoming as powerful but charming and kindly where her own mother had been cruel and domineering. Charlotte as the pretty, loving mother her own and Tina's had never been.

The wish to have a child (to be a mother) is also fulfilled—narratively motivated by Charlotte's claim that through his daughter, cared for by herself, she and Jerry can be together, for in Tina she will have a part of him! The perversity of this claim is barely concealed. An asexuality is posed in the appeal that in having Tina she has part of Jerry, has Jerry's child without having sex! On the other hand, motherhood is sexualized by this association, thus standing in for Charlotte and Jerry's passionate love. If this is seen alongside the aggressive fantasy of the eviction (which is ultimately the killing) of the mother, the film presents a clear Oedipal trajectory for Charlotte, but with a perverse twist. For instead of transferring her desire onto her father, and hence onto his substitutes by whom she can have a baby/phallus, Charlotte obtains the child but evicts the father (she promised Dr. Jacquith) and sets herself up as the "good" mother against Mrs. Vale's "bad" mother. Here, no man is the agent of the Father, no man successfully intervenes against this trajectory; on the contrary, the narration marshals Dr. Jacquith, Jerry, *for* it. Of course, she cannot marry Jerry, because he is already married; but this narrative motivation could easily be resolved by the ailing wife conveniently dying. That this device is not adopted turns the narrative back onto the excluding of the father in favor of the mother/child relationship (having rejected Elliot, as she goes upstairs to face her mother, Charlotte remembers the silence as being the same as the time her father died), now represented as admirable, all-fulfilling. No, indeed, why ask for the moon when you want the stars! In a sense, Dr. Jacquith, Jerry, are both substitutes for the phallic mother, and they are finally unnecessary once the conditions are set for Charlotte herself to be the phallic mother.

Such a reading implies a homosexual desire played across the film, and if this is the case (and my reading is not too farfetched), it is also a way of understanding the pleasure for the *masculine* spectator, since the film figures the eviction of the father and the reinstatement of the now "good" phallic mother. By suggesting this I am assuming that the place of the spectator is not one of simple identification with Charlotte Vale. Nor is my suggested reading an attempt to psychoanalyze that character. Rather it is an attempt to grasp how the film makes a series of narrative moves between its fantasy scenarios (which are not only successive, but also compounded, each containing elements of the others). Apparently fulfilling banal wishes, it thereby sets the term for another ("unconscious") scenario of desire, clearly Oedipal, but where the subject positions are not fixed or completed, Charlotte is both mother and daughter, Mrs. Vale and Tina. This is not Charlotte's fantasy, but the "film's" fantasy. It is an effect of its narration (of its *énonciation*). If we identify simply with Charlotte's desires, that series of social and erotic successes, then the final object, the child Tina, will be unsatisfactory. But if our identification is with the playing out of a desiring, in relation to the opposition (phallic) mother/child, the ending is very much more satisfying, I would suggest. A series of "daydream" fantasies enfold an Oedipal, original fantasy. The subject of this fantasy is then the spectator; inasmuch as we have been captured by the film's narration, its *énonciation*, we are the only place in which all the terms of the fantasy come to rest.

However, in order to bring about such a subject position, the narration must "bribe" us, to use Freud's term, to admit the perverse or rather *repressed* wish. This, as has been noted, is partly achieved through the preliminary of the more "normal" erotic and ambitious wishes, but whose banality often provokes rejection by "sophisticated" audiences (as shown in some of the contemporary reviews). But the film also produces a fore-pleasure through its aesthetic devices, which "hook" us to the play of desire rather than leading to an immediate release in laughter. The earlier examples from Freud involved puns and word substitutions, and *Now Voyager* presents comparable examples. A simple device is the parallelism of shots of Charlotte's shoes: first seen as she descends to join her mother and Dr. Jacquith at the beginning of the film, this shot of a close-up of her feet operates metonymically as a synecdoche for Charlotte and connotes her as an "old maid"—the shoes are sturdy brogues, her legs fat, her stockings are thick lisle. The same order of image is presented later, at Charlotte's first appearance on the cruise; other passengers are awaiting her (so that they can all go to shore), speculating about the mysterious Renée Beauchamp (for the ticket was booked in her name), and the cinema audience waits, for we last saw Charlotte in her usual unflattering clothes (though Lisa had noted she was thinner!), when Dr. Jacquith removed her ugly spectacles and spoke about "sign-posts." This second shot reiterates, puns, the first but with a difference: Charlotte's ankles and feet are again the object of view, but now slender, clad in fine silk stockings, and smart high-heeled shoes. The camera quickly pans up to her face (quickly, so that a salacious connotation is not produced), and a *beautiful* Charlotte is revealed. The same metonym, but different connotations. The shot ends with another "bribe," for Charlotte's face is delightfully now hidden, now revealed by her huge-brimmed hat, evoking our wish to *see*. The hat continues to offer a hide-and-seek effect when she first meets Jerry and later as they lunch.

The repeated signifying of Charlotte's social success on the cruise similarly works by the use of the device of a surrogate audience within the film, this time it is Lisa and June, who are meeting her at the dockside. In addition there is fore-pleasure in its excess: not one but several fellow-passengers come up to say goodbye, and not one boyfriend but several. Further there is the humor of the comeuppance delivered to June and the pleasure of the reversal in Charlotte's gentle teasing when she comments that June is becoming a roly-poly.

The trite staging of their enforced night together "bundling" as a result of the car accident during a shore trip to Rio de Janeiro is presented as a comic incident in the device of the incompetent and incomprehending Brazilian driver who misunderstands their instructions and eventually crashes the taxi. Coincidence and chance are central elements of cinematic fore-pleasure in melodrama. In this example, the accident also results in Charlotte missing the ship, and hence remaining with Jerry for three days before flying on to rejoin the cruise. Later in the film, on the train to the sanitorium, Charlotte wishes she could hear Jerry's voice just once. Chance fortuitously intervenes for at the sanitorium she finds Tina and, taking her to town for an ice cream, she obtains her own wish by helping Tina telephone her father.

Finally, there is the example of cigarettes, which works through a series of transformations. First of all smoking links Dr. Jacquith and Charlotte in being something they have in common, and as a common transgression in the Vale house (when he first entered he had knocked his pipe against a vase, the ash spilling onto the floor). Later, when Charlotte is showing Dr. Jacquith her room he finds the cigarette ash in her wastepaper bin that she had earlier covered over, and this discovery leads to Charlotte's angry confession of another secret when she shows him her diary record of the cruise she and her mother had taken and the sexual repression imposed on her by her mother. Connected to transgression, cigarettes come to signify Charlotte and Jerry's sexual desire: on the balcony of their hotel in Rio de Janeiro, late at night, Jerry lights two cigarettes and taking one, Charlotte thus agrees to stay with him. This gesture is reiterated at their leavetaking in Rio, and again at their meeting in Boston, and in the final sequence of the film; but this time when Jerry lights up the two cigarettes it now signifies his agreement to forswear his sexual desire in order to enable their union through Tina! The gesture of smoking thus accumulates a meaning of transgression and sexuality across the film, which is reorganized at the end to mark an asexual commitment that is nothing of the kind.

The scenario, the *mise-en-scène* of desire thus emerges for us not just in the story, but rather in its narrating: that series of images bound into the narrative structures, in the devices, delays, coincidences, etc., that make up the narration of the story. The pleasure then not in *what* wishes Charlotte obtains but *how*—a how that refers to a positioning, ultimately of the spectator rather than Charlotte, in relation to desire; an oscillation between mother and child. A series of banal fantasies embed another scenario: the eviction of the father and the usurpation of the mother, a scenario that fore-pleasure opens us to. When Charlotte forgoes the moon for the stars she fulfills every child's wish for the mother to forgo the father. Charlotte is "phallic" for the narrative in being bound to pre-Oedipal relations, rather than because of any male, "phallic" imaging of her. Though clearly the transformation of Charlotte in the hands, and through the words, of Dr. Jacquith, the refiguration of her body as beautiful, desirable, places her desire there as subordinate to masculine desire (Lea Jacobs's argument that Charlotte is spoken through the masculine discourses), this is true only insofar as it presents femininity as the masquerade.

The Reckless Moment

This film presents a rather different example of the workings of fantasy in film. It most closely approximates Laplanche and Pontalis's thesis that "Fantasy is not the object of desire but its setting. In fantasy the subject does not pursue the object or its sign: he appears caught up himself in the sequence of images. He forms no representation of the desired object but is himself represented as participating in the scene" ("Fantasy and the Origins of Sexuality," p. 17). For the film as fantasy, the subject is at one and the same time Lucia, Donnelly (the film's principle characters), and the spectator. The following discussion of *The Reckless Moment* will seek to exemplify this.

The Reckless Moment (made by Columbia and released in 1949, in Britain with an A certificate) was directed by Max Ophuls, or Opuls as he was styled on his American films, from a screenplay by Henry Garson and Robert W. Sodeberg, based on a *Ladies Home Journal* story, "The Blank Wall," by Elisabeth Sanxay Holding, adapted by Mel Dinelli and Robert E. Kent. The film concerns an American family, white, middle-class, and living in a seaside suburb of Los Angeles. The film opens with a man's voiceover (which does not recur in the film) describing the town and its inhabitants and speculating on how little it might take to shatter the peace of a family. The scene cuts from shots of boats to a boy fishing, he looks up and calls "Mother, Mother, where are you going?" The mother is Lucia Harper and she is driving to Los Angeles to see Ted Darby, a man of dubious character, to persuade him to stop seeing her daughter Bea. She is unsuccessful. On returning home she is greeted by her son David, the grandfather, and Sybil the maid in turn, each of whom asks her where she has been. She goes upstairs to tell Bea of her meeting with Darby, to forbid her to see him again, saying that he had asked for money as payment for not seeing her anymore. Bea disbelieves her mother, and has indeed already arranged to meet with Darby that night in the adjacent boathouse. But Darby shows himself to be the no-good that Lucia portrayed him as and Bea, horrified, rejects him. He struggles with her but she hits him with her flashlight and runs out. He stumbles after her, stunned by the blow, and clutching at the rail of the stairway, which we see is broken, he falls to the beach below.

The hysterical Bea is met by Lucia, who goes out to check if Darby is still in the boathouse. Finding no one, she returns to put Bea to bed. Very early the next morning, Lucia goes for a walk and discovers Darby's body speared by their boat anchor. She drags his body to their boat and takes it to marshes some way away. Having covered up the killing, she is visited later that day by Donnelly, who blackmails her over loveletters Bea had sent Darby and which came into his hands as collateral on a loan to Darby. Donnelly falls in love with Lucia, however, but he cannot withdraw the blackmail because of his partner Nagle. Lucia tries to raise the $5,000 demanded but cannot do so without her husband's signature. He is away and she adamantly refuses to contact him. When she meets Donnelly again he tells her that her problems are over since Darby's killer has been arrested. Conscience-stricken, Lucia tells Donnelly that the man couldn't have done it, and, taking the blame herself, confesses that she killed Darby. Donnelly, disbelieving, tells her that it doesn't matter and that she should let the man take the rap since he might have done it anyway. Later Donnelly finds out that the man had an alibi after all, and that Nagle has gone to see Lucia himself. Donnelly goes after Nagle, finds him in the boathouse with Lucia and after an argument strangles him in a struggle. Lucia finally believes in the now-wounded Donnelly and wants to clear him by going to the police and taking the blame. Donnelly, out of love for her, refuses to let her do so and drives off with Nagle's body, but crashes his car. Lucia has followed him but he demands she leave him to await the police alone or else his sacrifice will have been for nothing. She returns home. Crying on her bed, she is called down by the family to receive a phone call from her husband Tom, while Bea tells her that Donnelly was found by the police and died after confessing to killing Darby and Nagle.

A synopsis such as this, of the main elements of the action, elides the narrative drive of the film, which I shall summarize as: extraordinary events intervene into an ordinary family's life as the result of transgressive sexuality on the part of the women of the family. Bea's transgression, her liaison with the no-good Ted Darby, puts Lucia "out-of-place"—viz. her son David's urgent calling as she drives off to Los Angeles at

Mother and daughter argue over Bea's relationship with Ted Darby: "Mother, can't you trust me?"

A few moments later Tom Harper phones to say that he will be away in Germany for Christmas. The scene affirms the secret between mother and daughter.

Donnelly leaves the house after demanding money for Bea's letters. The film noir tone is evident in the lighting and framing.

Placing a call to a relative, Lucia runs out of coins and dashes back to ask Donnelly for change, suddenly putting him in the position of a quasi-husband and protector.

Donnelly phones Lucia just after she is questioned by the police. He explains that Nagle will not agree to more time and asks her to trust him. In the last frame, the spectator is given an indication (withheld from Lucia) of Donnelly's sincerity.

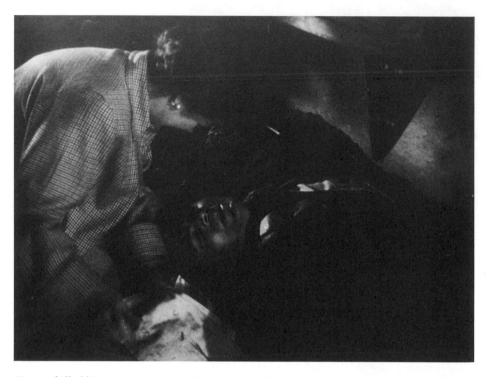

Having killed his partner to protect Lucia, Donnelly crashes the car containing Nagle's body. Lucia rushes to him, but Donnelly demands she leave or "it will all have been for nothing" and gives her Bea's letters.

*Back home, Bea tells Lucia that
Donnelly has been found beside a
crashed car and has confessed to
the murder of Darby and Nagle
before dying. In the final frame of
the film, Tom calls from Germany.*

the beginning of the film. Lucia seeks to confront Darby and takes on the role of the father, in seeking to be the keeper of her daughter's sexuality. But Darby flirts with her, commenting on how like Bea she is, how young she is to be Bea's mother, and Lucia's endeavors to warn Darby off appear impotent.

Later, arguing with Bea, Lucia shifts between acting as the stern father who nevertheless wants to talk things over reasonably, and playing the irrational mother who hysterically demands that Bea obey her without question in one breath as she instructs her to tidy her room in the next. And in addition mother and daughter are identified as she laments that "I've been stupid and indulgent, your father wanted you to go to college and I took your side and persuaded him to let you go to art school. . . . [shot changes from Lucia to Bea]. . . . He was right, and I was wrong. You'd never have met Darby if we'd have listened to him." And later she says "I probably would have felt the same way at your age." The moment of identification is interrupted by Tom's phone call giving her the news that he will be in Germany for Christmas, involved in building bridges for the Marshall Plan. He is not told of Bea's misdemeanors.

That evening Lucia writes to Tom (interrupted by her son David, she hides his Christmas presents, then asks him why he isn't wearing slippers—this reference to his clothing is an invariable element at each encounter of mother and son until the end of the film when Lucia is most out of control, and David proudly informs her, as he is about to go to a movie, that he is properly dressed; it is an example of the economic way in which the film narrates Lucia as mother and housekeeper). Lucia begins to write that she wishes David were older, or Tom's father younger, or that Tom were there to deal with Darby himself. The signifying of the lack of the father here is intercut with shots of Bea leaving the house to meet Darby—the cause of Lucia's "need" for the father. Lucia tears up her letter and writes another, anodyne, one; thus the father's absence is underscored at the same time as he is *excluded* by Lucia's keeping him in ignorance.

Lucia takes charge of Bea, hysterical after her meeting with Darby; firmly reassuring her, she goes to find another flashlight to go out to check the boathouse in an action that precisely mimes that of Bea minutes earlier. Lucia is authoritative after her investigation—"He's gone" (which she will later find is not the case)—and motherly in putting Bea to bed, and also identified with Bea through the repetition of their actions. The next day, by concealing Darby's body, Lucia assumes the responsibility for his death. This is her *reckless moment*. And the import of sexual transgression that originated with Bea is transferred to Lucia. Bea drops out of the narrative, which has always in any case been centered on Lucia. Meeting Bea on the stairs, Lucia orders her to forget about Darby after first ascertaining that Bea had not told anyone of the relationship. Bea, unaware of his death, is mortified at the thought of him, but Lucia tells her, "Stop it Bea, I know how you feel but you mustn't talk against him or about him to anyone. You mustn't even mention his name. Do you understand?" Lucia asks if there was anything else, Bea after a pause replies No, and Lucia continues on upstairs as Bea goes to her breakfast. For Bea, but not for Lucia, it is over.

Later that day, at the post office mailing her letter to Tom, Lucia hears that Darby's body has been found. The scene economically narrates both events of the thriller narrative and the melodrama-detail of Lucia's role as "Mrs. Harper" (distractedly, she buys the family's Christmas tree). Arriving home, a man has been waiting for her. Donnelly is initially presented as a threat, with a deep-focus shot of him in the darkened, shadow-filled room. Lucia is helpless—shown first in her attempts to deny the significance of the letters and then, after her talk with Bea in the kitchen, she slumps defeated into a chair. She feels she must accept the blackmail in order to protect Bea from the possible sexual scandal. But, given the identification I have suggested above, Lucia is equally guilty and thus she is also protecting herself, and this is the motivation for her adamant refusals to contact Tom. The family and the home come to appear as a prison for Lucia, a *mise-en-scène* of containment in the interconnecting tracking shots and framings that always place Lucia within her family, which prevents her from taking decisive and independent action against the external threat.

Meanwhile Donnelly is drawn into the family by the same means that Lucia is shown as entrapped. Lucia leaves Donnelly (introduced as a friend of Tom's) talking to the grandfather, framed together; as she returns from talking to Bea, the camera follows her, revealing Donnelly in big close-up next to the grandfather as she joins them. By this camera movement Donnelly has been included into the family, a portent of later events. (Donnelly also gives the grandfather a racing tip as he leaves and the latter subsequently repeats his request for Lucia to "invite that nice man" to dinner. At the end of the film Sybil reiterates how nice Donnelly had been, in contrast to her comment—ignorant of who he is—of Nagle as a nasty man.)

Seeing Donnelly off outside the house, Lucia tries to stall for time (a sign of her weak position), refuses to contact Tom, and says that she cannot act precipitously for fear of worrying the family. These elements are replayed in their meeting the next day, adding the further element of Lucia as the site of morality when she berates Donnelly for his way of earning a living, comparing it to David's honest work (for a pittance) during his vacation. "You'd never know about that," she says. He replies "Do you never get away from your family?" "No." The external threat represented by Donnelly and Nagle's blackmail is split into good and bad as Donnelly falls in love with Lucia, but it will ultimately be shown that he does so precisely in terms of her role in the family, as mother and wife. The following scene at the drugstore, for example, vividly shows Donnelly in the part of husband as Lucia rushes up to him from the phone booth (*not* calling Tom) and takes change from him. He buys her a cigarette holder to save her health, having commented that her chain smoking was bad for her.

Driving back, the theme of Lucia's entrapment by her family is repeated, she also again refuses to contact Tom, and the *new* position of Donnelly is represented when he tries to assure her that but for his partner he'd not pursue the blackmail, but he has his Nagle just as she has her family. Lucia angrily denies the comparison, refusing to believe him. Donnelly comments that Bea is lucky to have a mother like Lucia, but she retorts, "Everyone has a mother like me. You probably had one."

In this abbreviated gloss of the film I am forced to emphasize dialogue over the staging of the scenes. But staging, camera movement, the image track as a whole, etc., are crucial to the film's narration, producing fore-pleasure; for example in Donnelly's subsequent phone call to Lucia. Having promised her more time, he phones to tell her Nagle won't agree. We see Lucia take the phone from the grandfather who has answered the phone, and then cut to Donnelly in a phone booth saying he understands, that she can't talk because her family is there. As a result he *alone* talks, and there is no cut back to Lucia, and Donnelly repeats his wish that she believe him, *in* him: "I wish things could have been different in many ways. Only one good thing came of it. I met you." Donnelly leaves and goes to join Nagle; thus Donnelly's good faith is proven to the spectator before it is to Lucia.

Lucia's meeting with Donnelly at the bus station (after failing to raise any money except for $800 by pawning some jewels) presents her repositioning in relation to Donnelly, as he tells her that Darby's killer has been arrested. The scene is orchestrated by alternating tracking shots and reverse-field close-ups as they go to get a coffee, sit down as Lucia "confesses," and finally Lucia leaves to catch her bus. Donnelly has been accepted by Lucia in the role of "protector," surrogate father as Lucia had been to Bea. He takes charge morally and practically, telling Lucia in words that echo her own to Bea, "Forget about him [the arrested man]. What's the use of sacrificing your family for a man that's no good, that deserves what's coming to him?. . . . It's the right thing to do Lucy, the right thing. Just you forget this. . . . I'll have it out with Nagle, I'll have the letters back and bring them to the house." "No, please. No please mail them, I'm sorry but." Lucia accepts his help but denies him as part of her world. Donnelly has filled the place of the absent father but the place of the absent husband remains empty. Her denial is a delay, and sets up the audience to expect its retraction, desiring Lucia to recognize Donnelly as worthwhile, as we have done!

This is brought about in the scene following the killing of Nagle (the boathouse is the repeated site of death). To Donnelly's declaration of love ("I never did a decent thing in my life, never even wanted to until you came along"), Lucia responds with a corresponding offer of sacrifice: "I can't let you take this on yourself and be hounded for murder the rest of your life. I got you into this. It was my way of doing something that made everything wrong." Lucia is lover and mother to Donnelly at the end of the film, trying to tend his wound; he had spoken of his love for her immediately after referring to his mother's unconditional love for him ("she would never learn that I was the bad one"), and he has finally done something she could be proud of. In dying, he has the mother.

Rather than pointing to the various fantasy themes at work (for example, the nullifying of external threat by sexual seduction), I wish to emphasize the way in which the film clearly presents a series of positions through pairings and equivalences, the terms of which are successively taken up by Lucia and Donnelly, the two main protagonists. This not as a manifest narrative content, but a narrated signified. Thus

- Bea is to Darby as Lucia comes to be to Donnelly (lovers)
- Lucia is to Bea as Donnelly comes to be to Lucia (father)

Donnelly is the helpful father to David, showing him how to fix the car horn, and he is the helpful son to the grandfather with his racing tips. But Donnelly is not shown with Bea, this exception tending to confirm the system insofar as Bea and Lucia are identified as interchangeable. Thus

- Donnelly is to the family as Tom is to the family (father)
- Donnelly is to Lucia as Tom is to Lucia (husband/lover)
- Lucia is mother to Bea (and her family) as she comes to be to Donnelly

But the sliding of positions is unstoppable, and Donnelly's gestures of "caring" for Lucia, his concern over her smoking, as well as the formal motivation of inverted parallelism, bring him too into the position of mother. The work of the film is to transform Donnelly from being "bad" insofar as he substitutes for the no-good Darby in the first set of equivalences, into being "good" as the father and husband/lover. This is clearly a typical fantasy, in which censorship renders the adulterous love-object bad, and the fantasy reverses this, but with a cost—death. The perversity of the fantasy is suggested obliquely, in a way which the film does not underline as such. That is, the opposition and pairing of Nagle and Donnelly, which the latter himself compares to Lucia's relation with her family, and he does so in terms of it being a *constraint*. The pressure of the film's working, its drive, centers on such equivalences, so that though there is no other reference to this equivalence, and Nagle dies at the hands of Donnelly in order to save the family, the film system as a whole supports such an inference—an inference that is an attack on the family as imprisoning, as marked by the film's closing image of Lucia.

In *The Reckless Moment* the hermeneutic, the problem of Bea's letters to Darby and the blackmail, is displaced by the other hermeneutic, of the story of Donnelly and Lucia. At the end, Lucia has the letters back, on behalf of her daughter, but is crying over a new lack—Donnelly we presume. And the ostensible lack that "causes" the narrative, that is, the absence of the father, is only ironically made good, filled by the final phone call from Tom Harper. The staging of desire emerges through the series of figures, the exchanges and equivalences set up, produced, by the narrative.

The discussion of *The Reckless Moment* has sought to show the particular shifts of positioning in that film, so that it comes to seem that the film is *about* these, and Donnelly's death only halts this exchange, it does not resolve it. This is made clear by the irony of the closing shot. The "proper" father makes himself heard as the third term, putting an end to the imaginary play of dyadic relations, pairings. However, he is only heard by Lucia, the cinematic audience receive no aural or visual signification of the father except through Lucia's declaration of how much she loves him! The possibility of the imaginary play continuing thus remains. Further, the repositionings are not simply the substitution of Tom by Donnelly, but involve the diverse positions father, mother, child, lover, wife, husband, each of which are never finally contained by any one character. And any position only has meaning by its relation to the others (this can be seen in the sliding of "meaning" of the role "mother").

The film thus illustrates the way in which at its most radical, that is in the original fantasies, the staging of desire has multiple entries, where the subject is both present *in* the scene and interchangeable with any other character. Narrative in the film, just like secondary elaboration of the dream, organizes the material, restoring a minimum of order and coherence to the raw material and imposing on this heterogeneous assortment a facade, a scenario, which gives it relative coherence and continuity. A holding down, fixing, is performed in the production of a coherence, a continuity; the narrative seeks to *find* (produce) a proper place for the subject. What is interesting in the analysis of *Now Voyager* and *The Reckless Moment* is that, though in different ways, in each film the subject-positions shift across the boundary of sexual difference but do so always in terms of sexual difference. Thus while subject-positions are variable, the terms of sexual difference are fixed. It is the form of tension and play between the fixing of narrative—the secondary elaboration—and the lack of fixity of the subject in the original fantasies that would seem to be important, and not any already-given privileging of one over the other.

Furthermore the "fixing" produced by the narrative may not reproduce the fixed positions of sexual difference. In *Now Voyager*, Charlotte achieves a transgressive feminine position. *The Reckless Moment* presents a closure that replaces Lucia in the feminine position as wife and mother, but the irony of the final image and its figuring of Lucia framed behind the bannisters of the stairs, restates a wish presented in the film for the eviction of the Father, in his symbolic function. While the terms of sexual difference are fixed, the places of characters and spectators in relation to those terms are not.

Notes

1.   The decision in this article (apart from in quotations where the term is given as it occurs in the original) to use the spelling "fantasy" rather than "phantasy" has been adopted inasmuch as the former spelling is normally used in discussions of film and literature, and the intention of this article is to show that fantasy in film can be understood to work in the same way as fantasy in the daydream and in the unconscious. The "ph" spelling used within the English translation of Freud's works in the *Standard Edition* is sometimes also used to distinguish between conscious and unconscious fantasies. However, the French psychoanalysts Laplanche and Pontalis make a cogent argument for rejecting this distinction in the translating of Freud's work: "It betrays little respect for the text to render words such as *Phantasie* or *Phantasieren*, which Freud invariably employed, by different terms according to the context. Our opposition to this terminological and conceptual innovation rests on three grounds: i. the distinction should not be introduced into translations of Freud's work, even if the interpretation of his thought were correct; ii. this interpretation of Freud's thought is incorrect; iii. this distinction contributes less to the study of the problem than Freud's concept" ("Fantasy and the Origins of Sexuality," p. 11, footnote 24).

The usage of "fantasy" here follows the practice adopted by Elisabeth Lyon in "The Cinema of Lol V. Stein," and this article is indebted to her discussion there of fantasy as the circulation among positions of subject and object, the look and looked-at, which she notes are characteristic of the structure of the fantasy where the subject is at once included in the scene and excluded from it. While her discussion concerns Marguerite Duras's *India Song*, this article will seek to consider similar questions in relation to two Hollywood films.

2.   See here Raymond Bellour's discussion of *Psycho* in "Psychosis, Neurosis, Perversion."

3.   Lynne Segal's article "Sensual Uncertainty, or Why the Clitoris is Not Enough" is a very interesting discussion of similar ground from a heterosexual feminist perspective, which also argues for a more positive view of fantasy. "Perhaps then we could touch upon, rather than ignore, women's actual sexual longings. We could explore how power is entangled with desire and pleasure in ways which may foster, disconnect from, or seek to redress more general relations of dominance and submission between men and women, one person and another" (p. 41).

4.   See Paul Willemen's discussion, which concerns the role of fantasy and repression in *Pursued*.

5.   A comment by the director Howard Hawks seems to me to summarize this relation of fantasy and reality. Answering a question about why the men in his war and adventure films never question the impossible conditions under which they work, he said, "They know there's nothing to be gained by it. It's part of the game. They take planes up and test them, they take cars out and test them. And having been schooled to the Army, they accept commands, no matter what the command. And that's what makes any army function. It's just a calm acceptance of a fact. In *Only Angels Have Wings*, after Joe dies, Cary Grant says 'He just wasn't good enough.' Well, that's the only thing that keeps people going. They just have to say 'Joe wasn't good enough, and I'm better than Joe, so I go ahead and do it.' And they find out they're not any better than Joe, but then it's too late, you see."

6.   "What is realism as understood by the theoretician of art? It is an artistic trend which aims at conveying reality as closely as possible and strives for maximum verisimilitude. We call realistic those works which we feel accurately depict life by displaying verisimilitude." Roman Jakobson, from "On Realism in Art" (1921). Gérard Genette extends these points in his article "Verisimilitude and Motivation."

7.   The nature of cinematic spectatorship in relation to the specificity of the cinematic signifier is more fully explored in Christian Metz's *Psychoanalysis and Cinema: The Imaginary Signifier*.

8.   The following discussion is indebted to Lea Jacobs's article on this film, "*Now Voyager*: Some Problems of Enunciation and Sexual Difference," although the exploration here gives a different analysis and emphasis to Charlotte's desire in taking up the "subtext" referred to in Lea Jacobs's final sentences: "Yet the fact remains that Charlotte refuses the man. In a gloriously perverse gesture the narrative does not bring Charlotte's desire to fruition and an even more perverse subtext would lead one to suspect that she likes it that way" (p. 103).

References

R. Barthes, *The Pleasure of the Text*, trans. R. Miller, Hill & Wang, 1974 (1973).

R. Bellour, "Le blocage symbolique," *Psychanalyse et Cinéma, Communications*, no. 23, 1974 (on *North by Northwest*).

R. Bellour, "Hitchcock the Enunciator," *Camera Obscura*, no. 2, 1977 (on *Marnie*).

R. Bellour, "Psychosis, Neurosis, Perversion," *Camera Obscura*, no. 3–4, 1979.

P. Califia, "Feminism and Sado-Masochism," in *Heresies*, vol. 3, no. 4 (1981).

M. A. Doane, "Film and the Masquerade—Theorising the Female Spectator," *Screen*, vol. 23, no. 3–4 (1982).

S. Freud, *The Interpretation of Dreams* (1900) *The Standard Edition of the Complete Psychological Works of Sigmund Freud*, vol. V.

S. Freud, *Three Essays on the Theory of Sexuality* (1905) *SE*, vol. VII.

S. Freud, *Jokes and Their Relation to the Unconscious* (1905) *SE*, vol. VIII.

S. Freud, "Creative Writers and Day-Dreaming," (1908) *SE*, vol. IX.

S. Freud, "Hysterical Phantasies and their Relation to Bisexuality," (1908) *SE*, vol. IX.

S. Freud, "Family Romances," (1908) *SE*, vol. IX.

S. Freud, "A Case of Paranoia Running Counter to the Psycho-Analytic Theory of the Disease," (1915) *SE*, vol. XIV.

S. Freud, "A Child is Being Beaten: A Contribution to the Study of the Origin of the Perversions," (1919) *SE*, vol. XVII.

N. Friday, My Secret Garden, Pocket Books, 1974.

G. Genette, "Vraisemblance et motivation," *Figures II*, Seuil, 1969.

M. Haskell, *From Reverence to Rape*, New English Library, 1974.

H. Hawks, "Interview," *Movie*, no. 5 (1962).

S. Heath, "Difference," *Screen*, vol. 19, no. 3 (1978).

S. Heath, "Film and System, Terms of Analysis," *Screen*, vol. 16, no. 1 and vol. 16, no. 2 (1975).

Heresies, vol. 3, no. 4 (1981).

L. Jacobs, *"Now Voyager*: Some Problems of Enunciation and Sexual Difference," *Camera Obscura*, no. 7 (1981).

R. Jakobson, "On Realism in Art," *Readings in Russian Poetics*, eds. L. Matejka and K. Pomorska, MIT Press, 1971.

J. Lacan, *The Four Fundamental Concepts of Psychoanalysis*, trans. A. Sheridan, Hogarth Press, 1977.

J. Laplanche and J.-B. Pontalis, "Fantasy and the Origins of Sexuality," *International Journal of Psychoanalysis*, vol. 49 (1968).

J. Laplanche and J.-B. Pontalis, *The Language of Psycho-Analysis*, trans. D. Nicholson-Smith, Hogarth Press, 1973.

E. Lyon, "The Cinema of Lol V. Stein," *Camera Obscura*, no. 6 (1980).

C. Metz, *Psychoanalysis and Cinema: The Imaginary Signifier*, trans. C. Britton, A. Williams, B. Brewster, A. Guzzetti, Macmillan, 1982.

L. Segal, "Sensual Uncertainty, or Why the Clitoris is Not Enough," *Sex and Love*, eds. S. Cartledge and J. Ryan, The Women's Press, 1983.

H. Thorning, "The Mother-Daughter Relationship and Sexual Ambivalence," *Heresies*, vol. 3, no. 2 (1981).

P. Willeman, "The Fugitive Subject," *Raoul Walsh*, Edinburgh Festival, 1974.

This article derives from a paper presented in July 1982 as one of a series of m/f *workshops called* Re-opening the Case: Feminism and Psychoanalysis. *Some of the ideas in that paper were prompted by and drew upon lectures and discussions with Ben Brewster. This article has benefited from subsequent discussions with colleagues, friends, and students. I would especially like to acknowledge the invaluable intellectual and editorial help of Parveen Adams.*

from *m/f* 9, 1984

Femininity and Legal Decisions

m/f has consistently argued that there is no general theory and no set of rules for determining what should constitute a feminist politics. This applies as much to demands for equality as to anything else. Political choice is always a matter of calculation, since the effects of equality and inequality are different in different social fields. If in a particular case the political choice is in favor of formal equality, this does not rule out the adoption of a different means for working toward the reduction of discrimination in other cases. A politics of formal equality just cannot be a general solution. The article in this section urges the pursuit of formal legal equality between men and women as the calculation most likely to produce a politically acceptable outcome. But there is no truth about women within or without the law that establishes, by itself, the general necessity for equality before the law; if there is such a necessity it is a political one.

The argument that follows illustrates an anti-essentialist position within the premenstrual tension debate. It respects the discontinuities between discursive practices and thereby shows that legal statuses are quite particular to *law*. The question of legal responsibility cannot be answered by a naturalistic investigation into the mental and physical state of subjects but has to be decided as a matter of judicial policy. The forms of statement proper to psychology and medicine are discontinuous with those proper to law. It is true that the law has increasingly taken a psychological perspective on the question of legal responsibility, but this of course does not make legal responsibility a psychological attribute in itself, independent of the law, to which the law should defer. The argument for or against the premenstrual tension defense should not, then, concern psychological or medical "fact." Yet many feminists argue precisely as though doctors and psychologists could tell the law it had misconstrued the demarcation of legal responsibility. But the law does not investigate subjects in order to *find* whether they are responsible or otherwise, but in order to *hold* them responsible or otherwise. The medical question does not determine the issue.

Since legal statuses are not a natural attribute of subjects, it is open to us to press for formal equality regardless of the "facts." The political choice really has little to do with the existence or otherwise of premenstrual tension. The political choice is made on political grounds that have to do with the desirability or otherwise of excluding large numbers of subjects from responsibility to the law. Special exceptions may mean that punishment is meted out elsewhere, unforeseen and unexpected, in other spheres of activity—and in a punishing increase in other forms of social control to which the legally irresponsible are subject.

Parveen Adams

At the Mercy of Her Hormones:
Premenstrual Tension and the Law

HILARY ALLEN

Early in 1980 a young woman called Sandie Smith, who had a long history of recurrent violent and criminal behavior, stabbed to death a colleague after an argument at work. She was tried and found not guilty of murder but guilty of manslaughter due to diminished responsibility and was sentenced to a period of probation with supervised medical treatment. A year later, after being found guilty of threatening to kill a second person, she was again sentenced to a period of probation with medical treatment. The following day another woman, Christine English, who had killed her lover by running him down with a car, was found not guilty of murder but guilty of manslaughter due to diminished responsibility and was conditionally discharged without punishment. What links the legal biographies of these two women is that in each case a decisive factor in determining the imposition of conspicuously lenient sentences—rather than the custodial sentences that might otherwise be expected for such serious crimes—was the acceptance of medical evidence that the crimes had been committed while the defendants were suffering from severe symptoms of premenstrual tension.

This paper is concerned with the medical claims and legal doctrines that form the background to these cases, with the debates that have surrounded them, and with the relation of these to certain more general problems of theorizing the link between biology and social action. The field with which I am concerned is already transected by a series of arguments, some of which address directly the implications of these legal decisions for feminist politics. It is upon these feminist arguments that the main body of the paper is focused, and my object is to clarify them, to indicate their tensions, and to suggest how they might be further developed. In order to make sense of these arguments, however, it is first necessary to address the configurations of medical and legal orthodoxies that they overlay.

Premenstrual Tension and Medicine

The judicial leniency in these cases was consequent upon a depiction of pre-menstrual tension—or the premenstrual syndrome as it is sometimes known—as a determinate medical disorder, of limited incidence, biochemical etiology, and serious symptomatology. This conception of the "disease entity" of premenstrual tension can be dated to the work of Frank in the 1930s,[1] and has subsequently been taken up widely within the medical establishment, particularly through the extensive work of Katharina Dalton, to which I shall repeatedly refer.[2]

From the beginning the symptoms identified as typical of the disorder were strikingly diverse, and continuing research and reporting have produced an apparently ever-increasing range of symptoms occurring in almost every system of the body. According to Dalton, the only criteria for the admission of any complaint as a symptom of the disorder is its cyclical recurrence in the premenstrual phase, and its abatement at or soon after the onset of menstruation. Diagnosis is made on the basis of the temporal patterning of the symptoms, rather than their content: none of the recorded symptoms are unique to premenstrual tension, and no individual symptom is universal in all cases of the disorder.

The physical symptoms are not of relevance to the current discussion and will not be catalogued here; they are generally troublesome rather than incapacitating and rarely represent serious physiological threat.[3] The psychological symptoms, which are of more direct concern, are described as the commonest symptoms of the disorder, and Dalton suggests that some degree of premenstrual psychological disturbance is almost universal among sufferers. She mentions a gamut of possible symptoms, ranging in severity from the insignificant to the deeply incapacitating. These include symptoms of depression and lethargy, increased irritability, restlessness, tendencies to violence, loss of concentration and memory, impaired judgment, increased libido, unusual cravings, and schizophreniform symptoms such as derealization and paranoia. Altogether, the catalogue of possible symptoms is strikingly comprehensive.

Numerous attempts have been made to provide a unitary etiological explanation for the variety of physical and mental disturbances, but none have proved conclusive. The currently popular hypothesis, favored by Dalton, is that either a deficiency or an imbalance of the hormone progesterone is responsible, and this hypothesis is supported by the claimed effectiveness of progesterone treatment in relieving symptoms of the disorder. In this regard, however, two caveats must be raised. First, it is misleading to reason from effectiveness of treatment to etiology:

headaches are presumably not "caused" by a biogenic deficiency of paracetamol, although paracetamol may cure them; plaster casts are highly effective in treating broken limbs, but are irrelevant to their etiology. Secondly, there is no evidence *apart* from that of treatment that a progesterone abnormality is involved: no measurable differences have been found in the hormone levels of diagnosed sufferers of the disorder and normal controls, and despite certain suggestions to the contrary there exists no biochemical test by which to determine the presence or absence of the disorder. The enthusiastic reception accorded to the progesterone hypothesis and treatment merely parallels that received by numerous earlier therapies, now discredited, and already certain reports[4] are suggesting that this form of explanation and treatment may likewise prove disappointing.

Despite the lack of certainty concerning the disorder, the medical authorities[5] appear confident in asserting that the condition exists, can be positively diagnosed, and has a distinct and limited incidence

> More than 30 years of research into PMS [pre-menstrual syndrome] have produced a clear and precise definition . . . the diagnosis of PMS is confirmed in only half the women claiming to have PMS . . . A full medical history will reveal many characteristic features which confirm or refute the diagnosis. (Dalton 1982, pp. 93–94)

One might expect from this that a fairly clear picture of the rate of incidence could be established with relatively little difficulty. In practice, however, calculations of incidence vary widely, from less than 10 percent of women of menstrual age to almost 100 percent.[6] This disparity reflects the difficulty of drawing any clearcut line between the "normal" and the "abnormal" concomitants of the menstrual cycle, and the inability of researchers to agree on which mental or physical changes should be regarded as pathological and which as normal or even desirable.

This difficulty in establishing a line between normal and pathological premenstrual changes is neither trivial nor of purely technical significance. For upon this ambiguity hang two significantly different understandings of the condition. Ostensibly, the medical establishment treats premenstrual tension as a specific pathological entity to which certain unfortunate women are prone—an anomalous departure from a norm of female *health*. Yet to the extent that the medical establishment accepts that certain premenstrual changes are virtually universal, and leaves open the door to an understanding of these changes that makes all women to some extent sufferers of premenstrual *disorder,* the "norm of female health" recedes to a vanishing point where premenstrual tension reappears not as a limited pathology that may *afflict* the female constitution, but as part of an unlimited pathology that *is* the female constitution. The depiction of the female body and its functioning as inherently pathological, and of menstruation as a debilitation that renders the female subject physically, intellectually, and morally incompetent, is hardly an unfamiliar one, and its history and deployment have been widely discussed in feminist literature.[7] It is unsurprising, then, that many feminists should find within the supposedly modern and novel category of premenstrual tension a disturbing echo of all those earlier discourses that made menstruation a central signifier of female inferiority.

The suggestion of such a continuity would doubtless be denied by modern medical authorities, and yet if one compares the catalogue of complaints (in both senses of the word) that characterize the older and the more recent depictions of women's cyclical pathology, the parallels are more striking than the differences.[8] And at the very point of describing the pathological features of this ostensibly distinct and abnormal clinical condition, modern medical writers repeatedly seem to betray themselves by appealing to a common knowledge concerning women's nature in order to illustrate this pathology

> In its mildest form it [premenstrual tension] appears as no more than *the natural contrariness of women.* (Dalton 1964, p. 7, my italics). . . . All who read the findings set down in this book may understand the extent to which cyclical changes in the levels of a woman's hormones are responsible for her unpredictable changes of personality. The reader will begin to realize that there is a biological basis for much that has been written about the whims and vagaries of women . . . *every woman* is at the mercy of the constantly recurring ebb and flow of her hormones. (Dalton 1971, introduction, my italics)

In the light of such passages the flamboyant misbehaviors of a woman such as Ms. Smith appear to be not bizarre and anomalous products of some pathological aberration from female function but rather its paradigmatic example.

Even the construction of the disease category seems open to suspicion. For, as noted above, the condition has neither any unifying symptoms nor demonstrable unity of etiology, its only definite feature being the recurrence of symptoms—any symptoms—at a specific point in a biological cycle. This mode of construction of a disease category, solely by reference to its periodicity, is perhaps unique to premenstrual tension and oddly discrepant from the usual medical paradigm. By analogy one might pose the category of "pre-breakfast syndrome," in which to lump together all the various complaints that could ever, in any individual, be shown to appear regularly in the first hours after waking and then to subside. These would include such diverse problems as habitual hangover, morning sickness, smoker's cough, lethargy or excitability, reduced or increased libido, irritability, intellectual impairment, and numerous others. However widely demonstrable such a pattern of cyclical "abnormality" might be, it seems unlikely that the medical profession would grant it the status of a specific and unitary disease entity, or that the law would look kindly upon it as grounds for special treatment. With this in mind it is difficult to see what provides substance for the production of the category of premenstrual tension—unless, of course, some deep and insistent assumption of the determining and unitary influence of menstruation upon all women's ills, and the underlying homogeneity of all women in their shared cyclicity.

Certainly, the medically based studies that have claimed to demonstrate a statistical relationship between premenstrual tension and female crime[9] have done so in ways whose methodological coherence is dependent on the assumption of a *general* influence of premenstrual changes upon women as an anatomical category, and not on the assumption of a specific disorder whose behavioral disturbances will only be found in identifiable sufferers of the condition. In a typical study, for example, D'Orban and Dalton (1980) examined the relationship between menstrual phase and time of offense in fifty women convicted of crimes of violence, and found that almost half the offenses had been committed in the final week of the offender's cycle. These results are noteworthy, especially in the context of other studies that tend to confirm them. What should be clear, however, is that although these studies claim to address the relationship between premenstrual tension and crime, they are not designed in such a way as to allow them to show that sufferers of premenstrual tension (an independently diagnosable medical condition) are more prone than other women to committing crimes, but only that as a class women show a propensity to commit crimes during the premenstrual phase. In general these studies make no attempt to assess whether the women whose crimes were committed in this phase might by other medical criteria be considered sufferers from premenstrual tension. Indeed, one of the few researchers whose data collection included the subjects' own reports of their premenstrual patterns notes in passing that subjects whose crimes were committed premenstrually reported a *lower* incidence of premenstrual symptoms than controls.[10] Of course, given the way the disease entity is constructed, such a finding need in any case represent no threat to the general proposition that premenstrual tension leads to crime, since *anything* that might be identified as a premenstrual "symptom" (including, of course, a propensity to crime) will constitute grounds for a diagnosis of the condition—irrespective of other symptoms or their

lack. To rely on such reasoning therefore seems a little circular. In spite of these difficulties, these studies are routinely taken both by the medical profession and by the
popular press as evidence for a direct relationship between premenstrual tension
and crime, and provide the general background for "illustrative" medical
discussions[11] that deploy isolated individual case histories of women whose crimes
are restricted to the premenstruum, in order to substantiate claims of a general relationship between premenstrual tension and female crime.

Medical Evidence and Legal Decisions

Whatever its difficulties, the medical depiction of premenstrual tension as a
determinate hormonal disorder, causing serious psychological disturbance and
having a demonstrable relationship to crime, provides an essential background
against which the decisions in the cases of Ms. Smith and Ms. English are to be seen.
In each of the trials, Dr. Dalton herself gave evidence to the effect that these women
were extreme sufferers of the disorder, and that it was causally responsible for their
criminal behavior. In their summary comments on these cases the judges made clear
their acceptance of this formulation of the issues involved, and in the second Smith
case the judge went so far as to instruct the jury that they "should proceed on the
assumption that her behavior was attributable to the fact that she had insufficient of
this hormone . . . she knew what she was doing but she could not control herself . . .
she had lost her moral safeguards."

It thus appears that the judges accepted unequivocally that these women's
behavior would not have occurred but for the impact of illness upon their mental
state. In popular terms, this might be seen as constituting an absolution from responsibility and as legitimating the exemption of the individual from the sanctions
normally attached to such antisocial behavior. The legal position, however, is rather
less straightforward and the terms in which such considerations of pathological causation can influence the outcome of a criminal trial remain strictly circumscribed.
Since confusion over the legal issues involved has characterized many of the discussions of these cases, it may be useful at this point to outline briefly the different
points of law that limit the possible deployment of medical evidence such as that
provided by Dr. Dalton in these cases.

In principle there exist four main legal pathways by which such evidence, if
accepted, can influence the outcome of the trial. The first two of these are concerned
with the *legal responsibility* of the defendant and influence the *verdict* of the trial.

THE NECESSITY OF CRIMINAL INTENTION

Within most modern law there exists a general principle that in order for an action to constitute a *crime,* it is necessary not only for the act to be prohibited but also for the actor to have performed the action with a "guilty intention."[12] If such "guilty intention" can be shown to have been lacking in the commission of a prohibited act, as in certain cases of accidental action, no crime is deemed to have taken place and the defendant must be acquitted. And for the purposes of the law, certain abnormal mental states, viz., those of *automatism* and *insanity* are regarded as precluding the possibility of *forming* a "guilty intention," thus negating the defendant's responsibility for the action and requiring a verdict of not guilty. The state of automatism, which was claimed by Ms. Smith in relation to the charge of threatening to kill, has been legally defined as "connoting the state of a person who, though capable of action, is not conscious of what he is doing. . . . It means unconscious involuntary action and it is a defense because the mind does not go with what is being done."[13] In Ms. Smith's case, this defense was rejected by the judge on the grounds that despite the deleterious influence of her premenstrual tension over her *self control,* she none the less remained entirely *conscious* of her behavior, "knew exactly what she was doing, and intended to do it." Having thus instructed the jury that the defense of automatism was not open to Ms. Smith at point of law, and in the absence of any dispute as to the material facts of the case, the jury was obliged to return a verdict of guilty.

The defense of insanity might in principle also have been attempted in this case. The legal category of insanity is quite distinct from such medical notions as "mental illness" or "psychosis," and is defined as applicable when, as a result of a "disease of the mind . . . the accused was laboring under such a defect of reason . . . as not to know the nature and quality of the act he was doing, or, if he did know it, that he did not know that he was doing wrong." These cognitive criteria are not concerned with the defendant's ability to resist performing a criminal act; providing that the defendant is conscious of performing an illegal act, an inner compulsion to act in that way, however overwhelming and however much a product of mental disorder, does not provide grounds for a defense of insanity. Even if the strictness of these criteria did not prevent the widespread deployment of the insanity defense, the consequences of successfully pleading insanity would discourage the majority of offenders from claiming such a defense. For although the defense of insanity allows the defendant to be formally acquitted, as having lacked responsibility for her actions, it brings with it the obligation of an indefinite and possibly lifelong detention in a special hospital such as Broadmoor. It was in this context that the appeal judge remarked of Ms. Smith that her decision *not* to put forward a plea of insanity was "doubtless wise."

HOMICIDE AND THE PLEA OF DIMINISHED RESPONSIBILITY

In general the law recognizes only a simple distinction between full criminal responsibility and its complete absence. The one major exception to this is in cases of homicide, in which the defense of "diminished responsibility" entitles the accused to be found guilty not of murder (which carries a mandatory life sentence) but of the lesser charge of manslaughter (for which there exists a considerable discretion in sentencing ranging from discharge without punishment to imprisonment for life). The defense may be accepted in any instance where the court is satisfied that at the time of the killing the accused "was suffering from such abnormality of mind (whether arising from a condition of arrested or retarded development of mind or any inherent causes or induced by disease or injury) as substantially impaired his mental responsibility for his acts and omissions in doing or being party to the killing." This defense has been employed to cover a very wide range of circumstances, including cases where the defense amounts to a plea of "irresistible impulse" (not otherwise available under English law): it was this defense that was used by both Ms. Smith and Ms. English in the cases involving homicide. And it was the judicial acceptance of this defense that made possible the nugatory sentences they received—of probation in one case and a conditional discharge in the other— rather than the life sentences they would have received had they been regarded as of normal "responsibility" at the time of the offense.

The other two ways in which medical evidence can influence the outcome of the trial do not affect the *verdict* of the trial, but only the *sentence*. They are thus only of relevance in cases where the defendant has been tried and found guilty.

HOSPITAL ORDERS AND TREATMENT ORDERS

Although there is very little to prevent a seriously deranged defendant from being found legally responsible for her actions and guilty of a crime, the court may choose to sentence such an offender by making a compulsory hospital order (for a definite or indefinite period) or, as in Ms. Smith's case, by making medical treatment a condition of probation rather than imposing a penal sentence. In legal terms, such a sentencing decision in no way implies an exoneration from guilt or criminal responsibility; it merely implies that the court regards supervised medical treatment to be desirable in the interests of the individual or of public safety, and a pecuniary or prison sentence to be inappropriate.

In exercising its discretion at sentencing, the court is empowered to take into consideration a wide variety of factors that are not relevant to questions of legal guilt or responsibility. These may include aspects of the offender's current or past circumstances or conduct, the likely impact of particular forms of sentencing, and various features of the crime that influence "the extent of the moral guilt" of the offender. This was the phrase used by the judge in the context of his decision to pass a strikingly lenient sentence on Ms. Smith after her conviction for threatening to kill. Although he had virtually instructed the jury to find her *legally* guilty, since he deemed the legal criteria for a plea of nonresponsibility due to automatism to be unfulfilled, he made clear that he nonetheless regarded her as free from *moral* guilt for her actions, which he accepted were attributable to her premenstrual tension. Rather similarly, in sentencing Ms. English, the judge spoke of "the wholly exceptional circumstances" of the case, and by allowing her to go free without punishment he was widely perceived as having exonerated her from moral blame for the killing.

An important postscript to these cases, which has considerably intensified the popular confusion surrounding them, was Ms. Smith's appeal against the verdict of guilty in respect of the charge of threatening to kill. Although the lightness of her sentence might be seen as vindicating her from moral guilt, she had still been found criminally responsible and sustained a criminal conviction. In appealing against this conviction, her counsel urged the court either to allow a broader interpretation of automatism, which would allow this defense to be open to a woman in Ms. Smith's position as a sufferer of premenstrual tension, or else simply to establish a precedent of allowing the jury to return a verdict of not guilty in such cases because of the defendant's lack of moral guilt. The defense counsel pointed out "the great hardship that a woman suffering from this complaint may experience. She may, through no moral fault of her own, commit a number of violent offences as a result of being unable to control her impulses . . . if this occurs, she is morally blameless and it is quite wrong that she should suffer all the stigma and indignity of being branded as a criminal." The appeal judges, however, rejected the appeal. To have accepted it, they suggested, would have been contrary to all existing legal precedent and could not have been done without, in effect, introducing a major change in the law concerning criminal responsibility, and establishing a "special defense" of premenstrual tension. In conclusion, they reaffirmed their sympathy for Ms. Smith and commended the merciful treatment she had received by the original judge, but upheld the verdict.

That the court had *upheld* the original decision in all its aspects—including the striking leniency of sentence and the acknowledgment that Ms. Smith was "morally guiltless"—was far from clear in the press coverage of the decision. For what was stressed in the press was the court's stated objection to establishing a "special defense" of premenstrual tension, which would absolve women from criminal responsibility. Thus the *Times* article, which was headed "Judges reject pre-menstrual tension defence," opened by stating, "The Court of Appeal yesterday rejected a plea that tensions arising from menstruation should be a special defense for criminal acts." Given the widespread interpretation of the original decision as having provided a precedent for exactly such a defense, this reportage tended toward the impression that the Appeal Court had in some way *overturned* the original decision, and foreclosed the possibility of such evidence of premenstrual tension being used to gain a comparable result in future. It should by now be clear however, that if anything the reverse is the case: while declining to make *new* law, which would allow the outright acquittal of sufferers from premenstrual tension, the Court of Appeal *in no way challenged and in fact commended* the precedent established in these cases.

In practice, therefore, the option of claiming premenstrual tension as grounds for diminished responsibility in homicide cases and as a major mitigation in other cases remains completely open. The arguments that were raised at the point of the original judicial decision are thus not of merely historical interest, but concern existing precedents and practices in the treatment of female offenders. In the remainder of this paper I shall therefore be examining these arguments, and attempting to develop them.

Debate and Dissent

The debate and dissent that followed upon these decisions was not centrally concerned with their immediate effects—that is, the lenient treatment of two isolated female offenders—but rather with the "implications" of these decisions for women as an anatomical and legal category. In principle, of course, these decisions were at no point concerned with a category of women: in the terms of the law, nothing was granted to Ms. Smith or Ms. English *as women,* but only as extreme sufferers of a particular medical condition. It could hardly escape public notice, however, that this was a condition to which *only* women were subject and to which, in some interpretations, *all* women were subject. One popular interpretation of the cases was summed up in an article by Corinne Squire

> The medical evidence on which both cases relied, made these two women particular examples of a condition from which, it claimed, all women suffer to some extent. Implicitly, all women who menstruate are

at times not responsible for their actions, are close to madness and prone
to crime. (Squire 1981, p. 16)

It is not even necessary, however, to accept the view of premenstrual tension as a
universal female malady in order to regard the special treatment accorded to Ms.
Smith and Ms. English as having major implications for women, both within the criminal justice system and elsewhere. The following projection, for example, which considers only the direct legal implications, is based on one of the lower rates of
incidence commonly suggested in the medical literature, of around 25 percent.

Taking this rate of incidence, a straightforward calculation will reveal that at any
one time about one in every sixteen women of menstrual age will be both a sufferer
of the condition and currently in the relevant phase of her cycle. On this basis, even
if there were no statistical correlation between menstrual phase and crime, one in
sixteen female offenders in this age group could legitimately claim, by reference to
these precedents, that she had grounds for special treatment because of the
psychological disruptions caused by her condition. If we then compare this to the
rates of incidence of even the commonest of those psychological disorders that
would routinely be taken into account as possible grounds for such special treatment
(e.g., depression: one in thirty individuals; schizophrenia: one in a hundred), it
should be clear that the acceptance of premenstrual tension as a legally relevant disorder affecting 25 percent of women 25 percent of the time would be likely to have
major legal consequences. First, one would expect a major increase in the absolute
number of cases in which mental abnormality would be deemed relevant to legal
decision-making, and thus an absolute increase in the involvement of the medical
profession in the criminal law. Second, since this absolute increase would be entirely
restricted to women, it would result in a massive increase in the (already existing)
sexual *disparity* in the deployment of medical and psychiatric evidence in legal
actions. Third, and as a corollary, it would result in an overall change in the sentencing patterns of female offenders, with a significant reduction in the imposition
of severe and custodial sentences and an increase in the number of women receiving
compulsory medical treatment.

In the publicity that followed upon these cases, including a number of news-
paper and journal articles and a prolonged correspondence in the national press,
one finds these implications of the decision being criticized from two very different
perspectives. On one side there were those whose concern was characterized by a
fear lest the acceptance of the "defense" of premenstrual tension should lead to a
legal free-for-all in which women might too easily be exempted from legal account-

ability for their actions. There were numerous references to the possibility that premenstrual tension might become a woman's "all-purpose excuse,"[14] and the revelation by Ms. English's lawyer (subsequent to the trial) that he had hit upon this possible line of defense very much by serendipity and pursued it merely on the strength of the coincidence of Ms. English's crime with her premenstruum (rather than any clear medical history of premenstrual disorder) may well have fueled a suspicion that the appeal to premenstrual tension as a mitigating "excuse" would be open to considerable abuse and manipulation.

The other critical approach to the "implications" of these cases is less concerned with the ways in which premenstrual tension might be used to "excuse" female crime, at the expense of society, than with the ways in which the acceptance of premenstrual tension as a natural weakness of the female constitution might disadvantage women in their claims for sexual equality. It is this side of the coin that was widely emphasized in the feminist discussions of these cases and that most concerns us here. Various interrelated arguments were posed. It was suggested that the acceptance of these decisions could have retrograde ideological effects by reinforcing a conception of women as inherently irresponsible and unstable; more directly, it was felt that through their acceptance of what might be seen as an inherent female tendency toward cyclical instability and incapacity, these cases might provide a specific legal precedent by which to justify discriminatory treatment of women in employment, education, political life, and so on. Certainly, there have been American cases in which employers have argued against allowing female candidates to be considered for particular positions of responsibility on precisely these grounds. A further line of argument concerned the possible drawbacks of the "medicalization" of female deviance. Squire, for example, argued that the explanation of women's crimes by reference to a medical condition "puts women down," places women under the insidiously patriarchal control of the medical establishment, and denies both the social origins and the political meanings of women's deviance. The medical approach aligns conformity with health and deviance with disease, and there is no reason to suppose that in relation to the treatment of premenstrual "deviance" it would restrict itself to criminal matters, as the following heavily normative remarks by Dalton make clear

> Amongst PMS women increased libido is occasionally noticed in the premenstruum. . . . All too often it is this nymphomanic urge in adolescents which is responsible for young girls running away from home, or custody, only to be found wandering in the park or following the boys. These

girls can be helped, and their criminal [sic] career abruptly ended with hormone therapy. (Dalton 1982, p. 94)

Each of these unacceptable "implications" of the judicial decisions concerning premenstrual tension emerge from a single root: the reference to *female biology* as providing both a basis for explanations of women's behavior and a legitimation of practices that discriminate against women. I shall return to this matter later, since I wish to suggest that it is in relation to this issue of biology that the existing feminist challenge to these judicial precedents can best be developed. In the context of the feminist criticisms that were expressed at the time, however, this underlying issue was given little attention. Instead, criticism focused upon the enumeration and condemnation of these possible consequences themselves. In an important sense, it was the simple declaration of the insufferability of these consequences that *constituted the critique*: feminists were enjoined to oppose these legal decisions simply because of the unacceptable consequences that might arise from accepting them. What is most important—and potentially most subversive—about such a critique is its insistence upon treating these decisions as requiring a political rather than merely a "scientific" debate. It is worth noting something of the form of this critique.

Most importantly, the critique is in effect unconcerned with the "real" existence or otherwise of the phenomena that proponents of the disorder describe, including those relating to the claimed "breakdown" of these women's behavioral controls. The legal decisions were in principle based upon an acceptance of the scientific truth of the medical claims, but the challenge to these decisions is organized around the quite different criteria of the acceptability of the social and legal *effects* of these decisions. In relation to "scientific truth" the thrust of the challenge is at best indifferent and at worst simply repressive—its insistence upon the untenability of the knowledge claims concerned is in principle prior to any positivist demonstration of their falsity and *ultimately not dependent upon such a demonstration.* When one examines the position closely it is clear that what ultimately invalidates the claims of the proponents of the "premenstrual defense" is not the error or otherwise of their "facts," but their threat to particular values existing independently of facts.

Lurking in the background of this form of argument is either an epistemological distrust of the notion of scientific fact or at least a political refusal to prioritize the "factual" criteria of science in relation to problems that are somehow conceived as lying outside of that domain. Yet this distrust and this refusal are never directly articulated, and without the consolidation of that inchoate refusal, the argument is largely impotent against the inevitable rejoinder of an "appeal to the facts," such as is typified in the following letter to the *Guardian*

> It is disturbing to read that workers for women's equality are "aghast" because courts are beginning to recognize premenstrual problems as being desperately real and not imaginary. A century and a half ago we were still treating epileptics as victims of possession by devils. Until Banting and Best's discovery of insulin we did not know there was such a thing as sugar diabetes.
>
> The courts are presided over by tough trained minds, used to sifting evidence and to detecting spurious claims. Before Sandie Smith and Christine English were set free unpunished despite having killed, the judges were presented with cold hard facts. Those facts were that without a supplemental dose of progesterone those women were exposed with the regularity of clockwork to the risk that they would take leave of their normal senses. With that dose the risk was eliminated.
>
> . . . The miracle of reproducing the human species is principally a female miracle. The hormone patterns in a woman's biology reflect this, and it is like refusing to look through Galileo's telescope to deny the evidence that is there before us.
>
> Half the women in the world suffer all manner of physical and mental distortion because of hormonal imbalance and this can now be corrected. As the courts have seen, the treatment works. This discovery is probably the biggest step towards true equality of women and men that there has ever been. It is a tragic irony to hear women shouting it down. (Scotland et al., 1981)

The force of this rejoinder lies in its confident assertion that both the problem at hand and its solution can be unequivocally located in a domain of "cold hard facts" that the scrutiny of tough trained minds can reveal as simply "there" like Galileo's stars, awaiting discovery. These cold hard facts include: 1) the reality of premenstrual tension, like that of epilepsy or diabetes, as a determinate clinical "thing" (sic); 2) the location of that entity in woman's biology; 3) the unambiguous causative link—as straightforward as the workings of a clock—between women's unbalanced hormones and crime; and 4) the capacity of hormone treatment to "correct" this imbalance and thereby restore or produce a state of biological equity between women and men. Reference to each of these facts is legitimated by an appeal to scientific evidence that is "there before us," and the problem of determining the correct judicial response to sufferers from premenstrual tension is then treated as in principle no more equivocal than these facts themselves. All that is seen to be needed is a meticulous sifting of the evidence in order to separate the true claims from any spurious ones, and the correct solution is assumed to follow with the mechanical inevitability of an arithmetical equation. In this case the solution is the freedom of the defendants with provision for their compulsory medical treatment—and by extension, it would appear, the comparable treatment of "half the women in the world." In the terms of this solution jurisprudence, history, medicine, social policy, and women's interests are all required to appear as characters inscribed on a single surface of "cold hard facts" continuous with those of astronomy, mechanics, and biology. And like that of any equation, the truth of the solution is regarded as analytic: no grounds for dissent are conceivable except as a stubborn refusal to face the facts.

One response to this confident epistemological positivism—and one adopted by many feminists in the context of these arguments—is to meet the proponents of the "premenstrual defense" on their own terms and to challenge the scientificity of the facts themselves: to argue, for example, that the research on which they depend is methodologically unsound, or that the evidence produced is equivocal, or that the disease entity is itself somewhat suspect. Certainly, since the deployment of "scientific evidence" plays a central part in the legal and medical arguments with which we are concerned, there is clearly a value in interrogating this evidence, and it is even possible that a critique based solely upon a dispute over the empirical evidence could succeed in undermining the current medico-legal position. By joining the debate *on these terms,* however, feminists implicitly concede that in principle the issues involved, which concern the guilt, legal responsibility, and punishment of particular female offenders, can indeed be resolved by a calculated sifting of the scientific evidence. And by so doing, they effectively realign themselves with that very positivism which their initial refusal of the decisions—however inchoate in its theorization—was fundamentally challenging. What I wish to argue is that this realignment gains little or nothing for feminist arguments in this area, and instead threatens to obscure certain theoretical issues that are of fundamental importance to any feminist analysis of the operation of the law.

The original critical position, which sought to reject these judicial decisions because of their disturbing social implications, at least insisted on the political nature of the debate. In its indifference to the medical "facts" about the psychological effects of premenstrual tension, it implicitly repudiated the notion that a calculation of facts alone could ever be sufficient in deciding these cases. And instead it affirmed that the decision as to the proper treatment of these women belonged to a space of *argument,* whose solutions could neither be given in the facts to which they referred, nor be empty of political values. The weakness of the critique lay in its failure to explicate the grounds for this insistence. Its political thrust was clear but in the absence of any clear statement of its conceptual basis, its apparent disregard of the medical evidence could be dismissed as merely perverse, and its preoccupation with the "social implications" of the decisions could be registered as an unwarranted intrusion into the field of legal judgments of extraneous and improper considerations. What is at issue here is the way in which prescriptions for the organization of social relations (in this instance those related to judicial judgment and sentencing) either are or ought to be generated. What is implicitly questioned are the operations of reasoning that intervene between the establishment of the legal facts of a case and the conclusions that are drawn from them. I suggest that it is unfortunate that these issues were never directly explored in the course of the debate over these decisions, for I believe it is on *this* territory, rather than in the tangled terrain of the medical "facts," that feminist arguments concerning the proper treatment of such women can best be developed. It is therefore to these issues, which lie somehow behind and beyond the decisions themselves, that I shall turn in the remainder of this paper.

Biology, Intention, Responsibility

The positivist claims that are typified in the letter quoted above (Scotland et al.) depend upon the belief that conclusions as to the "correct" judicial treatment of a sufferer from premenstrual tension can be simply "read off" from the biological circumstances that surround the commission of her offense. I mean to argue that this belief rests upon a fallacy concerning the operations of reasoning that are involved.

At root the fallacy is that of assuming a natural continuity between the statements, processes of reasoning, and forms of rationality that are proper to different domains of discourse—in this case those of biology, of social behavior, and of the law. Substantively there is the conflation of the social and the biological, through a reductionist argument that allows social action to be presented as little more than a byproduct of biology. Rather differently, there is a conflation of disparate *forms* of statement—the descriptive and the prescriptive—that allows the disparate discourses to which they belong (in particular those of medical science and of jurisprudence) to be treated as if they shared a common logic and a common derivation from a domain of empirical facts. As I shall argue below, neither conflation is sustainable, either theoretically or empirically, and once this underlying untenability is made clear, the "logic" of the premenstrual tension defense simply collapses.

Put crudely, the conflation of the biological and the social requires that in the last instance biological states should provide a sufficient condition for the behavior of social actors. In the terms of this reductionism, to explain a behavior is thus to do little more than to elucidate the biological conditions of its occurrence, which are then treated as its determinants. In this sense, the forms of explanation of all human phenomena are homogenized. The statement that Ms. Smith's criminal behavior was "attributable" to her "insufficiency of the hormone progesterone" is treated as a statement of the same order as one that in certain instances lack of ovulation may be "attributable" to an excess of this same hormone. The complexity of the mechanisms involved may be acknowledged to differ, but no qualitative gap is seen to divide them.

The importance of this move, of course, is that once it is established that the behavior in question is "attributable" to a biological state, it is then treated as self-evidently inappropriate and, indeed *unjust,* to subject the behavior to the kinds of social sanctioning that are applied to crime. The logic of the conclusion is simple: the behavior is caused by a hormonal state; hormonal states are not under individual control, it is unjust to punish the individual for events that she cannot control; it is therefore unjust to punish for the behavior in question. When Ms. Smith, despite all such reasoning, was still convicted of a criminal offense by the Court of Appeal (albeit with only a nugatory sentence) it was against the apparent violation of this reasoning that she protested, complaining angrily as she left the court that "It's a crime to be ill in this country."

One must object, however, both to the initial claim of biological causation and to the subsequent deployment of this claim in arguing for the exclusion of the behavior from the domain of social evaluation and sanction. The reductionism of the original claim is conceptually bankrupt, and the reasoning into which the claim is then inserted is logically incoherent.

The central claim that Ms. Smith's behavior was "attributable" to her hormonal state depends upon the premise that her antisocial behavior was restricted to periods when she was in a particular hormonal state, and upon the resultant inference that she would not on this occasion have behaved as she did had her hormonal state been different. This premise was demonstrated to the satisfaction of the court, and it is here unnecessary to take issue either with the premise itself or with the inference that was drawn from it. What must be made clear, however, is that this demonstration establishes only a *necessary* and not a *sufficient* condition for her behavior; as far as the logic of this reasoning goes, one might as well argue that since her crimes only ever occurred during the cyclical state of cerebral arousal that we know as wakefulness, and presumably would not have occurred had she been asleep, her behavior was attributable to her wakefulness.

But of course, a rather stronger kind of claim is intended—equivalent in effect to the claim that Ms. Smith's premenstrual tension provided a *sufficient* condition for her behavior. We are asked to believe that her hormonal state not only made her behavior possible, but made it inevitable. She had no option but to behave as she did: biological state led to mental state led to social action in a single mechanical movement of causality, in which no other factors intervened. Against the tempting simplicity of this formulation it is only necessary to counterpose the evidence of empiricism itself. Although it is easy to demonstrate that everywhere biological states provide the *necessary* conditions for particular human behavior, their failure to provide *sufficient* conditions has repeatedly been demonstrated. Even such minimal units of "biologically programmed" behavior as the reflex action are subject to modification on the basis of external variables, and in humans can be exaggerated or suppressed, either willfully or unconsciously. Even these are not purely biological. Quite similarly, a number of now classic psychological experiments have demonstrated that hormonal states may modify but never determine behavior, and that the behavioral response to such states is neither uniform nor direct, but dependent upon a complex of social and psychological variables that are irreducible to biology. In the context of this insufficiency of biology in the explanation of individual behavior, the attribution of a woman's criminal behavior to her hormonal state offers at best only a misleading scientificity to the evaluation of her conduct. And as many feminists have pointed out in the context of biological arguments generally, this privileging of the biological serves inevitably to obscure (whether inadvertently or through more or less deliberate complicity) the whole political nexus of social factors that structure and influence the behavior of human actors.

However, even if one treats as unproblematic this claim to explain Ms. Smith's behavior as the product of her biological state, the way in which this claim is deployed in arguing for her exemption from punishment is itself theoretically untenable. The initial claim may have appeared to dissolve the distinctive territory of social action by making of it a mere continuation of the biological, but the conclusion that is then drawn from this claim is dependent upon the reassertion of a radical discontinuity between them. For the claim to demonstrate that Ms. Smith's behavior was biologically caused was never deployed as a challenge to the general notion of crime or to the appropriateness of punishing crime, but only as grounds for excluding *her* behavior from the category of crime and from its associated sanctions, whose appropriateness elsewhere the argument absolutely requires.

Indeed, the form of the argument is dependent upon establishing a conceptual antithesis between the domain of social action and the domain of biology such that disorderly behaviors can be conceived and categorized as emerging either from one or from the other, and thus as being proper objects for either the biological interventions of medicine or the social sanctions of judicial punishment. The opposition that thus structures the argument—that of nature against reason—is an old and venerable one and requires as its ground the familiar Manichaean subject in whose person the blind forces of nature and the reasoned forces of culture constantly struggle for dominance. When all is well, according to this model, reason is in control and action is "caused" by the (morally accountable) forces of intention, while the amoral forces of biology are subdued. Yet under certain conditions of pathology, of which the condition of premenstrual tension is only one, we are to assume that these forces of biology in some way usurp control, to overwhelm the forces of intention and expropriate the space of action. In the resultant situation, sometimes described as directly analogous to constraint from without, the individual cannot control what occurs; she is, in Dalton's words, "at the mercy of her hormones." As the defense counsel observed of Ms. Smith (a woman "normally sensible and benign"), at monthly intervals the "hidden animal" in her "escaped" and turned her to violence and aggression.

Having posed the matter in terms of the abnormal ascendency of biological forces (conceived as normally silent and lacking effectivity of their own), an ingenious operational tactic can then be introduced. Without in any sense displacing from the moral domain the categories of guilt and responsibility, it becomes possible under this formulation for the presence or absence of these to be established by reference elsewhere. Rather than requiring a demonstration of the *in*capacity of that in principle somewhat inaccessible domain of the defendant's intention, evidence as to her moral incapacity can be inferred from a kind of "overcapacity" of the biological. The hormonal changes attendant upon the menstrual cycle are then construed in precisely this way, as an intrusive excess of biology, whose impact, darkly registered in the shadowy terrain of "responsibility," can for operational purposes be detected by the positivity of biological investigation. This possibility of positivity is celebrated in an early and much quoted paper by Oleck

Temporary incompetence or insanity is primarily a matter of subjective evidence, is very difficult to prove and is easily subject to abuse. Pre-

menstrual tension, on the other hand, may well be a matter of objective
evidence, not too difficult in most cases to prove, if it exists, and can be
verified by scientific tests. . . . These latter facts largely remove premenstrual tension from the legal area of subjective and emotional argument
into the area of provable facts. (Oleck 1953, p. 494)

Yet despite the apparent claim to the legitimacy of biological science, the Manichaean
conception of the subject upon which the argument is grounded is entirely foreign
to this scientific discourse. For in the terms of biological science, the function of the
biological within the field of behavior can in no sense be conceptualized as disruptive, intrusive, or discontinuous, but is instead constant, necessary, and inevitable.
Independent of the will, there are constant biological changes, many of them cyclical,
which alter the conditions against which action can occur, and with which one can
quite routinely trace behavioral correlations. Some of these, like those associated
with night and day, the menstrual cycle, and maturation, as well as those associated
with certain states and processes that we identify as pathological, may also be shown
to correlate with changes in the individual's propensity to criminal behavior. Yet
there is no logical sense in which the observation of such changes allows one to conclude that the criminal behavior is therefore in some way "more" a product of biology and therefore "less social" than in acceptable behavior that may occur under
different biological conditions at other points in these cycles. The attempt to treat
the biological and the social as opposite and antithetical poles of a continuum along
which human behavior can be located—as more or less biological and more or less
social—is thus inherently misleading. The biological and the social are always and
necessarily imbricated within human behavior, and the demonstration of the operation of one is never a demonstration of the inactivity of the other. And the kinds of
statements that can be made about the two are discontinuous. The rationality of biological discourse allows us to draw certain conclusions as to the physiological conditions of certain actions; it does not allow us to draw conclusions as to the
accompanying intentionality of the actor, still less about the social and moral status
of the action.

Prescription and Description

What has been at issue so far has been the discontinuity between certain forms
of statement about the causes or origins of human behavior. Yet there remains a
sense in which statements about the defendant's biology and statements about her
intentions are inserted into the judicial discourse of the court in precisely similar

ways. For both are constituted as *descriptions of fact*: as establishing, within a problematic of truth/falsity, certain material components of the circumstances of the offense. In this sense, these statements are positioned in very much the same relationship to the judicial proceedings, as evidence concerning the concrete events. They may, as I have argued, be statements relating to substantively different and discontinuous domains, but they are none the less statements of the same *form*.

A characteristic—and misleading—assumption of those who adopt what I have identified as a "positivist" approach to legal decison-making is that the judicial discourse operates *wholly* upon a terrain of statements of this kind. The formal difference between descriptive and prescriptive statements is obscured, and it is assumed that statements as to the proper treatment of particular defendants and statements of the material facts of their cases are in principle statements of the same kind, predicated upon the same processes of observation and inference.

The fulcrum upon which this assumption turns is the reification of "responsibility" as an objective state of the subject, external to the law and as that to which the law is expected to *react*. From this perspective, the legal trial and the legal tests of responsibility are merely instruments of detection. The operation of the law is thus not to *make* an individual responsible or otherwise, but merely to *find* her so: the law, "like science" merely seeks to discover that which is already there. The conception of responsibility that is operant here is at once a psychological and a philosophical one: it refers to an ostensibly objective condition of the subject, conceived as deriving from a psychological state of intentionality and directly implying an objective moral condition—of guilt or its absence—to which the law must respond.

This moral and psychological conception of responsibility coincides with certain popular notions of the nature of justice, and is indeed reinforced both by the formulation of certain legal doctrines, including that of *mens rea,* and in much courtroom rhetoric and jurisprudential discussion. In articulating itself, the law certainly makes appeal to such ontological notions. What I wish to underline, however, is that there is a fundamental and a *necessary* disjunction between these broadly "philosophical" categories of guilt and responsibility and the operational categories that the law must deploy and sustain. The disjunction was made quite clear in the case of Ms. Smith, and formulated as a distinction between "moral" and "legal" guilt—Ms. Smith was not *morally* guilty for her actions, the judge conceded, but legally it was necessary to convict her as guilty none the less.

What must be recognized is that although the precise terms of this disjunction are open to criticism and in principle to readjustment—through changes in the formulation or the operation of the law—the disjunction itself is inevitable. For the problem that centrally concerns the law is not the philosophical or the scientific one of establishing the essential truth of "facts" (whether about events or states of mind or whatever) but the practical one of the management of certain social relations. The law does not operate, therefore, exclusively upon a terrain of "facts" and within the logic of inferences which can be read off from facts, but also within a space of *prescription,* whose statements are of a different order from statements of "fact," discontinuous from facts and irreducible to them. Thus in the case of responsibility, what the law must daily resolve is not an ontological question about whether the individual essentially "is" responsible, but the procedural one of whether the individual is to be *held* responsible, and with what consequences. Minimally we might say that in the terms of legal decision-making, "responsibility" exists only as a function of such procedures—as an imposed status whereby the individual is categorized as liable to particular social interventions. What the law establishes is thus in no sense a speculum with which to observe or detect a state of responsibility, but a constructive tool whereby to *establish* it.

This would necessarily remain the case even if the operational procedures whereby responsibility is established were precisely and exclusively organized around conceptualizations of moral guilt. In practice, however, there are a variety of other considerations that enter into the construction of such procedures as was made clear by the Appeal Court judges in relation to Ms. Smith. The defense counsel had urged that in view of her "moral blamelessness," it would be proper to introduce a change in legal precedent such that she could be exempted from legal responsibility and be found not guilty. To this submission the judge responded

> That is to look at only one side of the coin. Primarily the function of the
> law is to protect society, and if one asks oneself what would be the con-
> sequences if we accede to Mr. Evan's submission one would find this pic-
> ture. After she had stabbed the barmaid to death, the Appellant . . . [could
> legally be] . . . acquitted and discharged with all the consequent risks to
> society. There would be no control over her by society through the courts
> and she would continue to be a danger to all around her. That would be
> a totally unacceptable state of affairs.

The operation of the law in determining which individuals are held responsible is required to produce an "acceptable state of affairs," and what constitutes in a particular society an "acceptable state of affairs" is necessarily a *political* question that cannot be resolved "objectively" by any mechanical calculation of evidence or principle. The ethical requirement of our culture that the law should register certain moral and psychological characteristics of the defendant is one of the factors that influences the "acceptability" of legal decisions; others, including the wish to protect society from dangerous individuals, as stressed in the quotation above, are in principle quite distinct from this, and it is the part of the legal decision-maker to balance these sometimes competing considerations—an exercise of judgment that is inherently political rather than scientific.

Having thus recognized the inevitably political nature of the formulation and the application of legal procedure, then the form of argument of the feminist objections to the premenstrual tension "defense" is revealed as both more intelligible and more pertinent. The law is inherently concerned with constituting a particular field of effects, and not simply with registering and reacting to a field of existing circumstances. As I have already discussed, many of the feminist arguments were centrally concerned with this field of effects in relation to these judicial decisions. They rested, implicitly, on the demand that the law should avoid, in its attempts to produce an "acceptable state of affairs," establishing precedents that are liable to function in ways that are detrimental to women. And the imperative of that demand was in a sense quite distinct from any consideration of the moral guilt or otherwise of the women whom these judgments directly concerned. What I have attempted to make clear is that the unabashedly political form of the argument entails neither a perverse distortion of the proper concerns of the law nor a vacuous indifference to a demonstrable field of prior "facts." It merely restates certain concerns of the law—both *de facto* and inevitable—that are somewhat obscured by the positivist arguments, and challenges the privilege that these arguments accord to the prior facts (in this case those of the women's medical condition) in determining the necessary outcome of a judicial trial.

This paper has been concerned with a series of legal decisions and with the challenges and the criticisms that have been raised against them. It has argued for the necessity of recognizing a discontinuity between a domain of biological statements, as were offered in the medical evidence in these cases, and a domain of statements about the social status of particular actors and actions in relation to intentionality and responsibility. And it has stressed the pertinence and the legitimacy of a form of argument that evaluates legal decisions by reference to the acceptability of their effects, refusing the positivist suggestion that "correct" legal decisions can simply be read off from a "correct" calculation of the material facts of the individual case. Necessarily, it has therefore accepted that there can be no politically neutral, ethically unproblematic, or scientifically correct solutions to the problem of the disposal of such cases. Nonetheless it has been motivated throughout by an underlying pragmatic concern with how—from a feminist perspective—the legal response to such cases might best be organized. In the final section of this paper I therefore wish to make some specific suggestions regarding this.

Some Practical Suggestions

My basic position is that there should be *no premenstrual tension defense and no special judicial treatment of premenstrual tension sufferers as such*. This position is founded upon two quite different considerations, which jointly inform the practical suggestions that follow. First, as I have argued above, it is theoretically incoherent to treat the legal questions of responsibility, guilt, and proper punishment as reducible to any demonstration of biological state. Nothing of judicial relevance can properly be read off from evidence of the defendant's biological status as a sufferer from premenstrual tension, and there is every reason to resist the reductionism upon which the appeal to premenstrual tension depends. Second, there is the question of consistency in the treatment of male and female defendants. I begin from the assumption that it is desirable to avoid the differential treatment of male and female defendants, even where this implies the (politically uncomfortable) advocacy of severer treatment for women than that which they might currently receive. The general arguments against "chivalry" are familiar and need no rehearsal here; the more specific arguments concerning the unfavorable social implications of legal decisions that on the surface seem to favor female defendants have been alluded to earlier in this paper. On the basis of this general position I would make certain specific suggestions about the treatment of defendants who may be sufferers from this condition.

Concerning Responsibility

The Appeal Court judges insisted in their ruling that the legal responsibility of sufferers from premenstrual tension should be assessed by the same criteria as are applied to all other defendants. These are psychological criteria concerned with the defendant's *mental state at the time of the act* and are in principle indifferent to disease categories, biological abnormality, and the past legal and medical history of the defendant. Whatever the shortcomings of these criteria themselves, the judges' insistence that they should be applied no less to sufferers from premenstrual tension than to other defendants provides a precedent that seems both politically more desirable and procedurally less problematic than the establishment of any "special defense" of premenstrual tension, which would inevitably provide grounds for the differential assessment of male and female responsibility.

Granted, however, the refusal of any "special" defense of premenstrual tension, it remains entirely conceivable that certain female defendants who might be categorized as suffering from this disorder will also meet the existing psychological criteria for legal nonresponsibility by reason of automatism or insanity, or the less stringent criteria of diminished responsibility in cases of homicide.

Here again it must be noted that a diagnosis of the syndrome is irrelevant to the legal decision, which must be based upon evidence of the individual's psychological state at the time of the act, irrespective of the time of the month of her accompanying hormonal condition. An index of biological "abnormality" is not an index of legal irresponsibility. This argument notwithstanding, it might be objected that there are certain physiological states (such as epileptic seizure, for example) that are acknowledged as being so regularly accompanied by specific psychological effects that evidence of the physiological state can—at least for all practical purposes—be taken as implying that particular psychological conditions will have been in operation. Whatever the strengths and weaknesses of such an argument, premenstrual tension cannot in any case be seen as such a physiological state. As described in the medical literature, its symptoms are extremely variable, and even where the symptoms are extreme they do not always follow the same pattern. There is therefore no sense in which a diagnosis of premenstrual tension may be taken as implying that any particular psychological criteria have been met.

CONCERNING SENTENCING

Given the foregoing, the majority of cases where considerations of premenstrual tension arise will concern decisions at sentencing rather than technical issues of responsibility. In these cases the question of premenstrual tension is likely to enter either as mitigation (in the context of a general plea for leniency) or more specifically in connection with the possibility of ordering medical treatment as an alternative or an adjunct to other forms of sentence.

There are several ways in which premenstrual factors are represented as mitigating the "moral guilt" of these offenders, and thus as justifying more lenient treatment. These serve to reinforce, in different ways, the discrepancy in the treatment of male and female offenders, and embody other problems besides. First there is the appeal to the "abnormality" of the woman's state of mind during the premenstruum, as compared to other times, which allows the woman's behavior at this period to be "bracketed off" as outside the scope of her "normal" moral character, which is held to be blameless of the aberrations that may occur in the premenstruum. Yet to the extent that a cyclical fluctuation of mood may be seen as a "normal" characteristic of many women, such a bracketing off of their periods of greatest irritability, impulsiveness, etc., may offer women an undue protection from accountability for their behavior. As a slight analogy, one might be reluctant to suggest that a husband who regularly battered his wife, but only ever in the evening when his cyclical weariness made him irritable, should be less culpable than one whose violence was less regular. *Cyclically recurrent behaviors are not inherently less reprehensible than others.* Second, there is the claim that these women are less guilty and deserve more lenience on the ground that their biological disorder influences not only the distribution of their antisocial behavior, but also their absolute *propensity* to crime, making them less able to resist. Without returning to the debates as to the relation of biology to responsibility, it will here suffice to note that a simple proneness to crime, whether seen as biologically caused or otherwise, is not routinely taken as grounds either for an exemption from moral blame or for a reduction in punishment. This is vividly illustrated by the case of the XYY syndrome, whose sufferers (always male) have been statistically shown to be very much more prone to violent criminal behavior than normal controls—but the courts have been uniformly unwilling to treat evidence of the syndrome as grounds of mitigation. *An exceptional propensity to crime is thus not constituted elsewhere as grounds for special lenience*; to constitute it such in the case of premenstrual tension would inevitably result in a discriminatory favoring of women.

The question of treatability raises other issues. An important element in the claim for special treatment for sufferers is the assertion that the antisocial behaviors associated with the condition appear in many cases to be very effectively suppressed or prevented by regular administration of certain hormone preparations. It is thus widely argued that both the interests of the sufferer and those of society are best served by ensuring that this treatment is given, to prevent future crime, rather than by punishing the crimes already performed. In relation to this proposal two main points must be made.

First, the existence of an effective method of preventing future crime is in principle irrelevant to the question of whether past crime should be punished. To exempt from punishment a sufferer from premenstrual tension because her criminal tendencies are susceptible to medical control, while punishing, for example, an XYY sufferer because his are not, may have certain pragmatic advantages, but cannot so easily be justified by any moral argument. And pragmatically such exemption from punishment, even when accompanied by the medical prevention of further crime, will have certain effects upon the way both the crime and the criminal are perceived—effects that have been discussed earlier and that are not necessarily in the interests of women generally.

Second, there is no reason why an offender who is medically regarded as liable to benefit from this treatment and is willing to receive it should not receive it on the same basis as any other patient—and this irrespective of whatever other provision the law may make in relation to punitive sentencing. To the extent that such voluntary treatment may both increase the likelihood of an early release from a custodial sentence, on grounds of "good behavior," and reduce the likelihood of further convictions, it would appear that such treatment might prove attractive to those female offenders who themselves regard their behavior as arising from this condition rather than their own free choices, while leaving others to take responsibility for their behavior in other ways. Such a voluntary approach would both avoid the appearance of a discriminatory lenience in cases such as Ms. Smith (where after a most serious crime she was sentenced only to probation with a condition of outpatient medical treatment), and also avert some of the other problems associated with an increase of compulsory medical control applied differentially to women.

The approach to the legal disposal of such cases suggested here displaces legal attention from the legally irrelevant categorization of these women as sufferers from premenstrual tension and focuses instead on specific, legally relevant issues that may arise equally in cases where other disorders and difficulties are involved. The category of premenstrual tension itself—as a pathological condition of exclusively female incidence, linked to cyclical changes that all women share throughout much of their lives and associated in complex ways with unwelcome conceptions of female nature—is loaded with cultural meanings that have no necessary place in the operation of the law, and that might to advantage be rigorously excluded from it. By contrast, the antisocial behaviors of women such as Ms. Smith and Ms. English, and the mental states in which these behaviors occur, have a relevance to the law that is irrespective of their relationship to women's hormones in general. The law has already at its disposal a vast body of precedent concerning the treatment both of recurrent offenders and offenders whose mental and moral states pose problems of assessment. It may ultimately be of more advantage for premenstrual offenders to be treated in accordance with these more general precedents, rather than to be singled out, as victims of their own disordered femininity, for nugatory punishment but compulsory medical control.

Notes

1.   Frank 1931, p. 1053f.
2.   Dalton 1961, 1964, 1971, 1980, 1982.
3.   The only symptom claimed to be universal to sufferers is a degree of premenstrual consti-pation. Intracellular water retention, resulting in temporary weight gain in the premenstruum, is also said to be typical and may produce a variety of localized effects in individual sufferers, including mild abdominal discomfort, sore nipples, and aching legs. Mild hypoglycemia (low blood sugar) is also frequently mentioned as a symptom, and may produce a tendency to feel faint if meals are not taken regularly. Additionally, it is suggested that any preexisting or recurrent medical condition is likely to be exacerbated or to recur during the premenstruum. An exhaustive catalogue of physical symptoms is provided by Dalton 1964, pp. 7–14.
4.   See Swyer 1981.
5.   In addition to Dalton's work *passim,* see Friedman (ed.) 1982. Weideger 1976.
6.   Dalton 1982, Rees 1958.
7.   See Delaney et al. 1976, Shuttle 1978.
8.   Krafft-Ebbing, for example, in 1902, (p. 93f) described the following symptoms as the "com-monplace" concomitants of menstruation: irritability, melancholia, poor relationships with others, ill-treatment of offspring, emotional explosions, libel, breaches of the peace, resistance to authority, excessive jealousy, and abuse of alcohol. All these symptoms reappear as characteristic of the pre-menstrual syndrome in modern works.
9.   For example, D'Orban 1980, Dalton 1961.
10.   Dalton 1961.
11.   For example, Dalton 1980, Scott 1974.
12.   Literally translated, the Latin maxim that is routinely cited states that "An act does not make guilty unless the mind is guilty."
13.   Bratty 1962, 46 CR APP R 1.
14.   For example, Berlins and Smith 1981.

References

        M. Berlins and T. Smith, "Should PMT be a woman's all-purpose excuse?" Letter to the *Times,* 12 Nov. 1981, p. 12.
        K. Dalton, "Menstruation and Crime," *British Medical Journal,* 1961, p. 1752f.
        K. Dalton, *The Premenstrual Syndrome,* Charles Thomas, Illinois, 1964.
        K. Dalton, *The Menstrual Cycle,* Pantheon, 1971.
        K. Dalton, "Cyclical Criminal Acts in the Premenstrual Syndrome," *The Lancet,* vol. 2, pt. 3 (1980) p. 1070f.
        K. Dalton, "Legal Implications of PMS," *World Medicine,* 17 April 1982, p. 93f.
        J. Delaney, M. Lupton, and E. Toth, *The Curse: a cultural history of menstruation,* Dutton & Co. 1976.
        P. D'Orban and J. Dalton, "Violent Crime and the Menstrual Cycle," *Psychological Medicine* 10 (1980) p. 353f.
        E. Frank, "The Hormonal Causes of Premenstrual Tension," *Archives of Neurology & Psy-chiatry* 36 (1931) p. 1053f.
        J. Friedman (ed.), *Behavior and the Menstrual Cycle,* Marcel & Dekker, 1982.
        R. F. von Kraft-Ebbing, *Psychosis Menstrualis,* Ferdinand Enke Verlag, 1902.
        H. Oleck, "Legal Aspects of Premenstrual Tension' in A Symposium on Premenstrual Ten-sion," *International Record of Medicine* 166 (1953).

P. Redgrove and P. Shuttle, *The Wise Wound: Eve's Curse and Every Woman,* Putnam 1978.

L. Rees in M. Rees (ed.), *Psychoendocrinology,* Grune & Stratton, 1958.

P. Scotland, L. Fleischmann, and T. Hingston, "Premenstrual Tension and Equality," letter to the *Times* 19 Nov. 1981, p. 13.

J. Scutt, "A Factor in Female Crime," *Criminologist* 9 (Nov. 1974), p. 56f.

C. Squire, "Indescribable Tension," *The Leveller* 11 Dec. 1981, p. 16f.

G. Swyer, "Premenstrual Tension," letter to the *Times,* 25 Nov. 1981, p. 13.

P. Weideger, *Menstruation and the Menopause,* Hill, New York, 1976.

from *m/f* 9, 1984

Psychoanalysis and Feminism

The preceding sections have shown how much weight *m/f* attaches to two ideas: the heterogeneity of practices that bear upon the construction of gender and—to some extent consequentially—the heterogeneity of women. Now we can add a third, that of the heterogeneity of the woman in her singularity. This is the moment of *m/f*'s commitment to psychoanalysis. The human subject as conceived by psychoanalysis is always divided, split and ex-centric to itself, in a word nonunified. This is quite different from the philosophical or sociological accounts of the subject in which any alienation from an ideal unity is conceived as a deprivation imposed by social relations. It is also quite different from the subject of Foucault's analyses, where the practices of subjectivation are all social marks upon the body of the human. The subject, in psychoanalytic terms, is not deprived by lack; it is constituted by it. In Lacanian terms, the signifier produces the subject as that which lacks. From the point of view of political analysis, each thesis of the heterogeneity of women imposes constraints upon what feminist political calculation might be.

Taken together, the theses of the heterogeneity of women and the heterogeneity of the woman create a vast complication for feminism. For the similarity between women, on the one hand; and the difference between men and women, on the other, have become entirely problematic. Frequently, feminism has had recourse to the concept of patriarchy as the blunt solution to all problems. Such a concept invariably implies a mechanism that bears upon two preestablished and mutually exclusive groups—women and men—such that in one way or another men have power over women. But clearly this is not so much a solution as a repetition of the claim of the simplicity of the categories, men and women. At a sociological level, the concept of patriarchy always requires this reductionism.

Psychoanalysis is sometimes raided to buttress the concept of patriarchy. Here the reference must be to the way in which the relations between women and men are structured through the power of the father. But, in fact, psychoanalysis cannot be enlisted in this way. For within psychoanalysis there are already two fathers; there is the Oedipal father and there is a term we may call the Primal father. The Oedipal father, whatever unconscious powers he may possess, does not enslave his daughters and free his sons. On the contrary, his traces spell out the very heterogeneity of the woman's possible positions and thus dispel the system of patriarchy. The Primal father functions as the node of the fantasy of an original unity; but this only explains the *fantasy* of unity, not patriarchy. We might say that the concept of patriarchy should be approached not as a true or false account of reality but as part of the fantasy that always seeks to represent reality as a *unity*. Psychoanalytic theory is concerned to think out the relation between a split subject, its psychical structuring of the world of objects, and the way in which this is experienced through the fictions of unity. We might say that psychoanalytic theory treats the theory of patriarchy, with its identities of victor and victim, as a fantasy par excellence.

But if feminists seeking a theory of patriarchy have sometimes turned to psychoanalysis, they have often turned away from it, on the grounds that it offers an account of woman as lacking. What tends to precipitate this belief is a reading of psychoanalysis in which the issue of lack intersects with the issue of the phallus in such a way as to suggest that one sex is lacking, and the other not. But it is the human subject *as such* who is constituted by a relation to lack. And the phallus is not an anatomical attribute but a symbolic entity. Men and women both lack the phallus. Yet they do not lack it in the same way, and it is on this differential that the theory of sexual difference hinges. Certainly in Freud and Lacan there is a distinct relation between the penis and the phallus, just as there is a relation between the no-penis and the phallus. That is to say, there is a differential relation to castration between the sexes, a differential which is capable of yielding an almost infinite series of sexual identities and positions. But all this is to insist again that while psychoanalysis sets the terms for a description of the difference between the sexes, it is not a theory of two anatomical teams.

The fundamental concept of lack that organizes the description of the difference between the sexes also organizes the difference within the sexes. This means that women are not a homogeneous psychical group. The social practices of sexual differentiation, which are themselves heterogeneous, act upon psychic structures that are already differentiated for members of the same sex. Since the psychical heterogeneity of women follows from the heterogeneity of the woman in her singularity, that is, from the division of the subject, its nonunity, its lack, it can be seen that the subject lives its division in many ways. But they all necessitate an imaginary element, a fantasy of unity. This is food for political thought; for it is the division of the subject that makes the political personal.

Parveen Adams

Notes

1.   For the reworking of Freud's concept of the Primal father, see M. Silvestre "Le pere, sa fonction dans la psychanalyse," *Ornicar?* no. 34 (1985); reprinted in M. Silvestre, *Demain la psychanalyse,* Navarin, 1987. The argument for the fantasy of the Primal father as a fantasy of unity was developed by Parveen Adams in a paper for a panel on "Masochism" at the Modern Language Association Convention, New Orleans, 1988.

Representation and Sexuality

PARVEEN ADAMS

This article contains some general comments on psychoanalysis together with an account of some aspects of Lacanian theory that is necessary as the theoretical framework for Montrelay's "Inquiry into Femininity," which has been translated for this first issue of m/f, and a discussion of some problems central to that text.

Certain feminist positions challenge the Freudian, phallocentric view of feminine sexuality in favor of "a specifically feminine, primary, vaginal sexuality" (cf. Karen Horney). The concept of a feminine sexuality organized in relation to the phallus, often reduced to the notorious concept of penis envy, is seen as the mere rationalization of existing sexist realities. The fact that penis envy may appear in the analytic situation is admitted but it is argued that this is merely the effect of a particular culture that represses the free expression or development of femininity.

Phallocentrism challenges the concept of such a pre-given femininity (as indeed it challenges any idea of a pre-given masculinity) and argues that there is a single libido that is designated "male." Its opponents posit a specific female and a specific male libido (cf. Jones, Horney). What is the theoretical basis for the choice between the two positions?

If the thesis of a single libido designated "male" is to be maintained, it is required that the thesis of a pre-given femininity be rejected. The argument for a feminine essence is subject to the usual objections to the concept of a human essence or human nature. What is of concern here is that form of the argument where the concept of a feminine nature is buttressed by biological and physiological phenomena. To argue against this is not to question the importance of these phenomena, but is to question the place that they occupy in theoretical argument.

The biological frequently appears as the "irreducible," the "fixed," and the "inescapable." It is this appropriation of biology by essentialist forms of reasoning that has to be rejected. When the anatomical distinction between the sexes is thought to already designate masculinity and femininity, the thesis of two libidos may result. The argument from two libidos is essentially essentialist. The argument from a single (male) libido is not essentialist because it is not a natural effect of a biological condition.

To say that there are not two libidos is to say that there is no necessary representation of the anatomical distinction between the sexes at the psychic level. Sexual difference *comes* to be represented (and within psychoanalytic theory that representation is in relation to a common third term and that third term is the phallus). Freud very clearly distinguished instinct (*Instinckt*) which is given, from drive (*Trieb*),[1] which can only be known through its mental representative. There is no sexual instinct, only a sexual drive. The question is how sexuality and the polarity masculine/feminine can be represented at the psychic level.

The crucial concept in Freud's theory of representation is the castration complex, for the function of the castration complex is the representation of lack. This implies that the representation of lack is crucial to the function of representation in general. What is the lack that has to be represented? In the Lacanian reading, which makes clear this relation of representation to lack, the concept of the *subject* is central. And the field within which the subject appears is that of language (Lacan, "The function and field of speech and language in psychoanalysis"). The subject is neither a biological entity nor a physical entity. The subject is *not* that individual of the social, political, and theoretical discourses that designate the individual as a fundamental and coherent entity. It is an effect of the signifying chain and it is put in place through the coincidence of the *lack* in the signifying chain and the *lack* in the drive (*Scilicet* I, "La phase phallique"; Lacan, "The partial drive and its circuit"). These terms and the meaning of this coincidence will be explained in detail later in this article. What is important here is that the moment of the appearance of the subject in the signifying chain is also the moment of the differentiation of the unconscious and the conscious. To speak of unconscious sexual representations is thus to presuppose the subject. It will be shown how the putting in place of the subject through the representation of lack is the putting in place of the sexed subject. Sexuality can only be considered at the level of the symbolic processes. This lack is undifferentiated for both sexes and has nothing to do with the absence of a penis, a physical lack.

Nonetheless, the anatomical difference between the sexes does permit a differentiation within the symbolic process. The boy represents lack through the production of the phallic symbol. For him the real organ, the penis, lends itself to symbolization. He can do this, but at the price of his "pound of flesh." It is not the representation of lack by the phallus that is the problem here but the relation posited between the phallus and the real organ, the penis.

The phallus represents lack for both boys and girls. But the boy in having a penis has that which lends itself to the phallic symbol. The girl does not have a penis. What exactly she lacks is not a penis as such, but the means to represent lack. This means that the representation of lack that is the function of the castration complex is not produced for her in the same way as for the boy.

It can then be argued that the anatomical difference between the sexes permits a difference in the representation of the body. The girl's body does not lend itself to symbolization in the same way as the boy's does and Montrelay argues that it thereby remains "unrepresentable." Although this formulation is problematic, it nonetheless marks a difficulty in the conceptualization of feminine sexuality. This difficulty is designated in other ways; through notions of woman's "negative entry" into the symbolic (cf. R. Coward, S. Lipshitz, and E. Cowie), woman's privileged relation to narcissism, to the imaginary (cf. J. Kristeva; J. Rose; L. Irigaray). It is consistently recognized that there is an obstacle to a feminine sexuality ordered in the symbolic. In Montrelay this recognition is linked to the insistence of the real of the woman's body, that real that is by definition outside all symbolization, all representation.

Freud himself had discovered that the girl's passage through the Oedipus complex is more precarious than the boy's. He had attributed this to the fact that she was already castrated. As I have said, this has to be posed as a problem of representation, the problem of how woman in fact does enter castration. This does not treat woman as the already castrated object, but marks the importance of the domain of the symbolic process in which the sexed subject takes its place. The crucial problems are seen to be displaced into problems of representation, lack, and the differential entry of the sexes into these.

Why the relation between phallus and penis? It is said again and again that they must be distinguished from each other. And certainly, the phallus as unconscious representative is not the same thing as a bodily organ. But it is necessary to examine the point at which they are put in relation in psychoanalytic theory.

Lacan insists on the fact that desire is the desire of the Other, that desire being desire for the phallus. The child wishes to be phallus for the mother because her desire is that the child be the phallus for her. It is the step that differentiates between being-the-phallus and having-the-phallus that, in the same movement, differentiates femininity from masculinity. What part does the penis play in this?

The little boy who has the penis will one day accede to the function of the father. In psychoanalytic theory his having the penis explains having-the-phallus as opposed to being-the-phallus (both girl and boy initially *are* the phallus for the mother). What is defining of woman is that she continues to *be* the phallus. Why does the phallus symbolize the penis and not some other organ? The answer, which is necessarily circular, is that the boy, since he has the penis, can accede to that order which symbolically distinguishes between having and being the phallus. The penis is his ticket to masculinity, but the ticket does not determine the category of masculinity itself (nor does it necessitate the taking up of a masculine position). It is in this sense and this sense only that Freud remarks that anatomy is destiny. It does not mean that destiny is anatomical.

This indicates a problem of the hierarchy of categories being employed. Since psychoanalysis aims to displace anatomical determination, the social categories masculinity/femininity must be logically prior to that of the anatomical distinction between the sexes in order for boys and girls to embark upon their masculine and feminine destinies. The category phallus must have priority over the fact of the penis in order to render its possession significant. Yet psychoanalysis sometimes inverts the hierarchy in order to make the orders of masculinity and femininity as permanent and secure as those of anatomical differentiation itself. This leads to an incoherence whose attempted solution sometimes takes the form of an appeal to the mythical moment of the institution of culture and society. But there the categories "man," "woman" are already to be found—the primal father possesses all the women in *Totem and Taboo:* in Lévi-Strauss women are the object of exchange. The mythical moment describes what makes society possible, it is not a description of the difference between societies. Within the psychoanalytic framework the result is that the representation of masculinity and femininity is secured as a privileged object.

Any reply to the question of the privilege of the phallus in terms of the phallus as an effect of patriarchal relations is unsatisfactory. Psychoanalytic theory would argue that the Oedipus complex is not contingent upon limited sets of social and kinship relations. So psychoanalytic theory itself could only conceive patriarchal relations as eternal and that would entail that the centrality of the phallus could never be shifted. Therefore any position that both declares the truth of psychoanalysis and remains dependent on something elsewhere, designated as a noneternal patriarchy, is a contradictory position.

The notion of patriarchy conceived as a set of social relations has no explanatory value and cannot extricate psychoanalysis from the difficulties raised by the relation of the sexual to the social, the subordination of women, etc., which are not themselves deducible from psychoanalytic theory. For it can only be conceived as an epoch, a unity of historical being, a being given in its origins. This unity may be conceived in variant forms (e.g., feudal patriarchy, capitalist patriarchy) but these variants cannot exceed its basic identity.

In fact, psychoanalysis can always resist the importation of the term patriarchy conceived as a set of social relations by demonstrating the necessity of the phallus if the problems of the unconscious and representation are to be dealt with. But this can be done only on one condition, a theoretical condition. That is that the problems can and must be dealt with within an organized space designated as sexuality. The consequence of this is that psychoanalytic theory can speak of the sexual and the social only within the terms set up by the privileging of the sexual.

Even if the theses of psychoanalysis concerning feminine sexuality cannot be ignored, much clarification is needed concerning the reciprocal relations of feminine sexuality and the social relations of its existence. Indeed, even this formulation, specifying the problem in terms, on the one hand, of the realm of the social, on the other, of the realm of the sexual, marks a failure of conceptualization. It has to be noted that this problem stems from the ambiguous status of the concept of sexuality itself within psychoanalysis. Sexuality falls on the cusp of nature and culture. The link between sexuality and society in psychoanalytic theory is a botched affair where sexuality is put in place through the Oedipus complex. This is related to a myth of origin of society as in *Totem and Taboo*. Sexuality enjoys an autonomy that leaves it as a universal phenomenon, untouched by the specific forms of social relations. At the same time, sexuality is conceived as a positioning of the subject within social relations and never simply prior to them. As a consequence, sexuality acquires a contradictory unity because of its apparent nonreducibility to either nature or culture. It may be said to manifest a "relative autonomy" from both. This formulation is current in many theories of determination in historical materialism and should serve as a warning of its unsatisfactory nature.

This fundamental problem, will, of course, affect the specific questions that are at present formulated from the notion of an obstacle to a feminine sexuality in the symbolic. Does this put the woman in a particular relation to the symbolic order as a whole? And does that different relation to the symbolic order have effects outside the domain of sexual pleasure and the sexual relation to the man? Lacan's formulation in terms of the "questions to be posed on the social repercussions of feminine sexuality" ("Propos Directifs pour un Congrès sur la Sexualité Féminine) is equally

subject to the criticism raised above in that social relations are seen as the effect of
the sexual.

    This article attempts to elucidate the meaning of phallocentrism and the claim
for a single, male libido through the concepts made available by Lacan for this work.
This exposition is necessary for Montrelay's work on femininity. She reviews a collection of essays on feminine sexuality that offer clinical evidence in endorsing the
claims of both sides in the Jones-Freud dispute. What is at stake in this dispute is the
form of organization of sexuality. Within the collection it is recognized that feminine
sexuality sets itself up as a function of references to the phallus and at the same time
it is maintained that the woman remains dependent on "the intrication of archaic,
oral, anal and vaginal schemas." Montrelay asks whether the two positions are com-
patible or whether the evidence necessitates the hypothesis of an incompatibility that
is more than the divergence of the two theories. Her contention is that Jones's concentricity (where the girls' experiences of the vagina remain organized as a function
of oral-anal schemas)[2] and Freud's phallocentrism "coexist as incompatible and
that this incompatibility is specific to the feminine unconscious" ("Inquiry into
Femininity").

    Montrelay does not entertain the idea of disposing of the concept of phallo-
centrism as Jones in fact does so easily. Her feminism absolutely does not lead her
to a position of multiplying libidos or positing an essential femininity that will speak
out one day. In fact, it will be argued that all she shares with Jones is a certain description of clinical cases.

    This link, however, leads her to define *femininity* as the blind spot of the sym-
bolic processes; *woman* as the effect of these processes. Then the central question
for her is how this femininity is repressed, allowing the eroticism of woman to be
produced in the symbolic.

    The interest of Montrelay's text lies in her emphasis on this question. To elab-
orate on *femininity* is to specify the limits of what can be known of that which Freud
described as the "dark continent." To elaborate on *woman* is to give an account of
an organization that is necessarily phallocentric but specific to the feminine sex. It
is this specificity within phallocentrism that has been specifically lacking at the theoretical level.

    The limitations of Montrelay's text relate to the difficulty of defining the exact
status of the phallus and the differential relation of the phallus to the body of the man
and to the body of the woman. These problems of the phallus and of the body are
crucial for any feminist critique of sexuality.

Lack and the Subject

JONES AND FREUD

The Jones-Freud controversy is precisely about the problem of essential femininity and the phallus. The difference between Jones and Freud turns crucially on the place of the sexual *organ* in the theoretical account of masculinity and femininity. For in Jones's work there is a biological determination founded on the organ. For Freud, on the other hand, the organ receives its place in the psychic economy through the function of the castration complex, the representation of lack. This difference is directly related to the two opposing positions taken up in the controversy. On the one hand, a given feminine organization of sexuality related to early knowledge of the vagina is posited, and on the other, an organization of sexuality constructed in the symbolic. Some essential points can be specified:

For Jones:

1. The real organ has a direct effectivity.
2. There is a masculine libido *and* a specific feminine libido.
3. Penis envy in the girl is a secondary reaction against femininity.
4. In the course of the child's development there is an "adaptation to reality," which involves the growing possibility of the satisfaction of need.
5. This "adaptation to reality" enables the girl to "express" her femininity without fear, after the phallic phase.

For Freud:

1. The real organ finds its place through the representation of lack.
2. There is only one libido and it is male.
3. The girl is precipitated into penis envy by the path leading through lack.
4. The endlessly renewed search for the lost object makes the notion of satisfaction highly problematic. The drive is something other than need and there is something in the nature of the sexual drive that is resistant to satisfaction.
5. There is no essential femininity to be expressed. The feminine is an outcome of the Oedipus complex organized according to the phallic dialectic.

For Jones woman is born, not made; femininity is innate and natural. This thesis relies on the reduction of the masculine and the feminine to the biological sexual polarity. In "La Phase Phallique," (*Scilicet* I) it is argued on Freud's side that

it is obvious that analytic experience has no point of contact, demonstrates no direct connection with a bipolarity of the sexes such as would be given in nature ... the facts show that analysis tackles the question from a completely, and strictly subjective angle—we would say: from the angle of a subjective declaration of sex ... but if his (Jones') point of view strikes us as more naturalist than biologist, it is so in so far as biology itself seems to have progressed only by distancing itself from the affirmation of sexual bipolarity, separating it, e.g., into heterogeneous levels (chromosomes, hormonal levels, primary and secondary sexual characteristics) which leave room for some discontinuities and some questions concerning what is involved in a clear division into male and female.

Freud himself had affirmed that the only bipolarity at the psychic level was that of activity and passivity and that the masculine and the feminine were not to be assimilated to that opposition. If there is no necessary representation of the male being and the female being at the level of the psychic, an explanation of the mechanism by which sexuality installs itself in the field of the subject is required.

SUBJECT AND SIGNIFYING CHAIN

The concept of the subject for Lacan is crucially dependent on language. Language is understood as a system that preexists the subject and the subject is produced in the entry into language. The subject is constituted as the effect of the signifying chain and the place of the signifying chain, that is, language, that orders the appearance of the subject is the *Other*. "The Other is the locus in which is situated the chain of the signifier that governs whatever may be made present of the subject—it is the field of that living being in which the subject has to appear" (Lacan, "The Subject and the Other: Alienation"). The field of the Other is the field in which meaning is produced. Meaning is only possible when the subject constituted within the signifying chain situates itself as a sexed subject in the field of the Other.

Lacan's diagram illustrates how the subject is made present in language. The constant appearance and disappearance of the subject in language is described as the operation of alienation; "the operation of the realization of the subject in his signifying dependence in the locus of the Other" (Lacan, *ibid.*). The effect of this alienation is to produce a divided subject, a subject who appears only in the division: appearance (meaning) and disappearance. It is not a question of the appearance *or* the disappearance of the subject; it is always a question of both.

The field of being, the field of meaning and the area of union—the area of non-meaning—are illustrated below. What is involved is a situation of choice where, no

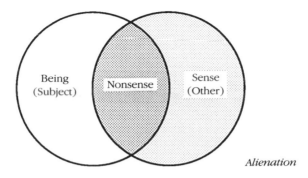

Alienation

matter what the choice, its consequence is a choice that is neither the one nor the other. Lacan uses the example *Your money or your life*! If the choice is money, both money and life are forfeit; if the choice is life, it is a life deprived of something, of money.

> Let us illustrate this with what we are dealing with here, namely, the being of the subject, that which is there beneath the meaning. If we choose being, the subject disappears, it eludes us, it falls into non-meaning. If we choose meaning, the meaning survives only deprived of that part of non-meaning that is, strictly speaking, that which constitutes in the realization of the subject, the unconscious. In other words, it is of the nature of this meaning, as it emerges in the field of the Other, to be in a large part of its field, eclipsed by the disappearance of being, induced by the very function of the signifier. (Lacan, *ibid.*)

What is meant, then, by the division of the subject is that the subject is constantly present and constantly fading. This is because of the structure of language. There is no preexisting meaning in language—only the differences between signifiers. The subject is produced in the signifying chain but the subject is only ever a signifier for another signifier. The subject, being no more than a signifier, "petrifies" in the same movement in which it is called to function as subject. This petrification, disappearance, fading is the *lack in the subject*.

The constitution of the subject in division is produced in the same movement as the constitution of the conscious and the unconscious. But the unconscious is more than this division. The subject not only arises in the field of the Other, but comes back on the field of the Other, effecting the superimposition of two lacks, the lack in the subject and the lack in the signifying chain, in the Other. From this emerges a further operation, which Lacan calls separation.[3] It is through the operation of separation that the subject locates the lack in the Other, in the interval between two signifiers. What has been said of the appearance and disappearance of the subject in the signifying chain is true of the Other as subject (in the first instance the Other as mother). And it is through the gaps and lapses in the discourse of the Other that the child finds the Other as a divided subject and the desire of the Other. The desire of the Other remains unknown in so far as something escapes articulation. It is at this point of lack that the subject rediscovers its lack, its disappearance. And it is at this point that the desire of the subject is born.

REPRESENTATION AND DESIRE

The lack in the first Other is the lack in the mother. The recognition of this lack is the recognition of her castration, of the fact that she does not have the phallus. The lack in the Other marks an instability of meaning that is of the nature of language itself; language being only the differences between signifiers. This instability corresponds to a fictional state (cf. Laplanche and Leclaire, "The Unconscious"), where the signifying chain produces a constant sliding of the signified under the signifier. This is the primary process Freud identified in the dreamwork. Stable meanings are only established by "key-signifiers" that have the property of ordering the whole chain of signifiers. Through the operation of metaphor a signifier S' is substituted for a given signifier S, which has the effect of maintaining S as a latent, unconscious signifier (Lacan, "The Agency of the Letter in the Unconscious or Reason since Freud").

The "key-signifier," Name-of-the-Father, put in a metaphorizing position through the Oedipus complex, produces the phallus as unconscious signifier. The Name-of-the-Father and thus paternal law is introduced through the representation of castration: through the production of the phallus as signifier. Thus the relations within the symbolic, including the prohibition on incest, determine the ordering of language. This ordering is given through the placing of the subject in the symbolic. It is in this sense that the Oedipus complex is the determining moment of the entry into language.

The phallic signifier ensures the fixing of meaning by setting itself up as unconscious representative. It is through the network of the signifier that the unconscious and the conscious are distinguished and desire emerges (the metaphorizing function is another way of describing the operations of alienation and separation). "The phallus is the privileged signifier of that mark in which the role of the logos is joined with the advent of desire" (Lacan, "The Signification of the Phallus"). Desire emerges through the putting in place of the phallic signifier, that is, through representation, the representation of lack (of the phallus). For representation is what produces the object as lost, re-presented but never present in the fullness, the plenitude of the mother/child dyad, a plenitude in which there is no subject. Freud had identified both the breast and the mother as lost object. The Oedipal prohibition on the child's incestuous relation with the mother is the definitive moment of representation and hence the moment of desire. The prohibition on the incestuous relation with the mother effected through representation is a prohibition on "enjoyment" (*jouissance*) of the mother. The phallus as signifier allows desire to emerge and prohibits *jouissance*.

The foregoing is a less familiar account of the Oedipus complex than the customary one. What has been said is that paternal law is to be identified in the "key-signifier" Name-of-the-Father, and it is this signifier that, in producing the phallus as unconscious representative, constitutes *jouissance* as prohibited. But this is at the same time to constitute the mother as the prohibited object, the lost object. Desire is by definition unfulfillable; representation ensures that the lost object remains lost. This links back to Freud's observation that there is something in the nature of the sexual drive that is resistant to satisfaction (where Jones had maintained the possibility of a growing satisfaction of need).

Thus, against Jones who assigned a direct effectivity to the real sexual organ, the Lacanian argument is that the real organ finds its place through the representation of lack. It is the phallic symbol that is placed at the point of the Other's lack. And it is here that the real organ, the penis is placed: "in order that its symbol can take the place of the signifier of this very point where the signifier is wanting; that is the price the subject must pay for his access to the world of desire" ("La Phase Phallique"). In other words, the *male* child's recognition of the lack in the mother, of her castration, produces the possibility of his castration, of the absence of his penis. It is only the possibility of this absence that allows the penis to be represented as present, to be produced as a signifier.

THE SEXUAL DRIVE AND THE BODY

It is clear that the anatomical difference between having and not having a penis permits a disparity in the symbolic process. Nonetheless, *it is a phallic mark that constitutes desire,* which is the meaning of Freud's claim that there is only one, male, libido.

To fully explain how "sexuality installs itself in the field of the subject by a path which is that of lack," it is necessary to show how a prior lack, the lack in the drive, in sexuality, coincides with the lack in the signifying chain. For it is through this coincidence that the drive can function in the unconscious, that the drive can manifest itself in the subject, thus establishing the relation between sexuality, subject, and lack. This is not fully taken up in this article but see Lacan, "The Partial Drive and its Circuit," and "Position de L'inconscient."

Here the question is about the way in which the drive relates to the phallic signifier, to the penis, and to the body. Freud established the importance of the erotogenic zones in infantile sexuality ("Three Essays on Sexuality"). The sexual drive (libido) is only partially represented by the erotogenic zones, that is by apertures at certain anatomical sites (mouth, anus, etc.). Freud also insisted that the drive had no object intrinsic to it. Precisely because drive is not instinct, the original object of the hunger instinct (milk) is *not* the object of the oral drive that is derived from it. The drive is formed in relation to the object that produces milk, the breast, but the breast is not the object of the drive in the same sense as milk is the object of the hunger instinct. The breast as object is what Lacan calls *objet petit a* (small object a). The drive can attain satisfaction only by the return of the trajectory of the drive around *objet petit a* onto the erotogenic zone. The pleasure obtained by the oral drive is the stimulation of the erotogenic zone, the mouth. The infantile sexual aim can only be the return of the drive onto the erotogenic zone.

The trajectory traced around *objet petit a* is like the trajectory proper to the signifying order. At first, the trajectory of the signifier has no object and no limit—there is only the ceaseless sliding of the signified under the signifier, pure primary process before the fixing of meaning through the phallus as signifier. But this is to say that it is only when the trajectory of the signifier bends around the absent and desired phallus and returns to the erotogenic zone that a limit is placed on it. In this way the trajectory of the signifier is "eroticized." It is the body, through the erotogenic zones, that restricts the trajectory of the signifier. This return onto the erotogenic zone is ultimately a function of the absent and desired phallus as discussed in the preceding section. The absent and desired phallus is the signifier that is lacking in the Other, that which will come to find its signifier in the phallic signifier. And it is a part of the body, the penis, which will be raised to the function of signifier.

The positing of a coincidence between the lack in the drive, for which the mother's breast is taken as prototype, and the lack in the signifying chain, raises again the question of how the phallus comes to represent all other forms of lack and severance. Within psychoanalytic theory desire is always the desire of the Other and the desire of the Other is desire of the phallus. But this is merely to repeat that that desire emerges from representation, more specifically, from the production of the phallic signifier which is always the signifier of the absent and desired phallus.

Within the theory, the structural homology between the lack in the drive and the lack in the signifying chain permits a definitive representation of lack only when the penis no longer belongs but circulates as a signifier for an other. The circulation of the penis as a signifier limits the ceaseless sliding of the signified under the signifier, thus ordering language and producing the subject as sexed subject. However, the fixing of meaning is never final: Barthes has emphasized the process of *signifiance,* the free play of signifiers in which the subject "struggles with meaning" and is "lost." This concept will be taken up later in relation to Montrelay's elaboration of feminine *jouissance.* For the girl's relation to language and to the body is seen to differ from the boy's inasmuch as the girl does not pay the price of her own body to produce the signifier of desire.

As has been shown, sexuality is installed in the subject through the path of lack, at the point where the signifier of signifiers, the signifier of desire, the phallic signifier is produced. Nonetheless, the structural homology works itself out differently for the two sexes. Yet this divergence does not mean that there are two libidos. The question of whether the subject is a man or a woman can only be referred to the representation of lack as the phallus. It should be clear by this point that this is the meaning of phallocentrism. The child of both sexes identifies with the mother's lack and thus with the imaginary object of the mother's desire—the phallus. The boy, by constructing the phallic signifier with a part of his own body, *has* it and ceases to *be* it. The girl can only continue to *be* the phallus. It is this that makes her a woman. This continuing identification accounts for the girl = phallus equation put forward by Fenichel, which means the girl's body as phallus remains outside the symbolic process.

Language is guaranteed by the boy's entry into castration and the production of the phallic signifier. The signifier of signifiers, by filling in the loss of the Other, produces the possibility of exchange at the symbolic level—at this level it is the phallus that is exchanged ("La Phase Phallique"). Exchange at the symbolic level represses the auto-erotic and incestuous enjoyment of *jouissance,* which is constituted as prohibited. The level of fixed meanings around the phallus represses *jouissance,* the fading, the loss of the subject. In this sense, the phallic symbol is constructed out of male *jouissance.*

The girl = phallus equation means that for her *jouissance* is not constituted as prohibited. However, it will be seen that the woman cannot partake of this auto-erotic, incestuous *jouissance*. Feminine *jouissance* has to be constituted elsewhere.

Montrelay and Feminine Jouissance

Montrelay attempts to specify feminine *jouissance,* avoiding the mistake of many concerned with feminine sexuality who would demand that women hold onto the auto-erotic, the pre-Oedipal. This solution to the dilemma of the woman in relation to phallocentrism assigns her to a regressive and psychotic space and forms the basis of a separatist politics and the notion of a "world" of women. Some aspects of this can be seen in an interview with Luce Irigaray, "Women's Exile" and in the recent film by Laura Mulvey and Peter Wollen, *Riddles of the Sphinx* (U.K., 1977).

Man and woman are both in the symbolic, constituted there through the representation of lack which is the function of the castration complex. Montrelay recognizes this when she designates the first representation as a castrating representation. This makes desire possible. Thus Montrelay says that "to desire is to represent the lacking object (the mother), that is to say, to "enjoy" (*"jouir"*) exclusively in the form of words" ("Inquiry into Femininity").

What Montrelay is interested in is the conditions under which representation fails. Here Montrelay distinguishes the case of the man and that of the woman. For the man, representation fails when the prohibition on incest fails—carnal knowledge of the mother is the realization, hence the annihilation of desire. For the woman, this habitually happens when, as object of the lover's desire, she recovers herself as maternal body and as phallus. Here representation is threatened by the real of the body. In both cases the lost object does not remain lost.

For Montrelay it is the condition of woman that representation habitually fails and it is this that has to be surpassed. It manifests itself in the "empty circulation" of words, in the failure of the discourse itself. Montrelay attempts to put this in relation to *femininity* and the *jouissance* that remains unrepressed in the woman. She describes a possible state of discourse in which, simultaneously, everything and nothing is said, where it appears empty of meaning and full of its materiality, only apparently symbolic. She also describes the effects of this seeming discourse in a woman patient:

> She does not know that the presence of the statement has become the
> real presence of her own body. That which resounds, so full yet so empty,
> unknown to her, is her femininity, or rather a certain sort of femininity,

where the body and discourse are confounded because they remain on this side of desire: in the Other.

There, where there is *jouissance,* real, to infinity, but there also where it cannot be appropriated. On the one hand, the body-word of Cecile says all, knows all, because it has been seized by this *jouissance,* on the other hand, the subject Cecile is expropriated from it: in the phase of the analysis when the statement becomes real, the body is there, but as Other. Castration, that is to say, the operation of detachment which would turn a little of this *jouissance* to Cecile's account, has no place. ("Parole de Femme sur le Transfert de L'hystérique")

There are two important questions in this account of the failure of representation. The first concerns the status of *femininity* in Montrelay's text. This is the point of Montrelay's support for Jones, through which she posits the coexistence of concentricity and phallocentrism in the feminine unconscious.

Femininity is defined as "the set of the 'feminine' drives (oral, anal, vaginal) in so far as these resist the processes of repression." In Montrelay's text *femininity* is an obstacle to the symbolic. But must *femininity* be positivized in this way? Even if there is early knowledge of the vagina, is this different from early knowledge of the mouth or the anus? Do we have to posit some *thing, femininity* that is the blind-spot of the symbolic process? Can precocious femininity not be constituted as the effect, not the cause of the failure to fully assume symbolic castration? This would put *femininity* in a different relation to the problem of the representation of the woman's body.

It is Montrelay's concept of *femininity* that bolsters Jones's thesis of a "precocious" organization of sexuality centered on a ceaseless oral, vaginal incorporation. But even if the concept of *femininity* is allowed, the implications of the thesis are wildly divergent. For Jones conceptualizes a femininity that can express itself and he attempts to make it "speak." Montrelay, on the other hand, designates Freud's achievement as the discovery of how to repress femininity: "we can ask whether psychoanalysis was not articulated precisely in order to repress femininity (in the sense of producing its symbolic repression)" ("Inquiry into Femininity").

How can *femininity* account for the "unrepresentability" of the body? There can be no representation outside the symbolic. Hence there cannot be a representation of *femininity,* an alternative form of representation that stands against the representation of lack. How *femininity* can otherwise function as an obstacle to the symbolic process is never elucidated. The coexistence of concentricity and phallocentrism, which Montrelay sees as defining of the feminine unconscious, remains an untheorized incompatibility.

However, the central difficulty in Montrelay's work on feminine sexuality does not concern *femininity* but the very concept of the "unrepresentable" body that she attempts to derive from *femininity*. Since the woman enters the symbolic through the representation of lack, what can it mean to say that the body nevertheless remains outside representation, outside the symbolic? No signified whatsoever can be produced except through language that involves castrating representations. The body must be signified through the entry into language. To speak of a body already organized sexually (i.e., concentrically) but which is not represented is to set up the unrepresented as already constituted outside of representation.

The problem with the concept of the body in Montrelay's work will become clearer in the following discussion of the production of feminine *jouissance*—the second question raised by the quotation above. Montrelay holds that the woman retains a certain direct relation to *jouissance*. Necessarily, there is no subject there to partake of it. It is only through castration that *jouissance* will be turned to the subject's account. Montrelay attempts to show how this castration is achieved.

She defines the "adult" woman as "one who reconstructs her sexuality in a field which goes beyond sex." This reconstruction means that all relation to *jouissance* is now of a sublimatory kind. Sublimation is defined as "an operation which consists in opening up new divisions and spaces in the material that it transforms."[4] It is the operation of metaphor that Freud used to explain the joke and the production of pleasure.

Montrelay distinguishes between a concentric economy of desire and a sublimated economy of desire. It follows that precocious pleasure and orgasm are to be distinguished from sublimated pleasure and orgasm. The former reactualizes the *jouissance* the woman has of herself and produces anxiety; the latter confirms the woman's access to the symbolic.

The distinction between concentric pleasure and sublimated pleasure is closely related to the problematic relation of woman's body to representation and hence to the representation of castration. There are always preconditions for pleasure (Montrelay's sublimated pleasure), preconditions that are precisely those of prohibition, repression, the representation of castration. It is the establishment of the secondary process that guarantees the stability of the pleasure principle (which governs the primary process) by setting limits on the play of the primary process. These limits are set by the stabilization of meaning through the operations described above. To the extent that something in the woman is resistant to symbolization, the preconditions for pleasure (Montrelay's sublimated pleasure) are absent. The pleasure that is possible in this case (Montrelay's concentric pleasure) is always problematic—in the woman it produces anxiety. (For the problem of pleasure in the man see Leclaire, "The Economic Standpoint—Recent Views").

Montrelay does not merely say that pleasure presupposes these operations; she identifies pleasure with these operations. She begins with an account of the pleasure that can be engendered in the analytic situation. The analyst can provide a representation of castration and thus produce repression. Sometimes this is followed by the analysand having a dream in which she has an orgasm. This effect of pleasure is explained by comparing it to the pleasure produced by the joke whose mechanism Freud elucidated in terms of metaphor. In the analytic situation metaphor is produced by the substitution of the analyst's text for the patient's text. Montrelay identifies pleasure as the meaning of metaphor. Pleasure lies *"in putting the dimension of repression into play on the level of the text itself"* ("Inquiry into Femininity").

All sublimation comes about through this pleasure of the joke. Just as the joke produces laughter, so the metaphor set up by the analyst's discourse produces the orgasm.

It is implicit in the argument that the analyst produces the representation of the concentrically organized body through its "repression." For Montrelay, this is a castrating representation. The body is thus assigned the function of lack. But the body itself is not lack. On the contrary, in Montrelay it is a fullness. However, the analogy with lack is the basis of Montrelay's account of feminine *jouissance* in the symbolic. Just as there is a relation between the representation of lack and the subject, so there is a relation between the representation of the body and the feminine subject of *jouissance*. But if the body is the effect of metaphor, why is the woman's body not "repressed" from the moment of the constituting metaphor, that is, the entry into language?

The relation between the representation of the body and the subject of *jouissance* is explicated in Montrelay's specification of the sexual act as another situation in which the woman can have sublimated pleasure and orgasm. The precocious form of orgasm bars access to the symbolic, leaving the woman locked into *jouissance*. There is no turning away from *jouissance* because there is no "representation" of the body. In the sublimated form of orgasm, the penis submits the body to a signifying articulation and pleasure and orgasm open out into the play of signifiers. This play of signifiers is a process, a production, a struggle with meaning. Thus "the act

of articulating produces on its own the meaning of the discourse, (meaning nothing)" ("Inquiry into Femininity"). The body of the woman can be "repressed" to produce sublimated pleasure and orgasm, which are in the field of the signifier.

Montrelay is arguing that feminine jouissance is like *écriture. Ecriture* is the
same as *signifiance* in Barthes's distinction between signification and *signifiance.*
Signification belongs to the realm of meanings fixed within society; *signifiance*
belongs to the realm of production through the play of signifiers:

> when the text is read (or written) as a moving play of signifiers, without
> any possible reference to one or some fixed signified, it becomes nec-
> essary to distinguish signification, which belongs to the plane of the
> product, of the enounced, of communication, and the work of the sig-
> nifier, which belongs to the plane of production, of the enunciation, of
> symbolisation—this work being called *signifiance. Signifiance* is a proc-
> ess in the course of which the "subject" of the text, escaping the logic of
> the *ego-cogito* and engaging in other logics (of the signifier, of contra-
> diction), struggles with meaning and is deconstructed ("lost") (quoted in
> Barthes, *Image—Music—Text*).

Signifiance is to be identified with the pleasure of *jouissance*. The "loss," the "disappearance" of the subject in *signifiance* is the production of *jouissance* within the
symbolic. The feminine subject can partake of this *jouissance* in the sexual act. The
sublimated orgasm produces the "disappearance" of the feminine subject and differs
from the precocious orgasm where the body remains "unrepresentable" and outside
discourse.

Montrelay's account of the *jouissance* of the "adult" woman clearly does not
rely on any notion of the expression of an essential femininity. Rather, it emphasizes
the necessity of relating the sexual act to the phallic signifier. Her position is thus
diametrically opposed to that of Jones, which relies on the notion of a genital maturation that takes place through a growing "adaptation to reality." Nonetheless, Montrelay's attempt to theorize the production of feminine *jouissance* fails. It
necessitates the production of the subject in two ways, analagous yet distinct. Here,
the production of the subject of feminine *jouissance* necessitates a theoretical priority of the body. The subject appears as a disembodied effect of the body.

The concept of the body remains extremely difficult for psychoanalytic or any
other theory to deal with. Yet it is not a problem that can be dismissed. Perhaps the
enigma of the woman is indeed to be conceived, not in terms of her relation to language but in terms of her relation to her body. The failure of the discourse Montrelay

speaks of in "Parole de Femme sur le Transfert de L'hystérique" has been identified by others including Robert Fliess in his "Silence and Verbalisation." Both authors relate what is happening at the level of speech to the body: Montrelay relates it to the real of the body, Fliess relates it to erotogenic zones. And perhaps it is not accidental that Fliess's "oral-erotic silence" and Montrelay's failure of the discourse are both illustrated with female hysteric patients.

I am indebted to Mark Cousins for critical discussions of certain psychoanalytic concepts which have helped me to write the first section of this article.

Notes

1.   In the English *Standard Edition* of Freud, *Trieb* is misleadingly translated as instinct.
2.   In Montrelay's "Inquiry into Femininity" the terms concentricity and precocious sexuality "turn" around a single orifice, "an organ that is both digestive and vaginal, which ceaselessly tends to absorb, to appropriate, to devour. We find again here the theme of concentricity."
3.   "*Separare*, to separate—I would point out at once the equivocation of the *se parare*, of the *se parer*, in all the fluctuating meanings it has in French. It means not only to dress oneself, but also to defend oneself, to provide oneself with what one needs to be on one's guard, and I will go further still, and Latinists will bear me out, to the *se parere*, the *s'engendrer*, the *to be engendered*, which is involved here. How, at this level, has the subject to procure himself? For that is the origin of the word that designates in Latin *to engender*. It is juridical, as indeed, curiously enough, are all the words in Indo-European that designate *to put into the world*. The word *parturition* itself originates in a word which, in its root, simply means to procure a child from the husband—a juridical and, it should be said, social operation." (Lacan, "The Subject and the Other: Alienation")
4.   This use of the term sublimation differs from Freud's.

References

R. Barthes, *Image-Music-Text,* trans. S. Heath, Fontana, 1977.

R. Coward, S. Lipshitz, and E. Cowie, "Psychoanalysis and Patriarchal Structures," *Papers on Patriarchy,* London Conference, 1976, Women's Publishing Collective, Lewes, 1977.

R. Fliess, "Silence and Verbalisation: A Supplement to the Theory of the 'Analytic Rule'," *International Journal of Psychoanalysis,* vol. XXX (1949).

S. Freud, "Three Essays on Sexuality," *The Standard Edition of the Complete Psychological Works of Sigmund Freud,* vol. VII, Hogarth, 1905.

K. Horney, *Feminine Psychology,* Routledge and Kegan Paul, 1967.

L. Irigaray, "Women's Exile," *Ideology & Consciousness,* no. 1 (1977).

E. Jones, "The Early Development of Female Sexuality," *IJP,* vol. VIII (1927).

E. Jones, "The Phallic Phase," *IJP,* vol. XIV (1933).

E. Jones, "Early Female Sexuality," *IJP,* vol. XVI (1935).

J. Kristeva, *Polylogue,* Seuil, 1977.

J. Lacan, "Propos directifs pour un congrès sur la sexualité féminine," *Ecrits,* Seuil, 1966; trans. in J. Mitchell and J. Rose (eds.), *Feminine Sexuality: Jacques Lacan and the école freudienne,* Macmillan, 1982.

J. Lacan, "Position de l'inconscient," *Ecrits,* Seuil, 1966.

J. Lacan, "The Agency of the Letter in the Unconscious or Reason Since Freud"; "The Function and Field of Speech and Language in Psychoanalysis"; and "The Signification of the Phallus," *Ecrits: A Selection,* trans. A. Sheridan, Tavistock, 1977.

J. Lacan, "The Subject and the Other: Alienation"; "The Partial Drive and Its Circuit," *The Four Fundamental Concepts of Psycho-Analysis,* trans. A. Sheridan, Hogarth, 1977.

J. Laplanche and S. Leclaire, "The Unconscious: A Psychoanalytic Study," *Yale French Studies,* 1972.

S. Leclaire, "The Economic Standpoint—Recent Views," *IJP,* vol. 45 (1964).

M. Montrelay, "Parole de femme sur le transfert de l'hystérique"; "Le rejeton de la pulsion," *L'ombre et le nom,* Minuit, 1977.

M. Montrelay, "Inquiry into Femininity," trans. P. Adams, this volume.

J. Rose, "Paranoia and the Film System," *Screen,* vol. 17, no. 4 (1976–1977).

Scilicet, "La Phase phallique," *Scilicet* I, 1968 (articles in this series were published anonymously); trans. in J. Mitchell and J. Rose (eds.), *Feminine Sexuality: Jacques Lacan and the école freudienne,* 1977.

from *m/f* 1, 1978

MICHÈLE MONTRELAY

> ... *like all women you think with your*
> *sex, not with your mind.*
>
> —A. Artaud

Why was the theory of femininity in psychoanalysis articulated from the start in the form of an alternative? What does it mean for analysts that they must choose between two contradictory conceptions of women: that of Jones and that of Freud?

The posing of these questions makes it necessary to recall briefly the contents of the two doctrines and the basis of their incompatibility. For Freud, libido is identical in the two sexes. Moreover, it is always male in essence. For it is the clitoris, an external and erectile part of the body, and hence homologous to the penis, which is the girl's erotic organ. And when, at the moment of the Oedipus complex, she desires a child from the father, this new object is again invested with a phallic value: the baby is nothing but a substitute for the penile organ of which the girl now knows she is deprived. Thus feminine sexuality is constantly elaborated as a function of phallic reference.[1]

For Jones, and for the English school (Klein, Horney, Muller), feminine libido is specific. From the start, the girl privileges the interior of the body and the vagina: hence the archaic experiences of femininity which leave an indelible trace. It is therefore not enough to give an account of feminine sexuality from a "phallocentric" point of view. It is also necessary to measure the impact that anatomy, and the sexual organ itself, has on the girl's unconscious.[2]

Thus Jones and his school were answering the Viennese school when they proposed the precocious, even innate character of femininity. Freud spoke of one libido, whereas Jones distinguished two types of libidinal organization, male and female.

Forty years have passed: the problem of femininity continues to be posed on the basis of the Jones-Freud contradiction. Can this contradiction in fact be surpassed?

PHALLOCENTRISM AND CONCENTRICITY

The investigations conducted by Smirgel and a team of analysts, published as the *Recherches psychanalytiques nouvelles sur la sexualité féminine,* have recently shown that it is possible to get past the contradiction. It is an advance which is possible from the moment one abandons all polemical preoccupation and sticks to clinical practice.

Predictably, the book starts with a detailed analysis of the confrontation of the two schools. But having completed the history of this long and burning dispute and disengaged its parameters, the authors do not take sides. Leaving the scene of the debate, they take us to the analyst's: there where the one who speaks is no longer the mouthpiece of a school, but the patient on the couch.

It is rare to be given an account of large fragments of the cure; still more rare for it to be given à propos of feminine cases. Here we have the freedom to follow the discourse of female patients in analysis in its rhythm, its style, and its meanderings. We are taken into the interior of the space that this discourse circumscribes, a space that is that of the unconscious where, as Freud has seen, negation does not exist, where consequently the terms of a contradiction, far from excluding one another, coexist and overlap. In fact, anyone who tries to take bearings from these researches is referred to Freud *and* to Jones. For this book not only talks of femininity according to Freud, but it also makes it speak in an immediate way that one does not forget. An *odor di femina* arises from it, which cannot be explained without reference to the work of the English and Viennese.

Thus the *Recherches* calls for a double locating, which is worth explicating at greater length here. Let us return to Freud: the essential modalities of the organization of feminine desire cannot be grasped without taking up in its own right the idea of phallocentrism so decried by Freud's contemporaries. The book makes constant and explicit reference to it—but specifying that the phallus cannot be identified with the penis. In fact, far from signifying an anatomical reality, the phallus designates, according to this book, the ideas and values that the penile organ represents. By freeing the concept of the phallus from the organic context with which it is still often confounded, the authors enable us truly to grasp the nature of phallocentrism: "There is every reason for separating the study of penis-envy from any consideration of the penis itself as a thing."[3] It is necessary, on the contrary, to specify the ideal dimension to which the male organ refers: "penis-envy is always envy of the idealized penis."[4]

Simultaneously, the models that are put forward in order to account for feminine desire make clear on the clinical level the real implications of "phallocentrism": the authors are not fooled by a patient who declares herself impotent and humiliated on the pretext that she is "only a woman." The penis envy latent in these remarks is not reducible to an instinct. It is impossible to legitimate it "through an alleged state of castration for which phylogenesis would bear the responsibility."[5]

On the contrary, the desire for the penis can be analyzed only in as much as it arises from a complex elaboration, constructed in order to maintain the phallic power of the father. Only those patients whose fathers' prestige and symbolic status had been threatened posit the possession of the penile organ as indispensable. Their sufferings and their symptoms appear in order to make plain that the essential is withdrawn from them, namely, the penis confounded in the imagination with the phallus. Thus the phallic power of the father is fantasmatically assured.

In the other accounts of homosexual or "normal" women, in every case, a particular form of relation to the paternal phallus can be traced, in which it is always a question of maintaining an inaccessible term, so that desire can subsist. It is a subtly constructed relation, but one that does not differ in its nature from that set up by the man: as the detailed account of a masculine case of perversion makes clear enough.[6]

In showing that desire is only ever pure artifice, the book thereby discards the hypothesis of the innateness of desire that the English school had advanced in relation to femininity. It confirms the correctness of Freud's reservations in regard to this "natural" femininity on which Jones insisted so much.[7]

And yet the *Recherches* takes up the main point of the clinical work of the English school. The article by Grunberger, especially, insists on the specifically *concentric* organization of feminine sexuality.[8] He shows that it is as if the woman, more so than the man, remains dependent on the drives, in which the authors see, like Jones, the intrication of archaic, oral, anal, and vaginal schemas.

"Often, for the little girl, it is the mouth which takes up symbolically, and for reasons on which Jones has insisted, the value of a vaginal organ," Luquet-Parat remarks.[9] And further on Maria Torok develops the theory of the English school:

> M. Klein, E. Jones and K. Horney have indicated long before we did, the precocity of the child's discovery and repression of vaginal sensations. We, for our part, have observed that the encounter with the other sex was

always a reminder of the awakening of our own. Clinically, penis-envy and the discovery of the sex of the boy are often seen associated with a repressed memory of orgasmic experiences.[10]

Thus two theoretical positions, hitherto considered incompatible, are both verified within the framework of a clinical study. The Jones-Freud contradiction therefore appears to be surpassed.

THE CONTRADICTION DISPLACED

But this transcendence remains implicit. The authors never formulate it as the outcome or culmination of their work. Let us look at these few lines where Grunberger analyses feminine narcissism, "That which," characterizes "... the libidinal cathexis of the woman, is its concentric character *and* at the same time the phallus."[11]

To simultaneously affirm the "concentric" and phallic character of feminine sexuality is to declare that both Freud and Jones are right. But surely it then becomes necessary to formulate a new point of view through which the truth of the two schools would be maintained?

This point of view is not formulated within the framework of the book; rather, the Freud-Jones contradiction seems to gradually lose its relevance in the face of clinical practice. And yet the verification of two incompatible propositions does not do away with the contradiction that links them. The fact that phallocentrism and concentricity may be equally constitutive of feminine sexuality does not prove that they make up a harmonious unit. It is my contention, that, on the contrary, they coexist as incompatible and that it is this incompatibility that is specific to the feminine unconscious.

Thus the most important thing about this work, that is, the displacement to which the authors submit the basic contradiction, is not sufficiently brought out. They should have stressed that the Freud-Jones incompatibility, although it was first articulated as a polemic, is far more than a disagreement of two schools. For, once this disagreement and the passions it arouses have subsided, the contradiction emerges again as a play of forces which structures the feminine unconscious itself. Phallocentrism and concentricity, both simultaneously constitutive of the unconscious, confront each other according to two modes: the first, the more spectacular, appears as *anxiety*; but the same relation of forces plays, inversely, in *sublimation*. Each of these determining processes of the unconscious economy will be seen at play in the incompatibility of the two aspects of femininity analyzed by Jones and Freud.

The Dark Continent

THE REPRESENTATION OF CASTRATION

Let us start with anxiety in general, from what we know of this state insofar as it is common to both sexes. This global approach will allow us to situate better in what follows the specifically feminine processes of anxiety.

Anxiety in psychoanalysis is most often described as "castration anxiety," that is to say, as the horror that seizes the child on discovering the penis-less body of the mother. It is this discovery that engenders the fear of one day undergoing the same fate.

It is true that in each cure, the analyst must reckon with the "imprescriptable" force of this fear of mutilation.[12] But this is not anxiety: to represent to oneself the motive of one's fear, is already to give a reason for it. But anxiety is *without reason*. What we mean is that it supposes the impossibility of any rational thought. In other words, anxiety appears as the limit-moment when conscious and unconscious representation are blocked off.

How are we to analyze this blockage? By specifying at first the nature of the representation that is its object. Three positions based on Lacanian theory will serve us as points of reference:

1. The unconscious is a structure or combinatory of desires articulated as representations.

2. These representations can be called representations of castration, inasmuch as their literal articulation effectively deprives the subject of a part of *jouissance*.[i]

3. The stake is this *jouissance,* whose loss is the price of representation.

Let us take these three propositions:

1. Unconscious representation, which is what this article is concerned with, refers to different processes from those currently designated by the term "representation." The latter, ordinarily, concerns the conscious; it explains the reflexive activity that applies itself to the reality of the (philosophic) subject and to objects. Unconscious representation, on the contrary, neither reflects nor signifies the subject and its objects. It is a pure cathexis of the word as such. How is this possible? An

example will make it clear to us: consider the distinction between conscious and unconscious representations of castration.

2. The conscious representation of castration in the child does not designate any real mutilation. It is an imaginary evocation: either it is the other who threatens by uttering a prohibition (the case of the boy); or the little girl in order to explain the absence of the penis to herself imagines: "someone must have taken it from me."

Such a representation takes on an unconscious status at the moment at which it no longer refers to anything but the words that constitute it. Taken out of reality, it no longer refers to anything other than its form: what is now cathected, both in the prohibiting utterance and the phantasmatic imagination, is their specific articulation and the multiple puns, the play of sonorities and images that this articulation makes possible. But how can words become the objects of such a cathexis? Why do they mobilize all the strength of the unconscious? Leaving these questions open and referring the reader back to Freud,[13] let us remark only that the words, in the first moments of life, extended the body of the mother and simultaneously circumscribed the place of *suspension* (suspense) of her desire. In words, therefore, the most real of *jouissance* and the furthest of the phallus were conjoined. Perhaps, in the unconscious, the power of words remains the same?

3. Consequently, the unconscious representation is only a text. But the text produces effects: since sexuality is organized as we have seen, not according to some instinct, some "tendency," but according to what has been said. Consequently, discourse makes impossible any direct and peaceable relation to the body, to the world, and to pleasure. It turns away from *jouissance*: it is in this sense that it is castrating. In other words, the unconscious representation of castration·is, in the first place, a castrating representation.

But, at the same time, the term representation must be taken in a second sense. For the sequence of discourse having once marked us, endlessly reproduces itself. And we can define the unconscious as the place where these re-presentations are indefinitely staged. This fact of repetition, of the eternal return of words, has been sufficiently demonstrated for us to take it as given here: if the representation then does not cease to represent itself, how can it disappear? Yet, the analyst must reckon with this effacement. For the patient, who expresses anxiety after the event, is speaking of a time when nothing was thinkable: then, the body and the world were confounded in one chaotic intimacy that was too present, too immediate—one continuous expanse of proximity or unbearable plenitude. What was lacking was a lack, an empty "space" somewhere. Indeed, it seems in these clinical cases that the castrating dimension of representation is missing. Consequently, it is as if representation, at least in its effects, had wiped itself out.

OEDIPUS AND THE STAKE

To explain the persistence of the representation as well as its vacillation in anxiety, let us pause at the hypothesis we set out a moment ago. Let us imagine that at certain moments, the representation is indeed produced, but without castrating effects: emptily circulating, it would lose the power of turning the subject away from *jouissance*. This, not as a function of facts inherent in representation itself, but from an intrusion, a violence, emanating from the real. Perhaps a reading of Sophocles' drama, *Oedipus Rex,* will serve as clarification.

At the beginning of the drama, Oedipus appears as he whose relation to representation is sufficiently assured to unravel the enigmas of the sphinx. And yet, the tragic action will progressively disclose the ruin of this representation.

The ancients used to say that this ruin was willed by the gods. The analyst declares that Oedipus was led to it by his incestuous desires. We must hold simultaneously to the idea of gods who persecute and to that of the subject who desires. For the theme of the fateful mistake, of the plan controlled by external forces, emphasizes this essential fact: that the realization of unconscious desire is always so catastrophic that the subject can never bring it about on its own.

It is one thing to desire, another to realize this desire. We have seen that to desire is to represent the lacking object (the other), that is to say, to "enjoy" (*"jouir"*) exclusively in the form of words. To satisfy this desire is, on the contrary, to decathect words to the profit of reality: in other words, enjoyment of the mother leads back to a recuperation of the stake that, endlessly replayed, is normally the guarantee of representation.

This is why it is necessary that desire should not be realized. Hence the repression that ensures that one does not think, nor see, nor take the desired object, even and above all if it is within reach: this object must remain lost.

But in Oedipus, the gods, or chance, restores the object of desire: Oedipus enjoys Jocasta. But, simultaneously, repression continues to take place, and in an ever more pressing manner: the successive recourses to Tiresias, to sacrifices, and to the law show a desperate effort to avoid seeing the cause of the pestilence. An effort that is ineffectual: repression is no longer anything but a gigantic pantomime, powerless to assure the throwing back into play of the stake of desire. We know that, for want of a stake, representation is not worth anything.

Thus Oedipus' tragedy enables us to emphasize both the economy and the failure of representation at the same time. But it also suggests the cause of this failure. Why does the encounter with the sphinx take place immediately before the drama? To what does the sphinx refer, this reasoning and devouring hybrid being, which beats its wings as it talks? Why does this monster, a woman with the body of a beast, take up her place at the gates of Thebes?

Does not the encounter with this enigmatic figure of femininity threaten every subject? Is it not she who is at the root of the ruin of representation?

Freud, asking himself about feminine sexuality and assessing the small purchase that it offers analytic investigation, compared it to a "dark continent."

The *Recherches nouvelles* begins by recalling this formula. How appropriate! And yet it is as if the authors do not see the threatening shadows that they call forth by these words. For feminine sexuality is not a dark, unexplored continent through any provisional insufficiency of research: it is unexplored to the extent that it is unexplorable.

Of course one can describe it, give an account of it in clinical or theoretical work. But it is elsewhere, in the framework of the cure, that femininity stubbornly resists analysis. On the couch, a discourse analagous to that whose style the book renders so well, is enunciated: "live" discourse, whose very immediacy seems to be a sign of life. But it is this immediacy, this life, which is an obstacle to analysis: the word is understood only as the extension of the body that is there in the process of speaking. It seems no longer to be hiding anything. To the extent that it does not know repression, femininity is the downfall of interpretation.

It is femininity, not women, that can take on such a status. Let us specify what meaning will be given here to the three terms: woman, femininity, repression:

• the word woman will designate the subject who, like the man, is an effect of unconscious representation;

• by femininity will be understood the set of the "feminine" drives (oral, anal, vaginal) in so far as these resist the processes of repression;

• finally, repression will be distinguished from *censorship*:[14] the latter is always submitted to; the former, on the contrary, has the value of an act. In fact, the obstacles the censor opposes to libidinal development appear as the result of the experiences of the Other's desire. Regressions or fixations have made it impossible for the mother or the father to symbolize this or that key-event in the child's sexuality. And from then on, this "blank," this unspoken, functions like a check: the censor that is set up appears as the effect of an absence of representation. It is therefore unrepresentable, and consequently "uninterpretable." Repression, on the contrary, presupposes a symbolization: as we have seen, it allows the representation to be cathected as such, while the real satisfaction, renounced, becomes its stake. Repression is always a process that structures on the level of the psychic economy.

As we will see, feminine eroticism is more censored, less repressed than that of the man. It lends itself less easily to a "losing itself" as the stake of unconscious representation. The drives whose force was demonstrated by the English school circumscribe a place or "continent" that can be called "dark" to the extent that it is outside the circumference of the symbolic economy (foreclosed).

What are the processes which maintain femininity "outside repression," in a state of nature as it were?

The first, of a social order, concerns the absence of prohibitions: the girl is less subject than the boy to the threats and to the defenses that penalize masturbation. We keep silent about her masturbation, all the more as it is less observable. Francoise Dolto[15] has shown that, sheltered by their privacy, the girl, the woman, can live a "protected" sexuality. One tends to refer to the anxiety of rape and penetration without emphasizing that, in reality, on the contrary, the girl risks little. The anatomy of the boy, on the other hand, exposes him very early to the realization that he is not master either of the manifestations of his desire or of the extent of his pleasures. He experiments, not only with chance but also with the law and with his sexual organ: his body itself takes on the value of stake.

In relation to castration, therefore, the position of the man differs from that of the woman whose sexuality is capable of remaining on the edge of all repression. Under certain circumstances then, the stake of castration for the woman finds itself displaced: it consists in the sexuality and the desire of the other sex, most often that of the father and then, of the masculine partner. Which is why Perrier and Granoff have been able to show "the extreme feminine sensibility to all experiences relating to the castration of the man."[16]

Yet other processes, of an instinctual and not a social order, maintain feminine sexuality outside the economy of representation—the intrication of the oral-anal drives with vaginal pleasure. Jones, Klein, and Dolto have insisted on the fact that the girl's archaic experiences of the vagina are organized as a function of preestablished oral-anal schemas. At the further extreme, precocious sexuality "turns" around a single orifice, an organ that is both digestive and vaginal, which ceaselessly tends to absorb, to appropriate, to devour. We find again here the theme of concentricity disengaged by the authors of the book.

If this insatiable organ-hole is at the center of precocious sexuality, if it inflects all psychic movement according to circular and closed schemas, it compromises woman's relation to castration and the law: to absorb, to take, to understand, is to reduce the world to the most archaic instinctual "laws." It is a movement opposed to that presupposed by castration: where the *jouissance* of the body loses itself "for" a discourse that is Other.

Here, we will not therefore question the truth of the clinical observations produced by the English school: all experience of child analysis confirms the precocity of the "knowledge" of the vagina. More generally, it is quite true that the very small girl experiences her femininity very early. But, simultaneously, it must be stressed that such a precocity, *far from favoring a possible "maturation," acts as an obstacle to it,* since it maintains eroticism outside the representation of castration.

Anxiety and the Relation to the Body

A third series of processes stand in the way of repression: those concerning the woman's relation to her own body, a relation simultaneously narcissistic and erotic. For the woman enjoys her body as she would the body of another. Every occurrence of a sexual kind (puberty, erotic experiences, maternity, etc.) happens *to* her as if it came from an other (woman): every occurrence is the fascinating actualization of *the*[ii] femininity of all women, but also and above all, of that of the mother. It is as if "to become woman," "to be woman" gave access to a *jouissance* of the body as feminine *and/or* maternal. In the self-love she bears herself, the woman cannot differentiate her own body from that which was "the first object."

We would have to specify further what is only intimated here: that the real of the body, in taking form at puberty, in charging itself with intensity and importance and presence, as object of the lover's desire, reactualizes, reincarnates, the real of that other body, which, at the beginning of life was the substance of words, the organizer of desire; which, later on, was also the material of archaic repression. Recovering herself as maternal body (and also as phallus), the woman can no longer repress, "lose," the first stake of representation. As in the tragedy, representation is threatened by ruin. But at the root of this threat there are different processes: for Oedipus, the restoration of the stake proceeded by chance, from the gods; it was effected *in spite of* a prohibition. Nothing, on the contrary, is forbidden for the woman; there is no statement or law that prohibits the recovery of the stake since the real which imposes itself and takes the place of repression and desire is, for her, the real of her own body.

From now on, anxiety, tied to the presence of this body, can only be insistent, continuous. This body, so close, which she has to occupy, is an object in excess that must be "lost," that is to say, repressed, in order to be symbolized. Hence the symptoms that so often simulate this loss: "there is no longer anything, only the hole, emptiness." Such is the *leitmotif* of all feminine cure, which it would be a mistake to see as the expression of an alleged "castration." On the contrary, it is a defense produced in order to parry the avatars, the deficiencies, of symbolic castration.

The analyst often finds a "fear of femininity" in connection with feminine anxiety, especially in the adolescent. We have tried to show that this fear is not a result of fantasies of violation and breaking in (effraction) alone. At bottom, it is fear of the feminine body as a nonrepressed and unrepresentable object. In other words, femininity, "according to Jones," that is, femininity experienced as real and immediate, is the blind spot of the symbolic processes analyzed by Freud. Two incompatible, heterogeneous territories coexist inside the feminine unconscious: that of representation and that which remains "the dark continent."

DEFENSES AND MASQUERADE

It is rare for anxiety to manifest itself as such in analysis. It is usually camouflaged by the defenses that it provokes. It is a question of organizing a representation of castration that is no longer symbolic, but imaginary: a lack is simulated and thereby the loss of some stake—an undertaking all the more easily accomplished precisely because feminine anatomy exhibits a lack, that of the penis. At the same time as being her own phallus, therefore, the woman will disguise herself with this lack, throwing into relief the dimension of castration as *trompe-l'oeil*.

The ways in which this can occur are multiple. One can play on the absence of the penis through silence just as well as through a resounding vanity. One can make it the model of erotic, mystical, and neurotic experiences. The anorexic refusal of food is a good example of the desire to reduce and to dissolve her own flesh, to take her own body as a cipher. Masochism also mimes the lack, through passivity, impotence, and doing nothing (*"ne rien faire"*). The observations of Helene Deutsch and those of the *Recherches nouvelles* could be understood in this way. Castration is similarly disguised in the register of erotic fiction: where the feminine orifice, O, is "falsely" represented in its successive metamorphoses.

Here, I would rather turn to the poets, those who have written in the novelistic or made films out of the feminine drama (*"cinéma"*), since the limitations of this article rule out any detailed consideration of clinical cases.

Take Fellini, the director of *Juliette of the Spirits,* a film so baffling, no doubt, because it brings out the presence of the "dark continent" so well. The dimension of femininity that Lacan designates as masquerade, taking the term from Joan Rivière,[iii] takes shape in this piling up of crazy things, feathers, hats, and strange baroque constructions, which rise up like so many silent insignias. But what we must see is that the objective of such a masquerade is to say nothing. Absolutely *nothing.* And in order to produce this nothing the woman uses her own body as disguise.

The novels of Marguerite Duras use the same world of stupor and silence. It could be shown that this silence, this nonspeech, again exhibits the fascinating dimension of feminine lack: Duras wants to make this lack "speak" as cry (*Moderato Cantabile*), or as "music." Here, let us simply recall what is said in the *Ravishment of Lol V Stein*: "what was needed was a word-absence, a word hole . . . it could not have been spoken, it could only be made to resound."[17]

Thus the sex, the vagino-oral organ of the woman, acts as obstacle to castration; at the same time, "falsely" representing the latter in its effects of allurement, which provoke anxiety. This is why man has always called the feminine defenses and masquerade *evil.*

Woman is not accused of thinking or of committing this evil, but of incarnating it.[iv] It is this evil that scandalizes whenever woman "plays out" her sex in order to evade the word and the law. Each time she subverts a law or a word that relies on the predominantly masculine structure of the look. Freud says that Evil is experienced as such when anxiety grips the child in front of the unveiled body of his mother. "Did his desire then refer only to this hole of flesh?" The woman affords a glimpse of the Real, by virtue of her relation to nothing—that is to say, to the Thing. At this moment, the Symbolic collapses into the Real. Freud also says that the pervert cannot see the castrated body of his mother. In this sense, every man is a pervert. On the one hand, he enjoys without saying so, without coming too close—for then he would have to take upon himself a terrible anxiety, or even hate—; he enjoys by proxy the thing he glimpses through the mother. On the other hand, he does not appear to understand that her relation to the thing is sublimated. It is this evil which has to be repressed.

A film like *Day of Wrath*[v] lays bare all the masculine "defenses" against femininity and woman's direct relation to *jouissance.* The man is terrorized by the threat that femininity raises for "his" repression. In order to reassure him and convince him, the woman always advances further along her own path by explaining herself, wishing to speak the truth. But she does not understand that her discourse will not and cannot be received. For the fact of bypassing the law of repression precisely by *saying all* contaminates the most precious truth and makes it suspect, odious, and condemnable. Hence masculine censure.

The frustrations, interdictions, and contempt that have weighed on women for centuries may indeed be absurd and arbitrary, but they do not matter. The main thing is the fact of imposing the definitive abandonment of *jouissance*. The scandal can then come to an end—the feminine sex bears witness to castration.

The analyst, for his part, cannot define feminine castration simply as the effect of his strictures. If the exemplar of the hysterical, neurotic woman is *one who never lets up wishing to be her sex,* inversely, isn't the "adult" woman *one who reconstructs her sexuality in a field that goes beyond sex*? The principle of a masculine libido upheld by Freud could be clarified as a function of this "extraterritoriality."

Jouissance and Sublimation

FEMININE CASTRATION: HYPOTHESES

Once again, let us take an example from literature. Klossowski's portraits of women easily lend themselves to a clinical commentary. We might be surprised at the astonishingly virile attributes (both anatomical and psychical) with which the author endows his heroines and deduce from them some perversion. It is also possible to see in these attributes the material of a moral fable outlining a type of perfected femininity: the "true" woman, the "femme" woman would be drawn as she who has *"forgotten" her femininity,* and who would entrust the *jouissance* and the representation of it to an other. For this reason, Klossowski's heroine, Roberte, could in no way talk about herself, her body or "the word that it conceals."[10] It is someone else's task to hold the discourse of femininity, in love and/or in a novel.

Under the sign of this forgetting, a second economy of desire, where the stake is no longer the same, can effectively be described. The stake is now precocious femininity and not the penis or masculine sexuality: precocious femininity becomes the material of repression. "According to Jones" one or several periods of latency correspond to this decathexis of sexuality, periods during which the little girl and the woman disentangle themselves from their own bodies and their pleasures. This is why periods of frigidity in analysis can often be considered as an index of progress: they mark the moment when the patient decathects the vaginal-oral schemas, which till then were alone capable of providing access to erotic pleasure.

The decisive step by which the feminine unconscious is modified lies, not so much in the change of love object[19] as in the change in the unconscious representative. Masculine, phallic representatives are substituted for the first "concentric" representatives. The law and the paternal ideals of the father that are articulated in her discourse constitute the new representatives capable of supplanting the models of archaic representations (feminine Oedipus).

Let us note that this substitution does not mutilate the woman and deprive her of a penis that she never had, but *deprives her of the sense* of precocious sexuality. Femininity is forgotten, indeed repressed, and this loss constitutes the symbolic castration of the woman.

For clarity's sake, let us draw a diagram of these hypotheses on the economy of the feminine unconscious.

	Stake	Representative	Relation to jouissance
Economy I (according to Jones)	masculine sexuality (phallocentrism)	vagino-oral orifice (concentricity)	anxiety
Economy II (according to Freud	precocious femininity (concentricity)	signifying order (phallocentrism)	sublimation

This diagram calls for three comments.

1. The parameters of the feminine economy still refer to Jones and to Freud, but in opposite directions.

2. In clinical practice, such a clear-cut distinction is not observed. The two forms of economy usually coexist, with one predominating (provisionally or definitively) over the other.

3. The notion of sublimation has been introduced.

If we can show that in an economy of type II all relation to *jouissance,* including sexual pleasure, is of a sublimatory kind, then not only will a specific dimension of feminine sexuality be clarified, but a misinterpretation of sublimation will also be avoided: that which consists in seeing in sublimation a passage from the sexual to the nonsexual.

SUBLIMATION AND METAPHOR

In the cure and more specifically, in the transference, (i.e., the set of unconscious modifications produced by the enunciation of discourse on the couch), the dimension of pleasure can emerge.

In the *Recherches* M. Torok speaks of its manifestation: "when one of my patients has understood an interpretation, when, consequently, an inhibition is lifted, a frequent indication of this advance is that the patient dreams and in this dream she has an orgasm" (a description of one of these dreams follows).[20]

M. Torok, by insisting on the fact that a pleasure arises when a new representation is elaborated, tells us what is essential about this pleasure. Contrary to what one might think, this pleasure does not lie in the lifting of an inhibition, that is, in the releasing of a tension, contained for too long. On the contrary, the pleasure, far from being explicable by the cliché of release ("défoulement"),[vi] arises from the putting in place of *new* representations. Let us note that these were first enunciated by the other, the analyst, who, in interpreting, verbally articulates something of a sexuality maintained till then in the state of nature, in the "dark."

Here, therefore, pleasure is the effect of the word of the other. More specifically, it occurs at the advent of a structuring discourse. For what is essential in the cure of a woman is not making sexuality more "conscious" or interpreting it, at least not in the sense normally given to this term. The analyst's word takes on a completely different function. It no longer explains, but from the sole fact of articulating, it structures. By verbally putting in place a representation of castration, the analyst's word makes sexuality pass into discourse. This type of interpretation therefore *represses,* at least in the sense given to the word here.

Understood in this way, interpretation can perhaps help us to locate a certain cultural and social function of psychoanalysis. The Freudian theory of sexuality was developed (*mise en place*) in relation to women and femininity. We can ask whether psychoanalysis was not articulated precisely in order to repress femininity (in the sense of producing its symbolic representation). At the same time, Freud's reservations about Jones would make sense: the attempts to "make" femininity "speak" would surely jeopardize the very repression that Freud had known how to achieve.

Let us return to our example. What pleasure can there be in the repression that is produced at the moment of interpretation? First, let us say that interpretation, as it is analyzed here, does not consist so much in explaining and commenting, as in articulating. Here again, it is the form of words which must be emphasized. In response to the analysand's fantasy, the analyst enunciates a certain number of signifiers necessarily relating to his own desire and his listening-place. These words are *other*: the analyst's discourse is not reflexive, but different. As such it is a *metaphor,* not a mirror, of the patient's discourse. And, precisely, metaphor is capable of engendering pleasure.

First Freud and then Lacan analyzed the motives of this pleasure with regard to the joke. We laugh when we perceive that the words speak a text other than that which we thought. And if the other laughs, if the misapprehension plays on one more register, the pleasure becomes keener still. What function does this other text, this other ear, have? It has the function of engendering a metaphor, that is to say, of substituting itself for the preceding text and listening-place. Pleasure arises the moment this metaphor is produced. Lacan says that it is identified with the very meaning of the metaphor.[21]

In what then, does this meaning, bereft of signification, consist? We can define it as the measure of the empty "space" induced by repression. The metaphor, by posing itself as that which is not spoken, hollows out and designates this space. Freud said that the pleasure of the joke lies in the return of the repressed. Does it not rather, lie *in putting the dimension of repression into play on the level of the text itself?*

It is this pleasure of the joke that can be evoked in relation to all sublimation. For it is an operation that consists in opening up new divisions and spaces in the material that it transforms. In the transference, the patient's orgasm took note of an interpretation. Surely this is best represented as a breath of air between two signifiers, suddenly opened up by the metaphor?

The orgasm, like a burst of laughter, testifies to the meaning—insignificant— of the analyst's word. We must now try to rediscover this dimension of "wit" in pleasure and *jouissance*.

PLEASURE AND JOUISSANCE

Feminine erotic pleasure varies considerably in its nature and effects. There is variety in the places of the body cathected, in the level of intensity, in the outcome (orgasm or not), and in the effects: a "successful" sexual relation can cause calm or anxiety. Let us also remember that a neurosis cannot necessarily be inferred from frigidity; and that, reciprocally, psychotics and very immature women have intense vaginal orgasms.[22]

How are we to make sense of the exuberance, the bizarreness, and the paradoxes of these pleasures? By referring less to the varieties of form and intensity than to their function in the psychic economy. Here again, we will distinguish two types of sexual pleasure: the precocious and the sublimated.

The first was earlier seen to be the effect of the experience of archaic sexuality. Even if it involves two people, even if it presents the appearance of an adult sexuality, it merely re-actualizes or raises to the highest pitch in orgasm, the *jouissance* that the woman has of herself.[23] In this type of pleasure, the other's look and his desire further reinforce the circularity of the erotic relation. Hence the anxiety that arises before and after the sexual act.

Inversely, pleasure can be structuring in its effects. The sort of "genius," of inspiration that the woman discovers after love, shows that an event of an unconscious nature has occurred, which has enabled her to take up a certain distance from the dark continent.

We will call sublimated pleasure that which takes the same forms as incestuous pleasure while nonetheless presupposing and confirming woman's access to the symbolic. This pleasure is no longer derived from femininity as such, but *from the signifier,* more precisely, *from the repression that it brings about*: this is why sublimated pleasure is identified with the pleasure derived from the joke.

Such a transformation is on a par with the mutation which has been outlined above as the passage from Type I to Type II sexual economy. The latter assumes, on the one hand, the forgetting of precocious femininity, and on the other, the setting in place of a new representative or signifier of castration. Does not the sublimated sexual act constitute for the woman, one of the ways of putting a Type II economy into place, where:

1. the signifier would be actualized in the rhythm, the periodic return of the penis;

2. the stake would consist of the repressed feminine drives,[24] inseparable from the penis itself.

3. pleasure would be the meaning of the metaphor through which the penis "would repress" the body, feminine sexuality.

Let us be more precise: the penis, its throbbing, its cadence, and the movements of love-making could be said to produce the purest and most elementary form of signifying articulation, that of a series of blows that mark out the space of the body.

It is this which opens up rhythms all the more ample and intense, a *jouissance* all the more keen and serious in that the penis, the object which is its instrument, is scarcely anything.

But to state this is to state a paradox: the penis produces *jouissance* because it incarnates a finitude. Sublimation always implies a de-idealization. The phallic signifier, detached from the terrifying representations of the superego that revolve around the imaginary phallus, must appear as an object of not-much-meaning.[25]

This step, usually suspended during childhood, takes place after the first sexual experiences of adulthood. Is it a question of unconscious processes? Provided the ground has been prepared, life and a certain ethic undertake this work. To the extent that romantic idealization is successfully mourned (relinquished), to the extent that the dimension of the gift predominates, the penis can objectify, by its very insignificance, the "difficulty to be" of the couple, in which *jouissance* is lost. Thus it can no longer be separated in its consistency from the material of this archaic, feminine *jouissance* that has been renounced. It embodies it as lost, and all of a sudden restores it a hundredfold. For it deploys this *jouissance* in direct proportion to the forgetting, which is in itself infinite.

Thus, ethics is indissociable from a "certain" relation to *jouissance*. The de-idealization that it implies alone makes possible the occasional coming together and binding of two perfectly distinct, heterogeneous spaces. The voluptuous sensation of an aspiration of the whole body in a space absolutely Other and consequently, infinite, cannot simply be explained as the effect of the perception of the vaginal cavity. It implies that this cavity is hollowed out by repression, that is to say, by a symbolic operation.

Consequently, pleasure, far from being reduced to the excitation of an organ, on the contrary, *transports* the woman into the field of the signifier. Sublimated pleasure, like the dream and hypnosis, like the poetic act, marks a moment when the unconscious representation takes on an absolute value: in other words, when the act of articulating produces on its own the meaning of discourse (meaning nothing). Sweeping away all signification, it lays hold of the woman and catches her in its progression and its rhythms.[26]

For the man, exceptions aside,[27] this transportation into the signifier cannot be produced in so violent and radical a way. In fact, how could he abandon himself to that which he himself controls, and from whose play he gives pleasure (*jouissance*). Moreover, this game (play) involves the risk of detumescence,[28] and also the vertigo and anxiety aroused by the absolute of feminine demand: the woman expects and receives all there is of the penis at the moment of love.

If we no longer consider what is properly called pleasure, but the orgasm usually designated as *"jouissance"* by the analyst, a similar distinction must be made between *jouissance* of Type I and the orgasm that is produced in a sublimated economy. In the former, the residue of pleasure comes to a dead end, since the woman again found herself powerless to maintain the unconscious economy. This form of orgasm, registering pleasure outside significance (*signifiance*), bars access to the symbolic. Sublimation, on the contrary, transports not only pleasure but the orgasm into metaphor. Orgasm, endlessly renewed, brought to a white heat, explodes at the moment of pleasure. It *bursts* in the double sense of the French term *éclater*: the sense of deflagration and that of a revelation. There is therefore a continuity of the ascent of pleasure and of its apogée in orgasm: the one carries the signifier to its maximum incandescence; the other marks the moment when the discourse, in exploding under the effect *of its own force,* comes to the point of breaking, of coming apart. It is no longer anything.

To break *itself,* to disjoint *itself,* in other words, to articulate itself through a meaning that endlessly escapes. Orgasm in discourse leads us to the point where feminine *jouissance* can be understood as *writing* (*écriture*)—to the point where it must appear that this *jouissance* and the literary text (which is also written like an orgasm produced from within discourse) are the effect of the same murder of the signifier.

Isn't this why Bataille, Jarry, and Jabès speak of writing as the jouissance of a woman? And why that which she is writing is the Name?[vii]

Notes

1. S. Freud, compare, on this subject in particular: "Three Essays," (1905) *The Standard Edition of the Complete Psychological Works of Sigmund Freud,* vol. VII; "Femininity," (1932), vol. XXII; "The dissolution of the Oedipus Complex," (1924), vol. XIX.

2. E. Jones, "The Early Development of Female Sexuality," *International Journal of Psychoanalysis* (1927) vol. VIII; "The Phallic Phase" (1933) vol XIV; "Early Female Sexuality" (1935) vol. XVI.

3. J. Chasseguet-Smirgel, C. J. Luquet-Parat, B. Grunberger, J. McDougall, M. Torok, C. David, *Recherches psychanalytiques nouvelles sur la sexualité féminine,* Payot, 1964. M. Torok "La signification de l'envie de phallus chez le femme," p. 184.

4. *Ibid.,* p. 186.

5. *Ibid.,* p. 132.

6. *Ibid.,* p. 65—90.

7. On phallocentrism and the innateness of desire, see "La phase phallique," *Scilicet* I, Seuil: a rigorous restatement of the theoretical positions of Freud and Jones on femininity from the position of Lacanian theory; trans. in J. Mitchell and J. Rose (eds.) *Feminine Sexuality: Jacques Lacan and the école freudienne,* Macmillan, 1982.

8. *Recherches,* p. 103.

9. *Ibid.,*pp. 124—125.

10. *Ibid.,* p. 191.

11. *Ibid.,* p. 103 (author's emphasis).

12. *Ibid.,* p. 67.

13. S. Freud, "Repression" and "The Unconscious," *SE,* vol. XIV.

14. This distinction is not always made. These two types of process are usually designated by the term "repression" (primary and secondary).

15. F. Dolto, "La libido et son destin féminin," *La psychanalyse,* VII.

16. W. Granoff and F. Perrier, "Le problème de la perversion chez la femme et les idéaux feminins," *La psychanlyse,* VII. This article is essential for theoretical work on feminine sexuality.

17. Marguerite Duras, *La Ravissement de Lol V. Stein,* Gallimard, p 54.

18.   P. Klossowski, *Les Lois de l'hospitalité,* p. 145.

19.   The "change of object" designates the renunciation of the first love object, the mother, in favor of the father. On this problem see J. Luquet-Parat, "Le changement d'objet," *Recherches,* p. 124ff.

20.   *Recherches,* p. 192.

21.   A propos of metaphor, see J. Lacan, "The agency of the letter in the unconscious," *Ecrits: A Selection,* trans. A. Sheridan, Tavistock, 1977 and "Les formations de l'inconscient," *Séminaire 1956—1957.* On pleasure by the same author: "Propos directifs pour un congrès sur la sexualité féminine," *Ecrits,* Seuil, 1966, trans. in J. Mitchell and J. Rose (eds.), *Feminine Sexuality: Jacques Lacan and the école freudienne.*

22.   See F. Dolto.

23.   See P. Aulagnier, *Le Desir et la perversion,* Seuil.

24.   Drives repressed both in the course of earlier Oedipal experiences as well as in the *present,* by the very fact of the *presence* of the penis.

25.   This paragraph and the following one were added to the earlier *Critique* article in 1976 in order to clear up a misunderstanding. Only someone who idealizes the signifier could interpret the fact of relating to *jouissance* to an operation of sublimation and to the putting into play of the signifier's "frenzied idealization" (C. David). I take as a tribute—no doubt unintended—what someone exclaimed à propos of this article: "So, the *jouissance* of the woman is produced by the operations of the Holy Ghost!" It can happen!

26.   If the woman, at the moment of orgasm, identifies herself radically with an unconscious representation, articulated by the other, then does she not find herself again precisely in the archaic situation where the maternal representation was the sole organizer of fantasy? The reply could be in the affirmative for orgasms of the psychotic or neurotic (acute hysteria) type. In these cases, pleasure and orgasm are nothing more than the manifestation of, among other things, a sort of *direct seizure* of the woman by the Other's discourse. For the woman, who, on the contrary, assumes her castration, this relation is *indirect*: it passes through the (paternal) metaphor of the maternal discourse, a metaphor that, as we have seen, presupposes an economy of desire in which the woman puts herself at stake.

27.   Except in the case of actual homosexuality. We must be careful, however, not to set up too clear-cut a distinction between the sexuality of the man and that of the woman. Without pretending to settle the whole problem of bisexuality here, let us only say that every masculine subject is cathected as the object and product of his mother: he was "part" of the maternal body. In relation to the masculine body and unconscious cathexis, then, one could also speak of "femininity" as implied in maternal femininity. Would not the sexual act be structuring for the male subject to the extent that, putting into play the repression of femininity, he would produce each time the *coupure* that separates the man from his mother, while "returning" to her the femininity of his partner.

28.   On the question of detumescence cf Lacan *Séminaire 1967—1968.* See also "The Signification of the Phallus," *Ecrits: A Selection* and "Propos directifs pour un congrès sur la sexualité féminine," *Ecrits,* Seuil.

Translator's Notes

i.   The word *jouissance* is impossible to translate. Its meanings include: enjoyment; enjoyment of property or privilege; pleasure; and the pleasure of orgasm. It is necessary, however to distinguish between *jouissance* and *plaisir* (pleasure), which are two theoretically distinct concepts in Montrelay's text.

ii.   The article *la* of *la* femininité is italicized in French; see J. Lacan, "Dieu et la jouissance de la femme,": *Séminaire livre XX: Encore,* Seuil, 1975.

iii.   In "Womanliness as Masquerade," *International Journal of Psychoanalysis,* X (1929), pp. 303—313.

iv.   In the earlier version of this article, which appeared in *Critique* 278 (1976), this sentence ends with "since it consists in confronting desire with a bodily lack (which is carnal)."

v.   Directed by Carl Dreyer, 1943.

vi.   The french is *défoulement,* a pun on the French word of repression: *refoulement.*

vii.   *Nom* puns on the French negative *non* and also refers to *Le Nom du Père* (Name of the Father).

Translated by Parveen Adams, with acknowledgment to Jacqueline Rose for her invaluable advice.

from *m/f* 1, 1978

Is the Oedipus Complex Universal?

MOUSTAFA SAFOUAŇ

My interest in the question inscribed in this title was aroused by a number of analytical observations that strongly encouraged me to consider whether certain more and more frequently encountered subjective positions might not be based on a mythical conception of paternity: the conception Freud lent his authority in *Totem and Taboo.*

Guided by these observations, I was led toward a relativization of the Oedipus complex. But a relativization carried out not externally, by opposition or juxtaposition, as when, for example, one says: "Democracy is not the only form of government, there are also tyranny, oligarchy and so on."

This was a *relativization* carried out *from within the Oedipus complex itself,* that is, from within psychoanalysis itself, insofar as I regard the latter as our experimental access to subjectivity, at the level of its most radical containment in the symbolic order.

In order to clarify this conclusion, let me remind you of three distinctions, which I shall then examine more closely;

The first is the distinction marked by the law of the prohibition of incest between *nature* and *culture,* to use the standard terminology, although the term "culture" in fact denotes two things we ought to distinguish: *society* and *language.*

The second is located between that form of frustration constituted by *imaginary castration* or the feeling of castration on the one hand, and on the other the *symbolic castration* thanks to which human desire emerges from its indeterminacy as the desire of the Other, that Other too being unable to state what its desire is.[1]

The third is the distinction between *opinion* and *knowledge*—a distinction inseparably linked, as we shall see, to that between knowledge and truth.

Let me begin with the first. As you will know, Claude Lévi-Strauss regards what he calls the elementary structures of kinship as codifications of alliance, the latter being for him a special case of the universal exchange that constitutes the fundamental social fact, and he envisages those structures as systems of exchange, of goods and services, or systems of communication, of messages.

Whereas this Indian conception—for Lévi-Strauss tells us he heard it from Indians—of the law of the prohibition of incest as a law of exchange is sufficient to explain exogamy, it does not explain the prohibition of incest. There is nothing in the perspective of this theory to prevent the initiation of the adolescent male by his mother before he is put on the market as a marriageable man or enters it as a wife-buyer: we can recognize here a fairly typical obsessional's fantasy.

In such a fantasy we are dealing with a problematic of desire. Although the unitary, simple character of the exchange model fulfilled the requirements of a sociological conceptualization by providing for the formalization of kinship structures, it would not absolve us of the necessity, the moment our perspective is that of psychoanalytic experience, to distinguish between the woman as a *good,* or object of exchange, and the woman as an object of *desire.*

It is hardly surprising that desire should be a problem for (the) human being. For there is certainly no shortage of analogies between human and animal behavior. Everything can be found in animal species: hunting, house-building, singing, dancing, even a certain delight in self-adornment, at least if we can believe what Kohler tells us about chimpanzees. There is even a bitter struggle not for life but for leadership. There is a rudimentary use of tools and artificially made objects. And a use of pretense and marks, notably for the delimitation of territory, etc.

But all this notwithstanding, once caught in the web of language, the relationship between the organism and its environment is transfigured into the relationship between the speaking subject and what is called his being; which being is not presented to him in the constitutive images of his *Umwelt* or even in his own image. In other words, there is nothing transparent to him about this being; as a result, the relationship between the subject and being is an interrogation.

So much so that the question we analysts (I mean the Lacanians) ask about psychotics is precisely what it is that happens to the human being when he has nothing to guide him in his conduct of his life but imaginary reference points.

Indeed, there is nothing to prevent a latent psychotic from marrying, that is, choosing a sexual object in conformity with the symbolic order insofar as all society is its custodian. Only this marriage would leave him confronting the object as something he literally does not know what to do with; so the marriage usually only helps to detonate his madness.

What does this mean? Surely that it is not the natural object that gives birth to desire (I would go so far as to say that to wish to include in oneself as an object the cause of the desire of the Other is a formula for the structure of hysteria), but on the contrary, desire (whose determinations, for that very reason, it therefore falls to us to investigate) that invests the object with its erotic value.

Perhaps it is appropriate here to recall that Lacan saw immediately that this demonstration of the function of the libido in the construction of the object was Freudianism's greatest merit. I say "immediately" because he was already emphasizing it in his thesis of 1931, that is, at a time when thought was still extraordinarily swayed by Bergsonianism and its "immediate data of consciousness."

The question I should now confront is why the subject's capture by the symbolic order produces unconscious effects which are precisely those of castration. But I shall leave this question aside for the moment. And approach the third distinction, formulating it as follows:

Where I "know" that the mother—the mother from whom the Other takes over, that Other being the man for the woman and vice versa—is castrated, I do not know that it is true. In other words, where it is true, there is no I to know it.

This is not a theoretical opinion; it is a formula that simply sums up a state of affairs confirmed by all analysis, that is, that the energy with which the subject declares himself man or woman is proportional to that with which the reverse is stated in the unconscious. For example, a certain woman repeats that her husband "obviously" has the phallus, to the extent that she denies it unconsciously.[2] She also repeats with the same insistence another "obvious fact" (the erroneous character of which, if judged from the standpoint, precisely, of reality, should, however, be immediately visible), that her mother, as well as herself, is castrated: a repetition or insistence whose dual function—exorcising (her fantasy, or more precisely, what she might know of that fantasy) and preserving (that same fantasy, in which she constitutes herself as phallus in and for the Other)—is then glaring. Appropriately, in such conditions, marriage becomes the main symptom of incestuous desire.

This distinction between a "knowledge" without truth and a truth without knowledge is inseparable from the ambiguity that affects the relationship between the subject and his sex. An ambiguity such that—as seems to have been anticipated by a painter of whom one wonders whether he attended Lacan's seminar, who has at any rate painted a rather astonishing canvas entitled *The Moebius Strip or Before the Separation* (a reproduction of the canvas can be found in Lo Duca's *Histoire de l'érotisme*—bisexuality might in some sense be materialized in a single-sided surface: that is, if we imagine a two-dimensional being moving on it, no division would signal to that being where the front ends and the back begins.

The question now is to know how our two-dimensional being, that is, our subject, embarks upon this movement.

I shall start my answer with a fable. If we dip a stick into water, it appears to be bent [*brisée*]. This is said to be an illusion. Nevertheless, it is in this manner that appearance conforms to what ought to be, and to what we expect. If the stick appeared to be curved or straight or whatever, one would be justified in suspecting some illusionism.

Suppose the illusionist is the stick itself. Is that enough to speak of a subject? Yes, if the stick is tormented by the question of how the spectator wishes to see it, in what form, that is, in general what form he likes most. Given this it is easy to imagine that the stick will adopt all possible and imaginable forms, including the bent form, that is, the true one, but one which is nonetheless falsely true, or falsely false.

Suppose the spectator is an incorrigible aesthete who believes there is one figure more perfect than any other, for example, the circle, and seeing the stick take this form himself dives into the water, in the belief that he can grasp his eternal object there.

It is clear that there will be absolutely nothing in this result like a reconciliation of the stick to itself, or between it and the spectator; since the only conclusion the stick will draw from what it regards as its successful deceit is that the spectator does not love it for itself, but for the false appearance it has put on.

You will be familiar with the lover's question: "Do you love me?" that is, "are you sure it isn't someone else or, why not, something else that you love?" or "can I ever be sure of that?"

Suppose on the contrary the spectator is sufficiently aware of the source of his aestheticism to maintain his *sang-froid* or apathy in the face of the act. Sooner or later the stick will come to realize that in that act it runs the risk of never knowing what it "truly" is, since it is in this last form—the form of its being—that it imagines its otherness with respect to the appearance in which it is apprehended. It therefore realizes that it runs the risk of never knowing it; hence its anxiety.

There is only one solution: to recognize the "bentness" [*brisure*] of its form as a law, a law both of its appearance and of that of the spectator, whom we shall also suppose to be dipped in the same water since he is made of the same clay. It is also necessary, if this solution is to be a possible one, that the law of refraction be inscribed, for the stick, somewhere.

The conclusion this fable is intended to illustrate is a dual one: on the one hand there is an integration of desire into the order of the law only on condition of an initial disorder, because, on the one hand, the demand for love is so powerful that the subject cannot avoid a miscognition that is systematized in the very genesis of his object: the ego; and, on the other, this miscognition cannot be reduced to the mere effect of the imaginary captations of the subject: it also implies an interrogation of the desire of the Other in its relations with the law.

Such an investigation was involved when Hans asked his mother "Do you have a widdler?" Of course he knew his mother was differently constructed. But what concerned him was to know how his mother's desire was located with respect to the real that was beginning to intrude, the widdler that was beginning to acquire an erection. Now, her answer was "Yes." After that, how could he avoid falling in love with the same illusion, the same form? More precisely, how could he avoid falling in love with his "little difference," a difference thus turned back into the same difference? Straightaway the birth of the same illusion; the same passion is explicable in the girl, who easily miscognizes her own forms, too, and for the same reasons.

We know what a storm has been unleashed by Freud's thesis as to the phallicism of the girl. But in the end, over and above anything that might be said about one person's feminism and another's misogyny, we are dealing with an indubitable analytical fact, even if it is not easy to make it intelligible, because after all, the penis is not such a wonderful thing as to force the girl to want to sacrifice her own nature.

It is just that the girl, too, is a subject whose desire must take the path of an investigation of the desire of the Other, a desire she, too, depends on, all the more radically in so far as not even the love she may have for herself, the love without which she could not even assume her own image, is not mediated by the love of the Other. In other words, she is not born with the self love that has been proposed as a definition of narcissism; a definition that, if it were true, would plunge the self into a closure from which it is impossible to see why and how it would ever emerge.

But the danger of a narcissistic closure that his mother's answer exposes him to would be no smaller if the subject were capable of discovering in his own image the object of the desire of the Other, and hence of his own.

We thus gain possession of the answer to the question I put to one side for a moment, the question as to the reasons for symbolic castration: only the latter lays the foundations for the object relation in the human being, in so far as it imposes not mourning for the primordial object, which is rather a matter of the law, but a *restriction on the narcissism* into which the relation to the object as such would otherwise set.

An answer I shall attempt to illustrate by analyzing the dream of a subject belonging to a rather different cultural region from the one in which we are accustomed to working. In *Sun Chief, the Autobiography of a Hopi Indian,* we read the following lines—this is the dream of a subject belonging to a different cultural region, but this does not absolve us of the need to locate it, like any dream in its context:

> We got a book from the YMCA on masturbation. It said that the practice ruined a boy's health and caused him to go insane. But I saw the boys doing it right along. They did not mind being watched by other fellows. I never masturbated much myself because I did not want to lose my strength. I had wet dreams, however, and continued to dream occasionally of a girl in bed with me who always turned out to be a boy. I would ask her, "How long have you been this way?" She would say "From my birth." I would stop caressing her and say, "I don't think I can have intercourse with you." I always felt disappointed in making this discovery, and when I awoke I wondered if I would be as unlucky in getting a girl. I was not.

The context suggests that the dream concerned the cynical question, why not masturbate? one orgasm is as good as another. It is not difficult to see that the facts do not confirm the YMCA's answer that it harms one's intellect.

But Don Talayesva's conscious answer, although more moderate, is no less beside the point. Its only virtue is to put the ball back into the questioner's court, asking *in toto* why should one retain one's strength for girls? The answer, if one can still be given, can thus only come from somewhere other than the location of the conscious.

According to Freud's indications, and still confirmed by our experience, an affect arising in the manifest content of a dream is linked in the latent content to a different idea, and the only hypothesis we can formulate from the material available to us here is that it is the disappointment at not finding a boy in his bed, that is, an object conforming to the phallic—and probably maternal—ideal of the subject that, moreover, would reflect in all its aspects the image in which the ego has been constituted "from its birth," to adopt the words of the dream. But our dreamer eventually found his consolation precisely in the fact that this encounter, the encounter with himself, failed to take place.

Let me conclude: the possibility of an object choice in the sense in which Freud counterposes it to a narcissistic choice presupposes a detour in two states:

1. the *genesis of an ideal* or model with which the subject identifies, to the satisfaction of his *narcissism,* but with respect to which he feels himself to be *castrated,* or which, since it is—by definition—distanced, injures that very same narcissism and makes the image of his own body appear "bent" [*brisée*], marked by a break. This condition is necessary both for the man and the woman, since neither can desire unless some anticipation of him or herself as satisfactory is implicit in that desire. But it is not sufficient. Also necessary is

2. a *break in this capture by the ideal,* without which the feeling of castration would threaten to become everlasting in the subject, motivating his revulsions and discouraging in him any erection of his desire.

This feeling of castration is experienced by the subject in comparison: but it does not arise from that comparison. If it did, the feeling would have to be resolved eventually for the boy and never resolved for the girl. Even less can this comparison give rise to the origin of the ideal as such. In fact, the function of the ideal, insofar as it penetrates the whole economy of desire, is rooted in the promotion of the *phallus,* that is, precisely, of that whose insufficiency is discovered for the boy and its nonexistence for the girl, at an early age, in an attribute of the father.

It is clear that this subordination of the phallus to a symbolic order has not the slightest relationship with a nature in which, so to speak, there are as many phalluses as there are males. Only the play of the signifier can explain this introduction of a phallus that is in some sense absolute, along with what follows from that introduction, that is, the subordination of access to genitality to a movement that the subject feels as an exclusion from that very phallus.

This is a special case of that *induction of the imaginary by the symbolic* that can be illustrated even in the formation of the "scientific mind." But to take an example from much nearer our own experience, imagine a subject who asks himself about what it is to be king, even though he is completely ignorant of the whole symbolic context in which monarchy is located. Inevitably a signifier will come to answer the question, for example, the eagle or the oak, the image of which will wrap the king in its redoubtable mantle, whose lack the subject will then immediately feel. The same goes for an interrogation about the father, except that, for the reasons I have just explained, it is a necessity that the metaphorical image be that of the phallus.

I am now immediately in a position to answer the question that constitutes my title. Not only does *the essence of the Oedipus complex not lie in the rivalry* for which it is the precondition, it is even that very rivalry that obscures its essence. The Oedipus complex is in the end no more than *one cultural form* among others, those others being equally possible providing they perform the same function of *promoting the function of castration* in the psyche.

For my own part I think that this form is destined to wither away once science has advanced to the point that it becomes possible to say who the father is, that is, to the point that the subject no longer has to give credence to every word that names him.

And without going quite so far as such a still remote but perhaps not entirely inconceivable extreme, we know that artificial insemination is already on the agenda, and it is hard to imagine the consequences that will follow once the "respectable proxy" has become customary, as the pill now is.

Whatever happens, whatever may be its cultural fate, there is nothing to prevent the phallic image being the unconscious effect of the authority of the maternal uncle, for example, if it pleases a society to designate he who occupies that symbolic position as the sovereign third party to whom the mother's word is referred.

Of course, quite a different pattern of conflict would result, if only by reason of the paradox that the subject will see in the fact that the third party in question is not the same as he who enjoys the mother. The "atypical" cases we encounter fairly frequently give us not the slightest notion of what such a configuration would be like.

And here I should like to clear up a misunderstanding. We often deal with subjects for whom the father, the grandfather, or an uncle have indeed occupied this position of prime authority, but in whom the result is connoted as the effect of an atypicality. But I am speaking of what would happen if this atypicality were the type itself. Here resort to the ethnographic or ethnopsychiatric literature is of no help to us, since these matters have never been conceived in the perspective advocated here. They have not been so conceived in the absence of a relativization of the Oedipus complex, which can only be correctly carried out if we start from psychoanalytic experience in so far as it brings to light *the conditions which govern the structuration of desire, and the moments through which that structuration proceeds.*

Elsewhere[3] I have examined the conditions in which the first moment is missing, and the disastrous results that follow. About the second moment, let me say that it is incumbent on whoever carries out the function of the third party to spare the child, as far as can be, the effects of the strange prestige that designates him, the third party, as having what is necessary to possess the mother, and hence the woman (every woman or any woman); in other words, as having the phallus, on the one hand insofar as it is signified in the metaphors of absolute weapon and card that never loses, and also in that of color and brilliance, and on the other in so far as it stamps desire with its metonymic structure. The failure of this second moment sometimes goes so far that a belief in a mythical figure who alternately exalts and mortifies the subject becomes for him the very condition of his existence, or of his assent to existence.

If it is admitted that myth, far from reflecting the psychology of an epoch, rather shapes it, are we analysts not called on to answer whether the myth of the Oedipus complex is not becoming the refuge of a pleasure [*jouissance*] which, in truth, can "be reached (only) on the inverted ladder [*échelle inversée*] of the Law of desire?"⁴

Notes

1.   If, on the contrary, we were to envisage the Other as the imaginary other or the like, or even "the little other," we would discover a state of which the least that can be said is that it is not viable, the state brilliantly described by Kant as follows: "In this way a harmony [*Seeleneintracht*] may result resembling that depicted in a certain satirical poem as existing between a married couple bent on going to ruin, Oh marvellous harmony, what he wants is what she wants; or like the pledge which is said to have been given by Francis I to the Emperor Charles V, 'What my brother Charles wants (Milan), that I want too,'" *Critique of Practical Reason and Other Writings in Moral Philosophy* trans. Lewis White Beck, University of Chicago Press, 1949, p. 139.

2.   A denial that has perfectly concrete consequences for the way this woman conducts her married life.

3.   *Études sur l'Oedipe,* Seuil, 1974, chapters VI and VII. Chapter VI has been translated as "Contribution to the Psychoanalysis of Transsexualism," in *Returning to Freud: Clinical Psychoanalysis in the School of Lacan,* ed. Stuart Schneiderman, Yale University Press, 1980.

4.   Jacques Lacan, *Écrits,* Seuil, 1966, p. 827; *Écrits, a Selection,* trans. Alan Sheridan, Tavistock, 1977, p. 324.

Translated by Ben Brewster

from *m/f* 5/6, 1981

Men and Women: A Psychoanalytic Point of View

MOUSTAFA SAFOUAN

The thesis I want to argue in this article is that the difficulties that characterize and have always characterized the relations between man and woman cannot be assimilated to a phenomenon of a social order; it is a vain hope that they might be suppressed by the adoption of concerted methods or the promulgation of laws that would guarantee, for example, equality of rights—even if such laws are desirable in other respects.

This thesis might seem surprising—are we not discussing two naturally complementary sexes, destined as such to understand one another, even to dissolve into one another, as in the diabolical and still effective myth that Plato puts in the mouth of Aristophanes (*The Symposium*)?[1] But to put it another way, the thesis that I am arguing here is as follows: neither sexual relations between man and woman nor the context in which society recognizes them as legitimate, that is, the family based on marriage, are in any way natural. This dual formulation requires me to answer the question: if something belongs neither to the order of society nor to that of nature, where can it be located?[2]

Consider the family. On the one hand its social character seems guaranteed by the variability of its forms; a variability that is infinite in the sense that in principle if not in fact it accommodates all the combinations open to it by the law of exchange. On the other hand, its universality, which is shared by no other institution, apparently obliges thought to assign it an extra-social and *hence* natural origin. Thus Lévi-Strauss can speak of the "biological family":

> Just as the principle of the division of labour establishes a mutual inter-dependence of the sexes, thus forcing them to collaborate within a household, the prohibition of incest institutes an interdependence of biological families and forces them to generate new families through whose offices alone the social group can succeed in perpetuating itself.[3]

This quotation calls for a number of comments. Firstly, the idea that society acts teleologically on nature to create society is hardly more tenable than the Hegelian vision of society as the expression of the Idea or the rational necessity underlying man and his world.[4] Let us note in passing that, if society had to institute the division of labor to establish a mutual interdependence of the sexes, that would imply that the relationship between society and nature consists not of the biological support that the former finds in the latter, but rather of the lack of such a support. Secondly, if the aim was just to establish a mutual interdependence, society, according to a principle of economy, should be content to institute the principle of the division of labor, without dictating certain tasks to man, certain others to woman. There is here an excess that seems rather to answer to a need to *say* who is man and who is woman.[5] Similarly, it cannot be claimed that the prohibition of incest institutes a mutual interdependence between biological families. The tendency to self-enclosure that Lévi-Strauss attributes to these families is rather a characteristic of the modern nuclear family, to the point that it is this very tendency that defines it in relation to the family under the *ancien régime.*[6] Animals do not hang on to their young once they are capable of movement. The biological family is a projection. Nature itself is a cultural idea; its separation from culture is as mythical as the separation of the upper and lower waters. Nor can the prohibition of incest be defined as a "division of marriage rights between families," as Lévi-Strauss suggests, in an attempt to demonstrate its positive character. For the main thing this law prohibits is not marriage between the child and its mother; it prohibits (and this prohibition is quite clearly addressed to the mother *before* it is addressed to the child) their sleeping together. In other words, this is not a law lying at the origins of the emergence of the human family but one which, within that very family, constituted according to the law of exchange, as Lévi-Strauss has taught us, sets limits to consanguines' enjoyment of each other. Unless one supposes that a consanguine is the most appetizing person in the world, the prohibition of incest goes beyond what is required by the law of exchange alone. It too contains an excess that is less easily explained than was the case with the division of labor.

But to say that the law of exchange governs the constitution of the family is also to say, with Claude Lévi-Strauss, that "in all human societies, it is an absolute precondition for the creation of a new family that there already exist two other families ready to provide here a man, there a woman whose marriage will give rise to a third family, and so on *ad infinitum,*"[7] a diachronic operation that is inconceivable without the existence of a nomenclature, that is, of language. Without being the origin of this nomenclature, the prohibition of incest is nonetheless signified in it. More precisely, it is signified either in the name of the one or ones to whom the ego's mother is supposed to belong, that is, in the name of the father, or in the names of the ones who are supposed to have her at their disposal, the grandfather or maternal uncle.

Unless the mother has decided to treat such a name as null and void, as seems indeed to be the case with transsexual children,[8] the presence or signifying effectivity of this name cannot fail to make itself felt in her relation to the child. If the term "hominization" has a meaning it is to this presence, in which Lacan sees, not without reason, the foundation of the symbolic function, that it must be attributed. Just as without language there is no prohibition of incest, so there is no speaking subject without that same prohibition. Indeed, the child's desire for its mother, on whose love it depends, is first of all a desire to be the object of her desire. Clear away any obstacles to the tendency to put it at the sexual service of its mother, and at once there is no longer a subject, just an appendix.

It is not for nothing that the wisdom of the nations says *tres faciunt ecclesiam*. For imagine two subjects. Either they kill one another or they intertwine, and they have no need of speech to do either; or else they can come to an agreement, which cannot be achieved without some speech determining their action and the rules of that action. But it is as clear that neither of these two subjects has any voice but its own to support this speech, as it is clear that that voice alone cannot suffice to give it the authority for it to be accepted as mutually agreeable. That is why he who enunciates that speech, even if he is only thereby enunciating a law to which he is himself subject, can only establish it as an object of agreement if he presents it as a speech received from elsewhere. So emerges the third party, He who speaks, the Other of the Other, to whom are assigned, as it were, the powers of enunciation. We are touching on the symbolic basis of the necessity of authority; a necessity lying in the last analysis in the lack of any Reason (*Raison*) that could prevail against (*avoir raison contre*) desire, and, in consequence, in the fact that speech cannot otherwise achieve any agreement between subjects—short of saying that it loses even the reference to truth, which is, however, essential to it.

The same idea can be formulated in other words by saying that the heteronomy of the moral law is unavoidable. If all the efforts of a Hegel seem to be exerted toward the suppression of this heteronomy, if the political theory of a Hobbes, on the contrary, appeals to the Sovereign, it is because the symbolic basis of authority (and this is to touch on the reason why Lacan has repeatedly stated that the complete formula of atheism is not that the father is dead but that he is unconscious) is usually hidden by the fact that the very nature of what is called meaning is such that the invocation of the third party is impossible without its imaginarization as master.

By distinguishing between the symbolic dimension of authority (the one founding the speaking subject) and its imaginary dimension (the one fixing it either in revendication or in "voluntary servitude"), I have by the same token demonstrated why the symbolic function can only be sustained by another name than the one that designates, in Lacan's words, "the Other of love and of primary dependence," in the event the mother or her surrogates. I have also demonstrated why it is men who exchange women and not *vice versa*.

On this point, Lévi-Strauss writes:

> Women readers who are alarmed to see themselves reduced to the role of objects of exchanges between masculine partners need not worry: the rules of the game would be the same if the reverse convention were adopted and men became objects of exchange between feminine partners.[9]

Actually, no one is deceived by the concession to an ideal of egalitarianism (only an "ideal" anyway because the structural conditions setting limits to its application are ignored). For the fact is (and it is a fact not unconnected with the rivalry between woman and man), the fact is that the theoretical possibility our author implies has remained a mere possibility. Who could fail to see the oddity, not to say contradiction, in the fact that the arrangement of the future of children as sexed beings is entrusted to their mothers, that is, to precisely the people supposed not to take them as objects of sexual desire?

I hope the reader will not regard the allusion made in the last paragraph to "structural conditions" as a way of reintroducing the Trojan horse of the natural relation. This is a point, however, that deserves more extended treatment.

Always on the lookout for a natural basis explaining the universality of the family, another anthropologist writes:

> It is a basic ground-rule for any primate species that, if we want healthy and effective adults, we have to associate mother and child safely and securely through the critical period of birth at least to the point where the children become independently mobile. In humans, with their extremely long dependency period, this is even more important, so that in a very real sense the mother-child tie is the basic bond in any system of social relationships and one that is really taken over from nature.[10]

This thesis gave rise to a discussion that is very relevant to us here:

> *Rapoport:* Surely the only irreducible unit is an adult-child unit? There
> has to be somebody older than the child to look after it, and that adult
> could be a man or a woman. We can look at history to get the possible
> range of patterns but we are here concerned with the future of the family.
> In technological fields it is a truism that the future is based on the past
> but equally that it may take new forms. The present form of nuclear family
> has evolved from the past but in future it may be the framework for new
> variations each of which may be functional for different purposes. We
> must begin to think about alternative forms in addition to all those Dr.
> Fox has discussed. There are many current social movements which are
> thinking up new organisational forms for different kinds of child care and
> child-and-adult arrangements where the mother-child unit is not the nec-
> essary irreducible unit.
>
> *Comfort:* But if you don't have the mother, you must at least have a lac-
> tating female.
>
> *Rapoport:* Not necessarily. You can bottle-feed babies, and some males
> may be as good as some females at doing so.[11]

There can be no doubt that Rhona Rapoport's thesis is basically correct. No one disputes that only females give birth. But there is a whole world of difference between
saying that and the statement that the desire for maternity and mothering is a natural
desire for the woman. Women who reject it are to be found in all sorts of societies.
To regard them as monsters is to presuppose the problem resolved in favor of the
naturalistic thesis.

Suppose, however, that the prospect Rapoport holds out as a possibility the
realization of which would tend toward more equality between the sexes, or rather
towards nondiscrimination (as if the relations between men and women were simply comparable to the relations between blacks and whites), suppose this prospect
became the general rule. In other words, suppose that it is the man who occupies
the place of the "Other of love and primary dependence." Apparently we could conceive that this would give rise to a kind of counter-Oedipus complex or generalised
inverted Oedipus complex, in which the identifications on which heterosexual
desire is built will take place: initially desirous of his father or of being the object of

his father's desire, the boy will come into competition with his mother, but as this rivalry is subject to a prohibition—which in this hypothesis can be conceived as supported by the name of the mother—the boy will be induced to renounce his homosexual desire so as to be able, if all goes well, to identify with his father as desiring. As for the girl, initially desirous of her father in the same way, she will be induced to renounce this primary heterosexual desire so as to be able, via an identification with her mother as desiring, to transfer it to other men.

What objection could there be to this hypothesis, the only truly matriarchal one? Precisely that it reintroduces the Trojan horse of the natural relation: the shifting of identifications (both the identification in rivalry with the mother and the normative or resolutory identification with the parent of the same sex) is supposed in this hypothesis to be governed by the perception of a *direct* desire binding the parents one to the other.

It will be noted that this objection applies just as much to the earlier of Freud's versions of the Oedipus complex. The two conceptions, that of the Oedipus complex and the one I have called a generalized inverted Oedipus complex, are superior to the anti-Oedipus in that they recognize that desire is, in the Hegelian formulation, desire of the Other, in the dual sense of desiring the thing the Other desires or being that thing itself. Only, up to this point, desire may emerge as a result of purely imaginary fascinations or on the basis of identification with the other as no more than the like. But the simplicity of this mediation that the image of the like offers desire is nothing less than subverted as soon as that like presents itself also as the locus of language and speech—what Lacan emphasizes by writing *Other* as opposed to *other,* the latter being reserved as the designation of the like. For once this is the case, instead of a tendency converging on the same object, the subject's desire becomes a search for a signifier, an interrogation as to the desire of the Other insofar as that desire is located beyond everything that, in the relationship between the Other and its own will, is articulable for it, that is, its demands.[12] This questioning, already located in a different chain from that of demands,[13] stabilizes in an interpetation of the ever-enigmatic desire of the Other; it is because desire is in essence interpretation that it is interpretable. In other words, and this is the locus of the subversion I have just mentioned, instead of being coopted to an object, desire is first coopted to a fantasy.

Now, the signifier the quest for which represents the initial moment in the constitution of desire is both a signifier lacking in the Other (since it is inarticulable) and a signifier of its lack (since there is desire). And what happens during the so-called phallic phase is that the child, who has undergone his or her first experience of love with a woman, begins to realize that the latter's desire is related, in what is no doubt to the child a more or less obscure way, to the phallus. Hence the hardly avoidable possibility of identifying with that signifier, which does not lack a corresponding image, an image which is borrowed from a perfectly real organ. Hence, in consequence, the need to restrain this identification, which would otherwise amount to the reabsorption of being—the being that language brings forth before any attributes: what am I?—into the phallic attribute alone. This restraint is supplied by the symbolic order. Just as there can be no agreement between subjects without a third term as support of the law, so there can be no subject of sexual desire without a signifier inscribing in some sense the prohibition of an identification with what, on the level of the Other of love as sexed being, appears as lack. That is why if the possibility suggested by Rhona Rapoport, that some men would find greater satisfaction than some women do in caring for children, became a general law, the result would not be a "Counter-Oedipus Complex" but a sexuality adrift at the mercy of narcissistic fascinations alone.

It seems inescapable that such a possibility is by no means remote. This is not the place for a detailed examination of the different explanations that have been offered for the birth of the modern nuclear family, but there is every reason to question the tendency of some writers to regard the emergence of this form of family as an advance.

Edward Shorter, for example, is probably right to state that:

Once the rules of market-place individualism had been learned, they easily took control of the whole arena of conscious attitudes. It is this *prise de pouvoir* that Fred Weinstein and Gerald M. Platt call the "wish to be free." My argument is that for young people in late eighteenth-century Europe, the sexual and emotional wish to be free came from the capitalist market-place.[14]

Now this desire for freedom is, to say the least, suspect when one remembers that Benedetto Croce, the philosopher of freedom, could only define the latter as a struggle against oppression, so much so that the destruction of all oppression would bring about a boredom worse than death[15]—which is to say that the only freedom available is that of dying . . . or worse.

In fact, what Shorter is forgetting and yet constitutes the decisive contribution of Marxism is that the rise of industrial society was accompanied by that of the labor market. In other words, labor has been suppressed as an activity enabling the individual, man or woman, to realize him or herself or to recognize him or herself in the product of that activity itself. If the division of labor between the sexes has actually helped in stabilizing their relations—even if its primary causes lie elsewhere—this is not because it established a mutual interdependence between them, but far rather because it opened to each of them a field for the exercise of its gifts. Besides, it is easy to perceive that without real satisfactions in labor for each of the partners, marriage is hardly a viable relationship at the present time. In the absence of a sufficient condition, which does not exist, it is at least a necessary one. Once dispossessed of their possibilities of becoming what they can be by the transformation of labor into a commodity, individuals are left in the lurch, their only remaining reference being the fixed and fixing one to themselves. And what can one make of this oneself except what Shorter expresses excellently but fails to perceive that in doing so he is handing us the very formula of love in its narcissistic structure: "You look into another person's eyes in the hope that you'll find yourself."[16]

Now, like King Midas transforming everything he touches into gold, love transforms everything into a gift; it defines itself as the gift of oneself. As Philippe Ariès has shown,[17] the birth of the modern family was accompanied by its increasing recentering around the child. But what is not so often noticed is that the child has itself become a gift object in which each parent not only rediscovers him or herself (again) but also a being totally subject to the exercise of his or her power—which, of course, is unfailingly motivated by the idea that all this is for the good of the child. As Ariès writes:

> The solicitude of family, Church, moralists and administrators deprived the child of the freedom he had hitherto enjoyed among adults. It inflicted on him the birch, the prison cell—in a word, the punishments usually reserved for convicts from the lowest strata of society. But this severity was the expression of a very different feeling from the old indifference: an obsessive love which was to dominate society from the eighteenth century on.[18]

It may be said that this centering of family organization around the child takes us as far as possible from the Christian ideal according to which husband and wife are "one flesh"—at least if one accepts Evald Lövestam's interpretation of this expression:

> This expression (one flesh) does not refer to the sexual relationship nor to the unity that comes out of having children together. It refers to man

and woman's entire concrete existence as human beings where they—in their unity with each other—with their different qualifications (*ish-ishah/zakhar-nekerah*) complement each other to live together as parts of the same body. The special quality of this union is strongly stressed: it has deeper dimensions than even the blood ties between parent and children.[19]

However, at the present time, when what Ivan Illich would call the "knowledge market"[20] is replacing the labor market and age classes the division between the sexes, when the satisfaction of demands is entrusted more and more to enterprises conceived in such a way that their carrying out can constitute the object of a technology, it can be asked what will become of the world when a new commandment declares them, the adult and child, one flesh. This fantastic prospect cannot be ruled out. Evidence for this is provided by the tendency to restrict the definition of the "family" to this couple alone: "a community composed of a child and one or more adults in close affective and physical relation which is expected to endure at least through childhood."[21] And it is a virtual certainty that paternity will soon be redefined in law to retain only the *Pater* component and to exclude that of *Genitor*.[22]

All this notwithstanding, any attempt to answer my question remains in the domain of science fiction. John Irving's now famous novel *The World According to Garp*[23] give us not the slightest notion about it. For the eponymous Garp's mother (a character living integrally in the dimension of response to demand, that is, a nurse who, in her one attempt to escape from her nurse's uniform, unwittingly dresses as a whore) has not only given her offspring the name of the invalid by whom she was impregnated, but also raised him by strict reference to her family tradition.

Until the artificial child-adult family proves to us that the family was never anything but a social institution without any link to nature, there is no one more qualified than the legislator to know the true reason for the difficulties between man and woman—which does not prevent him from acting as if no consequences followed from such knowledge: for otherwise he would not be able to act. He knows that his function is a necessary one, that the very idea of leaving it to the interested parties to establish their own marriage or cohabitation contract is, to say the least, "strange,"[24] if not classifiable as a masochistic practice. He also knows that his texts are always deceptive, as is clear merely from a reading of this commentary by an eminent jurist, Tony Honoré, on the term "consent," which turns up so frequently in those texts:

The talk of "consent" is of course pure fiction. A wife does not, merely by going through a ceremony of marriage, consent to sexual intercourse at any time or place which her husband may choose. What she and he agree to do is to develop and maintain a mutually tolerable sexual relationship. It may seem a little unambitious to put the duty so low. But the law is here concerned with minimum standards of conduct, not with the conduct of the ideal husband or wife.[25]

The misrecognition of each and everyone is inscribed in that reference to the ideal husband and wife when it is a question of their desires.

Without the Law, where would we be? And how can we recognize that words are vain to speak our desires without ceasing to deploy our weary pens in Its service?

Notes

1.   In today's humorless jargon one would talk of "establishing a couple identity" regarded as an "engagement transition task." See Rhona Rapoport: "The Study of Marriage" in Peter Lomas, ed., *The Predicament of the Family,* Hogarth Press and Institute of Psychoanalysis, 1972, p. 188.

2.   It is thus a matter of going beyond the "nature/culture" alternative from which Ernestine Friedl, for example, has not (see her *Women and Men, An Anthropologist's View,* Holt, Reinhart and Winston, 1975).

3.   Claude Lévi-Strauss, *Le regard éloigné,* Plon, 1983, p. 82; trans. by J. Neugroschel and P. Hoss as *The View from Afar,* Penguin, 1987.

4.   On this point see Charles Taylor's admirable account in *Hegel,* Cambridge University Press, 1983, pp. 378—388.

5.   There is no need to appeal to psychoanalysis to confirm the existence of uncertainty as to sex. Here is the testimony of an anthropologist, Robin Fox, in Katherine Elliott, ed., *The Family and Its Future,* J. A. Churchill, 1970, p. 133: "The pill does not render the woman infertile as much as it renders the man sterile. I have seen this amongst teenagers and college students in America where the young males have enough troubles anyway about their masculinity; they are always wondering whether they are really masculine and how to prove this." No one would claim that this need for proof is peculiar to young Americans; if it is more pronounced among them, it gives rise to all sorts of rituals elsewhere.

6.   See Philippe Ariès, *Centuries of Childhood,* Penguin, 1973.

7.   Lévi-Strauss, p. 83.

8.   See Moustafa Safouan, "Contribution a l'étude du transsexualisme," *Etudes sur l'Oedipe,* Seuil, 1974; trans. in S. Schneiderman, ed., *Returning to Freud: Clinical Psychoanalysis in the School of Lacan,* Yale University Press, 1980.

9.   Lévi-Strauss, p. 90.

10.   Robin Fox, "Comparative Family Patterns," *The Family and Its Future,* p. 2.

11.   *Ibid.,* p. 10.

12.   Hence the comparison Lacan makes between the French *Est-ce?* ("is it?") and the German *Es* ("id").

13.   The existence of a dual chain or, if you prefer, "words beneath words," constitutes the every-day experience of analysis, but evidence of it is available to everyone.

14.   Edward Shorter, *The Rise of the Modern Family,* Fontana, 1976, p. 254.

15.   See Benedetto Croce, *La Storia come pensiero e come azione,* Laterza Bari, 1965, p. 50.
16.   Shorter, p. 254.
17.   Ariès, *op cit.*
18.   *Ibid.,* p. 397.
19.   Evald Lovestam, "Divorce and Marriage in the New Testament," *The Jewish Law Annual,* vol. IV (1981), p. 51.
20.   Ivan Illich, *Deschooling Society,* Harper and Row, 1970.
21.   Ivan Illich, *Justine, Equal Opportunity and the Family,* Yale University Press, 1983, citing John E. Coons and Stephen D. Sugarman, *Education and Choice: The Case for Family Control,* University of California Press, 1978, p. 53.
22.   See R. Snowden and G. D. Mitchell, *The Artificial Family,* George Unwin and Unwin, 1981.
23.   John Irving, *The World According to Garp,* E. P. Dutton, 1978.
24.   See Tony Honore, *Sex Law,* Duckworth, 1978. pp. 50–51.
25.   *Ibid.,* p. 23.

Translated by Ben Brewster

from *m/f* 9, 1984

The Feminine Superego

CATHERINE MILLOT

Freud's statements as to the weakness of the superego in women have often been singled out as evidencing misogyny on his part rather than impartial clinical observation. At first sight they may indeed seem strange, given that there is abundant evidence that women are no more immune than men to the ravages of the superego that Lacan characterized as obscene and ferocious.

The Two Vicissitudes of the Love Object

On this point I shall attempt to clarify Freud's position by examining two vicissitudes of the Oedipus complex among girls. In "Some Psychical Consequences of the Anatomical Distinction between the Sexes," Freud makes the following statement:

> I cannot evade the notion (though I hesitate to give it expression) that for women the level of what is ethically normal is different from what it is in men. Their super-ego is never so inexorable, so impersonal, so independent of its emotional origins as we require it to be in men. Character-traits which critics of every epoch have brought up against women—that they show less sense of justice than men, that they are less ready to submit to the great exigencies of life, that they are more often influenced in their judgements by feelings of affection or hostility—all these would be amply accounted for by the modification in the formation of their super-ego which we have inferred above. We must not allow ourselves to be deflected from such conclusions by the demands of the feminists, who are anxious to force us to regard the two sexes as completely equal in position and worth.[2]

This difference between the superego among women and in man is linked by Freud to the Oedipus complex. Freud's reservations about the superego among women concern the post-Oedipal superego, not the early, maternal, superego to which Melanie Klein devoted so much attention.

Freud suggests that the Oedipus complex is asymmetric between the sexes: the boy leaves the Oedipus complex thanks to the castration complex, whereas the girl enters it via the same complex, the main point being castration anxiety, which Freud sees as lacking in women insofar as the castration threat has no object for them, given the lack of a real organ for it to find a purchase in. With the elimination of castration anxiety, "a powerful motive also drops out for the setting up of a super-ego and for the breaking-off of the infantile genital organisation."[3] These two points are interdependent: "In her, far more than in the boy, these changes seem to be the result of upbringing and of intimidation from outside which threatens her with a loss of love."[4]

Three essential notions should be noted in this short sentence. First, the link between the superego and castration anxiety; second, the girl's dependence on an instance located in the outside world; and lastly the notion—one of Freud's recurrent themes—that, for girls, fear of a loss of love takes the place of castration anxiety among men. Freud's central thesis is to link the formation of the superego to the dissolution of the Oedipus complex for the girl, insofar as castration anxiety does not affect her. Which implies that she retains her bond with her father, that is, her demand on her father survives, it retains its actuality.

The formation of the superego for the man is consequent on the dissolution of the Oedipus complex (one might even say the destruction of the Oedipus complex), that is, it implies the renunciation of incestuous objects, in other words the renunciation of the incestuous demand. The superego, in fact, is a substitute formation, taking the place of the Oedipal bond, Freud's notion being that there is a superego insofar as the bond with the object, the amorous bond with the parental objects, is destroyed. The Oedipus complex is dissolved insofar as castration anxiety brings to an end the erotic bond with the mother, and the loving bond with the father.

For the girl, on the contrary, the same castration complex, linked to the fact that she lacks the organ of the penis, creates the Oedipus complex, and not only creates it, but maintains it: "The girl is driven out of her attachment to her mother through the influence of her envy of the penis and she enters the Oedipus situation as though into a haven of refuge. In the absence of fear of castration the chief motive is lacking which leads boys to surmount the Oedipus complex. Girls remain in it for an indeterminate length of time; they demolish it late, and even so, incompletely. In these circumstances the formation of the superego must suffer; it cannot attain the strength and independence which give it its cultural significance."[5] The superego and the bond with the father are inversely proportionate—the superego forms insofar as the bond with the father dissolves.

Here I must make a detour to specify what is involved in the paternal function in the Oedipus complex, and the relations between the superego and the ego ideal (*idéal du moi*).

Remember that the Oedipus complex, for the boy as much as for the girl, consists in the preference granted, at a certain moment in the subject's history, to the father in comparison with the mother, a change of objects following on from the discovery of the mother's castration. Freud notes that what Lacan has called this turning to the father's side, this *père-version,* which is the very essence of the Oedipus complex in both sexes, in many cases does not take place for the girl, who remains fixated on her mother. Let us consider the case where, for the subject, this passage, consisting in the fact that at a certain moment, the father has been preferred to the mother, has taken place. This preference goes along with a transference of power: the place of the Other, as the place to which the demand is addressed, has shifted from the mother to the father. Once this *père-version,* this turn toward the father, has been achieved, the destinies of boys and girls separate. The boy is held back from the path of this love for his father by the barrier of castration anxiety, and produces the renunciation of his father as object—a renunciation that is sanctioned by his identification with his father.

This is the notorious identification of the second type, a regressive identification (insofar as it replaces an object choice) that leads to the formation of the ego ideal. The boy identifies with his father insofar as he has loved his father and renounced that love. More precisely, he identifies with the insignia of paternal power, making the slide from having him—having his father as love object—to being him. The superego, in the sense in which Freud speaks of the post-Oedipal superego, is the correlate of this formation of the ego ideal, and corresponds to the obligations henceforth imposed on the subject as attendant on that paternal function, in the manner: "*Noblesse oblige.*"

Ego Ideal: The Initial Demand

The articulation of the superego and the ego ideal is a tricky question. The superego and the ego ideal are both formations belonging to the symbolic register, but, whereas the ego ideal is sustained by a feature—*einziger Zug*—a feature that is of the order of the *insignum,* of the badge, that is, of something halfway between the sign and the signifier, on the contrary, the superego is more a matter of speech (*parole*). According to Freud, it is composed of things heard, of verbal residues, whereas the ego ideal commands the subject's narcissistic position. It is related to the specular register and represents that by which the subject restores the lost narcissistic satisfaction, that is, it implies a fantasy of omnipotence.

The superego is related to the voice, not to the look. If the ego ideal is closer to a model, the superego is essentially a demand presenting itself in the form of imperatives and prohibitions, which are correlated with the model constituted by the ego ideal. The Oedipal superego is a demand to which the subject submits insofar as he thereby makes a compact with the paternal power. I can formulate this demand using Lacan's words: "Thou shalt not desire what was my desire."

Note that the origin of the formation of the ego ideal also lies in a demand: a demand of the subject addressed to the Other, and which has met with a flat refusal. It is on the basis of this rejected demand, on the basis of a privation, that the subject identifies with the Other that had the power to respond to it. It is with the insignia of this power to respond that the subject identifies. Which is to say that (virtually, at least) there are as many identifications as there are rejected demands.

The question is one of the relationship between the initial demand, initiating the formation of the ego ideal, and the terminal demand, that of the superego. I shall suggest that this relationship depends on the fate of the initial demand, that is, on whether this demand has been repressed or truly renounced. Freud instances those cases in which the Oedipus complex has as it were exploded, in which it has been completely destroyed, I should say, insofar as the demand at the basis of the formation of the ego ideal has been actually renounced, and not just repressed, by the subject. In the second case it can be supposed to return in the form of superegoic demand, either in the mode of a direct turning round upon the subject's own self (along Kleinian lines, corresponding to an inversion, even a revision of the demand), or in a reversal into its opposite, announcing itself, for example, in the form of prohibitions. There is an echo here of instinctual vicissitudes—which suggests the possibility of a coordination of superego and *jouissance.*

When the demand has disappeared without repression, we would have the case of a true dissolution of the Oedipus complex, and in this case the superego would, in Lacan's terms, be reduced to the identity of desire and law. This would correspond to Freud's post-Oedipal superego, which constitutes the backbone of the subject, making him independent of all outside influence. Insofar as the demand for love on the father is rendered null and void, the essential springs of voluntary servitude also collapse. In a sense, after the dissolution of the Oedipus complex, the subject no longer has anything to demand of anyone.

This Freudian post-Oedipal superego is not the superego of transitivist retaliation, which is never anything but the turning on the subject of his own demand. It is the superego that, in the Lacanian perspective, hardly still deserves the name, since it results from the assimilation by the subject of the law insofar as that law frees him from demand and at the same time constitutes his desire.

In his commentary on the first scene of *Athalie*,[6] Lacan shows how Joad, the high priest, confronting Abner, prey to the terror of the superegoic figure represented by Athalie, substitutes for this fear, in a beautiful metaphor, the fear of God, which Lacan emphasizes is something quite different from a fear, is indeed its opposite. The fear of God is the signifier of the alliance that the Jewish people has made with God, and which places it on his side. The law it has made its own is identical with its desire, and now makes it inaccessible to fear as to pity, unsubjectable to any figure of tyranny whatsoever.

Penisneid: The Persistence of the Demand

It is this second form of the superego, linked to identification with the father and constitutive of the ego ideal, that Freud regards as not forming in the girl—precisely insofar as the girl is not required to proceed to this identification with her father. Falling outside the sphere of the threat of castration, the girl does not renounce her demand for love on her father, that is her demand for the penis or the child that is its substitute. The girl retains this demand, hangs onto it, even if it is subsequently addressed to substitutes for the father. She knows she does not have the phallus, and where she should go to get it: this is why there is something wild about "true" women, says Lacan.[7]

This fixity of demand has as a consequence a rigidity in the feminine character and tends to block women's developmental capacities, something Freud complains of at the end of the fifth of the New Introductory Lectures:

> A woman of [about thirty], however, often frightens us by her psychical rigidity and unchangeability. Her libido has taken up final positions and seems incapable of exchanging them for others. There are no paths open to further development; it is as though the whole process had already run its course and remains thenceforward insusceptible to influence—as though, indeed, the difficult development to femininity had exhausted the possibilities of the person concerned. As therapists we lament this

state of things, even if we succeed in putting an end to our patient's ailment by doing away with her neurotic conflict.[8]

In other words, this rigidity may be structural, but it is not pathological.

In addition, woman is, for Freud's taste, a little too matter of fact. She knows all too well what she wants, in the sense that there is no point in talking to her about it—she wants something more substantial. She is only accessible to "the logic of soup, with dumplings for arguments."[9]

The persistence of the demand has a further consequence: it leaves the woman dependent on a real Other, which may be her father or more often, of course, a substitute for her father. The identity of the object of satisfaction and the object of love for the woman, as Lacan puts it, makes her more dependent on the love of that Other from whom she expects the satisfaction of her demand for the phallus. To this extent the source of anxiety for her is the loss of this love, which would count for her at the same time as a refusal of her phallic demand. This being so, the Other to whom she addresses her demand—which can be anyone as soon as he is put in the place of the big Other—is in a position to subject her to ultimately limitless requirements. He is put in the place of the superego she lacks as an intrapsychical instance. Woman in some sense has her superego in the outside world.

In an article on the formation of the superego in women,[10] Hanns Sachs has described this subjection. The article is essentially devoted to the masculinity complex, but as a contrast the writer evokes what he regards as an opposite character type to the masculinity complex in which the ego ideal is particularly underdeveloped. Thus he evokes a whole category of women, whom he has not analyzed, however, but only observed. These women are presented as having the charm of narcissistic women, closed in on themselves. They are especially seductive socially and have a special capacity to enter into what the writer calls the idiosyncrasies of the men to whom they are attached. "They make themselves a mere echo of the man they are with," he says. A series of layers can be detected in their remarks. They have rather heteroclite knowledge on a whole variety of subjects. They have opinions whose diversity is not limited by contradiction. This psychical mosaic corresponds to the different men these women have known. From each man they have borrowed some ideas.

For Sachs, this should be seen as a kind of rudimentary formation of the super-ego, an adumbration constituted via the sexual act with men. These women make their own the ideas of men via the ephemeral appropriation of their phallic organs. The sexual act is the precondition for their being able to exalt the man so as to be able to put him in the place of the superego. But it is a superego that remains external, only reaches a rather low level, and never becomes personal, exerting no real influence on the ego. In fact it is a matter of a mode of appropriation of the phallus on both planes—the sexual act and the acquisition of ideas being here equivalent. This theory is not lacking in humor, but it is not very profound clinically: Sachs himself points out that he has not analyzed these women.

If one takes the consequences of what Freud suggests, it follows that there is no post-Oedipal maternal ego ideal for the girl, and hence no post-Oedipal maternal superego. Indeed, if the Oedipus complex includes a turn to the side of the father, it implies an abandonment of the mother as a point to which the demand is addressed precisely insofar as the mother's castration makes her forfeit the power and place from which she might respond to the demand—she forfeits the power of response. A maternal ego ideal forms in the girl only insofar as the subject has not assumed her mother's castration and has maintained her in her omnipotent status. In this case—I am thinking of Kleinian developments—the father is no more than an appurtenance of the mother, one of the attributes of maternal power, the equivalent of a fetish. Let me add that cures of children such as are reported by Melanie Klein seem to me to be directed toward such an issue for the girl—she is to identify with her mother as omnipotent and possessor of various phallic appendices, including the father's sex. In this case, the girl is subject to the first kind of retaliatory maternal superego, that is, the "obscene and ferocious" superego.

The Masculinity Complex

One can see the difficulties of the girl's position in respect to identification at the end of the Oedipus complex. For her there is no ideal feminine identification possible other than the phallic woman; but this is precisely a "pre-Oedipal" identification. This is because the ideal precisely includes phallic power. This does not facilitate the girl's relations with femininity, and often leads her to a solution close to that of the boy: this is what is known as the masculinity complex, and I want to turn to it now.

The masculinity complex is one of the three ways out of the castration complex produced in the girl by her confrontation with the reality of her lack of a penis. The first consists in an abandonment of sexuality altogether, the second corresponds to the masculinity complex that consists in her nonrenunciation of possession of the phallic organ, either in the form of a persistent expectation of it or in that of a disavowal of her deprivation of it.

The masculinity complex eventually came to designate the second of these forms in particular, the illusion that in one way or another she possesses the insignia of virility: "A girl may refuse to accept the fact of being castrated, may harden herself in the conviction that she *does* possess a penis, and may subsequently be compelled to behave as though she were a man."[11] The third way out is the one that leads toward femininity, orienting the girl toward the man from whom she will receive, in the form of a child, the symbolic substitute for the penis she lacks.

In 1925 and after,[12] Freud noted the existence of the masculinity complex in women, following a series of articles by Van Ophuijsen,[13] who introduced the term in 1917, and by Abraham, on the manifestations of the female castration complex, in 1920.[14] Van Ophuijsen based his description of this complex on a series of five cases of feminine obsessional neurosis in which analysis revealed the unconscious conviction of the possession of the male organ. In three of them this conviction was linked to the fact of having "Hottentot nymphae" that constituted the feature that distinguished them radically from other women. These patients behaved as men, and competed with them in intellectual or artistic activities. They presented marked homosexual tendencies. The fantasy of phallic possession was linked with their identification with their fathers.

For his part, Abraham listed the different feminine positions vis-à-vis the absence of the penis, from hope to renunciation, from disavowal to vengeance. On the neurotic side he distinguished two types, that of wish-fulfillment (corresponding to Freud's disavowal) and that of revenge. The first represents the neurotic version the perverse aspect of which is homosexuality. It corresponds to the masculinity complex, depending on the unconscious fantasy of being in possession of the virile organ. This fantasy is expressed in various symptoms such as eneuresis—in which the emission of urine symbolizes the possession of the "widdler."

No more than Freud do Abraham and Ophuijsen stress the castration anxiety accompanying such a fantasy. Inversely, the writers who examined the question of the superego among women related the formation of the superego to the existence of a castration anxiety in women, as a correlate of the masculinity complex—an anxiety leaving nothing to be desired in rigor (in this respect) to its analogue in the man. This is what Carl Müller-Braunschweig claimed: "If we emphasize the indestructible feminine fantasy of the possession of a penis, and if we admit, as we ought to do, the *psychical* reality of the imagined penis in the case of a girl alongside the corporeal reality of the penis in the case of the boy, then we can speak positively of a feminine castration-anxiety as well as of a masculine. Many adult women, in their parapraxes and dreams, behave entirely 'as if' they possess a member, the loss of which they have constantly to fear."[15]

Müller-Braunschweig, following on from Karen Horney, regarded such a fantasy in women as constituting a reaction formation with its source not so much in the disappointment consequent on the privation of the phallic organ as in the anxieties aroused by "feminine" desires, constituting a threat to their integrity and to their internal organs (fear of rape). Castration anxiety being preferable in the last resort to anxiety at the prospect of a much more radical destruction. Sandor Radó[16] takes up a similar perspective, but closer to Helene Deutsch, in making the masculinity complex a defensive formation vis-à-vis the woman's masochistic genital drives.

Ernest Jones returns to this dispute (primary or reaction-formed phallicism) in his article on the phallic phase.[17] In 1927, he had already[18] associated the masculinity complex, which he called the penis complex, with the homosexual position by distinguishing between two possible types, one retaining the masculine (paternal) object in the mode of identification and seeking from him a recognition of that virile identity, the other giving rise to a homosexual object choice by which the femininity lost by the subject identified with her father is rediscovered notwithstanding in the partner. Identification with the father, he stresses, is common to all forms of homosexuality, its function being to repress feminine desires, and it constitutes the most complete denegation of the latter: "I cannot possibly desire a man's penis for my gratification, since I already possess one of my own, or at all events I want nothing else than one of my own.[19]

It was Joan Rivière who contributed to the rubric "masculinity complex" the most developed case study in her article on "Womanliness as a Masquerade,"[20] The case presented an extra twist as compared with those usually described. The masculine position here was concealed behind the appearances of perfect womanliness. Thus we have a three-fold construction: a woman regards herself as a man who passes for a woman, a construction which cannot fail to evoke the Jewish joke reported by Freud: "If you say you're going to Cracow, you want me to believe you're going to Lemberg. But I know that in fact you're going to Cracow. So why are you lying to me?"[21]

Joan Rivière's patient combined a brilliant professional career and the life of a perfect wife and housekeeper. Nevertheless, she suffered from one symptom: required by her profession to speak in public, the night after giving a lecture, usually with great success, she would generally be seized by an anxiety state consisting of the fear that she had made a fool of herself, and she would then feel a compulsive need to seek reassurance. Which would also be expressed in sexual provocations addressed to men after the lectures she gave.

Joan Rivière summarizes her analysis of the fantasy underlying this symptom as follows: "The exhibition in public of her intellectual proficiency, which was in itself carried through successfully, signified an exhibition of herself in possession of the father's penis, having castrated him. The display once over, she was seized by horrible dread of the retribution the father would then exact. Obviously it was a step towards propitiating the avenger to endeavor to offer herself to him sexually."[22] By disguising herself as a castrated woman she assumed the mask of innocence and guaranteed her impunity. Her behavior with men after lectures thus constituted the obsessional cancellation of her intellectual performance.

Castration Anxiety: The Demand Inverted

As Lacan shows, in his seminar on the *Formations of the Unconscious,* in the case of the masculinity complex one is dealing with a completed Oedipus complex, and one which finds a resolution, but a resolution that can be described as atypical and neuroticising.

The girl has reached the *père-version,* corresponding to the third moment of the Oedipus complex: she applies to her father as he who can give her what she lacks. At this point a reversal occurs: instead of clinging indefinitely to the demand emerging from *Penisneid,* the girl renounces it. At any rate, as it is the demand of a child addressed to its father, it is already destined to meet with a refusal, in the form of the disappointment of the expectation. Freud thought it was the degree of constitutional masculinity in the girl that caused this disappointment to lead, not to the persistence of the demand, but to its renunciation. The girl renounces the maintenance of her demand and thereby identifies with that Other that has refused her satisfaction, and especially with the insignia of his power, thereby constituting a paternal, masculine, ego ideal. Nevertheless, writers such as Ophuijsen and Müller-Braunschweig noted that these women do not necessarily demonstrate masculine behavior.

It may be asked whether the renunciation of this demand is due to a special intolerance to the disappointment occasioned by the vain expectation, or whether it might not proceed from love for the father. The girl renounces her demand insofar as she feels that it constitutes a castration threat for her father. Having constituted this paternal ego ideal, she is henceforth endowed with the phallus at the fantasy level, but one should rather speak, as Müller-Braunschweig does, of a sort of illusory penis.

This has a whole series of consequences, and first of all castration anxiety which, at the level of neurotic manifestations, has to be distinguished from *Penisneid* insofar as it is not a matter of demand on the Other but rather of the subject's anxiety at the prospect of the loss of this illusory organ. Analysts have widely demonstrated that castration anxiety is certainly to be found in certain women. An anxiety which may manifest itself in the form of anxiety in the face of the superego, insofar as castration anxiety provides a purchase for the formation of the superego. Castration anxiety in women can also have the function of demonstrating the existence of something to be castrated, as in Joan Rivière's patient's case: the anxiety is one of the proofs of the existence of the phallus.

How does the superego manifest itself in the masculinity complex? Referring to the article by Hanns Sachs already mentioned, it seems to reduce itself to a prohibition bearing on the demand. Having renounced their demand for their father's phallus or a substitute for it, these women feel constrained to renounce every demand. This is what this writer designates as the "ideal of a renunciation." He presents the case of a woman patient who leads an ascetic life, full of toil and abnegation. In this case it is not a matter of the style of exhibitionist self-sacrifice that enables the subject to tyrannize her associates. On the contrary, it is a question of an ascetic attitude that is presented as a matter of course.

This woman feels perfectly satisfied, even parading a kind of fullness. The renunciation goes without question, to the point that the sacrifices are not experienced as such. This ideal of a renunciation conceals an ideal of self-sufficiency: if one has the phallus, one needs nothing else. The manifestations of autonomy in patients of this type are in sharp contrast to the dependence of Freud's woman. The renunciation of the demand is directed at the father and functions as a reassurance: he need not worry, nobody is going to ask him for anything! Joan Rivière points out that this kind of woman is particularly attractive to men who don't like to have too much asked of them.

Identification with the father has as a corollary the fact that the paternal Other is reduced, precisely by that identification, to the status of a little other, while the mother is restored to the place of the big Other. Henceforth, the girl, identified with her father, will replay with her partners and with her own real mother, the history of her pre-Oedipal relations. With that maternal Other she will rediscover her initial demand, but in an inverted form, that is, she will feel herself addressed with the demand for a phallus that she had addressed to her mother before turning towards her father. She then becomes liable to a superegoic requirement that it is impossible to satisfy, precisely that of giving the phallus to her mother, a requirement that must inevitably hold her in constant anxiety at a threat in which are fused the fear of being castrated of this imaginary phallus and the fear lest the truth of her lack be revealed. The writers note that castration anxiety, when it is present, is more severe in women than in men.

On the one hand, these women are in some sense more apt than others to find a social and professional niche, more given to cultural realizations, but, on the other, they are especially severely subject to inhibition. The choice of love object for these women—and I refer here to Jones's article on this, on the phallic phase in women—may be heterosexual, or homosexual. If it is heterosexual, it is so to the extent that they aim to make a man recognize their virility. It is as men that these subjects propose themselves as lovable. In fact, the object of desire—and not the object of love—is feminine. Traces of this renunciation at the symptomatological level can often be found in the form, for example, of occasional feelings of persecution, in all sorts of transactions, of having been swindled. They have, indeed, abandoned the substance for the shadow.

Something Beyond the Oedipus Complex?

The two most frequent vicissitudes of the castration complex in women correspond to *Penisneid* on the one hand, that is, the persistence of the demand addressed to the father, and to the masculinity complex on the other, based on the repression of penis envy.

In the first outcome, the dominant part is played by the demand on the Other by which the subject places herself in a dependence on an external instance fulfilling the function of a superego which is otherwise absent as an intrapsychical instance.

In the second outcome the demand of the Other has the upper hand, giving a superego with features close to those found in the treatment of obsessional neurosis in men.

In the first case the girl does not emerge from the Oedipus complex. On the other hand, it might be asked what happens to the Oedipus complex in the second. Are we dealing with its resolution, insofar as the girl seems to have renounced her demand on her father? The reemergence of pre-Oedipal relations to the mother undermines such a conclusion. The ultimate question thus remains open where the existence of something beyond the Oedipus complex for women is concerned.

Notes

1.   Translated from "Le surmoi féminin," *Ornicar?*, no. 29 (summer 1984), pp. 111–124.
2.   Sigmund Freud, "Some Psychical Consequences of the Anatomical Distinction Between the Sexes," (1925) *The Standard Edition of the Complete Psychological Works of Sigmund Freud*, vol. XIX, pp. 257–258. See also "The Dissolution of the Oedipus Complex" (1924) vol. XIX, pp. 173–179; "Female Sexuality" (1934), *SE*, XXI, pp. 223–224; and "Femininity" (1932), *SE*, XXII, pp. 112–135.
3.   "The Dissolution of the Oedipus Complex," p. 178.
4.   *Ibid.*
5.   "Femininity," p. 129.
6.   Jacques lacan *Le Séminaire livre III: Les Psychoses*, Seuil, 1981, pp. 298–304.
7.   Jacques Lacan *Le Séminaire livre V: Les formations de l'inconscient*, unpublished seminar (1957–1958).
8.   Freud, *SE*, XXII, pp. 134–135.
9.   Freud, *SE*, XXII, pp. 134–135.
10.   Hanns Sachs, "One of the Motive Factors in the Formation of the Super-Ego in Women," *International Journal of Psychoanalysis*, X (1929), p. 39.
11.   Freud, "Some Psychical Consequences" *SE* XIX p 253.
12.   Freud, "Some Psychical Consequences," "Female Sexuality," and "Femininity."
13.   J. H. W. Van Ophuijsen, "Contributions to the Masculinity Complex in Women," *IJP*, V (1924), pp. 39–49.
14.   Karl Abraham, *Selected Papers*, London, 1968, pp. 338–369.
15.   Carl Müller-Braunschweig, "The Genesis of the Feminine Super-Ego," *IJP*, VII (1926), p. 361.
16.   Sandor Radó, "Fear of Castration on Women," *Psychoanalytic Quarterly* 2 (1933), p. 425 and in *Psychoanalysis of Behaviour, Collected Papers*, vol. I (1922–1926), pp. 83–120.
17.   Ernest Jones, "The Phallic Phase," *IJP*, XIV (1933) and in *Papers in Psychoanalysis*, 5th ed., pp. 452–484.
18.   Ernest Jones, "The Early Development of Feminine Sexuality," in *Papers in Psychoanalysis*, pp. 438–451.
19.   *Ibid.*, p. 447.
20.   Joan Rivière, "Womanliness as Masquerade," *IJP*, X (1929), pp. 303–313.
21.   Freud, *SE*, VIII, p. 115.
22.   Joan Rivière, pp. 305–306.

Translated by Ben Brewster

Discussion

Juliet Mitchell: I'd like to start by asking for some clarification. What status are you giving to the superego itself, after all it's the subject of the paper. At one point you talk about what Hanns Sachs said about the superego. You are quite dismissive of Sachs where he suggests that the girl uses the superego in the real world as an external superego. Yet I thought that earlier you had been suggesting something similar and that you came back to this again at the end. At the end you argue that Freud is saying that the girl, lacking castration anxiety, is dependent on real objects, and you suggest that the real object is in some ways equated with the paternal superego, well with the father as an external superego, as though the father could become in reality the superego. I think that this is a very problematic interpretation. As I understand it, what Freud is saying is not that the father or even the function of the father (in a more Lacanian sense) is the source of the superego. In the boy's resolution of the Oedipus complex it is the superego of the father that becomes the superego of the child. It is not the father, it is the father's superego. This is how Freud explains the whole transmission of culture as well as the often extraordinary dislocation between the real father and the superego. The superego of the "ideal" little boy after the castration complex might be an extraordinarily severe superego bearing no relation to the father, for what is being transmitted, in the presencee or absence of any real father, is the paternal superego. So I don't see how that paternal superego could then become the real object for the little girl.

Catherine Millot: Yes, it's not in the same sense. There are two types of superego. Lacan speaks of a superego which is very tyrannical, the pre-Oedipal type of superego which is essentially maternal.

Juliet Mitchell: You mean the superego that Melanie Klein writes about?

Catherine Millot: A Kleinian superego, yes. And maybe the father could be at the place of that superego—the tyrannical pre-Oedipal superego—then the father is at exactly the same place as the mother for the girl. It is just a passing from mother to father but there is no superego formation in the sense of Freud's post-Oedipal superego. And I think that when Freud talked about the superego of the father, the boy identifies himself with the superego—not only with the father but with the superego of the father. It designates the link of his father to the law for the father is also subject to the law and in that sense the boy identifies/constitutes his superego in relation to the law.

Juliet Mitchell: I agree with that—but my point was that there can't be such a thing as an external superego, by definition. The little girl has not got a post-Oedipal castration anxiety superego, so that the object that she becomes dependent on is not a superego. It must be actually something else—something that is making and creating real demands to and from her.

Catherine Millot: We may say that there are two types of superego, the one, the pre-Oedipal type maintains the Other with a big O, big Other, and the post-Oedipal superego introduces the other with the big O crossed through. There is no longer a big Other for someone who has a superego in the second sense. There is no continuation of demand because there is no Other at all, the big Other is quite suppressed.

Jacqueline Rose: Can I try and say what I think Juliet's question is? Running through Catherine's paper there was a constant reference to the idea of an external point of reference for the girl child, and how her psychological and psychic development depends on that concrete and locatable reference in the real world. Insofar as the whole formation of the superego is a problem of a relationship to the symbolic order and is a relationship to the law, what does it mean to make all these distinctions on the basis of an outside and external reference? Indeed, Freud does seem to be saying something like this when he says the girl is dependent on a loss of love—so that the whole of the girl's development seems to go into the axis of demand and real others whereas the whole point of the superego is that it is in a symbolic register. Is that your question, Juliet?

Juliet Mitchell: Yes, exactly. This Other that is *not* crossed through in this paper becomes a real other. Catherine's argument invites an interepretation on that level.

Catherine Millot: I think the problem arises because of the mixture of Freudian and Lacanian terms within which I am working. Certainly it is the case that Freud makes constant reference to the idea of an external object which I myself used in my paper. But it might help if the question was transposed into Lacanian terms—it clarifies the matter because the opposition isn't between an internal superego and an external superego who would be locatable in the outside world, but it is an opposition between the Other capital O and the Øther with the capital crossed through. The advantage of Lacanian terms lies in their simplicity! In Lacanian terms, what Freud is trying to say is that the woman has a particular difficulty in acceding to the idea of the Other as somebody who is crossed through. Originally, the Other is fantasied as a place of truth which can both receive and satisfy the demands of the subject or the child. The formation of the superego in the sense in which I described it for the boy, is the point where the Other is seen to be also lacking and that is what it means to talk about the Other as crossed through, that is, there is no place in which demand can be fulfilled and no place in which desire can be completed. So reading Freud's account of the superego development (or nondevelopment) of the girl, in Lacanian terms, it could be said that the girl tends to remain in a position of demand vis-à-vis the Other who then is constantly perceived as always in need of completion or always able to complete the girl. That is to say that her relationship to the Other does not pass into that final stage where the Other is recognized to be lacking and therefore she maintains a relationship toward demand.

The dissolution of the Oedipus complex does imply moving into the domain which is the beyond of hope or in a sense the no hope, which means the collapse of this whole register of the fantasy of completetude or completeness. In relationship to the girl that hope remains anchored or tied onto the body—that relinquishment of hope is a stage through which she doesn't pass.

Juliet Mitchell: It is not quite clear whether in some cases she does not pass through it. It seems to me that there were two uses of the ego ideal for the girl: one in which there is an identification with the phallic mother and one in which there is an identification with the phallic father. Those are two different aspects of the masculinity complex as you are trying to analyze it, and they are different in status and they would also seem to me to be different in relation to the formation of the superego—which superego the girl does or doesn't develop. If the masculinity complex is based on an identification with the father then the girl does have castration anxiety and does, in that sense, have the possibility of a superego. If the masculinity complex is based on a maternal identification with a phallic mother (Klein's argument about the little girl), then there can be no castration anxiety because it is repudiated, denied, disavowed, and there could therefore be no superego in the girl, nor no hope. But in the masculinity complex based on an identification with the father I can't see why there can't be a superego for the girl and no hope as well—she has an imaginary penis, but what difference does that make?

Catherine Millot: This is the very important question that I was coming to at the end of my paper, the question as to why the masculinity complex for the girl cannot be seen as a true dissolution of the Oedipus complex. I stress that what I am saying are only hypotheses and speculations around this question. But in the case of the description which Juliet gave of the masculinity complex (identification with the father, castration anxiety, therefore superego and no hope) nonetheless it is not a true dissolution because the desire has been repressed but not renounced and comes back in the form of anxiety, and to that extent is not a true *dépassement* of the Oedipus complex for the girl in the same way as it is for the boy, even though there is superego formation.

Jacqueline Rose: What worried me about Catherine's paper, which I also found fascinating, was not what was said about the girl, which I realize is causing vibrations enough in the room as it is, but actually what she said about the boy. It is precisely this concept of a full and satisfactory dissolution of the Oedipus complex for the boy which I've always thought was a problem in Freud's formulation. Lacan has a term for the idea that something disappears out of existence completely—it's foreclosure and it leads to psychosis. So the notion that the boy somehow goes through the Oedipus complex and it all disappears without trace is an extremely worrying one for me and also it implies that he moves into the position of recognizing that the Other can't satisfy him and all demand drops out of his psychic economy. I wanted to say two things about that, one that it reminded me of Christopher Lasch's use of psychoanalysis which is about the necessary passing through of the Oedipus complex as being the precondition of free political activity for the man, which means that you can then reject tyranny, you can reject the state, you can reject all these hideous advanced American internalisations which are being imposed upon you. It seemed to have the notion of a kind of development out and into true subjecthood. So there was that problem for me and the other one is that it seems to leave out of the account that the passage through the Oedipus complex for the boy brings him up against what in Lacanian terms would be described as the real of sexual difference which will always persist as a problem or as an anxiety point for the subject—witness indeed what Catherine was saying yesterday about cinema as the place in which the fantasy that the woman exists is reinscribed for the subject. So that in a sense even if the boy goes through and out of the Oedipus complex it is not all neatly resolved and passed through without trace and especially at the point of the relationship to sexual difference.

Catherine Millot: The first thing is that the idea of a complete disappearance of the Oedipus complex in the boy is a limit case—is the absolute limit of the description—and Freud himself says there are only, in fact, some cases where the Oedipus complex seems to disappear. Secondly, foreclosure is the opposite of what I was describing because foreclosure, far from being a case where you recognize the Other as lacking, is where you cannot countenance the Other at all because there is no question of any recognition of lack and it leads to psychosis. It is a much bigger denial than the normal neurotic resolution where you do and don't know, as it were. Finally I would say that the question for me is—can we do without, can we get past the father? That is the political, social, and ethical question which in a sense underlay the whole of my paper. What Freud was saying in relationship to women is that they have a too matter-of-fact relationship to the literal father; the man is dealing with his father when he is dealing with his boss. And in Lacan's last seminars on Joyce he did, in fact, turn his attention to this question of the paternal function and said in his classical, enigmatic fashion that one can only get past him if one can make use of him and that the paternal function in the way I have been describing it can be replaced by the *"symptôme,"* not in the sense of symptom but a classical Lacanian pun *le sainte homme,* the holy man. But it is a pun on symptom, and that of course raises the whole question of what such a substitution should be, of a getting past of the father which wouldn't be a symptom. Joyce was taken as an example of a way of writing through that problem, writing and displacing that problem—but writing isn't necessary, what is required is a certain *savoir-faire,* a certain know-how, a certain play on the paternal register. The question of getting beyond, the idea of getting beyond the Oedipus complex is in no sense settled for the boy at all and that issue is wide open for the man as well.

Louisa Murano: My question is what prevents Lacanians from assuming that women are psychotic, since what remains for her is a real lack which fails to be symbolized.

Catherine Millot: It is not possible to take from Lacan the idea that women are psychotic or that they lack access to lack. Because if there is a lack it's only insofar as there is a symbolic register. There is nothing missing in the real; the phallus itself is the symbol of sexual difference and the woman could be said to experience penis envy insofar as she registered a symbolic lack and is therefore in the register of the symbolic. So there is nothing in Lacanian discourse which means that the woman does not have access to the realm of the symbolic. Secondly, regarding the idea that in the sexual act the woman sees the phallus in the body of the man and makes her own body a phallus for the man—there is no accusation of error in stake in that because, after all, these are imaginary equations which are valid for both sexes and men are also quite capable in the sexual act of equating their penis with the phallus. Furthermore, they are capable of putting the woman in the place of the imaginary phallus and indeed it is insofar as they do that, that the woman makes that identification.

Geneviève Fraisse: Could you develop the end of your article, in particular at the point when you said that the woman will be led in the masculinity complex to substitute the shadow for the substance.

Catherine Millot Once the masculinity complex has been surpassed, there is no longer any demand and this leads the woman to renounce, precisely, all the same, the fact of imagining herself to have the phallus which had been set against the desire for a child. The fantasy of phallic possession can lead to the repression of an older desire or demand for a child vis-à-vis the father. Consequently, she could be said to have renounced the substance for the shadow—in the sense that the woman has been led to attach herself to a sort of fantasy, a phallic possession which has existed to the detriment of the satisfaction of her initial demand.

Constance Penley: I am still puzzled about the two superegos that you set up. How are you constructing the maternal superego as a superego?

Catherine Millot: The distinction between the maternal and paternal superego is best formulated by Melanie Klein. In her theorization of the maternal superego, what is feared is not castration but destruction—related to the fantasies about the inside of the mother's body—which would then lead to retaliation. There's no difference in the relation to that anxiety for boys and girls except insofar as the different journeys through the Oedipus complex leaves the girl more prone to the ravages of that maternal superego in her later life, and that's a clinical fact.

Juliet Mitchell: I think that one of the problems of reading Lacan onto Freud on the question of femininity is that the Lacanian description refers to an earlier point of Freud's theory. Freud's writings on femininity are *late* writings, after his structural model of the mind. I know that with Jacqueline Rose I've written that Lacan refers to Freud's latest papers and not, as it is often argued, that he goes only to Freud's earliest work. However, on the question of the feminine superego, I believe he does do this. What is missing from a Lacanian account is any place for Freud's change in his theory of anxiety.

In Freud's paper to which Catherine is mainly referring—the 1933 essay on femininity in the *New Introductory Lectures*—there are two themes. One, Catherine has spoken to—how is it that a girl comes into being? We cannot say what a woman is, only how the girl comes into being from a child with a bisexual disposition. I think Catherine has spoken to that dimension of Freud's essay. But there is another dimension to the essay which is set up at the beginning. Freud is addressing his audience of men and women and saying to men that the problem of femininity is something "we've" always knocked our heads against; as for you women in the audience, you yourselves are the riddle. I think he's talking, as he has done since the 1880s, to this question of the riddle of femininity *seen from a masculine perspective.*

If you leave out that dimension—which involves Freud's changed theory of anxiety, in which he changes from the notion that because we repress things we become anxious to the notion that it's because we are anxious that we repress things—you get to the untenable contradiction in Lacan's and Catherine's formulation. It can't be that the girl can't have castration anxiety because she can't repress something and that repression (in the masculinity complex) then makes her anxious. It's the other way around in Freud, anxiety produces repression. Omitting Freud's last theory of anxiety entails leaving out Freud's concept of the ego at this period, of the ego as a system of defenses formed on the bed of anxiety. Something the same but different from oneself causes intense anxiety. Remembering Freud's thesis of pre-Oedipal "masculinity" of both sexes in relation to the mother, then, at the point where the mother becomes the point of difference for the child, or something other than oneself, we have anxiety and the defense against it. The "castrated" mother or femininity are the names that the defenses which constitute the ego of the post-Oedipal child give to this point of difference. In omitting to discuss anxiety and the ego you are therefore leaving out the masculine perspective—*for both sexes.*

You are not addressing the fact that—for Freud—both sexes repudiate femininity. (Who wouldn't reject it—given that it is the perspective from which the feminine is seen as problematic, as "the riddle"; who wants to be a riddle?) The Lacanian account omits Freud's changed theory of anxiety and Freud's new theories about the ego which came at the exact period when he is writing all his essays on femininity. I do think the Lacanian theory simplifies certain things; I actually do think the concept of the Other and of the Ø crossed through is a simplification—yet reverting to Freud's early model of anxiety at this point means that an important dimension is left out.

Catherine Millot: The first thing is that in a sense Freud was joking when he said the woman is the enigma for you and you yourselves, women, are the enigma (jokes are very serious indeed) because of three points which I hope will clarify all the questions raised by this paper. First of all, all sexed subjects are in the same place as regards the enigma of femininity insofar as what is being represented there is Lacan's question of what is the desire of the Other—which is how he formulated Freud's question, what does a woman want? That desire will always be the desire of the mother; the father comes into the question in a completely different way and both the girl and the boy will be suspended in identical ways in relation to the mother's desire. That they are both in the same position is the first point—there is a lack of differentiation in relation to that primordial desire. Secondly, and overlaying this comes the question which Lacan addressed later in his work when he said "there is no signifier Woman in the unconscious," no signifier Woman with a capital W, that the woman is unsymbolizable for both sexes. Now obviously insofar as women are women this touches them somewhat more closely than it might be seen to touch men but in a sense what I was doing in my paper today was giving the Lacanian and Freudian approach to that statement "Woman does not exist." What that means, and this is my third point, is that there is available for women, and this was the whole drift of the paper about the superego, no possibility of a post-Oedipal feminine iden-tification because the journey which I described through the Oedipus complex, the recognition of castration, the problem of the fantasies and desires that that unleashes, leaves no possibility for the woman of a straightforward post-Oedipal identification with the woman, it becomes a contradiction in terms. I am saying that both sexes are at this same point of impossibility but that in a sense what might be a dissolution or getting beyond of the Oedipus complex for the girl is precisely a renunciation of the existence of femininity in that sense of Woman with a capital W. Is that not a good conclusion?

from *m/f* 10, 1985

PARVEEN ADAMS

A dilemma that faces feminists is that while on the one hand we want to be good mothers, on the other hand we struggle against many of the attributes of she who is represented as the "good" mother. These representations are the more difficult to resist to the extent that the mother is defined in psychological terms for they amount to a claim that there are universal attributes of mothering. Yet we have recognized that the "good" mother is not a universal figure but is a product of particular social practices and we have made some attempts to analyze these practices.

Of course, social practices include theoretical discourses and the specific practices associated with them—in analyzing the construction of mothering feminists have often implicated psychoanalysis in the inculcation of social norms in individuals, including mothers. However, this is not obviously true and it should be noted that Freud himself specifically disclaims any wish to establish normative criteria either at the level of theory or at the level of clinical practice. If psychoanalysis frees the person from the disabling effects of pathology, this is by no means through effecting the demands of social norms, and Freud is quite clear that meeting society's stringent demands may itself generate neurosis.

Other forms of psychoanalysis might take a different position especially where the mother-child relation is concerned. Indeed, Freud's theories have been invoked left, right, and center to prop up pedagogical norms and to justify a wide variety of therapeutic interventions whose aim is the regulation of the behavior of both parents and children. So it can be said that normative criteria have been introduced through the notion of mothering and its elaborations since the eighteenth century; and it might be said that psychoanalysis sustains a discourse that makes the woman responsible. But it is crucial to distinguish between those theoretical psychoanalytic positions that are formed within and generalized to a practice of mothering and those theories like Freud's that have always avoided this precisely by demonstrating that the level of psychical life is not the same as the level of reality at which a mother "manages" her child.

The former positions may take the form of giving recipes for maternal behavior (the child should not be given a feeding dummy) or may confine themselves to enjoining on the mother a general responsibility for conducting herself along a pre-defined path. Both these forms of advice are in the name of the child's healthy development. In contrast, Freud's work does not emphasize the individual mother's performance in respect to her child. The mother, no matter what she does, will necessarily provoke ambivalences that are crucial to the child's normal development, though they might also become obstacles to it. The very nature of the tasks the mother performs: bathing, feeding, procreating, link them to seduction, dissatisfaction at being given insufficient milk, jealousy of siblings, and a fear of the loss of love. Freud is speaking of the mother in the unconscious, a mother who introduces the child to lack, to castration, to representation. Freud's concept of psychical reality requires repression of the desire for the mother, an instinctual renunciation which is the price of "Civilization."

To say that this figure of the mother does not constrain the real mother is not to say that the way a particular mother relates to her child is irrelevant to the child's psychic life. It is, rather, to insist that the child cannot escape the play of its mother's *psychic* life across its own. Freud writes:

> To the uninitiated it is hardly credible how seldom normal potency is to be found in a husband and how often a wife is frigid among married couples who live under the dominance of our civilized sexual morality, what a degree of renunciation, often of both sides, is entailed by marriage, and to what narrow limits married life—the happiness that is so ardently desired—is narrowed down. I have already explained that in these circumstances the most obvious outcome is nervous illness; but I must further point out the way in which a marriage of this kind continues to exercise its influence on the few children, or the only child born of it. At a first glance, it seems to be a case of transmission by inheritance; but closer inspection shows that it is really a question of the effect of powerful infantile impressions. A neurotic wife who is unsatisfied by her husband is, as a mother, over-tender and over-anxious towards her child, on to whom she transfers her need for love; and she awakens it to sexual precocity. The bad relations between its parents, moreover, excite its emotional life and cause it to feel love and hatred to an intense degree

while it is still at a very tender age. Its strict upbringing, which tolerates
no activity of the sexual life that has been aroused so early, lends support
to the suppressing force and this conflict at such an age contains everything necessary for bringing about lifelong nervous illness. ("Civilized
Sexual Morality and Modern Nervous Illness," pp. 201—20)

Of course all quotations are out of context. What is important here is not that a "neurotic wife who is unsatisfied by her husband" will produce a neurotic child. Certainly
the quotation is about individual cases, but the argument within which it is embed-
ded is about "civilized" sexual morality in Freud's time; it is an argument about an
organization of social relations in which the child's sexual curiosity is unappeased,
in which there is sexual abstinence followed by late monogamous marriage, and in
which the suppression of the unmarried woman's sexuality "often goes too far" so
that "the preparation for marriage frustrates the aims of marriage itself."

This organization of social relations can encourage neurosis. For though Freud
endows instincts with a capacity for transformations, repressions, and sublimations,
this lability of the instincts, the toleration of instinctual renunciations, varies with the
individual's "constitution." Hence some are normal while others succumb to neurosis. But even "normality" has its limits—the instinct is never infinitely malleable.
Freud writes of the demands of the cultural superego that it

does not trouble itself enough about the facts of the mental constitution
of human beings. It issues a command and does not ask whether it is possible for people to obey it. On the contrary, it assumes that a man's ego
is psychologically capable of anything that is required of it, that his ego
has unlimited mastery over his id. This is a mistake; and even in what are
known as normal people the id cannot be controlled beyond certain
limits. If more is demanded of a man, a revolt will be produced in him
or a neurosis, or he will be made unhappy. (*Civilization and its Discontents,* p. 143)

This suggests that social demands should take some account of what psychoanalysis
has discovered about psychical life. Freud's argument is partly based on his clinical
work where he found himself often obliged to oppose and reduce the claims of the
individual superego for therapeutic purposes. It is clear here that Freud is not fitting
his patient to social norms. Nor, in treating the individual case, which is presumed
to contrast with the "normal," is he unaware of the possibility of "social neuroses"

and he expects that "one day someone will venture to embark upon a pathology of cultural communities."

It must be borne in mind that Freud's own arguments on the relation between mental constitution and cultural demands follow the path set by his conception of "Civilization." But by that very token, cultural orderings will never satisfy psychical demands and psychical life will never fit neatly into cultural demands. For Civilization means that *any* set of social orderings requires primary repression, desire, and the unconscious. It is a further consideration that some social orderings may produce a more neurotic society than others; the basic conditions for individual neurosis are already given.

It should be clear that Freud could not and did not hold the real mother responsible for the health of her child's psychic life. Two things are fundamental here: the concept· of psychical reality and the nature of the relation between the psychic and the social.

When psychical reality and social reality are left out of account an altogether different figure of the mother is produced—the mother whose biology fits her for her task; who will initially be in a state of "primary maternal preoccupation," a state amounting to an illness; who will have such a sensitivity to her child that she exists only as part of a mother-child dyad; who will have a husband who relieves her of all extraneous pressures, allowing her to devote herself to her child. The mother who accepts this picture will certainly feel responsible.

This is one example of the "good" mother as universal figure. No unconscious desire of her own insists to disturb her good management of her child. No shadow of the social dims her natural ability to have a good relation to her child. This characterization is not a travesty of the "good-enough" mother constructed by the British pediatrician and psychoanalyst D. W. Winnicott. He is infinitely sensitive, insightful, and modest in his writings; but all the care and all the clinical skill and all the moderation can only serve to define, albeit in general terms, the path the good mother takes.

I am not attempting a general evaluation of Winnicott's thought or of his clinical practice. I have chosen to comment on an aspect of his theories in order to highlight the fact that there is more than one "psychoanalysis" and the implications of this. I would add that if we conceive of his account as part and parcel of contemporary practices of mothering, we have thereby to recognize that it *is* part of our social reality. And if that reality and its normative criteria are set up successfully through a variety of practices of intervention in family life, so are its failures. Hence the particular form of problems for mothers. So the organization of social relations necessitates further interventions that alleviate particular problems and forms of suffering—that these interventions are in the service of social norms is a tautology. The transformation of this intricate network of relations is a massively complex task and it would be unwise to just dispose of Winnicott's insights and the therapeutic practices elaborated from them.

Despite these remarks, it must be insisted that the child's psychic health is not in the gift of the mother. The *desire* of the mother will ensure a perturbation that makes the "good-enough" mother into a figure that beckons merely to ensnare the real mother. Winnicott does not see this because he leaves out any consideration of the unconscious and any consideration of the social. He believes that the mother has a "natural," if not a conscious, intellectual knowledge of what she is required to do. Presumably he thinks that she acts on this knowledge subject only to external accidents. It hardly seems as though the vast array of different child-rearing practices historically and cross-culturally, could all conform to a "natural" knowledge. While psychic health and ill health are distinguished in all cultures, what counts as the one or the other is by no means universal. That is to say that no child-rearing practice can guarantee normality. Indeed, that would be to abolish the unconscious.

I want to clarify the Freudian concept of psychical reality by contrasting the theories of Winnicott and Freud insofar as they are concerned with the relation between mother and child. I will start with Winnicott, one of whose major concerns is the initial period in the child's life that he calls the period of absolute dependency. During this period the mother has a number of tasks in relation to the mental growth of her child and what is essential to performing these tasks successfully is the capacity for a deep identification with the infant. Winnicott is in no doubt that the biological mother is the best person for the job. He believes that the maternal function is natural in the natural mother. The special ability to identify closely with her particular infant comes from the special way in which her body and her self have been and are involved with the infant. So, for example, during pregnancy, her bodily involvement with its accompanying fantasies links up with her own early infantile experiences, and the baby in the womb is linked with the "good internal object," the expectant mother's own good-enough mother in early infancy. There are also early shared experiences: the birth itself, breathing movements, heartbeats, all of which contribute to close identification. This links with Winnicott's conception of the "ordinary devoted mother" who has no need for intellectual comprehension of her work—her biological orientation has already prepared her for her baby. This appeal to biology is complicit with the normative thrust of Winnicott's work. For the mental health of the human being is said to be laid down in infancy by the mother who Winnicott holds to be theoretically responsible for certain conditions of both normality and pathology. That he adds "though of course are not to blame" is hardly convincing.

What precisely, must the mother be like who identifies closely with the infant and what are the tasks for which that is a precondition? Winnicott has a very definite answer to the first question. The mother must be in a state of Primary Maternal Pre-occupation, which is a particular state of heightened sensitivity toward the end of her pregnancy and during the first few weeks of the infant's life. A state, Winnicott says, which is "almost an illness." It is necessary that the mother be in this state to meet the infant's needs that are body needs. But by this, Winnicott is not referring to the functions of feeding, cleaning, etc., as such. Rather, the infant's needs are in relation to the building of an ego, of becoming an experiencing person with "a live rela-tionship between inner reality and external reality, between innate primary creativity and the world at large which is shared by all." It is important to note here that this notion of need is neatly and deliberately separated off from any notion of desire, Winnicott going out of his way to give thanks that child therapists increasingly sub-stitute the term "need" for "desire."

The mother then, has the task of meeting the child's needs, building its ego on the basis of the infant's experiencing a "continuity of being." It is the mother's task to guarantee this personal continuity of the child. Since the building up of the infant's ego involves its coming to accept the body as part of the self, the mother has to make whole the infant's unintegrated body. She does this both by having "the child in her mind as a whole person" and by holding the baby in a natural way so that the baby does "not have to know about being made up of a collection of parts . . . all these parts are gathered together by the mother who is holding the child and in her hands they add up to one." Perhaps it is now somewhat clearer how the mother provides for the infant's body needs, a provision described by Winnicott as ego-support.

Another aspect of ego-support through which the baby can "go-on-being" is the manipulation of objects so that the baby is not threatened by them but feels it has created them. This implies the existence in the baby of a simple, unmediated, con-scious perception of external objects, the possibility of what Winnicott calls "objec-tive objects." Nonetheless, Winnicott holds that such objects exist only as threat of annihilation, and lack of predictability. As such, "objective objects" fail to provide the grounding of self, introducing instead a false self, a compliant child, a sense of unreality. In other words, such objects hinder the growth of the ego. The mother's management of the child includes then, her management of objects. To her is assigned the task of introducing the world in small doses to the child, of establishing predictabilities, of creating a world of "subjective objects." Thus the mother has to provide security and illusion at the same time, the illusion of security, by allowing the infant to experience the world as *its* creation and under *its* control. The baby's ability to create the milk, the breast, or whatever almost becomes a matter of timing, the arrival of the milk and the breast when the baby is hungry and expecting it.

Winnicott's account of the early mother-infant relation makes the mother responsible for the growth of the infant into a coherent and confident individual, one who is certain of itself and can thus take its place in the world of shared reality. In sharp contrast, Freud has a view of the individual subject as essentially divided and split, in a world where objects and reality are not unproblematically given, where unconscious wishes are always bound to signs and where the notion of satisfaction is itself problematic. For Freud, these three elements are crucially connected with each other through the concept of "drive." Winnicott claims that he is interested in what comes *before* this, that is, an experiencing person, an ego. But the primacy accorded to the coherent, certain ego is precisely what Freud subverted as long ago as 1905 in his theory of the drive (crucial developments are to be found in his 1915 paper, *Instincts and their Vicissitudes*). This is a difference that means that Winnicott can produce a theory of what mothers should and shouldn't do in the name of adaptation and mental health, where Freud's theory marks the importance of desire, desire being that which can't be managed. It is not an accident that it is the term desire that Winnicott so happily displaces in favor of need.

I will try to explain exactly what the crucial difference in the two positions is by starting with the different views of the function of the object. I have already said something about Winnicott's view. For Freud, the finding of an object is always the refinding of it. What this means is that the drive, and we will consider the oral drive here (which many theorists mistake for an oral instinct), does not bear the same simple relation to the object as the instinct does. Instincts operate on needs and needs can be satisfied. So, for example, the instinct of hunger can be satisfied with nutritional objects. And indeed this instinct is important in Freud insofar as it sets up an experience of satisfaction that the child wishes to repeat. But we cannot say when the child hallucinates milk or the breast or when he sucks his thumb that he is satisfied. Furthermore, the reason for this is not merely that in fact the real object is missing. For the real object is the object of the instinct and here Freud is talking about the object of the drive. Having once experienced satisfaction, the hungry child will evoke particular memory traces and will re-evoke the original perception. A psychical impulse of this kind Freud calls a wish. Wishes then, are fulfilled by *signs* of satisfaction. The drive is not the instinct precisely because it exists at the level of representation. The drive, Freud wrote, can only be known through its mental representations.

What are the consequences of this view for the maternal object and for the fate of Winnicott's list of maternal tasks? Insofar as the mother introduces the infant to a fundamental division between the object looked for and the object found, the maternal object is itself a refound object. As such, what can it mean to demand that she prove herself to be a predictable object? For Winnicott, the mother's predictability is an essential part of that ego-support without which the child is doomed to mental ill health. One could almost say that for Freud unpredictability, which he would call loss, is a constitutive feature of psychical reality, an irreparable phenomenon, a phenomenon that makes us human.

We can also see the difference between Freud and Winnicott in relation to the mechanism of hallucination. For Winnicott, it is a sustaining illusion of omnipotence, of continuity of being, a grounding for the ego and certainty; at least, it is a phenomenon that can be used by the mother, to these ends. For Freud, hallucination is a mechanism by which the oral drive operates at the level of wish-fulfilment. It thus marks the subject's relation to the lost object. What is at stake is the constitution of a split subject through the play of presence and absence. The split subject is precisely that which does *not* have that continuity of being that Winnicott deems so essential for the ego.

To mark the notion of a split subject more precisely, I will briefly refer to Jacques Lacan who displaces the commonsense meaning of "object" altogether. Where Freud referred to a refound object that nevertheless remained as the object which satisfied desire; Lacan's use of the term no longer refers at all to that which satisfies desire. Rather, the object, the lost object, is the *cause* of desire. Lacan calls it *petit objet a,* cause of desire. To try to show what this means I will summarize Lacan's account of the *fort-da* game. This game is described by Freud (1920), who observed his grandson playing with a cotton-reel attached to a thread. The child's game consisted in throwing the reel over the edge of its cot and saying o-o-o for the German "*fort,*" which means "gone" and then drawing up the thread and greeting the reappearance of the reel with "*da,*" which means "here." This game has often been interpreted as instituting a function of mastery or control. Lacan rejects this as of secondary importance although Freud does point out that the child is making himself the agent of the mother's disappearance. Instead, Lacan stresses what he calls the ever-open gap that results from the mother's absence. The game with the cotton-reel linked to itself by the thread that it holds, expresses a self-mutilation. For the reel is not the mother, but a small part of the subject that detaches itself while still being retained by it. Thus the reel is the lost object, Lacan's *petit objet a.* And the repetition of the endless game marks the mother's disappearance, her absence, as the cause of the splitting of the subject. Lacan says: "the game of the cotton-reel is the subject's answer to what the mother's absence has created on the frontier of his domain—the edge of the cradle—namely, a *ditch,* around which one can only play at jumping." The game is essentially about something that is not there and will never be there. The child can jump across the ditch, that is, it can begin to speak, but the loss itself is constantly replayed in language and remains the cause of desire. Desire, then, being essentially unfulfillable.

If desire is the radical oscillation of the subject in the fort-da game, an oscillation set up and replayed around the lost object, then what is at stake is the *lack-in-being* of the subject. It should be redundant by now to point out that this is diametrically opposed to Winnicott's notion of the infant's *continuity of being.* And certainly the play of desire can allow no certainty of or about the subject. The mother can hardly manage desire. And once desire is admitted, you have to allow not only the child's desire but also the mother's unconscious desire, which the mother can't manage either.

Freud's concept of psychical reality establishes a psychical domain that makes no claim to determining the social domain. Social norms remain open to dispute and feminism must concern itself with the question of the establishment of different norms, less disadvantageous to women. But some feminists have made large claims for the *psychical* effects of such social changes. They have done so only at the cost of disregarding Freud's concept of psychical reality and of making the social determining of the psychical. Such a simplification of the problem of the relation of the social to the psychical is well exemplified by Nancy Chodorow's *The Reproduction of Mothering* which privileges the social by avoiding the concepts of desire and the unconscious in relation to sexual difference. At the same time, on the question of what constitutes good mothering for the infant, Chodorow's picture is curiously close to Winnicott's. It will be argued that in the final analysis both the psychical and the social get short shrift in Chodorow's account. Her book is very well known, has been much discussed, and has exercised a wide influence. I will assume a familiarity with it and will confine myself to a few pertinent points.

It is of particular interest in that Nancy Chodorow is well aware of the dangers in considerations of the relation between the social and the psychical. She argues that while psychical reality does not determine social relations, neither do social

relations determine the psyche. There is to be no isomorphism between social reality and psychical reality. However, this is not to say that ultimately she herself avoids
the dangers.

Chodorow's basic contention is that the fact that *women* mother is the single
most important factor in their subordination. This connection, of course, is not conceived as direct and unmediated. It is conceived in psychoanalytic terms, that is to
say, in this case, in the terminology of object-relations theory. Again, the crucial concept of desire is displaced. For it is argued that there is a primary and fundamental
sociality in the infant, a need for human contact that is fundamental to development.
All development, from the start, is affected by "social relational experiences"; she is
saying that experience is social by virtue of its being of the relations between persons.

The argument being that persons are informed by their own childhood history,
past and present relations inside the family and outside it. As Talcott Parsons would
have it, persons have places within higher-order social systems. Thus through the
relation with persons, the child comes to be integrated into larger social units. It is
the woman who first mediates *her* social because of the *social* fact that women
mother.

What are the consequences of the fact that women mother? No less than the
differences between masculinity and femininity. We see here that the social fact that
women mother is said to produce a *psychical subordination* in the girl, in the form
of femininity.

Chodorow argues that while good mother-child experiences lead to the development of parenting activities in children of both sexes in early life, the pre-Oedipal
and Oedipal periods ensure that parenting capacities persist in women alone. It
should be noted that for Chodorow the Oedipus complex is not the constituting
moment of sexual difference through the intervention of the third term (symbolic
father), but the effects of a psychical problem of dependence/independence, effects
contingent on family organization in the sense of who is there to turn to, etc. What
is primarily at stake here are social factors affecting the separation from the mother
and hence the different "relational potential" of the genders.

Chodorow claims that the importance of the girl's pre-Oedipal attachment to
the mother is generally recognized but not explained. It is to be explained by the
fact that women mother. According to Chodorow, mothers of daughters, because
they are of the same gender and have been girls, tend not to experience them as separate in the same way as do mothers of infant sons. The daughter is experienced as
an extension or double of the mother herself and the daughter as a sexual other

remains a weaker theme. Sons, however, are experienced as male opposites. Sons are experienced as differentiated and this differentiation is encouraged. What this means is that girls are caught up in early mother-infant relational issues, while maternal behavior propels boys into sexualized genitally toned relationships. In some sense, the girl is trapped within the relation to the mother; whereas the boy is drawn into a triangular situation, with the mother as sexual opposite and the father as rival.

It is in the Oedipal period proper that the girl assumes her femininity and the boy his masculinity. For Chodorow, the differences arise because the girl's situation in the family is different from the boy's. The boy's developmental task of separation from the mother is simpler both because of the way his mother responds to him and because that separation carries with it the advantage of an identification with masculine power: "the carrot of the masculine Oedipus complex is identification with the father and the superiority of masculine identification and prerogatives over feminine." Thus the boy has a power to pit against the threat of the omnipotent mother of early childhood. His separation is secured.

The question of the feminine Oedipus complex is the question of why the girl turns to the father. Chodorow's answer is that the girl turns to the father as symbol of freedom from dependence on and merging with the mother. Whatever its sexual meaning, this turn to the father concerns emotional issues of self and other. But Chodorow insists that these issues are resolved by persons in roles that are systematically gender-linked because of family organization (women's mothering). *Hence* the characteristics and complications of the pre-Oedipal and Oedipal periods. The girl, in the Oedipal period, maintains both her parents as love-objects and as rivals. The girl, in fact, never gives up her mother and she oscillates between mother and father. And the reasons that the father does not activate exclusive heterosexual love are the fact that he is not the girl's primary caretaker and the shortcomings of his own emotional qualities. As Chodorow puts it, he is a different and less available Oedipal object than the mother.

Parenting capacities, then, are different in children of different sexes because given the nature of the masculinity of fathers and the femininity of mothers, identification processes are different for the two sexes. The girl's identification is predominantly *parental,* based on a "real relationship" with the mother. This determines what it is like to be womanlike. The boy's identification is predominantly a *gender-role* identification. But since the boy has no real affective tie with the father, there is an element of masculinity that is defined negatively—a differentiation from others, a denial of relationship. The girl, then, retains the parenting capacities set up in the early mother-child relation; the boy does not.

Given this analysis, it is not surprising that Chodorow proceeds with the specific suggestion of *shared parenting*. Shared parenting will allow the male to develop parenting capacities, identify with the father on the basis of a real tie and activate exclusive heterosexual love in the girl. The female will not be trapped in issues of separation and primary identification and will relinquish her daughter more easily. Issues of differentiation will no longer be intertwined with sexual issues. Gender identity will be more stable while both sexes will be free to choose what they want to do. Thus it is social conditions which will allow the characteristics of the pre-Oedipal and Oedipal periods to change. It should be noted that this is the abolition of masculinity and femininity as traditionally understood. The psychoanalytic explanation of sexual difference has completely collapsed. It would be difficult to hold that the psychical has maintained its autonomy from the social in Chodorow's account.

What is left is an androgyny of the emotions, an equalization of "relational potential," organized around a biological sex difference (Chodorow's object relations account heavily relies on *sex* differences though I have not elaborated on this). The social fact of shared parenting reduces sexual difference to sex differences. The move away from psychoanalysis and back to sociology is complete.

Yet, paradoxically, it is what Chodorow retains of the psychical that makes it impossible for her to consider *social relations* in any but the most simplistic way. By confering the status of unquestionable truth on some aspects of the parent's relation to the infant, she narrows the domain within which the social can have effects. Let man and women both be parents! She misses the point that the role of the parent is itself a construction that needs to be understood in historical terms. Her rough and ready justice rules that the man should also do what the woman has done hitherto, and she appears to think that this principle of equality is in itself a critical alteration of social relations. It would seem at least as important to recognize that the characteristics of present-day "mothering" are not universals, that "mothering" is constituted through a diverse set of practices, not unified in its origins or in its effects.

We cannot have shared parenting by decree. Perhaps we cannot have shared parenting at all, where shared parenting is an equalization of "relational potential." Chodorow might well be absolutely right in thinking that relational potential plays a major part in the lives of women (hence women as mothers). But is it not possible that "relational potential," far from being a natural outcome of a naturally organized parent-child relation in early life, might itself be the effect of the practices that have constructed the modern mother and bound her to a set of tasks? That the father is not in this position is more than a matter of the manner of the boy's separation from the mother. Do we want to intervene in social practices so as to ensure that the man is also bound to the same set of tasks (even if it were possible that both the mother and father could be so bound), or might we wish to relinquish the notion of relational potential in its present form? This is not to deny the principle of sharing; it is to say that the possible forms of the relation between parent and child and indeed between mother and father should not be prejudged.

It is not being claimed that such an analysis leads directly to the means of transformation; indeed it is unclear what purchase political action would have here. But when the model of "mothering" itself escapes questioning, we as feminists have abdicated the infinitely complicated task of seeking the means toward the institution of new norms. This would be a pity as would the premature rejection of the psychoanalytic conception of sexual difference, which has done so much to undermine traditional notions of what women and men are and which has been used to develop feminist argument beyond the questioning of social roles alone.

References

N. Chodorow, *The Reproduction of Mothering,* University of California Press, 1978.

S. Freud, "Three Essays on the Theory of Sexuality" (1905), *The Standard Edition of the Complete Psychological Works of Sigmund Freud,* vol. VIII.

S. Freud, "Civilized Sexual Morality and Modern Nervous Illness" (1908), *SE,* vol. IX.

S. Freud, *Beyond the Pleasure Principle* (1920), *SE,* vol. XVIII.

S. Freud, *Civilization and Its Discontents* (1930), *SE,* vol. XXI.

J. Lacan, *The Four Fundamental Concepts of Psychoanalysis,* trans. Alan Sheridan, Hogarth Press, 1977 (1973).

D. W. Winnicott, *The Child, the Family and the Outside World,* Penguin, 1964.

D. W. Winnicott, *Collected Papers: Through Paediatrics to Psychoanalysis,* Tavistock, 1958.

This article is an expanded version of a paper first presented in July 1982 in London as one of a series of m/f *workshops called* Reopening the Case: Feminism and Psychoanalysis.

from *m/f* 8, 1983

The Train of Thought in Freud's "Case of Homosexuality in a Woman"

MANDY MERCK

Nearly twenty years after the first of Freud's six celebrated case histories, "Fragments of an Analysis of a Case of Hysteria" (completed on January 25, 1901), he wrote the final one—"The Psychogenesis of a Case of Homosexuality in a Woman."[1] "The last case," notes Ernest Jones, "resembled the first one in so far as the patient was a girl of eighteen and the analysis a short one. But this time it was Freud, more alive to the significance of resistance than twenty years earlier, who broke off the treatment" (*The Life and Works of Sigmund Freud,* vol. II, P. 314).

The invitation to compare this analysis with the more famous case of "Dora" has proved "irresistible" to commentators[2]—not least because of the much debated significance of Freud's own footnoted revision to the earlier study:

> The longer the interval of time that separates me from the end of this analysis, the more probable it seems to me that the fault in my technique lay in this omission: I failed to discover in time and to inform the patient that her homosexual (gynaecophilic) love for Frau K. was the strongest unconscious current in her mental life. (1905)

Freud's failure to discover Dora's homosexual tendency "which he none the less tells us is so constant in hysterics that its subjective role cannot be overestimated"—the exasperation is Lacan's[3]—seems difficult to detach from his own involvement with his patient, his famous countertransference. The fact that nineteen years later he could break off the analysis of another "beautiful and clever girl of eighteen" (Dora's "intelligent and engaging looks" are also made much of) seems to support Jones's interpretation—that Freud had learned from a clear precedent. But as his analysis of the origins of homosexuality in this case suggests, there are many pathways for libidinal investment. It is upon these, particularly upon questions of identification, that I wish to focus here.

I

Like Dora, the young woman in this case was "handed over" to Freud by her father—and also by her mother, slightly less the neglected party in this analysis than in Dora's. This was six months after an "undoubtedly serious attempt at suicide" precipitated by a not-very-chance meeting of father and daughter while she was out walking with the woman she loved, an upper-class courtesan about ten years older whom "the girl" (as Freud describes her throughout) "pursued" with "devoted adoration." Although "the lady," as Freud terms the courtesan, carried on numerous affairs with men, she lived with a woman lover, but her relations with Freud's patient were never more than friendly. Despite—or indeed, because of—this distance, the girl had become so infatuated with her that she had abandoned studies, social functions, and most of her friends in order to conduct a courtship that seemed to consist of sending flowers, waiting at tramstops, and occasionally taking walks "in the most frequented streets" with her beloved. Here—inevitably—the pair were one day discovered by the girl's furious father, who had already become aware of her past and present attractions to women—including this woman of ill repute. "Immediately afterwards," Freud writes, "the girl rushed off and flung herself over a wall down the side of a cutting on to the suburban railway line which ran close by."

Six months later, after an extended convalescence and a related softening on the part of her parents, the girl agreed to analysis for their sake—an unpropitious start, in Freud's view, for what he anyway saw as a difficult project. For he believed that the girl "was not in any way ill"—not neurotic, but its negative, perverse. (As early as 1905, in "Three Essays on Sexuality," Freud had opposed the neuroses to the perversions, arguing that neurotic symptoms are formed at the cost of abnormal sexuality [p. 160]. As Otto Rank reiterated in 1924, the neuroses can function to block the perversions ["Perversion and Neurosis" p. 273]. This girl had no such block on her homosexual object choice.) And so, Freud speculated, unless the libidinal impulses that led the girl to mollify her parents were as strong as those invested in her conscious sexual objects, or unless she retained enough bisexual organization to provide compensatory heterosexual attachments, the prognosis wasn't good. Indeed, it was as bad as that for converting a convinced heterosexual to homosexuality, "except that for good practical reasons the latter is never attempted."

Thus Freud undertook a rather skeptical analysis of eleven weeks (Dora's also lasted eleven weeks), during which he nevertheless believed it possible to trace the "origin and development" of female homosexuality "with complete certainty and almost without a gap." This "remarkable" situation is explained by Jones as the result of the patient's determination "to retain the sole 'symptom' for which she was being analyzed (so) that she could afford to let the analysis of it proceed quite freely: her resistance was not against the analysis itself, only against it having any effect" (Jones, p. 312). And in a fascinating comparison, Freud likens the process of analysis to the stages of a train journey to a distant country: the first, which this girl managed so well, is like the traveler's preparation—booking the ticket, acquiring a passport, packing, and finally arriving at the station (i.e., the analyst extracts the necessary information and interprets it to the patient). "But after all these preliminary exertions one is not a single mile nearer one's goal." The second stage of analysis requires the patient "to make the journey itself."

Before he relates the first stage of this analysis, Freud addresses himself to the "fruitless and inapposite" question of the biological determination of homosexuality—a question to which, despite his own preference for a psychogenetic explanation, he will return in this case study. Here we are told that the "beautiful and well-made" girl's appearance and menstrual cycle are feminine, although she is tall, sharp-featured, and conspicuously intelligent and objective (conventional, rather than scientific, signs of masculinity, argues Freud). More importantly—and this ostensibly nonphysical evidence follows on immediately in the text—she takes the masculine part not only in her object (a woman) but in her attitude towards it (technically, her aim), greatly overvaluing the loved one and humbly renouncing all narcissistic satisfaction.[4]

II

Freud's account of his patient's psychic development is yet another of the frustrating consequences of his first theory of the Oedipus complex. (Lacan's commentary on this case refers to "the . . . prejudice which falsifies the conception of the Oedipus complex from the start, by making it define as natural, rather than normative, the predominance of the paternal figure," "Intervention on Transference," p. 69.) Although in his 1905 "Essays" Freud acknowledges the primacy of the mother's breast as an object for all infants, it is not until 1925—five years after this case study—that the mother is posed as the original Oedipal object for both sexes.

("Some Psychical Consequences of the Anatomical Difference between the Sexes," p. 251). Thus Freud assumes here that the father is the first normal Oedipal object for girls—including this one. After her father, in a trauma-free childhood, she turned to her older brother, with whom she compared genitals at the age of five—an event whose "far reaching after-effects" Freud doesn't explain for several pages (in a writing strategy that effectively divides his patient's heterosexual history from her homosexual one). At five and a half a second brother was born, then at school the girl discovered "the facts of sex" with the usual reactions of fascination and loathing. At thirteen to fourteen, she displayed a markedly maternal affection for a small boy in the local playground. But after a short time she grew indifferent to him and began to take a romantic interest in older women—mothers in their early thirties—and was chastised for this by her father.

Freud attributes this change in object to the birth of a third brother when the patient was sixteen, an affront to the girl's pubescent desire for a child of her own from her father. "Furiously resentful and embittered, she turned away from her father and from men altogether. After this first great reverse she foreswore her womanhood and sought another goal for her libido." The consequent transformation, Freud points out, was severe: "She changed into a man and took her mother in place of her father as the object of her love."

This interpretation sets up several major themes that will reappear in the psychoanalytic literature on homosexuality:

(1) its heterosexual origins (Jones refers to the "discovery that homosexuals always have to begin with a profound fixation on the parent of the opposite sex," p. 134);

(2) the "motive of evasion," or what Freud calls "retiring in favour of someone else"—withdrawing from a painful competition for a heterosexual object into homosexuality;

(3) and finally, the identification of the homosexual with the opposite sex ("she changes into a man").

In the girl's case, her renunciation of her father served to improve relations with her mother, a youngish woman who had hitherto favored her three sons and treated her daughter quite harshly. And her blatant behavior also produced a libidinal gain in regard to her father—namely, the pleasure of revenge for his betrayal of her.

III

The third section of this case study opens with the author's complaint about his previous linear presentation of the patient's development as an inadequate "means of describing complicated mental processes going on in different layers of the mind." The ensuing topographical digression (on the masculinity of the girl's attitude toward her objects and her resistance to the analysis) raises two more influential themes in the psychoanalysis of specifically female homosexuality—courtly love and the question of transference to a male analyst.

In describing his patient's attitude toward her lover, Freud repeatedly employs the terms of courtly love, at one point citing the Italian Renaissance poet Tasso's description in the *Gerusalemme Liberata* of a male lover who "hopes for little and asks for nothing." This idealization of the beloved and neglect for one's own satisfaction is a broadly masculine tendency, in Freud's scheme, which divided anaclitic and narcissistic object choice along gender lines. And courtly love, which places "unsatisfied desire in the centre of the poetic conception of love" (Johan Huizinga), also connects Lacan's analysis of female homosexuality to his theory of the excessive nature of all desire and the impossibility of its gratification. The homosexual woman, whose courtly love "prides itself more than any other on being the love which gives what it does not have" ("Guiding Remarks for a Congress" p. 96) is phallic precisely in that lack. For it is lack, the threatened lack of castration, which constructs the masculine identity in Lacan's theory (*The Four Fundamental Concepts of Psychoanalysis* p. 38).[5] What neither Freud's homosexual patient nor Dora will accept is the mystery of the Raphael Madonna contemplated at such length by the latter in the Dresden museum: that of accepting oneself as idol rather than idolator, as object of the man's desire, rather than worshipper of woman ("Intervention on Transference," p. 68).

In Freud's view this homosexual girl's idealization of an unavailable woman of ill repute corresponds "to the smallest details" with that special type of masculine object choice discussed in his 1910 essay "A Special Type of choice of Object Made by Men"—the exclusive attraction to women who are both already attached and who suffer from a dubious sexual reputation. This he traces to a profound mother fixation challenged by the son's discovery of his mother's "infidelity" with his father. Concluding "that the difference between his mother and a whore is not after all so great," the boy elides their functions, combining genital desire and filial tenderness with fantasies of both rescue and revenge.

Now this allusion fleetingly reopens the question of early mother love only briefly mentioned thus far in the homosexual case study. But again it is deferred in favor of a discussion of the motives for the patient's suicide attempt—not simply the conscious despair she felt when the lady perceived her father's anger that day and broke off their relationship, but also, according to Freud, self-punishment and the fulfillment of a wish. The girl's fall onto the railway line, Freud argues, gratified her desire to "fall"—to become pregnant—through her father's fault. (The pun works in both English and German.) Her own death-wish represented the turning against herself of her desire to punish her parents, and its coincidence with a fall indicated the girl's identification with her mother, "who should have died at the birth of the child denied to herself."

Underlying all this Freud perceives the girl's desire for revenge on her father, an emotion so strong that it actually permitted her coolly intellectual cooperation with the first stage of the analysis—while absolutely refusing to go further, and in particular to make anything but a negative transference onto the analyst. The patient's only ostensible gestures at a positive transference, a series of dreams that seem to suggest heterosexual wishes, are rejected by the analyst as lies—intended to deceive both father and father-substitute. And here Freud's own identification with his patient's father takes on an almost paranoiac tinge, as he speculates that the girl may have sought his good opinion of her "perhaps in order to disappoint me all the more thoroughly later on." His subsequent termination of the analysis has a strong emotional charge, as he accuses his patient of transferring to him "the sweeping repudiation of men which had dominated her ever since the disappointment she had suffered from her father." The parents are advised to take their daughter to a woman analyst and the case study moves on to its conclusion.

IV

In this final recapitulation of the psychogenesis of the girl's homosexuality, Freud notes the advantages of hindsight in tracing causation. Taken in reverse, no factor seems wholly determining, no result inevitable. So why were the patient's reactions to her mother's last pregnancy so extreme? The story of the girl's development is told again, but this time with an emphasis on the continuity of her homosexual attachments, which go back from the courtesan, to one of her teachers, to a number of young mothers, to a probable infantile fixation on her own mother. Because this history is conscious, Freud regards it as superficial, the surface eddies of a river that also has its deeper—unconscious—heterosexual current. And the fact that the deeper current has been deflected into the shallower one, rather than vice-versa, seems to require an explanation—the only one available being that of a congenital disposition to homosexuality.

To this end, albeit with some difficulty, Freud cites his patient's early "masculinity complex," her reluctance to be second to her slightly older brother and her envy of his penis upon the genital inspection conducted at age five. But he also retains the belief of the term's originator—Van Ophuijsen—that the complex is the result of a girl's sense of injustice at her parents' preference for a son, and he associates this sense of injustice with a political protest:

> She was in fact a feminist; she felt it to be unjust that girls should not enjoy the same freedom as boys, and rebelled against the lot of women in general. (p. 169)

The notion of an inborn sense of injustice seems untenable, and Freud goes on to admit that the "girl's behaviour . . . would follow from the combined effect in a person with a strong mother-fixation of the two influences of her mother's neglect and her comparison of her genital organs with her brother's." But the explanation for the mother-fixation in the first place? Despite the sophistication of Freud's final critique of the "Third Sex" theory of homosexuality in his conclusion to this study, the idea of a congenital—if not necessarily hermaphroditic—bias towards homosexuality is explicitly retained: "on the other hand, a part even of this acquired disposition (if it was really acquired) has to be ascribed to inborn constitution."

Afterword

The truncated character of Freud's analysis, and the ambiguous biologism with which the case study concludes, leave important questions unanswered. In the first place, the stated seriousness of the girl's suicide attempt, and the severity of her feelings about her father, do not fit comfortably with Freud's nonpathological diagnosis. Jacqueline Rose's discussion of this case argues that "his explanation of this last factor—the lack of neurosis ascribed to the fact that the object choice was established not in infancy but after puberty—is then undermined by his being obliged to trace back the homosexual attraction to a moment prior to the Oedipal instance, the early attachment to the mother, in which case either the girl is neurotic (which she clearly isn't) or all women are neurotic (which indeed they might be)" (Jacqueline Rose, p. 10—11). But I wonder if there's a third possibility—which is to say that this girl may not suffer conflict about her object choice, but instead about the "masculine" identification with which she carries it off, an identification presented in the case as a singular and unproblematic concomitant of that choice.

The question of whether a masculine identification is actually necessary to female homosexuality has preoccupied commentators from Havelock Ellis to Helene Deutsch. *Cherchez* les femmes, we might say, since the historical difficulty has been how to explain those "feminine" women whom the "masculine" kind are supposed to desire. If a masculine libido is what produces female homosexuality, what makes these other women do it? Ellis's answer in 1897 was to distinguish the (masculine) "actively inverted woman" from the (feminine) woman "open to homosexual advances," "a womanly woman . . . not quite attractive enough to appeal to the average man"[6] (pp. 87–88). Thirty-five years later, Helene Deutsch solved the problem in a different way: while acknowledging the predominance of the "phallic masculine form" of female homosexuality, she argued that this is often a cover for a joint infantilism reflecting a prephallic mother fixation, which displays itself in reciprocal mother-child role play ("On Female Homosexuality").

In the "Three Essays" Freud challenges Ellis's views on physical and psychical hermaphroditism in inverts, with one significant exception: "it is only in inverted women that character-inversion of this kind can be looked for with any regularity. In men the most complete mental masculinity can be combined with inversion" (p. 142). Although this case study includes a general qualification of the view ("The same is true of women; here also mental sexual character and object-choice do not necessarily coincide"), it argues repeatedly for the masculinity of this patient's identifications. Indeed, Freud points out that the girl's masculine identification produced a "gain from illness"; it improved the girl's relations with her mother, who evidently preferred to function as confidante to a homosexual daughter rather than competitor with a heterosexual one. He doesn't, however, count as related "losses from illness" his patient's neglect of her own friends, her studies, and her appearance; her attraction to impossible objects; and her "undoubtedly serious" attempt to end her own life.

This may be the result of the positively narcissistic character of the girl's "masculinity complex," with its suggestions of a robust refusal of inferiority. But this phallic identification, a five-year-old's rebellion against castration prior to the installation of mature gender identification at puberty, is not the only "masculine" identification in this case. There is also the girl's psychical transformation "into a man" after puberty, when her mother bore the child she desired from her father. This process corresponds to that described in "Mourning and Melancholia," whereby the lost object is not relinquished, but instead absorbed into the ego through a process of identification. Like the jilted melancholic, the homosexual girl could be seen to preserve her love for her father by this method. But in identifying with an object that she also hates for the pain it has caused her, she may suffer, like the melancholic, from an excess of self-denigration. Such a "powerfully cathected and destructive" paternal introject is also remarked by Joyce MacDougall in the clinical material presented by her analyses of four homosexual women.[7]

Thus we see, in an analysis structured on a simple masculine/feminine dichotomy, at least two different "masculine" identifications: one with the father after puberty, the stage at which Freud would three years later identify the accession into the masculine/feminine division; and another, at five, via the masculinity complex, with a phallic principle that disavows castration and sexual division and may well be an identification with the "phallic mother"—in short, a "masculine" identification with a female *imago*.

This brings me to my second observation, which is that this case study closes where you think it really must continue, with the question of the girl's apparently fundamental (but largely unexamined) attachment to her mother. Delving into this area—that of Freud's 1931 "Female Sexuality" and 1933 "Femininity" discussions of the pre-Oedipal development of girls—may not answer the question "What does the little girl require of her mother?" Especially if, as Jacqueline Rose points out—after Lacan—the answer is only the unanswerability of desire. But the hypothesis that girls do focus their early desires on their mothers, and refocus them with such difficulty, seems to contradict Freud's assumption of the dominance of the heterosexual current in his homosexual patient's psychic life. (It might also facilitate a less symmetrical account of male and female homosexuality than that in which both have an original love object of the opposite sex.) Furthermore, the 1931 essay's discussion of the active sexual aim[8] involved in early play with dolls (in which the little girl enacts the rituals that the mother performs on her—dressing, feeding, spanking, etc.) would also contradict the presentation of the homosexual girl's later interest in small children as her accession to a heterosexual passivity, which is then so thoroughly (and inexplicably) reversed.

Here it is instructive to compare Freud's famous comments in the "Case of Homosexuality" with the relevant passage in "Female Sexuality":

> psychoanalysis cannot elucidate the intrinsic nature of what in conventional or in biological phraseology is termed "masculine" and "feminine": it simply takes over the two concepts and makes them the foundation of its work. When we attempt to reduce them further, we find

> masculinity vanishing into activity and femininity into passivity and that
> does not tell us enough. (1920, p. 171)

> The fondness girls have for playing with dolls, in contrast to boys, is com-
> monly regarded as a sign of early awakened femininity. Not unjustly so;
> but we must not overlook the fact that what finds expression here is the
> active side of femininity, and that the little girl's preference for dolls is
> probably evidence of the exclusiveness of her attachment to her mother,
> with complete neglect of her father object. (1931, p. 367)

I should stress here that these references to the pre-Oedipal are not intended to propose it as either a possible place of refuge from the demands of mature womanhood
or as the location of a "true" femininity. I simply want to argue that it may offer an
active sexual aim after the example of the mother, rather than the father, which may
be preserved (along with others) into later life. Does the girl's impersonation of the
courtly lover indicate a transformation of such early feminine activity into a masculine mode—and thus a recognition of bravado (and libido) as a male preroga-
tive—at the expense of her own self-esteem? Does this amount to an inevitable
splitting of the ego under the pressure of a conflict between a demand (to be active)
and a threat (to relinquish her femininity in the process)? (In which case Lacan has
the last word: "in order to be the phallus, that is to say, the signifier of the desire of
the Other . . . the woman will reject an essential part of her femininity. . . . It is for what
she is not that she expects to be desired as well as loved, ("The Meaning of the
Phallus," p. 84). Or was there any therapeutic possibility of reconciling the girl's activity with her femininity?

   I suspect that the failure to raise these questions makes this influential case
study a somewhat less radical approach to female sexuality than its rejection of a
"cure" might suggest. Lacan argues that Freud played a part in this failure by not perceiving here, and with Dora, the identity of his patient's desire with that of the father,
and her commensurate need to be seen as an "abstract, heroic, unique phallus,
devoted to the service of a lady" (*The Four Fundamental Concepts of Psychoanalysis,*
p. 39). Yet, as we have seen, Freud seems to have no difficulty identifying his homosexual patient's "masculine" ambitions (her desire *for* the mother)—the trick is to
square them with her "feminine" ones (her desire to *be* a mother). Does her mature
homosexuality represent a displacement of an earlier heterosexual desire, or does
the heterosexual episode (her desire for a child by her father) represent the usual
displacement of what Freud sees as evidence of an early current of homosexuality?

(The child as surrogate for the phallus which this patient, in her youthful "masculinity complex," was so reluctant to relinquish.) Given the original "bisexuality" of the infant, perhaps we should insist upon both.

As I pointed out earlier, the logic of his analysis leads Freud back to biology, and to his reflections at the end of this case on contemporary attempts to surgically modify male inversion (presumably through the replacement of "hermaphroditic" testicles). Could an analogous ovary transplant be successful in cases of female homosexuality? Freud thinks the solution impractical, and his explanation is the final sentence of the case study:

> A woman who has felt herself to be a man, and has loved in masculine fashion, will hardly let herself be forced into playing the part of a woman, when she must pay for this transformation, which is not in every way advantageous, by renouncing all hope of motherhood.

Note here how motherhood has finally been gathered under the phallic aegis. In this strange hypothesis of biological causation, the subject's original—suspect—ovaries apparently enable both homosexual love ("in the masculine fashion") *and* heterosexual reproduction. On this assumption, female heterosexuality could only be achieved surgically at the price of one of its major compensations, motherhood. Without acknowledging it, this speculation inverts the equation heterosexuality = fertility/homosexuality = sterility ("at the time of the analysis the idea of pregnancy and childbirth was disagreeable to her") that has structured the entire case.

And this brings me back to an earlier point, the remarkable extent to which the homosexual patient has been masculinized. Might this say as much about the analyst as the analysand? In her discussion of "Dora" and this case, Suzanne Gearhart points out that Freud's solution for the homosexual girl—a woman analyst—is as biologistic as his solution for the hysteric—a husband. Neither analysis comes to terms with early bisexuality, and thus female homosexuality is assumed to present "an absolute obstacle" to positive transference to a male analyst (pp. 105—107). In insisting upon a woman analyst, isn't Freud acting precisely as he accuses his homosexual patient of doing? Retiring in favor of someone else when a rivalry for a loved object becomes intolerable? If this is so, it would suggest two things: that here, as in the case of Dora, countertransference is an important factor; and that in addition to Freud's conscious identification with the homosexual girl's father there is an unconscious one with the patient herself. (Similarly, Toril Moi has referred to Dora as both Freud's "opponent and alter ego. She possesses the secret Freud is trying to uncover, but she is also a curious person in search of sexual information—a quest oddly similar to Freud's own quest for the secrets of sexuality" ("Feminist Readings of Dora," p. 17).

Two aspects of Freud's own biography—if they are admissible to this sort of discussion—might support this argument. The first applies to his peculiar description of the surgical treatment of female homosexuality in the last sentence of the study: "A woman who . . . has loved in masculine fashion, will hardly let herself be forced into playing the part of a woman." During the month that this study was written—January 1920—and the previous December, Freud was visiting a dying friend every day. The friend was Anton von Freund, still in his early forties, a former patient and member of the private "Committee" formed to support Freud's work. Freud had treated von Freund in 1918–19 for a severe neurosis that followed an operation for the cancer that eventually killed him. The operation that precipitated the neurosis involved the removal of a tumor of the testicle (Jones, vol. II, p. 22). Could this contribute to the air of castration anxiety that pervades Freud's conclusion to this case?

The metonymical slide from castration to death (not so metonymical in the case of the unfortunate von Freund, who died on January 20) brings us to the second biographical detail, an experience of the three-year-old Freud when his family was emigrating from Freiberg to Leipzig in 1859:

> the train passed through Breslau, where Freud saw gas jets for the first time; they made him think of souls burning in hell! From this journey also dated the beginning of a "phobia" of travelling by train, from which he suffered a good deal for about a dozen years (1887–99) before he was able to dispel it by analysis. It turned out to be connected with the fear of losing his home (and ultimately his mother's breast). . . . Traces of it remained in later life in the form of slightly undue anxiety about catching trains. (Jones, vol. I, p. 14)

So . . . a man with an abiding fear of train travel undertakes the analysis of a woman brought to him because of her suicidal leap onto a railway line. After weeks of preparation, they reach what he terms the station—but then their reservation is canceled. And who shall we say was more reluctant to make the journey?

Notes

1.   Sections I–IV in this article follow Freud's significant divisions of this study. All citations from Freud are from *The Standard Edition of the Complete Psychological Works of Sigmund Freud*, Hogarth Press.
2.   See Jacqueline Rose, "Dora"—Fragment of an Analysis," p. 10.
3.   In "Intervention on Transference," p. 69.

4.   Two remarks from the 1905 "Three Essays" should be borne in mind here: Freud's dictum that "no one single aim can be laid down as applying in cases of inversion, (pp. 145, 58) and his listing of the overvaluation of the sexual object" as simply one of many perverse aims (pp. 150, 62).

5.   Jacques Lacan argues that both Dora and the homosexual girl desire "to sustain the desire of the father" in *The Four Fundamental Concepts of Psychoanalysis,* p. 38.

6.   The paraphrase is from Sonja Ruehl, "Inverts and Experts: Radclyffe Hall and the Lesbian Identity," p. 19.

7.   Joyce MacDougall, "Homosexuality in Women." But MacDougall's patients exhibit much more serious symptoms—severe disorganization, phobias, self-mutilation— than Freud's patient, and she posits the paternal introject at an early stage of childhood.

8.   Freud's periodization of the sexual stages of childhood is complicated by a number of revisions. Three years after this case study, in "The Infantile Genital Organization" he recategorized these into active/passive (at the anal stage), phallic/castrated (at the infantile genital stage, which would be clitoral for girls), and masculine/feminine only at the final organization of puberty. There, he writes, "maleness combines [the factors of] subject, activity and possession of the penis; femaleness takes over [those of] object and passivity" (pp. 145, 312). It's worth noting that the respective analysts cited propose three different paradigms of female homosexuality: phallic (Freud), oral (Deutsch), and anal-sadistic (MacDougall).

References

Henry Havelock Ellis (and John Addington Symonds), *Sexual Inversion, Studies in the Psychology of Sex,* vol. 1, Wilson and Macmillan, 1897.

Helene Deutsch, "On Female Homosexuality," in *The Psychoanalytic Quarterly,* vol. 1, 1932.

Sigmund Freud, "The Psychogenesis of a Case of Homosexuality in Woman" (1920), *The Standard Edition of the Complete Psychological Works of Sigmund Freud,* vol. XVIII, The Hogarth Press, 1961.

Sigmund Freud, "Fragment of an Analysis of a Case of Hysteria" ("Dora") (1905), *SE,* vol. VII.

Sigmund Freud, "Three Essays on Sexuality" (1905), *SE,* vol. VII.

Sigmund Freud, "Some Psychical Consequences of the Anatomical Distinction between the Sexes" (1925), *SE,* vol. XIX.

Sigmund Freud, "A Special Type of Choice of Object Made by Men" (1910), *SE,* vol. XI.

Sigmund Freud, "Mourning and Melancholia" (1917), *SE,* vol. XIV.

Sigmund Freud, "Female Sexuality" (1931), *SE,* vol. XXI.

Sigmund Freud, "Femininity" (1933), *SE,* vol. XXII.

Sigmund Freud, "The Infantile Genital Organisation: an Interpolation into the Theory of Sexuality" (1923), *SE,* vol. XIX.

Suzanne Gearhart, "The Scene of Psychoanalysis: the Unanswered Questions of Dora," in Charles Bernheimer and Claire Kahane (eds.), *In Dora's Case,* Virago, 1985, pp. 105–127.

Johan Huizinga, *The Waning of the Middle Ages,* Peregrine, 1965.

Ernest Jones, *The Life and Works of Sigmund Freud,* vol. I and II (unabridged edition), Hogarth Press, 1955.

Jacques Lacan, "Intervention on Transference," "Guiding Remarks for a Congress," and "The Meaning of the Phallus," in Juliet Mitchell and Jacqueline Rose (eds.), *Feminine Sexuality,* Macmillan, 1982.

Jacques Lacan, *The Four Fundamental Concepts of Psychoanalysis,* Penguin, 1977.

Joyce MacDougall, "Homosexuality in Women," in Janine Chasseguet-Smirgel (ed.), *Female Sexuality: New Psychoanalytic Views,* pp. 171—220, Virago, 1981.

Toril Moi, "Feminist Readings of Dora," in *Desire,* Institute of Contemporary Arts Publications (London), 1984.

J. H. W. Van Ophuijsen, "Contributions to the Masculinity Complex in Women" (1917), in *The International Journal of Psychoanalysis*, vol. 5 (1924), pp. 39—49.

Otto Rank, "Perversion and Neurosis," in *The International Journal of Psychoanalysis*, vol. 4 (1923).

Jacqueline Rose, "Dora"—Fragment of an Analysis," in *m/f*, no. 2 (1978) and reprinted in *In Dora's Case*, eds. Bernheimer and Kahane, Virago, 1985.

Sonja Ruehl, "Inverts and Experts: Radclyffe Hall and the Lesbian Identity," in Rosalind Brunt and Caroline Rowan (eds.), *Feminism, Culture and Politics*, Lawrence and Wishart, 1982.

Many thanks to Jean Fraser and Barbara Taylor for their helpful comments on this piece, which was originally presented at one of a series of seminars on Psychoanalysis and History organized by the History Workshop *in London in 1985.*

from *m/f* 11/12 1986

Interview

m/f was set up by Parveen Adams, Rosalind Coward, and Elizabeth Cowie, and the first issue appeared in February 1978 with a joint editorial by all three. Rosalind Coward left the journal later in the same year, shortly after the second issue. Meanwhile Beverley Brown had joined the editorial group. We continued the practice of joint editorials till number 5/6 in 1981.

In 1983 Beverley Brown took up a post in Australia, and she was still abroad in June 1984 when this interview took place.

The interview was for the Dutch women's journal, *Tijdschrift voor Vrouwen Studies* and was conducted by Mieke Aerts and Saskia Grotenhuis. The interview was published in Dutch in 1985 in no. 21 of the journal.

Although the interview was not produced for *m/f,* we think it useful to publish it in our last issue as an explication of our view of *m/f*'s work. We would like to thank Mieke Aerts and Saskia Grotenhuis for their well-informed, probing, yet sympathetic questions.

Parveen Adams and Elizabeth Cowie

Q: In Holland there has been some speculation about the exact meaning of the letters m/f on the cover of you journal. Some people think that it means Marxism versus feminism, others are in favor of masculinity versus femininity, and still others presume m/f to be nothing more than the initials of an important contemporary French philosopher. Which of these explanations comes closest to being the truth?

Elizabeth Cowie: We had great difficulty in trying to think of a title for the journal and decided upon *m/f* precisely because it did not mean just one thing and was therefore open in terms of defining the program of the journal. The *m* and the *f* for us have always stood primarily for masculine and feminine and the idea of the slash was not that it should mean versus but that it should mark a difference, a separation. We also considered the order of the letters but decided against reversing them—it might have led to the journal being taken for a radio magazine since *FM* is a broadcasting frequency!

Parveen Adams: The first response I had was from an American feminist living in Paris who wrote that she was very disappointed that men came first. And my initial reaction was—why men? It could be mother/father. But anyhow, the important point is precisely that *m/f* makes possible a large number of readings.

Q: In that case, what about the relation of m/f *to Marxism/Feminism?*

Elizabeth Cowie: The debates around, and critiques of Marxism were certainly important to our discussions. Nevertheless our perspective, as we stated in the first editorial, was *socialist-feminist.* If we had wished to be taken as anything else we would not have simply used "a feminist journal" as our secondary title.

Parveen Adams: In the years we were working on the idea of bringing out the journal, from 1976 to 1978, a lot of women were associated with Marxism and socialism. There was the domestic labor debate, a great deal of feminist-socialist history writing and socialist-feminist conferences. We were involved in these conferences. I myself was in a woman's Marx reading group for some years. Rosalind Coward, Elizabeth, and myself studied the new critiques of traditional arguments on the left and were influenced by the work of Cutler, Hindess, Hirst, and Hussain.

So we were engaged in many different sorts of argument in relation to Marxism. And it became clear to us that the Marxist-Feminist position was a paradoxical one, impossible to sustain. We certainly did *not* intend *m/f* to be read as Marxist-Feminist!

Elizabeth Cowie: There were other discussions too, for example around Juliet Mitchell's book *Psychoanalysis and Feminism* and around Foucault's work in the journal *Ideology and Consciousness,* which first came out in 1977.

Q: What you are saying suggests that all three of our suggested readings of m/f *are important to the project of your journal. Would you also agree if we were to describe its development as a moving away from a critique of Marxist-Feminist general the-*

ory, in the process of which you lost interest in a Foucauldian approach (of discourse analysis) but started to pay more attention to psychoanalysis?

Elizabeth Cowie: No, the critique of Marxism/Feminism is still important—the article as recently as no. 7 on the question of women as a reserve army of labor indicates that. And the commitment to exploring psychoanalysis has been there from the first issue. Our development has, I think, been a consolidation of the approach outlined in our first issues. The work of Foucault, too, is certainly not something which we've lost interest in, but nor do we see it as constituting our general theory or approach.

Parveen Adams: The question is a very complex one because so much is implicated. It is true that from the beginning a general theory of women's oppression was rejected and explicitly argued against. The first four issues were important for staking out a position, but having done that, we tried to map out a terrain in which we could do more "positive" work. Indeed, we had been severely criticized by feminists for being extremely negative in our first issues, of only hitting out at things. So then there was more emphasis on articles in which theoretical and political analyses were brought together, because that exactly is something we very much want to do. I think our double issue nos. 5/6 has some good examples of this type of article.

Now, about our interest in psychoanalysis. Of course, it is central to us. But first I would like to say that for me a lot of other things are important that don't have anything to do with psychoanalysis. For example, the areas of work, unemployment, education, the law, the relation of feminism to socialism, and antiracism. I agree that we have not published very much about those areas, but from the very beginning we have paid attention to them. We are of course dependent on the sort of articles we can lay our hands on.

Secondly, I would agree that direct references to psychoanalysis abound because we engage directly with it. We do not have such a relation to Foucault's work. I do not think however that you can draw any simple conclusion from that. The article on mothering I wrote for *m/f* no. 8, for instance, shows not only a maybe rather odd use of psychoanalysis, but also a use of Foucault and Donzelot when it comes to a critique of Chodorow. There I try to argue not only that she has a very simple notion of psychoanalysis, but also that it is very unclear what kind of "social" she is talking about. Compared to Foucault's and Donzelot's notions about how norms are set up, and how "feminine mothering" gets set up in the midst of a web of relations—parent-child, mother-father, mother-doctor, state-family—Chodorow has a very simple idea of sex differences in the social. Certainly, Foucault and Donzelot represent a decisive advance in the analysis of such problems.

Thirdly, our interest in psychoanalysis does not mean that we propose a general psychoanalytic theory of women's oppression. You can already see part of this in my article on the distinction between sexual division and sexual differences, in *m/f* no. 3. This is of course an argument against a general theory of women's oppression. But the important point here is my disagreement with Juliet Mitchell, where I say that, no matter how sophisticated her use of psychoanalysis, by treating it as part of a theory of ideology she finally returns to men, women, and patriarchy. The central question here is the famous slide from what is said about masculinity and femininity in psychoanalysis to the subordination of women. Now I don't think you can make that move. Juliet Mitchell would probably say that the interesting problem is precisely that slide between the phallus, the penis, and the father (and so into the social) and that this is a problem both for feminism and psychoanalysis to address themselves to. But I don't stand in that position.

Psychoanalysis makes a statement about femininity and masculinity. I agree with what both Juliet Mitchell and Jacqueline Rose argue strongly and powerfully, which is that femininity is not defined by a content but by a difference from masculinity, and that this is very problematic, because nobody wants to be in the position of the feminine, be they man or woman.

But it must also be the case that the "feminine" when talked about in that way, does not exhaust, equal or define women. Femininity is a political problem, but it is only one of many problems within feminism. As it is not coextensive with women, it is certainly not coextensive will all the arenas of women's subordination.

Q: Do you intend to say that within m/f's *project psychoanalysis can handle the psychic and other theoretical approaches are to handle the social?*

Parveen Adams: No, not exactly. Let me put it like this. It is not a question of saying that psychoanalysis elucidates psychical relations but stops short of social relations. Clearly, psychoanalysis makes strong claims about culture or the symbolic. I don't want to get into boundary disputes within the human sciences which may be important, but are not *our* starting point as feminists. Let us rather start from the claim that the personal is political. There you have a strong impetus to try and think about an area that is called the personal, and to rethink its articulation with the political. Now in a way, psychoanalysis is almost the only kind of discourse available and fits with this feminist interest. Because the concepts that feminism wants to develop on that count have to do with sexuality, sexual difference, psychic reality, childbearing, parents, desire, sexual desire, and so on. Now these are also the terms around which psychoanalysis—that is classical Freudian analysis—revolves. What I am insisting is that there is this curious isomorphism—I don't mean to say that psychoanalysis is feminist or that feminist discourse should be a psychoanalytic discourse—but there is this isomorphism nonetheless. Of course, if you come to psychoanalysis because of your feminist interest in "the personal," perhaps you are bound to end up with a problem of the psychic and the social, partly because you get the feeling that in psychoanalysis you have left out all those vast concerns of feminist politics. Psychoanalysis can certainly speak to some areas like sexuality, motherhood, sexual difference, in some way, but there are other areas, of employment, social policy, nuclear weapons, that psychoanalysis has little to say about.

Q: But isn't that exactly setting up the problem in terms of the psychic versus the social? And what happens then to your proposed rethinking of their interrelationship?

Elizabeth Cowie: I think that Parveen is stressing this demarcation in order to get away from any suggestion that psychoanalysis would be our general theory. And I certainly don't think it suggests a return to posing the social versus the psychic. We had argued in the editorial to nos. 5/6 and in my introduction to Mary Kelly's work in the same issue that we need to address the forms of connection that might exist between psychic relations and social relations. But I think now that there is still a difficulty in posing the issue in that way because you always end up asking which was first and which determines which and thus end up speaking of this versus that without even considering what led you to oppose those two terms. Within the theoretical terms we have at present I don't think we can tackle this problem directly. Instead, we have to examine the social practices themselves and consider why we've lined up some as social, some as psychical, some personal, some political.

Parveen Adams: Well, that is true of course. But a further problem is that what psychoanalysis means by the "social" is quite different from what sociology and Marxism mean by it. And conversely, what they imply about the psyche is quite different. Clearly, one cannot combine the approaches happily. Obviously it would be wrong to argue that the psychic and the social are ontologically distinct realms; rather, it is a question of adopting one or other term as a strategic vantage point from which to analyze a particular question.

Elizabeth Cowie: Yes, though it can't be a question of simply becoming more and more sophisticated at determining which is psychical and which is social, not least because the presumption that ultimately the latter is really the most important can return. We have to rethink that opposition, that division. In the context of my own area of work on film, the concept of fantasy is particularly interesting because it seems to me to exist or work across the division of psychic and social. Fantasies may be individual but they involve within their scenarios social relations. And they may be public, involving a mass audience as with cinema, or the novel. Psychoanalytically, fantasy is both a conscious and an unconscious process, presenting to and for the subject a mise-en-scène of its desire. I don't mean by this to propose fantasy as a general concept of analysis—reading the social or the political as fantasy. Rather it seems to me to pose a disruption of these categories by introducing the issue of desire.

Parveen Adams: Exactly. The important point here is that we do not see psychoanalysis as a general theory of patriarchy, but maintain that there are many different uses of psychoanalytic insights to be made. Two examples: Elizabeth's work on film and fantasy and my article on mothering. These do not rely on psychoanalysis as a general theory of patriarchy and thus they are completely different from the traditional feminist concerns that someone like Gayle Rubin has in the context of psychoanalysis.

Elizabeth Cowie: Yes Parveen, but surely you do not wish to so radically exclude psychoanalysis from certain questions? I don't mean by this that I think that psychoanalysis necessarily has something to say about other domains, though it may well do—rape is perhaps one such area. Rather, I think its importance—as it has been developed by Lacan and others—is as a theory of human subjectivity—it speaks of the human subject as a subject of desire. Psychoanalysis describes the stake of desire (for desire is constructed for the subject) in relation to the instituting of difference and especially sexual difference. And obviously the subordination of women arises from a production of women as different in particular ways. This cannot imply an identity in the production of difference addressed by psychoanalysis and by feminism, as is sometimes attempted, but it does seem to me to pose their interrelationship.

In this sense psychoanalysis is for me not just a body of knowledge we can import into other domains. But nor is it simply an interpretive tool which can be used to psychoanalyze social discourses as if they were discourses of the couch. I think that Lacan's reworking of Freud in relation to a theory of language and signification shows the way in which the subject is spoken by the structure of desire rather than simply how the subject speaks his or her desire.

Parveen Adams: Of course, ultimately everything has to be social and psychic at the same time, so in that sense I've got to be wrong. But to take up your example—of course psychoanalysis speaks to rape; but the article we had on rape in the double issue does not speak of psychoanalysis. It tries to show how certain legal and pretrial practices and that which is permissible as evidence come to construct sexual difference in court, which is of course always overlaid with an already given sexual difference, but still has its own manner of being constructed. So the problems of sexual difference are not hegemonized by psychoanalytic thought; at least, I don't want it to be that way for feminism in general. It may be that psychoanalysis has something to say about rape but the problems which feminists raise within the context of rape slip out of the grasp of a purely psychoanalytic point of view. A similar argument can be made about the topic of pornography and Beverley Brown's article on it in the same double issue of *m/f,* nos. 5/6.

Q: But Parveen, you would not agree with Elizabeth's view on the broad range of domains psychoanalysis could speak to?

Parveen Adams: Yes, as I said, I *would* agree in principle. I would hardly claim that psychoanalysis could not speak to the problem of rape. But I wouldn't agree that other forms of analysis are therefore any the less necessary. I would tend to be suspicious of any primordial analytic tool, whether that is psychoanalysis or anything else. I don't see what is wrong with using one theory for this and another theory for that.

Q: But doesn't a statement like this one, even as the insistence on the study of particular objects Elizabeth argued for earlier on, bring you very close to the sort of empiricist analysis traditional history writing got famous for? Has your refusal of general theory landed you in Flat land, where the facts speak for themselves?

Elizabeth Cowie: What I think you are indicating as a problem is that if you don't have a general theory you can only talk about the contingent. But I don't think we are quite doing that! Objects of knowledge only emerge within particular theoretical frameworks. Therefore, there is an issue of what objects of knowledge can be. And it is the analysis of the conditions of the production of such objects that is politically pertinent. There is therefore no necessary choice between general theory on the one hand and the contingent on the other.

Parveen Adams: So you see how Foucault still informs the whole project, even if he doesn't get mentioned!

Q: Could you relate that to the objects of feminist theorizing, for instance "men" and "women"?

Parveen Adams: Of course, everybody "knows" what or rather who men and women are. That's not the problem. The problem is whether or not this knowledge is adequate to ground a feminist politics. To what extent do women constitute a real or potential unity by being that entity we call women? I would like to answer that in two ways. First, I would like to repeat something Elizabeth, Beverley, and I wrote in reply to Rosalind Coward and Michèle Barrett (Correspondence, *m/f* no. 7), who are both claiming that difference as a historical construction is very important *and* insisting on something called the concrete collectivity of women. That is, they want to insist on the specificity of the historical while grounding that at the same time in the obviousness of the unity of women. It is the difficulty of holding both these positions that we really addressed.

Now we assumed that their appeal to the historical and the social means that they are not grounding the distinction of men and women in biology. So there must be something else. So what we said was that in order to establish a concrete collectivity of the kind that they wanted, they would have to demonstrate 1) that the collectivity was socially produced; and 2) that it was produced as a unity, which means that each and every person in it is constructed in the same way, as a unity; and 3) that social relations produce just those groups of people and no other groups. And then, all that would have to add up to the conclusion that these effects of the socially produced equals oppression. Now you have to demonstrate all those things before you can produce a notion of collectivity which is not biological. I personally think that this is not possible.

What I think is this: the common condition of woman is a perception which is not so much dependent on a theoretical argument, but is based on the obviousness of experience to some women. Now there you have your empiricism. But the problem is that not all women share this experience.

There is more, and this is the second thing I would like to say. Playing devil's advocate to myself I was thinking: now what did I do in 1970 or 1971? I was in New

York then, and I picked up some of the radical feminist papers around. And all the way one immediately "recognized"—that is the word—oneself and one would say: good heavens, this is me! Now what one was doing there is appealing to experience, openly in this case. But you would have to say that it was not just an experience of women. It was a socially constructed, experience of white, Western, middle-class women, one that I, even though a Parsi, shared and recognized by virtue of my own formation. None of this constitutes an accusation however, precisely because these women are talking in terms of a specific experience. It can only become ground for an accusation the moment this experience is universalized. Then other women, from other backgrounds, constructed in other social relations can come along and say: you have not included us in your experience, and you have to, because it is supposed to cover all of us. Now I say it would be absurd to accuse white women of formulating their experience and calling it oppression, but it is also absurd for white women to claim a universal oppression.

And actually, if I may get experiential for a moment, the construction of "woman" we are trying to argue for fits far better with the ongoing proliferation of women's groups and female identities than the attempt to subsume everything under one homogeneous sign of oppression. Which is of course not the same as saying that our approach has produced this kind of fragmentation.

Q: To us it would seem very difficult to use the fragmentation of the women's movement as an argument in favor of your project, of deconstructing the idea of a general theory of women's oppression. For one, this fragmentation is really a proliferation of general theories, and secondly, the problem seems more to be how to grow beyond all those separate groups. How do you feel about that?

Parveen Adams: It seems almost the implication of your question that we would oppose the unity of the movement. But of course you need a unity. What we are trying to say is that if there is a unity, it is not given by being women, you have to work for that unity.

Elizabeth Cowie: I would say that people tend to see this question in terms of a simple alternative between necessity ("one day the underlying unity will become clear") and voluntarism ("we just have to be one").

Parveen Adams: And it is at this point that once again theoretical activities become important. Because when you want to discuss the fragmentation of the women's movement in terms more meaningful than either "the decline of feminism" or "a question of priorities," you have to ask the question what the notion of women's oppression means, which is a theoretical question.

Now at this point our refusal of general theory means mostly two things. First of all we are saying that the political objectives that you formulate cannot be read off from a general position. There is no such thing as having a nice, safe position in which a theory gives you your explanations, your justifications, your audience, and your politics. Marxism may have been one of the last theories that tried to do all this, and it just doesn't work. Secondly, and more specifically, we are questioning easy formulas like: why does it always have to be women who are discriminated against? Such formulas presuppose something like a notion of the universal oppression of women. All we say is that women are not universally given as women, and that the notion of oppression itself is a constructed notion. So we have to pay careful attention to what it means to construct concepts like "men," "women," and "oppression" within a specific given theoretical and political conjuncture.

Q: Well, there are some feminists who say that as long as one half of the population goes through the same toilet doors, at least about the concept of women there cannot be much misunderstanding.

Elizabeth Cowie: But that is exactly the conflation of sexual division and sexual difference which we are arguing against. The point is to try and articulate the ways in which the construction of oppression relates to the construction of the category women, and not to try to deduce one from the other.

But to go back to the question of unity and fragmentation. I think that the unity of the early British Women's Movement—symbolized perhaps in the way in which the original Four Demands met such general agreement—emerged from a specific conjuncture and had a specific history. That conjuncture included the awareness of the position women had found themselves assigned to in relation to the new socialist struggles of the 1960s, a position as ancilliary helpers in that struggle. The rejection of that role was later a powerful factor in the arguments for the autonomy of the Women's Movement from socialist parties. The history was of consciousness-raising in small groups as our form of organizing and political practice. Do we find an original unity of all women here? The fact is that a woman would have had to have already recognized herself as being in the position where she is motivated to join a group—and many, many women didn't join. You had to nominate yourself in some way as a person who should join a consciousness-raising group. And you might do that if you had had a particular set of experiences. What I am suggesting is that the original unity of the Women's Movement which we have been accused of fragmenting was itself a very contingent unity.

Q: May we see this as an invitation to ask you about your views on the developments of feminist politics, in the near future?

Parveen Adams: That can't really be answered in a general way, but it would seem to me that two of the things that would be important to discuss are what constitutes socialist-feminism and at what point can feminist objectives be put into relation with the antiracist struggle? It is these questions which necessitate the forging of political objectives which will be difficult but which will yield perhaps a more unified feminism.

Elizabeth Cowie: I think it extremely important for feminism to question the assumption that there is some necessary connection between women's struggles and other struggles. Of course, feminism can and must be connected to other struggles, which would themselves be all the stronger for the alliance. But it is important that we always *explicitly* recognize these as alliances. Rights, for example, rights to benefits, can be argued for in various ways. It makes a big difference if one is doing it by claiming a specific interest for women or by posing something like a general or socialist interest. The kind of argument one chooses to make will depend on the alliances one chooses to make.

Parveen Adams: Modern feminism puts a great deal of emphasis on the political and the personal. That means it not only has to do with questions of equality, but also with the construction of new norms. That is indeed an incredibly difficult idea. What kind of political undertaking is it? How do you do it? How do you guarantee that it gets anywhere? You can see the need to develop arguments around this kind of problem when you look at the kind of solution Nancy Chodorow offers to the question of mothering. She makes it into a question of equality of the simplest kind. But as I see it, feminism is not just about getting the chores evenly shared, it is about new forms of mother-child, parent-child interaction. But that reminds me of one other thing I want to say.

It could be that feminist objectives are not all of one order. I mean this: while I certainly would not say that I wanted an androgynous human being to emerge as the overall solution to women's subordination, maybe we ought to say that there are certain domains (law, work) where we do wish a somewhat androgynous figure to emerge. Our problem then is how to construct our objectives in terms of sexual difference while struggling for effects of equality. Yes, maybe the shortest answer to your question goes like this: in some cases the objectives of feminist politics go against sexual differences, in other cases they do not, and the problem is to find out which is which.

from *m/f* 11/12, 1986

Postscript

RACHEL BOWLBY

Une Passante

To Baudelaire's poem, "A une passante," "To a Passing Woman," there may be no more to add.

The deafening street around me was screaming.
Tall, slender, in heavy mourning, majestic grief,
A woman passed, with a proud hand
Lifting, balancing the garland and the hem;

Agile and noble, with her statue's leg.
And I, tense like a madman, was drinking
In her eye, livid sky where the hurricane germinates,
The gentleness that fascinates and the pleasure that kills.

One flash . . . then night!—Fleeting beauty
Whose look made me suddenly reborn,
Will I see you no more but in eternity?

Elsewhere, very far from here! too late! *never* perhaps!
For I know not where you are fleeing, you know not where I am going

O you whom I would have loved, o you who knew it![1]

Amid the clatter and din of the street, there she is; or there she was, no sooner there than gone, vanishing, disappearing, here only in what is now the loss of her.

But the poem brings her back: gone/here, *fort/da*: brings her back fixed and no longer fleeing, but fixed as one who flees, fleeting (*"fugitive"*), runaway (*"tu fuis"*).

He looked, she looked; I looked, you looked; there was an instant, it could have been forever, it is past.

You knew, "you who knew it," you didn't say. Silent woman who knows, whom he sees knowing, who will not (cannot?) say.

He looks at her, she looks at him. Two looks that make one? Or two different, incommensurable looks? Or one look, his that sees her seeing him (seeing her (seeing him . . .)?

She brought new life ("made me suddenly reborn"), and is also a murderer ("the pleasure which kills") coming in funeral garments, who fled away free (*"Fugitive beaute,"* *"tu fuis"*). Death-dealer and life-giver, a mother.

A twofold mother: *"Moi, je buvais,"* "I was drinking," in her eye, nourishing eye and evil eye, "the gentleness that fascinates and the pleasure that kills."

In mourning, she has lost someone; she transmits her loss to him, leaving him marked by her passing.

Anonymous: any woman, *une femme.* And also the one and only, the unique woman, love eternal, at first and last sight.[2]

Two women seen in one. The woman of the street. A fast (*"fugitive"*) lady. The whore, undomesticated, whose home is the *maison de passe,* the street inside. At the same time *"noble"* and unavailable, inaccessible: not to be approached. She is *"majestueuse,"* a queen or goddess with her statuesque leg.

From the third person, "a woman," to the second, "you," addressed at the end, *toi que j'eusse aimée*!," you whom I would have loved, past unfulfilled conditional, if what? No answer, she disappeared, never to return, consecrated in the restoration of the imaginary moment when it might have been that she was there. Unconditional love: under no conditions could it be, its possibility is past, ruled out, from the start; and also without interference from external conditions of space and time, in eternity.

The timing puts her definitively in the past, as the one who passed, irrevocably, and yet will have marked him forever. She is out of time, no sooner here than gone, represented only in her absence. And out of time because only "in eternity," in the timeless, will he see her again. There was a flash of light, "un éclair," then darkness, *"puis la nuit."* The snapshot of what looked like a woman, caught, taken, in an instant, remaining only in an image, the picture of her.

In the distance between them, only their eyes "meet": otherwise they are apart. He is fixed, transfixed (*"crispé"*); she moves, "passed" across the field of his vision. On this separation between them, in space as in time, depends her perfection, and the unconditional quality of the love.

The Passante

This *passante,* a *passante*: we have not heard the last of her. She turns up again, and repeatedly, in Proust. Here is one such occasion.

> The charms of the *passante* are generally directly related to the rapidity
> of the passing. It only takes night to be falling and the vehicle to be going
> fast, in the country, in a city, and there is not one female torso, mutilated
> like an ancient marble by the speed that carries us forward and the dusk
> which darkens it, which does not aim at our heart, at every corner on the
> way, in the depths of every shop, the arrows of Beauty, of Beauty of which
> it might sometimes be tempting to wonder whether in this world it is any-
> thing else but the complementary part added to a fragmentary and fleet-
> ing *passante* by our imagination overexcited by regret.[3]

Proust's *passante* might be a direct descendant of Baudelaire's. "*Fugitive*" once more, she is the fleeting impression, only there in the moment that she is already gone. She is statuesque, "*comme un marbre antique,*" both noble and dead, her own monument, like the "statue's leg" of the sonnet. But the "mutilated," "fragmentary" nature of Proust's *passante* also, now, looking back, seems to have been shared by the "statue's leg," just one leg, one part, singled out by Baudelaire. The "regret" here is like what is inferred from the poet's "O you whom I would have loved," her loss the condition for the desire of her, and for the conditional's being necessarily in the odd time of the "past unfulfilled."

The *passante* here seems to have moved on or away from her Baudelairean singularity, fixed now into a type: not *a,* but *the* passante. There is not even a question, this time, of a look in return, from her. "*Fugitive*" still, her appearance is fleeting not because she passes—she may be quite stationary, in the back of a shop—but because he does—or "we" do, a community of (masculine) readers invoked for the occasion as sharing in, recognizing, this as a commonplace experience, and the appeal to whom is a further reinforcement of the generalization of the scene.[4] And if we ignore generic differences between lyric poetry and narrative prose, we could note that whereas the poem, in its title and in the concluding apostrophe ("O you . . .") is addressed to a particular *passante,* Proust's narrator addresses "us" who are not *passantes* but viewers of *passantes,* on the subject of *passantes,* a general category. The generality of the experience, recognized as an example of a common type, removes its apparent uniqueness and irrevocability: one *passante* is like another in that she can be replaced, that another and another will figure in the same way, without there being any single constitutive event, even in retrospect.

Putting the two together, Proust's spectator appears to extend and confirm what was only a possibility in the Baudelaire poem. Quite explicitly, the *passante* is now (in every sense) a mere projection from the spectator.[5] Her passing is really his, as he zooms by just catching sight of her; her partial and fleeting appearance belongs to the same phenomenon. Whence the hypothesis that Beauty might just be "the complementary part added to a fragmentary and fugitive *passante* by our overexcited imagination." The "Beauty" is not out there, but born of "our" own "overexcited" imagination; it is added as the missing, "complementary" part to make a whole of what would otherwise be just the fragmentary vision. It is this addition, carried over to her from us, which completes her, raising her up to the heights of a capitalized essence. "Beauty" substantializes her fragmentariness and puts a stop to her disappearance, her passing (*"fugitive"*). It fits her to him, makes her in the image of his "overexcited imagination" prompted by her loss, "regret."

The Eternal Passante

Seen in this light, the *passante* does not seem at all like a localized figure. And once she has been drawn out in this way, an identification to be projected potentially onto any woman, anywhere, we might take this still further and look at her as quasi-mythological, a timeless figure.

For there are in this scenario some rather familiar elements. First—in the beginning—there is *the* woman created out of an extra bit added on from and by the man. The rib is removed from Adam to make Eve, beautiful and whole, but made from a fragment. She is a lost piece of him, the primordial "complementary part": in the beginning, they were one. But as long as she lives they cannot be reunited, for her very existence depends on their separation.

The Biblical genesis of woman is not the only mythical echo called forth by the *passante*. Baudelaire's *passante,* irretrievably lost, is as though dead: in her disappearance, she passes on her loss to the poet. Like the widowed Orpheus, who descends into Hades in quest of Eurydice, he can seek her only in her death. And just as Orpheus can have her back only on condition that he does not look at her—one glimpse, and she will be gone—so the writing which brings back the *passante* can only follow after a sighting that is never to be repeated.[6]

"The" Woman, Encore

And if Baudelaire and Proust have said it already, perhaps Lacan says it some more, *encore*. For we seem to have been approaching a point where the *passante* has come to look indistinguishable from the psychoanalytic figure of femininity, in all her fantasmatic ambiguity.

Several features that may be glimpsed in the *Encore* seminars would seem to lend support to at least a partial identification of the Lacanian "woman" with the *passante*:

> We could in theory write *x R y,* and say that *x* is the man, *y* is the woman, and *R* is the sexual relation. Why not? Only there's this, it's stupid, because what is supported under the signifying function, of *man* and of *woman,* are only signifiers completely bound up with the current-run [*courcourant*] usage of language. If there is a discourse which demonstrates this to you, it must be psychoanalytic discourse, in making an issue of this, that the woman will never be taken other than *quoad matrem.* The woman only does her job [*entre en fonction*] in the sexual relationship as the mother.[7]

There is no sexual relation, "*Il n'y a pas de rapport sexuel.*" The poet and his *passante* never meet, there is nothing more than what he sees in her. But at the same time, it is the fantasy of their complementarity, their being made for each other, which engenders the endless wish for their unity.

The mother: no getting away from her, but she has always left you. You, the man: from the moment that the mother turns out to be "a woman," there is no going back, nothing for it but to seek her again, hopelessly, for what now seems to have been the perfect link is broken forever. So—the most usual outcome—"women," one after the other, all the same in that they are not her, the one and only, but could or should have been, "O you whom I would have loved!" (You, the woman, a woman, too, from the moment that the mother turns out to be one. A different story, into which the *passante* seen by the poet enters rather as a problem of identification: to be or not to be [like] her.) "There is not *the* woman, the woman is *not all* [*pas toute*]."[8] "The" woman does not exist, the woman as perfect complement, but she is seen as potentially this, as truth, all, from the man's projection. The "fragmentary" *passante* who *would have been* all is projected as all by what the imagination supplies to her appearance—both in that she is seen as lacking, and that she makes up for a lack in the man.

What leaves some likelihood for what I am putting forward, namely, that of this *jouissance,* the woman knows nothing, is that all the time we've been begging them, begging them on our knees—last time I was talking about women psychoanalysts—to try to tell us, well, not a word! We have never been able to get anything out of them.[9]

Who knows what she wants? Her *jouissance* may be other than phallic, but she won't say or can't. "*O toi qui le savais,*" you knew it but you said not a word. "If the libido is only masculine, the dear woman, it is only from where she is all, which is to say from where the man sees her, from nowhere but there that the dear woman can have an unconscious."[10] Only masculine libido, phallic organization of *jouissance* as far as it can be articulated. It is all seen from the masculine side: no desire, no imagining from her side can be represented.

Ça, a Woman

There is more to it than that. Sometimes it seems as if Lacan is also presenting the unconscious itself, and not only the (impossible) woman, as something not unlike a *passante* in one of her aspects:

Here we find again the rhythmic structure of this opening and shutting of the crack. . . . The evanescent apparition occurs between two points, the start, the finish of this logical time—between that instant of seeing where something is always elided, even lost, of the intuition itself, and that elusive moment when, precisely, the grasp [*saisie*] of the unconscious does not end, where it is always a matter of a deceptive recuperation.[11]

In my preceding statements, I have been continually stressing the, in a sense, *pulsative* function of the unconscious, the necessity of vanishing which seems to be in a sense inherent to it—all that, for an instant, appears in its crack seeming to be destined, by a sort of preempting, to close up again, the metaphor Freud himself used, to whisk away, to disappear.[12]

Like the *passante*—"one flash, then darkness"—the unconscious for Lacan is something that no sooner flickers into view than it is gone again. We might dwell for a moment on the striking similarities in the image. First, that is it indeed an image, a *visual* analogy: the unconscious is seen/not seen, appearing/disappearing—despite the fact that psychoanalysis is a practice whose medium is entirely one of words. The vanishing unconscious is also like the *passante* in that it is always ungraspable—in the very moment, the instant, you have it, it closes off again. And yet it is also what the analyst is seeking, endlessly, and by the very fact of its being "lost," unattainable as such: no "recuperation" or recovery other than one that is deceptive, false in its appearance. It slips away, tricky and evasive (there are many different words for this: *se dérober, évanouissante, évasif, élusif, élidé*: it is quite an emphatic betrayal or escape). The impossible feminine apparition is not confined to the manifest consideration of sexuality and sexual difference, but seems to have passed or seeped into the depths of the psychoanalytic account of subjectivity, to produce a covertly gendered unconscious. Or overtly: "Eurydice twice lost, such is the most tangible image we could give, in myth, of what the relationship is of Orpheus the analyst to the unconscious."[13]

So many representations from the masculine point of view, of the view as masculine: it is as if Lacanian psychoanalysis provided a culmination to the series of *passante* passages, exposing the terms of her (non)existence in all their intractability.

Pas Ça, Not That

"*Une femme passa,*" "a woman passed," a woman seen from the masculine position; heard in a different way, "*une femme, pas ça,*" "a woman, not *that,*" no thank you. And if we hear "*pas ça*" in a different way again, we find the further objection: not the "*ça,*" the usual French translation of Freud's "id": "not the unconscious," to which femininity sometimes, at moments, seems to be all but assimilated. If it is taken as a critical exposure of the structure rather than an admiring exposition of it, psychoanalysis seems to offer the perfect account of the cul-de-sacs of a femininity that is conceived simply as a projection of masculine desire. But it offers no immediate ways out, no other place, either female or neutral, outside the given patriarchal or phallocentric scene.

Impasse. Where do "we"—women? feminists? *passantes?*—go from here? No step seems possible. No step: *pas de pas. Pas pas, papa:* only the old patriarchal story. Unless we said no to all that and looked in a different direction altogether. *Pas:* a no that would also be a step? Or a step that would only represent a denial?

The Modern Passante

The Freudian/Lacanian line treats the woman/*passante* as the masculine fantasy of femininity, but other feminist approaches have taken different directions. For in another sense, the *passante* could be seen not as universal figure of fantasy, but as a preeminently historical figure, a woman of her time.

Looked at in this way, Baudelaire's *passante* comes across almost as a tableau of the experience of modernity. It is an anonymous encounter which takes place apparently in a large, modern city: the street, anything but a neutral background, is the first subject of the poem, and it is an active, shouting milieu where the couple themselves are silent. There is the fleeting, unforeseen event that shocks, and the peculiar temporality (the sighting is retrospectively fixed as *having* happened, irrevocable in that nothing will alter its significance, and also in that it cannot be recovered in its pristine originality, which is represented only insofar as it is past, or passed away).[14]

Proust's version is differently situated. Unlike Baudelaire's *flâneur,* on foot, noises from the street surrounding him, the viewer here is traveling in a vehicle, and the sighting of the *passante* is an effect of his own speed, his own passage. The *passante* can be anywhere at all along the route, in town or the country; Baudelaire's was a particular, urban *passante.* Proust's *passante* is potentially ubiquitous, *"dans la ville, à la campagne"*: another of the *passante* scenes in *A la recherche du temps perdu* concerns the very type of the country girl, a milkmaid, seen from a train. If it is a crucial part of the poet's experience that this woman emerges and disappears in the street, Proust's narrator seems to be no longer restricted to this setting: the *passante* could be any woman, anywhere—or just anything momentarily seen "as" a passing woman. The train, the vehicle (horse-drawn here, elsewhere in Proust an automobile) expands the reach of the urban sighting, making the country, too, into a possible site for the glimpse in passing of an unknown woman. The landscape (itself an aesthetic metaphor, implying an externally placed spectator) is turned into a passing scene (cinema, the "moving picture," is on the horizon already). And the vehicle in which the viewer is situated removes him from any sensory contact with the street itself: the scene in which *passantes* appear is a spectacle seen at a safe, and thereby even more untraversable, distance.

Taking this more historical line, two avenues of analysis open up, two feminist turnings. One would treat the *passante* as a distortion, symptomatic of the patriarchal misrepresentation or misrecognition of women in comparison with what they really are. Look again, look at her as she really is, and you will see something very different from what appears from the perspective of the masculine writer. The *passante* or woman is *not that,* not what she has been shown to be, seen through male eyes; instead, whether already or potentially, there are other, more true-to-life women concealed behind this view of her. This line of investigation might then look at the diversity of the women who actually walked the city streets or the country lanes in this period—of different races or social classes, but united by an oppression that subordinates them all as women, and/or which prevents the expression of their underlying femininity.

The second type of historical approach would not compare the *passante* with another, more accurate picture of women masked by her image, but would look instead at the conditions of representation that made it possible for the woman to be seen as a *passante*, and which, by the same token, might preclude the figure of the *flâneur,* the strolling spectator, from being represented as a woman.[15] This approach would not presuppose a different, more realistic identification of the woman as other than a *passante,* but would, rather, explore the different discourses that construct and constrain various modes of identification, not consistently divided along a line of sexual division.

The *passante:* perhaps the most ancient and the most modern figure for a woman? Perhaps the figure who throws into confusion any easy distinction between the historical and the timeless, between changing conditions and eternal forms; or between the social and the psychic.

The fable of the *passante* I have just recounted and of the separation of psychic and social forms of analysis has been leading up, step by step, to one view of where *m/f* came in. For, looked at with hindsight (a backward glance, or postscript, to which we shall return), *m/f*'s questioning of the figure of woman can be seen as having pointed feminist debates not only toward a distinction between psychic and social questions, but also toward the impossibility of leaving them at that. In thinking p/s, the psychic and the social, *m/f* refused to treat them as either/or alternatives, and at the same time insisted on the need to think each of them through, on its own terms. After this, the *passante* was never going to look the same again; nor were the eyes of the onlooker going to be simply identifiable as those of a man, or indeed of a woman.

The mysteriousness of *m/f*'s name is a promise, or threat, of the disturbances of these categories. In a sense, the name might seem, provocatively, to flaunt the enigma of femininity in person. Some of its possible senses, clearly never meant to be fixed, are mentioned in the interview in the "Last Issue" given by an *m/f* now personified by Parveen Adams and Elizabeth Cowie, to a group of Dutch feminists. Male/female, masculine/feminine seem the most obvious; but mother/father, Marxism/Feminism, and even Michel Foucault are also raised as possibilities. There is also a hint of s/s, in its Saussurian and Lacanian versions, to suggest a semiotic or psychoanalytic orientation. At any rate, it is clear that *m/f* is no univocal figure, and no univocally female figure either.

Pas Ça Encore

From the beginning *m/f*'s project consisted of both a questioning of existing theories of feminism, and a building upon possibilities that had recently been opened up: via psychoanalysis (as an aid rather than a hindrance to feminist understanding) and via new methods of historical analysis. The principal target was the essentialism implied by the first of the two historical lines sketched above. *Essentialism* designated any theory or politics presupposing either a biological or a social unity of women: either their bodies or a consistently operating social "oppression" determines a unified group identity on the basis of which political demands "for" women can then be made.

m/f countered this with a double move, which involved both the psychical and the second of the historical lines. On the one hand, there was psychoanalysis, and a concept of a psychical reality that was different from social reality and that rendered problematic any simple reading of the political field. At the same time, the psychoanalytic disruption of the categories of masculinity and femininity as readily transposable to actual men and women challenged the justification for feminist demands in the name of a common identity, whether femininity was seen as the problem (a false identity imposed by patriarchal culture) or the goal (the chance of being real women at last), or both.

On the other hand, and against the same monolithic explanations, there was the notion of a multiplicity of sexual differences, set up in different ways according to the different discourses—the medical and the legal were the most often mentioned—in which they appeared. This second model, which was fairly explicitly taken from Foucault, and in particular from *The Archaeology of Knowledge,* made it possible to talk about social questions, but was not directly hooked onto the first.

Psychoanalysis gave "woman" as fantasy, as a construction without any essential identity based on either biology or ideology. The Foucauldian model gave "women" of many kinds, infinitely proliferated as different discourses set up particular categories, open to challenge and, by the same token, infinitely mutable.

Both lines were used strategically to unsettle the assumptions of other arguments that relied on unexamined notions of individual or social identity. Psychoanalysis was also examined in its own right, and internal arguments within psychoanalysis theory were presented and discussed on their own terms. The aim here again was to root out residual elements of biologism or normativity so that psychoanalysis (and it was a Lacanian psychoanalysis that predominated) emerged as the theory that offered the most thorough challenge to any pinning down, by her body or by social norms, of the identity of woman.

Yet, although psychoanalysis lends itself very well to the undoing of all easy assimilations of femininity to femaleness, and of all invocations of a unified identity as one sex or the other, it does still require the sexual differentiation of bodies as the material on which the Oedipus complex and castration will have their effects, even though these effects will not necessarily follow the usual—anatomically predictable—paths. A girl who turns out psychically like a heterosexual man is not in the same situation, socially or psychically, as a boy to whom this occurs. But because of its anti-essentialist position, *m/f* at first refrained from emphasizing this aspect of psychoanalysis (which came more to the fore toward the end), preferring rather to concentrate on how psychoanalysis could be used as a means of criticising the notions of the body implied in other theories.

The separation of psychoanalytic from social concerns seems much less simple in view of the fact that so many manifestly feminist issues cut across these concerns: issues of sexuality and social regulation, of violence against women, abortion, mothering, etc. This was part of the original argument for the pertinence of psychoanalysis to a movement articulating itself through the slogan "The personal is political." But given this situation, it would be more difficult to maintain the strict separation of areas with their corresponding forms of analysis (a question that comes up explicitly in the interview published in the last issue). Psychoanalysis was never presented as providing answers or solutions on a political level, or as deciding, either *a priori* or in particular cases, whether or not different areas of concern should be regarded as provinces for psychic or social investigation, since it would always be a question of both. But nor was the notion of a multiplicity of heterogeneous discourses going to supply a theory or practice of something that could be unified as "feminism." This notion did not allow any special rights to a concept of psychical reality either—since in these terms psychoanalysis, from which the concept was derived, could only be considered as one social discourse among others. In practice, psychoanalysis was exempt from treatment as one social discourse among others, because that would have made it impossible to use it as an account of a psychic reality fundamentally different from social reality.

It was its recognition of the difficulty of femininity and its lack of fixity that made psychoanalysis attractive to feminists; but psychoanalysis did not propose the means to a general resolution or reform (which would be outside its psychical territory), and could not be used as a basis for feminism other than negatively ("woman is not *that,*" "'woman' is a fantasy"). Yet it was not clear that a Foucauldian analysis could yield a feminist politics either. If women were differently specified in different discourses, every response must be local and nothing could unify them all as "feminist." But *m/f*—"a *feminist* journal"—certainly did want to maintain the political force of that word. Thus when Beverley Brown and Parveen Adams raise the question of how in a community of women the wish or choice to have a child can be assessed, they make clear that

> There are no obvious right and wrong positions here. The organisation of these social relations will indeed affect women and mothers and what we are saying is that it has to be worked out from a *feminist,* not an individual point of view.[16]

The emphatic *feminist* has no given content or program but keeps its place as an opposing argument, here against the "individual" point of view.

The question of the nature or necessity of feminist groundings is raised directly from the beginning, but especially in the editorial for issue 5/6 and in the final interview of issue 11/12. It may be focused particularly well from the editorial of issue 4:

> A further criticism has been that our analysis produces a political problem of the unity of the Women's Movement. Clearly the Women's Movement is not a coherent expression of oppressed womanhood or a universal condition, but itself a system of alliances between groupings of interests of mothers, workers, lesbians, battered wives, etc., and this does produce the problem of the basis for these alliances, a problem already recognized within socialist feminism. Once this is recognized, it is surprising that the very possibility of using the term "woman" across a range

of constructions is itself raised as an insuperable problem unique to *m/f*.[17]

"Mothers, workers, lesbians, battered wives, etc."—this particular collectivity is almost the exact antithesis of the *passante,* the negative of the fantasy of "woman." These women do not flit by, a look but not a word; instead, they form a "hetero-geneous" grouping of "a range of constructions" in the social, assorted "interests" with nothing to consolidate their common identity as women.

The fantasies of "woman" to be analyzed in the register of psychical reality; and/or a proliferation of "women" constructed through various distinct social discourses: this twofold feminist strategy of questioning might now be seen as having been both *m/f*'s contribution and, perhaps, the point at which it left us divided as to how to pro-ceed from there.

A New Passante?

And what if *m/f* was itself (herself?) a sort of *passante,* who briefly came and went, marking feminism forever in her passing? The final editorial: "The moment of *m/f*'s project has now passed."[18] And so, *m/f*, or several *m/fs*, passed, or passed away: for the body it constituted could only be conceived as a whole once the "Last Issue" had officially heralded its departure from the scene. What impression did she leave? And what impact will she make now, on her reappearance?

But was she, is she, a woman at all? For this doubt as to *m/f*'s sex was surely the greatest disturbance produced by its interrogation of psychic and social cate-gories. If *m/f* as *passante* was not simply, recognizably, a woman, perhaps its effect was to make it impossible to see the *passante* in the same old ways: sexual identi-fications had undergone a kind of mutation. This is one crucial sense in which *m/f* both recalls the *passante* and complicates her representation: to the extent that *m/f* is a *passante,* it seems to have challenged the grounds on which the *passante* might clearly be seen as the figure of a woman. *m/f* now seems to have represented a turning point, a disruption of the assumed differentiations of male and female places. Not only was the identity of the woman less immediately ascertainable, but the reader as would-be double of the viewer, the theorist, or his/her object was no longer simply assigned to one sex either. For one thing, like feminist writings before, *m/f* had dislocated the ready positionings in taking up the place of the theorist. But this did not mean *m/f* was seeking to identify a woman, or indeed that it identified itself as being simply one or the other.

To all appearances, this disturbance of clearly marked sexual boundaries was the source of much of the criticism of the journal at the time of its first publication, taken up implicitly and explicitly within its pages. How *can* it be a good move, a valid step, for feminism to put in question the unity of women, the identity of women as a political group? Doesn't this just leave "us" in the lurch, without a collective, even less an individual, body to grow from or cling to? Without some anchor, some theory of a general oppression of women to steady its passage, is not feminism left adrift amid a sea of floating signifiers? Against which, painstakingly and methodically, *m/f* insisted, over and over again, on the need to distinguish between sexual divisions and sexual differences, a distinction that was related to the problem of how to conceptualize the relations between the social and the psychic, or of how to formulate a "feminist" politics when the very identity of woman or women was understood as being open to question. The force of the criticisms the journal encountered at the time and subsequently (for it continues to be read and debated), the way it was perceived as going *too far,* is itself some measure of what it did to shake up the set ways of feminist thinking that turned on an already given sexual division. Something was in the process of being changed.

But not in the same ways for everyone. For some who turned away from *m/f* to begin with, seeing in it the grotesque opposite of a positive image of woman, a sort of ugly sister bent on impeding the harmonious progress of feminism, the journal's questions later came to seem important, even inescapable. Here the second look at a figure who could hardly have seemed more repulsive has revealed instead something irresistible that went unremarked in the rapid dismissal of the first glance or first reading.

And then there were those for whom, at the time, *m/f* was like a feminist *passante* in person, a fleeting apparition of something that seemed as if it might be going to answer to every hitherto unarticulated wish for something else. A momentary passing, a last glimpse, and then s/he is gone, "Fleeting Beauty/Whose look made me suddenly reborn." *m/f* seemed to breathe new life into feminism, for those of "us" seeing in "her" a different and new way of putting the questions, turning or twisting the settled patterns of looking and thinking about where feminism might possibly be going. But if she made her mark then, indelibly and irrevocably, to look at her now "as she first appeared" would be quite impossible. To the extent that *m/f*'s new questions were taken up, taken in, she became part of feminism, part of us. That means that it is hopeless to try to see, from where we stand now, exactly what *m/f* was: for she is still here, part of the place from which we ask the question.

As with the changed evaluation on the part of some who initially rejected *m/f*, this complicates the question that would ask what the journal's effect *was, then,* as definitively in the past, having happened once and for all. And for the very reason that s/he has become part of us, to see her again, now, might for such admiring readers produce a quite different impression from the one that is remembered as that of the first, formative view. If *m/f* has been fully incorporated into our ways of thinking, so that s/he is no longer separate as the new addition, out there, that we remember, it is likely that if she turned up once more, s/he would not live up to the memory of her youthful beauty, might even seem slightly aged or *passé:* to see a *passante* again might entail some unpleasant surprises that would detract from the image of her as perfect. (This is in fact what happens to Proust's narrator, the one time he actually decides to chase a *passante* through the streets of Paris to get a second look. When he catches up with her, she turns out to be not a beautiful, unknown young girl but someone he knows very well, Madame Verdurin—an opinionated and unappealing old lady.[19]) And in this case the position is even more complicated. If the *passante* turns out to have lost some of the freshness for which we remember her, it is not because she has aged but because she has not changed one iota or one wrinkle. Yet this is also what makes her seem out of date for us who have changed, moved on— and changed partly through the mark that *m/f* herself made on us then.

And so, reading *m/f* again, now, ten years after the first issue, some things seem oddly distant. Parts of *m/f* return as though with a lag in their step: was *this* the one who looked so bright and promised so much? It seems to have something to do with the style. Rereading the early editorials, there is an impression of firm control, a sort of pedagogical decidedness that seems to brook no opposition or even reply,[20] and to reduce each sentence to the barest, most minimal bones of a discourse sternly connoted as plain. This raises questions, I think, about the rhetoric of feminist argument, which were not *m/f*'s concern at the time, and which perhaps show up in this way only now, when the first moment of the journal is past, and when some of the particular debates conducted or mentioned in its pages are no longer current. In these early statements of position, it is as if something in the nature of feminist argument was assumed to rule out the possibility of textual play or "give": it is all solemnly declarative and strictly circumscribed. This is all the more striking, hard-hitting, in that the absence of play in the writing goes hand in hand, or at least side by side, with the advocacy of theories that refuse ideas of language as a straightforward, transparent medium of theoretical or political argument, as simply expressing one unequivocal thing. It is as though the exhilarating opening up of new questions in place of old protocols could only be achieved through a definitive form of declaration that partially shut them up again.

This might be connected to the intransigent styles of other left journals at the time, in whose context or terms *m/f* had to claim its right to a place and a hearing. Instead, or in addition, it might have to do with the very inadmissibility of *m/f*'s questions, whose lack of fit with feminist orthodoxies led to a form of statement that had to be all the stronger to get its point across. This raises the further question of the extent to which forms of writing or argument inflect the style of their response: *m/f*'s rejection of dogmas sometimes took quite a dogmatic form. This in turn probably had something to do with the "all or nothing" quality of the reactions for and against the journal at the time.

P.S.

m/f thus resists not only the obviousness of sexual division, but also the simple chronology of sequential time. There is no easy temporal distinction between its appearances as young or old, new or dated; by the same token, the journal cannot straightforwardly be either forgotten, dead and buried as "past history," or brought to new life as though it had never had any previous existence. In one way, as we have found, its reemergence now, the *passante* returning, brings into focus as many further questions as did its first appearance. It is the first reader who is now more likely to be disappointed, and the later ones for whom *m/f* can appear, once again, in all its originality.

If the journal's effects still, in both senses, "remain to be seen," then that is itself a sign of the challenge that *m/f* made and makes to existing ways of looking. Coupled with the use of psychoanalysis, *m/f*'s anti-essentialist crusade undermined many of the then-accepted bases of feminism. That this was taken as a threat, as well as a promise, is suggested by the force of the criticism directed against the journal. *m/f* never declared its project to be one of proposing final answers, assumptions about which were part of what it identified as problematic in the contemporary women's movement. That it was and is a source of new questions and new discussions is suggested by the appearance now of this volume, and the ambivalent legacy is in keeping with *m/f*'s enigmatic name and open questions. In one sense it left feminism without a leg to stand on, not even one, by pointing out the ways in which its apparent unity, a "whole" body of women, was not as complete and perfect as it might look.[21] But this was also its great achievement, opening up feminist engagements that might not always involve the search for single (or even double) explanatory models. Not yet that, *pas encore*—*m/f* was not the last to be seen or heard of the question of woman, but the questioning of woman after *m/f*'s passing can no longer be what it was.

Notes

1.   The poem is one of the collection *Les fleurs du mal,* and was first published in 1856.

2.   "Love—not at first sight but at last sight," from Walter Benjamin, "On Some Motifs in Baudelaire," in *Illuminations,* trans. Harry Zohn, Schocken, 1969, p. 169.

3.   Proust, *A l'ombre des jeunes filles en fleurs,* II (1918), 5th vol. of *A la recherche du temps perdu,* Flammarion, 1987, p. 87. An article by Francis S. Heck ("Baudelaire and Proust: Chance Encounters of the Same Kind," *Nottingham French Studies,* vol. 23, no. 2 (May 1984) pp. 17–26), which I thank Diana Knight for pointing out to me, usefully describes some of the key *passante* episodes in Proust as influenced by the Baudelaire sonnet.

4.   Many of the *passante* passages in Proust involve women (or *jeunes filles*) looking at women, but seen through the jealous look of the male narrator, who is never not overlooking the scene.

5.   In another *passante* episode, Proust uses the word himself, as the narrator wonders if pleasure with a *passante* might turn out not to be something unknown, but "a projection, a mirage of desire" (*A l'ombre,* II, p. 182).

6.   Other partial mythological or epic echoes and sightings may then be suggested. In book 11 of *The Odyssey,* the first of the souls whom Odysseus encounters is his mother who, in her death, gives him hope to go on by telling him news from home. Three times he stretches out to embrace her, and "three times she flitted from my hands, like a shadow or like a dream" (ll. 206–208). The episode is echoed in *The Aeneid,* first in book 2 when the hero is vindicated in quitting Troy by the ghost of his wife Creusa ("'Three times I tried to cast my arms around her neck where she had been; but three times, embraced in vain, the image fled my hands, like gentle winds or like a fleeting dream" [ll. 792—795]), and later when, like Odysseus, he is granted a descent into the underworld. Among the shades Aeneas sees is that of Dido, whose being in this place means that she did indeed kill herself when he left her. She appears out of the shadows, says nothing in answer to his questions but "flees back hostile into the shadowy grove" (*Aeneid,* book 6, ll. 472f.). A widow and a queen, this woman, like Creusa, is the one who must have been left behind for history to be made, as Aeneas pursues his mission of founding Rome. There must be no regrets, and her passing appearance, dead, puts her out of the way once and for all.

7.   Lacan *Le Séminaire, livre XX: Encore,* Seuil, p. 36.

8.   *ibid.,* p. 13.

9.   *Ibid.,* p. 69, trans. Jacqueline Rose, in Juliet Mitchell and J. Rose (eds), *Feminine Sexuality: Jacques Lacan and the école freudienne,* Norton, 1982.

10.   *Ibid.,* p. 90.

11.   Lacan, *Le Séminaire, livre XI: Les quatre concepts fondamentaux de la psychanalyse,* Seuil, 1973 p. 33. This volume is translated by Alan Sheridan as *The Four Fundamental Concepts of Psychoanalysis,* Hogarth Press, 1977.

12.   *Ibid.,* p. 44.

13.   *Ibid.,* p. 27.

14.   This is the modernity of Benjamin (see note 2, above), partly developed out of Baudelaire's own conception.

15.   On the absence of representations of female *flânerie,* see Janet Wolff's suggestive article, "The Invisible *Flâneuse:* Women and the Literature of Modernity," *Theory, Culture and Society,* Vol. 2, no. 3 (1985), pp. 37–46.

16.   *m/f* 3, p. 48.

17.   *m/f* 4, p. 4.

18.   *m/f* 11/12, p. 3.

19.   Proust, *A l'ombre,* II, pp. 87–88.
20.   A "worst case" example might be this extract from the first editorial, describing one of three current "tendencies within Marxist feminism":

> Firstly, there is the attempt to argue that women as a consistently deprived social group constitute an economic class. And because of a certain position within Marxism which asserts that transformation will be effected when a class becomes conscious of itself as a class (a class for itself) this position assumes that political changes in the position of women will be effected when women become conscious of themselves as a class. The consciousness of belonging to an oppressed class is seen to be the basis of political action. Against this argument it can simply be stated that class divisions cut across "women as a social group."

Three substantial explanatory sentences and then suddenly that's it—finished, dealt with (the paragraph ends there and the next goes on to a "second tendency"). The speediness of the dismissal seems to permit no further response: it is almost a reprimand, and the quailing reader is really put in no position to think she might reasonably pay attention to this line. This is even more noticeable because it is not clear that the point is established at all. The refutation is made "simply" by returning to the straight Marxist position that it is only the classical class contradictions that count, which is where Marxist feminist questions began in the first place.
21.   If the problem of putting the psychic alongside the social was both *m/f*'s stumbling block and its most fruitful contribution to feminist debate, it might be worth glancing back at the fleeting appearance of a different kind of *passante* within its pages, one whose identity is not constrained by the impossible choice between an eternal, mythological fantasy of woman and a historically specific construction. The editorial of issue 4 mentions an article by Parveen Adams and Beverley Brown, but there is something funny about the reference. In the third issue, where it appeared, the article is entitled "The Feminine Body and Feminist Politics." Now it has slipped into something a little less predictable: "The Feminist Body and Feminist Politics." And what a slip! Has *m/f* suddenly blown its cover, let the bag out of the bag, revealing the truth by lifting up the petticoat of anti-essentialism for just a second? Perhaps this is the first and last time that anyone, reader or spectator, ever got a glimpse of this barely imaginable entity, the feminist body. For it has never been seen again, and though no one, feminist, woman or man, can remember what it looked like, it has assuredly left an indelible mark on the mind of every discerning reader. Love at first sight—who can doubt that the feminist body would have provided the answers to all our questions, had she but stayed awhile?

m/f Contents Nos. 1–12

PARVEEN ADAMS cofounded *m/f* in 1978 and continued as one of its editors until it ceased publication in 1986. Editor of *Language in Thinking* (Penguin, 1972) and author of many articles on psychoanalysis and feminist politics, she is currently working on a book on masochism, culture, and the unconscious (Routledge). She teaches in the Department of Human Sciences at Brunel University, England.

HILARY ALLEN is a sociologist who lectures in the Department of Criminology at the University of Keele, England, works for the Labour Party and as a psychiatric nurse. She is the author of *Justice Unbalanced* (Open University, 1987) and several articles on women, psychiatry, and law.

RACHEL BOWLBY teaches English at the University of Sussex, England. She is the author of a book on femininity and consumer culture, *Just Looking* (Methuen, 1985), and of *Virginia Woolf: Feminist Destinations* (Blackwell, 1988). She is also an editor of *Oxford Literary Review* and cotranslator of a number of books of French theory. The essay in this volume forms part of a larger study of the *flâneur* and the *passante*.

BEVERLEY BROWN joined the editorial group of *m/f* in 1978. She has published widely on feminism, philosophy, and sociology. In 1985 she took up her current position at the Centre for Criminology and the Social and Philosophical Study of Law at Edinburgh University.

JOAN COPJEC is an editor of *October* and the author of many articles on psychoanalysis, film theory, and feminism. She is the author of *Apparatus and Umbra* (forthcoming, MIT Press) and is currently writing a book on Marguerite Duras and the "cinematic sublime" for Indiana University Press.

MARK COUSINS studied at Oxford University and the Warburg Institute. Head of the Department of Sociology at Thames Polytechnic, London, he also teaches at the Architectural Association. He has contributed essays on law, history, and political theory to a number of books and is the coauthor, with Athar Hussain, of *Michel Foucault* (Macmillan, 1984).

ELIZABETH COWIE cofounded *m/f* and coedited it from 1978 to 1986. She also worked for the journal *Screen* from 1972 to 1976 and was a member of its editorial board. Author of a forthcoming book on psychoanalysis, film theory, and the representation of women (Macmillan), she teaches film studies at the University of Kent, England.

MANDY MERCK edited the film and media studies journal *Screen* from 1982 to 1988. She is Series Editor of "Out on Tuesday," a gay magazine program that airs on the British independent television network Channel Four. A collection of her essays is forthcoming from Virago Press.

CATHERINE MILLOT is a practicing psychoanalyst and Maître de Conference at the University of Paris VIII. Her books include *Freud: Anti-Pedagogue* (Bibliothèque d' *Ornicar?*, 1979); *Horsexe* (Point Hors Ligne, 1983); *Nobodaddy* (Point Hors Ligne, 1988); and a forthcoming study of writing as a vocation.

JEFFREY MINSON teaches in the Division of the Humanities, Griffith University, Australia. He is the author of a critical study and application of Foucault's work, *Genealogies of Morals* (Macmillan, 1985) and is completing a book of essays on politics and ethics.

MICHÈLE MONTRELAY is a practicing psychoanalysis working in Paris. She is the author of *L'Ombre et le nom* (Minuit, 1976) as well as several major articles on psychoanalysis and feminism.

CHANTAL MOUFFE is a political philosopher who has taught at universities in England and the United States and at the National University of Colombia. She is the editor of *Gramsci and Marxist Theory* (New Left Books, 1979) and author, with Ernesto Laclau, of *Hegemony and Socialist Strategy: Towards a Radical Democratic Politics* (Verso, 1985).

CONSTANCE PENLEY teaches film studies at the University of Rochester. She is a cofounder and editor of the feminist film journal *Camera Obscura* and has published widely on film and feminism. She is the editor of *Feminism and Film Theory* (Routledge, 1988) and author of *The Future of an Illusion* (University of Minnesota Press, 1989).

MOUSTAFA SAFOUAN is a well-known psychoanalyst and writer working in Paris. A native Egyptian, he has translated Freud's *Interpretation of Dreams* and Hegel's *Phenomenology of Spirit* into Arabic. His own books include *Études sur l'Oedipe* (Seuil, 1974); *La sexualité féminine dans la doctrine freudienne* (Seuil, 1976) and *Pleasure and Being* (Macmillan, 1983).